The Body and Social Theory

Theory, Culture & Society

Theory, Culture & Society caters for the resurgence of interest in culture within contemporary social science and the humanities. Building on the heritage of classical social theory, the book series examines ways in which this tradition has been reshaped by a new generation of theorists. It also publishes theoretically informed analyses of everyday life, popular culture, and new intellectual movements.

EDITOR: Mike Featherstone, *Nottingham Trent University*

SERIES EDITORIAL BOARD
Roy Boyne, *University of Durham*
Mike Hepworth, *University of Aberdeen*
Scott Lash, *Goldsmiths College, University of London*
Roland Robertson, *University of Aberdeen*
Bryan S. Turner, *University of Cambridge*

THE TCS CENTRE
The Theory, Culture & Society book series, the journals *Theory, Culture & Society* and *Body & Society*, and related conference, seminar and post-graduate programmes operate from the TCS Centre at Nottingham Trent University. For further details of the TCS Centre's activities please contact:

Centre Administrator
The TCS Centre, Room 175
Faculty of Humanities
Nottingham Trent University
Clifton Lane, Nottingham, NG11 8NS, UK
e-mail: tcs@ntu.ac.uk
web: http://www.tcs.ntu.ac.uk

Recent volumes include:

The Tourist Gaze
John Urry

Critique of Information
Scott Lash

Commodifying Bodies
Nancy Scheper-Hughes and Loïc Wacquant

The Body and Social Theory

Second Edition

Chris Shilling

SAGE Publications

London ● Thousand Oaks ● New Delhi

ISBN 0-7619-4284-X (hbk)
ISBN 0-7619-4285-8 (pbk)
© Chris Shilling 1993, 2003
First published 1993
Reprinted seven times
Second edition 2003
Reprinted 2004, 2005

SAGE Publications Ltd
1 Oliver's Yard
55 City Road
London EC1Y 1SP

SAGE Publications Inc
2455 Teller Road
Thousand Oaks
California 91320

SAGE Publications India Pvt. Ltd
B–42 Panchsheel Enclave
PO Box 4109
New Delhi 110 017

British Library Cataloguing in Publication data
A catalogue record for this book is available from the British Library

Library of Congress Control Number: 2002115869

Printed on paper from sustainable sources

Typeset by Mayhew Typesetting, Rhayader, Powys
Printed and bound in Great Britain by
Cromwell Press Limited, Trowbridge, Wiltshire

Contents

Acknowledgements   vii

Preface to the Second Edition   viii

1   Introduction   1

2   The Body in Sociology   17

3   The Naturalistic Body   37

4   The Socially Constructed Body   62

5   The Body and Social Inequalities   88

6   The Body and Physical Capital   111

7   The Civilized Body   131

8   The Body, Self-Identity and Death   152

9   Concluding Comments   172

Afterword: Embodiment, Identity and Theory   178

References   212

Index   231

To
Max and Katie

Acknowledgements

I am indebted to those colleagues and friends who have assisted my work on the body. In particular, Philip A. Mellor and Keith Tester have long provided valued insight, encouragement and guidance, while Chris Rojek has provided all the help and discernment one would want from an editor. This new edition has benefited from their comments, and from the astute observations of Ian Burkitt and Paul Sweetman. Thanks also to Mike Featherstone, Bryan S. Turner and the rest of the *Theory, Culture & Society* editorial group for continuing to support my theoretical project. On a different level, I have been waiting for some opportunity to acknowledge my gratitude for the help and considerable skills of XueLong Li and Colin Ingram: two experts within their respective fields who have demonstrated practically to me how bodies think. The largest debt of support I have accrued while working on the body, however, is to my wife, Debbie.

Preface to the Second Edition

During the ten years that have passed since the publication of the first edition of *The Body and Social Theory* there has been a massive proliferation of writings on embodiment. It is now no longer possible to dismiss study of the subject as a luxurious curiosity to be classified alongside the 'bizarre' topics that periodically interest the outer reaches of the sociological imagination. Reflecting its social and cultural significance, the body has moved to the very centre of academic analysis. The existence of a healthy and thriving field of 'body studies' has been supplemented by multiple analyses of embodiment across a growing number of disciplines including sociology, history, anthropology, cultural studies, sports and leisure studies, philosophy, theology and religious studies. The subject of the body has served as an important stimulus for interdisciplinary work, and has been recognized as a notable development within mainstream surveys of the sociological tradition (e.g. Levine, 1995). It has also become foundational to general social theories of the creativity of human action and the human condition (e.g. Archer, 2000; Joas, 1996). Just as important as these positive manifestations of the body's significance to the social sciences and humanities, are the intractable problems faced by those theories that seek to explain social action *without* accounting for the embodied character of humans. Rational choice theory is a particularly pertinent example of this phenomena. It is highly influential within sociology and other social sciences in and outside of America, but is flawed by a series of untenable assumptions it makes about the bodily constitution of humans (Shilling and Mellor, 2001).[1]

The huge growth of work within the broad area of body studies has not, however, rendered irrelevant early key texts on the subject. In addition to Bryan S. Turner's (1984) *The Body & Society*, for example, Paul Hirst and Penny Woolley's (1982) *Social Relations and Human Attributes*, Peter Freund's (1982) *The Civilized Body*, and John O'Neill's (1985) *Five Bodies*, contain important insights and analyses that retain their relevance to the field. We can still learn from their respective discussions of the importance of the body to governance, the relationship between biology, psychology and sociology, the impact of social relationships on health and illness, and the symbolic importance of the body. It was in the context of studies such as these that I sought in the first edition of this book to identify an emerging field of body studies, and to develop a broad approach towards embodiment that built on the insights of such works as well as on the writings of a number of classical and contemporary thinkers who had yet to be fully associated with the area.

Rereading the original text of *The Body and Social Theory* in the light of subsequent developments in the field, I did not want to change what I felt remained of value to the area of body studies. Far from losing their impact, for example, naturalistic approaches to the body (see Chapter 3) have been given renewed impetus by those who view the Human Genome Project as revealing how the genetic constitution of our bodies determines our identity and destiny. There remains a need to reveal the limitations of such thinking and to demonstrate that *social* processes entered into human evolution and remain vitally important in affecting the health, well-being and life chances of people born into the twenty-first century.

If the excesses of naturalistic approaches towards the body still need curbing, so too do those associated with the reductionisms that remain evident in many cultural, technological and sociological approaches to the body (see Chapter 4). While usefully highlighting how our bodily identities and relationships are irreducible to 'natural' or 'biological' factors, there is still a tendency for these social theories of the body to imagine that our embodied being is somehow reducible to discourse, to technological advances, or to the structures of society. Such perspectives may have made a valuable 'epistemological break' from common sense thinking about what is supposedly 'natural' or 'inevitable' about the bodily capacities of women and men, gays, lesbians and heterosexuals, and those belonging to different 'racial' groups. In so doing, however, they ignore how the body is not only a location for social classifications but is actually *generative* of social relations and human knowledge.

In critically evaluating the limitations of naturalistic and social constructionist approaches, the original text sought to go beyond these alternatives by outlining a view of the body as a material phenomena which shaped, as well as being shaped by, its social environment. The body is central to our ability to 'make a difference' to, to intervene in, or to exercise agency in the world, and our bodily emotions, preferences, sensory capacities and actions are a fundamental *source* of 'social forms' (even if many of these social forms have ossified and become separated from their founding desires and dispositions). Thus, while Turner (1996: 34) has argued that 'we do not have to develop a sociological understanding of the physicality of the body since the "natural body" is always and already injected with cultural understandings and social history', this position threatens to underplay those physical capacities of the body that are productive of creative action and social relations, yet cannot be simply 'read off' from 'purely' cultural or social factors. Far from endorsing the need for an embodied social theory, indeed, such arguments run the risk of removing from our theoretical concerns the facticity and materiality of human embodiment, and turning issues of human need and well-being into matters of cultural preference (Soper, 1995). This is the context in which I still believe it is worth returning to the approach outlined in Chapters 5 to 9 of the first edition (which explore writings that can contribute to a view of the body as an irreducibly physical phenomenon engaged in a dynamic relationship with its social surroundings), and is the reason that I have decided to leave intact the structure and most of the content of the main text.

There have been a number of important developments in the field since *The Body and Social Theory* was first published, however, and I have taken the opportunity in this new edition to engage with some of the most important of them and to update the text in a number of respects. Significant feminist contributions to the subject were developed after I had written the original manuscript, while action-oriented and phenomenological approaches to the body have also increased in popularity. Furthermore, those theoretically dominant approaches which helped impart an identity to the area developed in such a way that they have contributed subsequently to a fragmentation of body studies and a growing confusion about what is meant by 'the body'. The new Afterword engages with these issues as it revisits and develops several of the most influential themes in the original text in the light of subsequent work. In additon, I have used this Afterword to introduce the outlines of a general approach to the body as a multi-dimensional medium for the constitution of society. This builds on the approach developed in the first edition, draws on my ongoing work in the area, and can serve as a basis for the consolidation of body studies.

Note

1. Theories of rational action tend to assume, in their stronger formulations, that actors cognitively establish goals before acting (and thereby propose that the normal state of the body is lethargy). They view the body as a permanently available instrument of action (that is autonomous vis-a-vis other people and the environment), and also reduce the body to a mere medium of preference-maximizing self-expression (underestimating the importance of human frailty, revelatory experience, and other unintended and unexpected events of life) (Joas, 1996).

1

Introduction

This book is intended to be a theoretical contribution to the rapidly growing area of the sociology of the body. In what follows I shall examine the changing status of the body in sociology; describe and evaluate the major perspectives which have been drawn on by sociological studies of the body; and offer my own analysis of how we might best conceptualize the relationship between the body, self-identity and death in the contemporary period that Anthony Giddens has termed 'late' or 'high' modernity. My argument here is that, in conditions of high modernity, there is a tendency for the body to become increasingly central to the modern person's sense of self-identity. In this context, the prospect of death assumes an importance which has rarely been acknowledged or investigated by sociology and yet is central to our contemporary understanding of the body. This opening chapter provides a brief introduction to these issues, while also familiarizing the reader with some of the main themes which inform this study.

In recent years there has been a large increase in academic interest in the body. The sociology of the body has emerged as a distinct area of study, a new journal devoted to the subject, *Body & Society*, was launched in 1995, and it has even been suggested that the body should serve as an organizing principle for sociology. With this aim in mind, Bryan Turner has coined the term 'somatic society' to describe how the body in modern social systems has become 'the principal field of political and cultural activity' (Turner, 1992a: 12, 162).

There has also been a massive rise of popular interest in the body. Newspapers, magazines and television are replete with features on body image, plastic surgery and how to keep the body looking young, sexy and beautiful, while the business of weight loss and keep-fit is now a multi-million dollar industry. In the UK alone, the gym and health club business is now worth an estimated £1.5 billion a year.[1] It is important to note that interest in the body is not new. In times of war, for example, governments have traditionally displayed concern about the physical health and fitness of the nation. Nevertheless, the position of the body within contemporary popular culture reflects an unprecedented *individualization* of the body. Growing numbers of people are increasingly concerned with the health, shape and appearance of their own bodies as expressions of individual identity. As Pierre Bourdieu (1984) notes, this concern may be especially acute among the 'new' middle classes. However, in recent years it has spread well beyond these narrow confines.

The body in high modernity

Any serious attempt to understand this increased interest in the body must come to terms with the conditions which have formed the context for this trend. In this respect, it is instructive to mention some of the developments which have accompanied the rise of modernity, and which have been radicalized in the contemporary period of high modernity.

Modernity has been referred to generally as those modes of social life and organization which emerged in post-feudal Europe, but which have in the twentieth century become increasingly global in their impact. Modernity can be understood roughly as the 'industrialized world', although it consists of several institutional dimensions which have their own specific trajectories (Giddens, 1990; Hall and Gieben, 1992). Among its many effects, modernity has facilitated an increase in the degree of control that nation states in general, and medical professions in particular, have been able to exert over the bodies of their citizens. It has also led to a reduction in the power of religious authorities to define and regulate bodies (Turner, 1982). Indeed, the relationship between modernity and religion has considerable implications for our contemporary concern with the body.

Theorists of modernity have long argued that while the modern age has developed alongside a gradual desacralization of social life, it has failed to replace religious certainties with scientific certainties of the same order. Science may have increased our control over life (though, crucially, it has not conquered death), yet it has failed to provide us with values to guide our lives (Weber, 1948 [1919]). Instead, there has been a gradual privatization of meaning in modernity. This has left increasing numbers of individuals alone with the task of establishing and maintaining values to make sense out of their daily lives.

The term 'high modernity' has been used by Anthony Giddens to describe the radicalization of these modern trends in the late twentieth century. In contrast to certain theories of post modernity, Giddens suggests that neither modernity nor the self are anachronistic sociological concerns. Social life is still shaped by modern concerns even though it is only now that the implications of these are becoming fully apparent. With the decline of formal religious frameworks in the West which constructed and sustained existential and ontological certainties residing *outside* the individual, and the massive rise of the body in consumer culture as a bearer of symbolic value, there is a tendency for people in high modernity to place ever more importance on the body as constitutive of the self. For those who have lost their faith in religious authorities and grand political narratives, and are no longer provided with a clear world view or self-identity by these trans-personal meaning structures, at least the body initially appears to provide a firm foundation on which to reconstruct a reliable sense of self in the modern world. Indeed, the increasingly reflexive ways in which people are relating to their bodies can be seen as one of the defining features of high modernity. Furthermore, it is the exterior territories, or surfaces, of the body that symbolize the self at a time when unprecedented value is placed on the youthful, trim and sexual body.

The uncertain body

These introductory comments can only begin to sketch out the context in which the body has emerged as a fundamental social and academic issue in the contemporary period. However, of all the factors which have contributed to the visibility of the body, two apparently paradoxical developments seem to have been particularly important. *We now have the means to exert an unprecedented degree of control over bodies, yet we are also living in an age which has thrown into radical doubt our knowledge of what bodies are and how we should control them.*

As a result of developments in spheres as diverse as biological reproduction, genetic engineering, plastic surgery and sports science, the body is becoming increasingly a phenomenon of options and choices. These developments have advanced the potential many people have to control their own bodies, and to have them controlled by others. This does not mean that we all possess the resources, or the interest, which would enable us radically to reconstruct our bodies. Indeed, the methods by which people seek to control their bodies usually take the more mundane forms of diet and keep-fit. Furthermore, the bodily concerns of the business executive and the homeless are likely to be very different. Nonetheless, we are living in a media age where knowledge of these developments is widespread, and the subjective deprivation of those without the resources to control and care for their bodies is likely to be accentuated by their possession of this knowledge. Quite simply, the body is potentially no longer subject to the constraints and limitations that once characterized its existence. Nevertheless, as well as providing people with the potential to control their bodies, this situation has also stimulated among individuals a heightened degree of reflexivity about what the body is, and an uncertainty about how it should be controlled. As science facilitates greater degrees of intervention into the body, it destabilizes our knowledge of what bodies are, and runs ahead of our ability to make moral judgements about how far science should be allowed to reconstruct the body.

Indeed, it would not be too much of an oversimplification to argue that the more we have been able to control and alter the limits of the body, the greater has been our uncertainty about what constitutes an individual's body, and what is 'natural' about a body. For example, artificial insemination and *in vitro* fertilization have enabled reproduction to be separated from the corporeal relations which have traditionally defined heterosexual experience. The moral panics over 'virgin births' in Britain illustrate the threat that these developments pose to many people's sense of what is natural about the body. As the front page of one of Britain's popular tabloid newspapers, the *Daily Mail*, fulminated, 'In a scheme which strikes at the very heart of family life, women who have never had sex are being given the chance to have a baby' (Golden and Hope, 1991).

Advances in such areas as transplant surgery and virtual reality exacerbate this uncertainty about the body by threatening to collapse the boundaries which have traditionally existed between bodies, and between technology and the body (Bell and Kennedy, 2000). This has very real consequences. As Turner notes, in a future society where implants and transplants are widespread and highly developed, 'the hypothetical puzzles in classical philosophy about identities and parts will be issues of major legal and political importance. Can I be held responsible for the actions of a body which is substantially not my own body?' (Turner, 1992a: 37). These developments also promise to increase those dilemmas surrounding the *ownership* of bodies which have already been raised in relation to such issues as abortion and surrogacy (Diprose, 1994).

Body projects

In this time of uncertainty, knowledge about what bodies are increasingly takes the form of hypotheses: 'claims which may very well be true, but which are in principle always open to revision and may have at some point to be abandoned' (Giddens, 1991: 3). This situation is not inconsequential for the modern individual's sense of self-identity – their sense of self as reflexively understood in terms of their own embodied biography. In the affluent West, there is a tendency for the body to be seen as an entity which is in the process of becoming; a *project* which should be worked at and accomplished as part of an *individual's* self-identity. We can trace individuals' attempts to shape and mould their bodies back to the early Christian era and even to Classical Antiquity (Brown, 1988; Foucault, 1988). However, body projects differ from how the flesh was decorated, inscribed and altered in traditional societies as they involve a reflexivity which is cut adrift from traditional models of socially acceptable bodies which were forged through rituals in communal ceremonies (Rudofsky, 1986 [1971]). Body projects still vary along social lines, especially in the case of gender, but there has in recent years been a proliferation of the ways in which both women and men have developed their bodies.

Recognizing that the body has become a project for many modern persons entails accepting that its appearance, size, shape and even its contents, are potentially open to reconstruction in line with the designs of its owner. Treating the body as a project does not necessarily entail a full-time preoccupation with its wholesale transformation, although it has the potentiality to do so. However, it does involve individuals being conscious of and actively concerned about the management, maintenance and appearance of their bodies. This involves a practical recognition of the significance of bodies; both as personal resources and as social symbols which give off messages about a person's self-identity. In this context, bodies become malleable entities which can be shaped and honed by the vigilance and hard work of their owners.

Perhaps the most common example of the body as a project can be found in the unprecedented amount of attention given to the personal construction of healthy bodies (Shilling, 2002a). At a time when our health is threatened increasingly by *global* dangers, we are exhorted ever more to take *individual* responsibility for our bodies by engaging in strict self-care regimes. Heart disease, cancer and a host of other diseases are increasingly portrayed as avoidable by individuals who eat the right foods, stop smoking and take sufficient quantities of exercise. Self-care regimes require individuals to take on board the notion that the body is a project whose interiors and exteriors can be monitored, nurtured and maintained as fully functioning. These regimes promote an image of the body as an island of security in a global system characterized by multiple and inescapable risks (Beck, 1992).

Self-care regimes are not simply about preventing disease. They are also concerned with making us feel good about how our bodies appear to ourselves and others. Health has become increasingly associated with appearances and what Erving Goffman (1969) has termed the 'presentation of self'. These concerns have been facilitated by the production of what appears to be an almost limitless number of self-help books, make-up guides, dietary supplements and exercise plans. Consumer goods battle with each other in their attempts to make people's bodies look and feel reliable and sensuous, and provide programmes for people to achieve a skin quality and muscle tone which give off messages about health by *looking* healthy and youthful (Banner, 1983). Indeed, the influence of this particular body project is such that even those who smoke and drink heavily, and consume other drugs, find it difficult not to reflect on the effects such actions are having on the health and appearance of their bodies. In an era characterized by a political emphasis on 'self-help' and 'personal responsibility', and a cultural emphasis on the 'body beautiful', those who engage in such habits have become the new moral deviants. However, the pervasive influence on us of what Robert Crawford (1987) refers to as 'the new health consciousness' is not the only way in which the body has become a project to be moulded in line with people's self-identities.

Plastic surgery has provided a much smaller, but fast growing number of individuals with the opportunity for a more radical and direct way of reconstructing their bodies in line with particular notions of youthfulness, femininity and masculinity. Face-lifts, liposuction, tummy tucks, nose and chin 'jobs' are just a small selection of the operations and procedures open to people with money who want to reconstruct their bodies. Well over two million breast implant operations have been performed in the United States since the early 1960s on women seeking to achieve bodies that are more 'feminine'. Increasing numbers of men have followed their example by having chest implants in search of a more muscular appearance. Penile engorgement operations are also available for those willing to pay for a more 'fully masculine' body (Grant, 1992).

Plastic surgery raises, in a particularly acute form, the question, 'What is the body?' by enabling people to add to or subtract from the fat, flesh and bones in their body. In this respect, newspapers and magazines have carried a number of articles about people who, by undergoing multiple operations, have become obsessed with changing the appearances and boundaries of their bodies in line with some idealized version of the self. Perhaps the most newsworthy example of this can be found in the much altered features of pop singer Michael Jackson.

For those not willing or able to undergo the risks involved in surgery, there is the increasingly popular activity of bodybuilding; an activity which used to reside on the deviant margins of the exercise industry. Bodybuilding is a good illustrative example of the body as a project precisely because the quality and sheer size of the muscles achieved by bodybuilders challenges accepted notions of what is natural about male and female bodies. At a time when machines are increasingly taking over the manual work traditionally carried out by men in factories, and when women continue to challenge the limited roles of wife and mother available to them in society, the construction and display of 'unnaturally' large or highly defined bodies appears to allow people to make strong, public and personal statements about who and what they are (Fussell, 1991). As one of the women in Rosen's study of women bodybuilders remarked, 'When I look in the mirror I see somebody who's finding herself, who has said once and for all it doesn't really matter what role society said I should play. l can do anything I want and feel proud about doing it' (Rosen, 1983: 72).

The projects of health, plastic surgery and bodybuilding are just three examples of how modern individuals are placing increasing emphasis on their bodies. Nevertheless, they serve at least to illustrate some of the opportunities and limitations which accompany the tightening relationship between the body and self-identity. Investing in the body provides people with a means of self expression and a way of potentially feeling good and increasing the control they have over their bodies. If one feels unable to exert influence over an increasingly complex society, at least one can have some effect on the size, shape and appearance of one's body. The benefits of this opportunity may be qualified in the absence of ultimate criteria for deciding *how* the body should be treated, or even what the body is, but it would be too easy to dismiss out of hand the advantages that can accrue to people as a result of the rise of the body as a project in modern society.

Investment in the body also has its limitations. Indeed, in one sense the effort expended by individuals on the body is doomed to failure. Bodies age and decay, and the inescapable reality of death appears particularly disturbing to modern people who are concerned with a self-identity which has at its centre the body. After all, what could signal to us more effectively the limitations of our concern with the young and fit, ideally feminine or masculine body than the brute facts of its thickening waistline, sagging flesh and inevitable death?

Bodies are limited not only in the sense that they ultimately die, but in their frequent refusal to be moulded in accordance with our intentions. Susie Orbach (1988) and Kim Chernin (1983) are just two of the many writers who have pointed to the difficulties involved in changing the shape of the body by dieting, and Emily Martin (1989 [1987]) has demonstrated how women frequently experience their bodies in a number of ways as being beyond control. It is also clear that attempts to change the size and shape of our bodies carry with them their own risks (for example, increasing evidence attests to the dangers associated with plastic surgery and frequent dieting). Another problem associated with our reflexive concern with the body involves the effects it can have on children. The age at which people experience anxiety about their body shape and weight appears to be getting younger, and research suggests that a substantial number of girls and boys as young as nine are unhappy with their bodies (Hall, 1992). It is, perhaps, not surprising that our contemporary obsession with the body has been associated with a worrying rise in eating disorders (Gordon, 2001; Grogan, 1999).

In these senses our bodies are *constraining*, as well as *facilitating*, while they are alive and not simply because they die. None the less, Zygmunt Bauman's point about the relationship between the body and death is applicable generally to our concern with the body as a project. As he argues in the case of health and self-care regimes, the modern obsession with the body 'is an attempt to belie the ultimate limits of the body by breaking, successively, its *currently* encountered, *specific* limitations' (Bauman, 1992a: 18). This pragmatic focus is an attempt to defer worrying existential questions about the *ultimate* limitation of the body (that is, death), about *why* the body should have become so significant to our self-identity, and about *what* the body is.

Another limitation in the rise of the body as a project is the way in which individual images of the desirable body can become harnessed to the perpetuation of pre-existing social inequalities. In this respect, the way in which the body has become a project for some women would appear to be more reflective of male designs and fantasies than an expression of individuality. For example, it could be argued that acting and modelling encourages women to change their bodies in line with male notions of beauty. As Robert Gerber (1992: 46) notes, 'Today the super-endowed, surgically altered woman has become a reference point of fashion'.

Sociology and the body

For these, and other reasons to be examined later in Chapter 2, the body has become an important social issue. However, it is only recently that the body has moved centre-stage to general theoretical debates in Europe and

Australia, while there still exists a strong degree of ambivalence towards the subject in North America. Contemporary explanations for this late and still incomplete 'arrival' of the body tend to suggest that it exists because of the *disembodied* approach classical sociology has traditionally adopted towards its subject matter. Bryan Turner, among others, adopts this position in *Regulating Bodies* (Turner, 1992a). Having been influenced profoundly by Cartesian thought, sociology has followed a longstanding tradition in philosophy by accepting a mind/body dichotomy and focusing on the mind as that which defines humans as social beings.

There is much of value in this explanation, which accurately describes how a significant portion of sociology has tended to approach the relationship between the mind and the body. However, this does less than full justice to sociology's specific dealings with human embodiment as a subject in its own right. Equally unsatisfactory is the view that the body can simply be 'recovered' by revisiting the classics (Williams and Bendelow, 1998). At the very least, a substantial work of elaboration and development is required if we are to fashion comprehensive classical sociological theories of the body. In contrast to these two approaches, I suggest that it is more accurate to describe classical sociology as having displayed a *dual approach* to the body. Instead of being neglected completely, the body has historically been something of an *absent presence* in sociology. The body has been absent from classical sociology in the sense that the discipline has rarely focused in a sustained manner on the body as an area of investigation in its own right. For example, sociological theory seldom takes into account the fact that we have fleshy bodies which allow us to taste, smell, touch and exchange bodily fluids (Connell and Dowsett, 1992). Classical sociology's concern with the structure and functioning of societies and the nature of human action, however, has inevitably led it to deal with important aspects of human *embodiment*.

The concern of classical sociology with the body has all too frequently been implicit, rather than explicit. Furthermore, it has tended to focus selectively on certain aspects of human embodiment. For example, sociology has focused on such issues as language and consciousness without recognizing that these capacities are themselves embodied. As Norbert Elias (1991) has argued, our capacities for language and consciousness are contained within, are part of, and are limited by our bodies. A related point concerns classical sociology's neglect of the body as an integral component of human agency. It is our bodies which allow us to act, to intervene in, and to alter the flow of daily life. Indeed, it is impossible to have an adequate theory of human agency without taking into account the body. In a very important sense, acting people are acting bodies.

Nonetheless, while classical sociology has not yet dealt adequately with the full implications of human embodiment, this does not justify the statement that sociology has adopted an entirely disembodied approach towards its subject matter. For example, Karl Marx (1954 [1887]) was concerned with the assimilation of the body into capitalist technology.

Georg Simmel (1990 [1907]; 1950) wrote about the embodied dispositions that propelled people towards others, and the social emotions that helped maintain relationships, as well as examining the deleterious effects of the money economy in eroding these emotions. Max Weber's (1985 [1904–05]; 1948 [1915]) writings displayed an interest in the rationalization of the body, and the 'shelters' from physical instrumentalism provided by art, love and eroticism. Emile Durkheim (1995 [1912]) viewed the body as a source of, as well as a location for, those sacred phenomena that served to bind together individuals into moral wholes. Indeed, the implicit presence of the body in sociology is illustrated by the fact that much recent work on the body has been able to draw productively on the legacy of classical sociology. Pierre Bourdieu's writings on the body, for instance, developed from a Marxian concern with social class and social reproduction, a Durkheimian interest in the social and cognitive functions of 'collective representations' and 'primitive classifications', and a Weberian focus on the particular styles of life and attributions of honour or dishonour that define status groups (Brubaker, 1985; Shilling, 1992).

Defending classical sociology from accusations that it has adopted an entirely disembodied approach to its subject matter is clearly not an endorsement of its treatment of the body. In this respect, it is important to mention some of those more recent social theorists who have sought to overcome the dual approach that sociology has traditionally adopted to the body. Erving Goffman and Michel Foucault, for example, have placed the body at the core of their respective analyses of the 'interaction order' and disciplinary systems.

These two writers have exerted a very considerable influence on con-temporary analyses of the body as a socially constructed phenomenon. However, rather than overcoming fully the deficiencies of classical socio-logy, much of their work can be seen as *reproducing in a different form* the dual approach sociology has tended to adopt towards the body. Social constructionist views of the body tend to tell us much about how society has invaded, shaped, classified and made the body meaningful, but we learn much less from them about what the body is and why it is able to assume such social importance. The body is named as a theoretical space, but often remains relatively neglected as an actual object of analysis. Indeed, it would probably be more accurate to categorize the more extreme social constructionist views of the body as symptoms, rather than analyses, of our modern concern with the body.

It should be clear from this that I think social constructionist approaches have, to date, provided us with less than fully satisfactory views of the body. It is all very well saying that the body is socially constructed, but this tends to tell us little about the specific character of the body. What is it, exactly, that is being constructed? Instead of addressing this question, and allowing us to understand how social forces mould and shape our physical selves, constructionism has tended to evacuate the embodied agent from social theory. In this respect, I agree with Turner when he argues that we need a foundationalist view of the body (Turner, 1992a). To begin to achieve an adequate analysis of the body we need to regard it as a material, physical and biological phenomenon which is irreducible to immediate social processes or classifications. Furthermore, our senses, knowledge-ability and capability to act are integrally related to the fact that we are embodied beings. Social relations may profoundly affect the development of our bodies in almost every respect; in terms of their size and shape and in terms of how we see, hear, touch, smell and think (Duroche, 1990; Elias, 1991), but bodies cannot simply be 'explained away' by these relations. Human bodies are taken up and transformed as a result of living in society, but they remain material, physical and biological entities.

Embodying sociology

Having touched on some of the main themes that run throughout this study, I want now to outline the five main aims of this book and provide a brief description of its individual chapters.

First, as mentioned previously in this introduction, I intend to provide a distinctive analysis of the position and treatment of the body in sociology which argues that the body has traditionally been something of an *absent presence* in the discipline.

Second, a major task I have set myself is to provide a clear, critical overview of some of the main perspectives and theories relevant to the sociology of the body. In contrast to a number of recent books on the body, I have decided against organizing the chapters in this study thematically. Instead, I have deliberately arranged the book in a manner which provides chapter by chapter access to different perspectives on the body. It seemed to me that this would be a useful way of organizing and interrogating some of the great diversity of studies published in recent years which are relevant to the sociology of the body. These studies have not always been seen as sociological works on the body, but I present them in this way and seek to explain how they constitute important contributions to this area.

In evaluating these perspectives, I am primarily interested in exploring what they do and do not allow us to say about the body in society. What do they reveal about the body, and what are the silences of these approaches? In Talcott Parson's terms (1968 [1937]: 17), what are the 'residual cate-gories'; the facts or observations which cannot be explained or accounted for by the main 'positively defined categories' of an approach to the body? For example, does a particular approach allow us to take into account the body's importance to human agency? Can it account for the changing historical importance of the body to social systems? Does it help explain why it is that the body has become such a concern for many modern people? Will a particular perspective on the body allow us to examine why social systems in the West appear still to be concerned with maintaining the view that women's bodies are different from and inferior to men's bodies?

This approach may be criticized by those who prefer a neat list of pre-set criteria against which theories are to be evaluated. However, its advantage lies in facilitating a broad and general overview of the strengths and weaknesses of particular perspectives on the body at a time when the sociology of the body is still relatively youthful.

The third major goal of this book involves attempting to go beyond the description and analysis of existing perspectives on the body in sociology by developing the outlines of what I consider to be a more satisfactory approach. This approach builds on the very considerable gains which have already been made in analysing the body in sociology and philosophical anthropology, and I work towards it by taking what I consider to be most useful from the perspectives outlined in the early chapters of this book. As I describe and assess existing work on the sociology of the body, I also seek to develop its insights in a significantly new direction. Although I do not intend to develop a full blown theory of the body in this book, it is worth saying something briefly here about the approach I will be promoting.

I shall be arguing that the body is most profitably conceptualized as an unfinished biological and social phenomenon which is transformed, within certain limits, as a result of its entry into, and participation in, society. It is this biological and social quality that makes the body at once such an obvious, and yet such an elusive phenomenon. On the one hand, we 'all know' that the body consists of such features as flesh, muscles, bones and blood, and contains species-specific capacities which identify us as humans. On the other hand, though, even the most 'natural' features of the body change over the lifetime of an individual. For example, as we get older our faces change, our eyesight deteriorates, our bones can become brittle, and our flesh starts to sag. The sizes, shapes and heights of bodies vary according to the care and nutrition they receive, while the openness of the body to social relationships and environments also contributes to its elusiveness. Our upbringing, for example, affects our bodies in a myriad of ways: our development as girls and boys who walk, talk, look, argue, fight and urinate differently all depends on the patterns of body training we receive from our parents and others (Haug, 1987). Medical and other technical interventions into the body also highlight the biological and social character of the body and have made it even more difficult to grasp exactly what the body is.

The biological and social constitution of bodies points to another component of the general approach to the body I want to promote in this book. In its attempts to avoid the pitfalls of biological reductionism, sociology has traditionally treated 'nature' and 'culture' as if they were distinct spheres, the analysis of which belonged to different disciplines. As Arthur Frank (1991) has pointed out, this division unhappily reflects the nature/culture bifurcation which pervades the body literature, and which tends to assume that the body can be analysed and explained without reference to its 'natural' properties and dispositions. However, this nature/culture dualism is an unnecessary and unhelpful split. The human body has been evolving for thousands of years and forms a very real base for social relations. In contrast to social constructionism, it is important to recognize that the body is not simply constrained by or invested with social relations, but also actually forms a basis for and possesses productive capacities which *contribute towards* these relations. The species capacities we are provided with at birth, such as the capacity for upright walking, speech and tool use, provide us with the ability to forge social relations. They also serve to shape those relations. For example, our embodiment means that we cannot be in two places at once, and imposes limits on the number of people we can meet and communicate with at any one time (Giddens, 1984). Social relations may take up and transform our embodied capacities in all manner of ways, but they still have a basis in human bodies.

In promoting a general approach towards the body, I also want to suggest that the sociology of the body needs to say something about the mind/body relationship. This is a subject which is often neglected by those sociologists who have focused on the body as flesh, but have not developed this into a consideration of human embodiment in general. My preference, as will become clear later, is for a view of the mind and body as inextricably linked as a result of the mind's location within the body. However, I shall not be exploring in any detail the long and detailed *philosophical* debates which have focused on this subject. Instead, drawing on the work of George Lakoff, Mark Johnson and Bob Connell, I will consider the *sociological* implications of the close relationship which exists between the categories and classificatory schemes we work with, and our bodily existence. This will be accomplished through an explicit discussion of the issues in Chapter 5, and by an implicit concern with the sociological consequences of the mind's location within the body in Chapters 6–8.

In establishing the outlines of this general approach towards the body, Chapter 5 is something of a key chapter as it seeks to move beyond what I consider to be the limitations of both naturalistic and social constructionist approaches to the body. I briefly consider the role of human evolution in providing us with species-specific capacities, and draw freely on the work of Bob Connell and Peter Freund. These two writers have provided important analyses of the 'gendered body' and the 'emotional body'. Taken together, their work suggests how social divisions become embodied in women and men. These gendered bodies then form the basis for subsequent social relationships, partly because of the ways in which they give rise to particular conceptions about the body. In Chapters 6 and 7, I shall also make the more controversial argument that the work of Pierre Bourdieu and Norbert Elias can be used to help overcome many of the biology/society, mind/body and nature/culture splits apparent in naturalistic and social constructionist approaches to the body. Furthermore, rather than simply providing general methodological approaches toward the body, the analyses of these writers can be interpreted as offering to us actual theories of the body in society.

The works of Bourdieu and Elias have been interpreted in many ways, but they are not usually regarded as providing us with theories of the body, and have yet to be fully utilized by sociologists of the body. My fourth main aim in this book, however, is to suggest in some detail that at the very core of their respective writings lie specific views of the body which take very seriously the sociological consequences of human embodiment as a physical phenomenon. I have already suggested that classical sociology adopted a dual approach to the body, and it is certainly the case that this approach continues to characterize a great deal of contemporary sociology. There are exceptions, though, and I suggest that Bourdieu's writings can be read as providing us with a theory of the body as a form of *physical capital*, while Elias's work is centrally concerned with elaborating what I refer to as a theory of the *civilized body*. Both of these authors provide sociologists with powerful, contrasting approaches to the body which help overcome the dual approach sociology has traditionally adopted to the body. They also have much to say about the position of the body in society and its implication in people's sense of self-identity.

Bourdieu's notion of the body as a form of physical capital points to the pervasive commodification of the body; a situation which links people's identities in with the social values accorded to the sizes, shapes and appearances of their bodies. In contrast, Elias shows us how our bodies have become increasingly individualized and now serve to separate us from others. He combines this with an analysis of how many conflicts which used to occur *between* bodies now take place *within* the embodied individual as a result of the rising demands of affect control. These processes serve to leave us alone with our bodies; investing more effort in their monitoring, management and appearance, and yet losing the satisfaction we once gained from indulging our senses and satiating our bodily desires. Elias has much more to say about the 'lived body' than Bourdieu; about how we experience ourselves and our environment through our bodies. However, the work of both theorists can be read as having much to say about the modern tendency for us to adopt a heightened reflexivity towards our bodies and why, in this context, the prospect of death should appear so disturbing to the modern individual.

This brings me to the fifth and final goal of this study: to promote the analysis of death as being of central importance to the sociology of the body. In contrast to existing studies of the body, I suggest that it is only by taking into account the prospect of death that we can fully understand the conditions associated with living as an embodied person in high modernity.

Outlining the body

Although I have not organized this book formally into sections, its contents divide into four broadly related areas. First, Chapter 2 provides a general overview of the body's position and portrayal in sociology. Second, Chapters 3, 4 and 5 examine separate methodological approaches to analysing the body in society. Third, while continuing to examine contrasting approaches to the body, Chapters 6, 7, 8 and 9 also look at why it is that the body has become a project for many people in the current period of high modernity, and analyse the limits of this orientation towards our physical selves. Fourth, the Afterword analyses the fate of body projects in the context of recent technological innovations, and at alternative conceptions of the body and self-identity, and seeks to develop further the broad approach adopted in this book. This involves reappraising some of the major theories examined in the main sections of the text, and identifying what I consider to be an important new direction in theorizing the body.

Chapter 2 provides a detailed examination of the body's dual status in sociology and of the rise of the body as an object of study. After exploring the body's absent presence in contemporary and classical sociology, I look at some of the reasons for the growing popularity of the body in sociology. These include the rise of 'second wave' feminism; the ageing of Western populations; a shift in the structure of advanced capitalist social systems; and the previously mentioned problem concerning our knowledge of what bodies are, which is connected to the rationalization of the body in modernity. This 'crisis' is reflected in recent post-modernist writings on the body which, despite their useful focus on difference, have actually given up the attempt to understand the body as a material phenomenon. It is also reflected in representations of the body in popular culture.

In Chapters 3 and 4, I examine two of the most important traditions of thinking that contemporary studies of the body have looked toward, drawn on and reacted against. Chapter 3 focuses on naturalistic views of the body. The naturalistic approach is an umbrella term which refers to a wide range of views which conceptualize the body as the biological base on which arises the superstructure of society. Society springs from the body and is constrained by the body which is, in turn, formed by the unchanging realities of nature. While most usually associated with sociobiology, naturalistic views have a long and varied history and have influenced, mostly in a negative sense, how contemporary sociologists conceptualize the body. Naturalistic views have been, and still are, extremely influential in legitimizing social inequalities. However, they have also been adapted by oppressed groups in order to justify their own embodiment as privileged.

Most recent sociological work on the body, though, has reacted against naturalistic views and has drawn instead on what appear to be a radically different set of writings. Chapter 4 examines a selection of social constructionist views of the body. These perceive the meanings, importance and even existence of the body to be social phenomena. Instead of being the natural base of society, the body is the *outcome* of social forces and relations.

Four main sources have influenced social constructionist views of the body in sociology: the anthropology of Mary Douglas; the writings of social historians on the body; the analyses of Michel Foucault; and the studies of Erving Goffman. After summarizing briefly this work, Chapter 4 then focuses on Foucault and Goffman. Foucault's work is often portrayed as providing us with profound insights into the body and it is undoubtedly the case that Foucault has done much to make sociologists take the body seriously. However, I argue that his epistemological view of the body as existing only in discourse is ultimately less of a help than a hindrance to sociology. In conclusion, I examine two contemporary theories of the body which can be seen as building on the work of Foucault and Goffman; Turner's theory of 'bodily order' and Arthur Frank's 'action problems' approach to the body. Because of its importance and influence, it is worth saying something here about how I intend to examine Bryan Turner's work on the body.

In *Regulating Bodies*, Turner describes three of his previous books (*Religion and Social Theory, The Body and Society* and *Medical Power and Social Knowledge*) as constituting a 'three volume work on the body' (Turner, 1992a: 254). However, as Turner himself notes, there has been a considerable degree of development and change in the approaches he takes towards the body in these studies. This is equally apparent in *Regulating Bodies*. As a result, Turner provides us with not one, but a number of sometimes incompatible views of the body. If we look at his major contributions, Turner has formulated a major theory of the body, and a very different methodological approach to the body. I first examine his 1984 theory of 'bodily order' in Chapter 4. Turner's 1992 methodology, which seeks to combine foundationalist and anti-foundationalist views of the body, comes under brief critical scrutiny in Chapter 5. My basic argument is that Turner's initial 1984 theory suffers from the limitations that tend to beset 'core problems' perspectives in sociology. In contrast, his latest approach represents an improvement on much previous theorizing about the body, but is ultimately unable to overcome the dualism which appears in his attempt to combine foundationalist and anti-foundationalist views of the body.

Returning to the outline of this book, Chapter 5 begins by making the case for a bridge to be built between the naturalistic view of the body as a biological phenomenon and the social constructionist view of the body as infinitely malleable. 1 then examine the work of Bob Connell and Peter Freund, two writers whose respective work on the gendered body and emotional body goes some way toward meeting this goal. 1 argue that their work can be developed in a direction that helps overcome the mind/body and nature/culture divisions which have characterized the body literature. Chapter 5 then focuses briefly on the relationship between work and the body and looks in particular at Arlie Hochschild's excellent study of the 'managed heart' (Hochschild, 1983).

My analyses of Bourdieu and Elias in Chapters 6 and 7 are intended to build on Chapter 5 by examining how a general approach towards the body may be extended into a theory of the body in society. I consider that these writers provide us with two of the most powerful theories of the body that presently exist. As mentioned previously in this introduction, 1 also feel that their work can be read as having much of value to say about the body in modernity which is of relevance to my general discussion of self-identity and death in the final chapter of this book. This is despite the fact that neither writer is concerned with developing explicit theories of modernity (Bogner, 1992; Lash, 1990: 237–65).

Chapter 8 seeks to bring together many of the themes of this study by focusing on the relationship between the body, self-identity and death in high modernity. Three different approaches are described which allow us to take seriously the importance of death and the body. The first derives from the work of philosophical anthropologists and Peter Berger; the second from the writings of Anthony Giddens on modernity; and the third from the previously examined work of Bourdieu and, more particularly, Elias.

Sociology has traditionally been concerned with issues of life, rather than with the subject of death. However, I suggest that the importance of the body in the contemporary age can only be understood fully by taking into account the modern individual's confrontation with death. In a time which has witnessed a decline in the attraction of religious authority and other totalizing narratives in the West, there is a tendency for modern individuals to be left increasingly alone with their bodies in the face of death. Our bodies come simultaneously to assume great importance, as carriers of life, and to appear acutely fragile and insignificant, as mortal entities which will inevitably die.

Finally, in the afterword, I review some of the major themes of this study in the light of developments in the sociology of the body that have taken place since the first edition of this book was published. This includes an analysis of the relationship between the body and self-identity, a reappraisal of the contribution of classical sociology, and a more critical view of contemporary developments such as structuration theory. My aim here is to build on the approach developed in the first nine chapters of this book by outlining the parameters of a view of the body as a simultaneously social and natural phenomenon which can also be analysed as a multi-dimensional medium for the constitution of society.

Note

1. According to research conducted for *The Times* (19 October 2002), the UK fitness market grew by 81% between 1994 and 1999. There are now nearly 2,000 private health clubs in the UK, and a record 156 clubs were opened in 2001.

2

The Body in Sociology

Throughout its establishment and development, sociology has adopted a disembodied approach towards its subject matter. At least, that is the picture which is usually constructed from the writings of those social theorists who have grown accustomed to regarding the body variously as the province of another discipline, an uninteresting prerequisite of human action, or simply a target of social control. It would probably be more accurate, though, to portray the body as having a dual status in sociology. Instead of being missing entirely from the discipline, the body has historically been something of an 'absent presence' in sociology.

It has been absent in the sense that sociology has rarely focused in a sustained manner on the embodied human as an object of importance in its own right. As bodies were commonly regarded as both natural and individual possessions which lay outside of the legitimate social concerns of the discipline this should come as no great surprise. It was only when sociology began to question the divide between nature and society that theorists conceptualized the body as central both to the human actor and to the sociological enterprise. However, it is also possible to argue that the body has been present at the very heart of the sociological imagination.

Like the human heart, the body in sociology tended to remain hidden from view, yet at the same time it served ultimately to keep alive and nourish that which surrounded it. In being concerned with human societies sociology was inevitably concerned, if only implicitly, with the ways in which embodied subjects externalized, objectified and internalized social institutions (Berger, 1990 [1967]). Although the physical, fleshy body was rarely an object of explicit sociological concern, facets of human embodiment (e.g. language and consciousness, and the dispositions and emotions that motivated action), became central to the development of the discipline. Furthermore, the efforts of contemporary sociologists to address and overcome the dual status of the body in social theory, have now led to a growing collection of work concerned with putting the body back into sociology.

None of this is to argue that classical sociology accomplished anything like an adequate conceptualization of the body. In this chapter I want to describe in more detail the dual status of the body in sociology, and trace the rise of the body as an object of study.

The dual status of the body in sociology is illustrated by the briefest of glances at some of the core areas of the discipline. The study of social mobility, of racism, the formation of the 'underclass', social inequalities in health and schooling, and globalization, are all concerned implicitly with the movement, location, care and education of bodies. In different ways, all these areas of study are interested in how and why the social opportunities and life expectancies of people are shaped by the classification and treatment of their bodies as belonging to a particular 'race', sex, class or nationality. In the study of health and illness, for example, inequalities in morbidity and mortality rates have prompted sociologists to ask what it is about the social existence of people that affects their bodies in such dramatic ways. Clearly bodies matter, and they matter enough to form the 'hidden' base of many sociological studies.

Despite this, though, sociologists have until recently tended to shy away from specific analyses of the body. Rather, they have in the examples above concentrated on questions concerned with the social structure of particular nation-states, prejudice and discrimination, attachment to work and family, access to services, and the interlocking of local and global processes in the spheres of culture, economics and politics. If it can be argued that the body is the base of sociological investigations, it is has all too frequently been a hidden base, undertheorized and taken for granted. For example, in the case of globalism, international trade is centrally concerned with global circuits of bodies, body images and body servicing (e.g. Phizacklea, 1990). This includes mail order brides, holiday sex tours to Bangkok, and even child slavery. Less dramatic instances of body trading exist in the case of sport. For example, the American baseball major leagues have academies in the Dominican Republic which, according to Klein (1991), systematically rob this nation of its best sporting talent. These are all quite different phenomena, yet they can be seen as lying on a continuum of body exploitation which is at the very core of globalizing processes. Nonetheless, it is rare to find the body given the explicit importance it deserves in theoretical accounts of globalization. Instead, the body once again assumes the status of an absent presence whose importance to the processes under study is rarely explored in any detail.

While the human body may act in certain respects as a stimulus to the sociological imagination, both the inclusiveness and the quality of sociological research have suffered when it fails to take sufficient account of the body. The sociology of education exemplifies this point. Education systems in the economically advanced West have passed through them virtually every young person living within the boundaries of a nation-state. Indeed, the compulsory nature of schooling is one of the main reasons why social policy analysts such as Janet Finch have identified schools as prime vehicles for the delivery of welfare services (Finch, 1984). Schools are places which can potentially ensure that children are inoculated against life-threatening diseases, are monitored for signs of physical abuse, have made available to them nutritionally balanced meals, and engage in physical education. To put it simply, schools are not just places which educate the minds of children, they are also implicated in monitoring and shaping the bodies of young people.

The bodily implications of schooling have been examined in general terms by the leading French sociologist, Pierre Bourdieu. He has analysed how the development of 'cultural capital' is embodied within children through their acquisition of particular dispositions, tastes and abilities (e.g. Bourdieu, 1984, 1986). Despite the influence of Bourdieu's work, however, sociologists in North America and Britain have developed theories of schooling which focus on language and the mind, rather than on other features of human embodiment (Shilling, 1992). For example, the sociology of education has traditionally been concerned with the multiple relationships which exist between social class, cognitive development, ideology, certification and social mobility. This approach has produced a wealth of important data about educational opportunities within societies, yet has also compounded the mistaken view that schooling is concerned only with the mind, and with one sort of knowledge – the abstract and academic. This proposition is found in the writings of both liberals, who tend to equate education with intellectual development, and most reproduction theorists, who see schools functioning to inculcate dominant ideologies in the minds of pupils. Neither of these perspectives, which otherwise share very little in their analyses, take adequate note of the embodied nature of schooling or the corporeal implications of educational knowledge. Yet one has only to think of the attempts of teachers to get young children to dress themselves 'properly', ask to go to the toilet in time for accidents to be avoided, sit still and be quiet during lessons, and respect daily rituals such as morning prayers or saluting the national flag, to realize that the *moving, managed* and *disciplined body*, and not just the speaking and listening body, is central to the daily business of schooling.

The importance of the processes involved in the schooling of bodies should not be underestimated. As Bourdieu (1988a) argues, schools are involved in the production of particular forms of bodily control and expression which can serve to obtain from children and adults forms of consent that the mind could otherwise refuse. For sociologists to ignore such features of education leads to a partial and misleading view of these institutions.

I have concentrated so far on one side of the dual status of the body in sociology; on how sociology rarely focuses explicitly on the body as subject matter. I have also argued, however, that the body can be conceptualized as occupying a place at the centre of the sociological imagination. The fundamental reasons for the body's importance are based on the assumption – derived in part from the concerns of philosophical anthropology and the phenomenology of Merleau-Ponty – that the capacities and senses, experiences and management of bodies are not only central to the exercise of human agency and constraint, but also to the formation and maintenance of social systems. It is these conditions of embodiment which have provided a potent stimulus for sociological work.

Our experience of life is inevitably mediated through our bodies. As Goffman has clearly demonstrated, our very ability to intervene in social life – to make a difference to the flow of daily affairs – is dependent on the management of our bodies through time and space. To put it another way, we have bodies and we act with our bodies. Our daily experiences of living – be they derived from learning in schools, travelling to a place of employment, working in an office, buying and preparing food for a meal, or making love with a partner – are inextricably bound up with experiencing and managing our own and other people's bodies. The birth and death of bodies represents start and end points in human existence, and from the cradle to the crematorium individuals depend upon the multiple caring and inter-dependent relationships which exist between bodies. The embodiment of humans is central to the intricate techniques involved in the formation and maintenance of families and friendships, and societies depend for their very existence on the reproduction of existing and new bodies.

Bodies, then, have occupied a place in the sociological imagination as our experience and management of them form part of the general material out of which social life and social theory are forged. Our experiences of embodiment provide a basis for theorizing social commonality, social inequalities and the construction of difference. We all have bodies and this constitutes part of what makes us human beings possessed of the ability to communicate with each other, and experience common needs, desires, satisfactions and frustrations (Doyal and Gough, 1991).

While human embodiment provides at least the potential for communication and shared experiences, however, bodies are inhabited and treated differently both within and between social systems. As Marcel Mauss pointed out in 1934, cultures have specific 'techniques of the body' which provide their members with identities, govern infancy and adolescence and old age, and inform such activities as resting, talking and walking (1973 [1934]). Furthermore, as the work of Norbert Elias demonstrates, bodily differences vary historically as well as cross-culturally. For example, in the Western world our sensitivity to bodily waste has increased enormously in recent centuries, as has the tendency to perceive the surface of our bodies as an immovable barrier between ourselves and the outside world (Corbin, 1986; Elias, 1978b). Bodies also vary on an individual basis. We all have bodies but we are not all able to see, hear, feel, speak and move about independently. Having a body is constraining as well as enabling, and people who are old and disabled often feel more constrained by their bodies than do those who are young and able-bodied (Campling, 1981; Featherstone, 1995). This point about individual bodies is linked to the more general condition that in addition to the possibilities of agency that exist by virtue of us *having* bodies, we are also constrained by the brute fact of *being* bodies. They constitute a condition which both provides us with life and ensures our ultimate death (Berger and Luckmann, 1967).

The body, then, is present in, as well as absent from, sociology. It is present in that the very subject matter of sociology is embodied and shaped by the opportunities and constraints that follow from having and being a body. While sociology may have, until recently, rarely focused explicitly on the body, it has examined aspects of embodiment and the consequences of embodiment. The sociology of health and illness, for example, is concerned with evaluations which are ultimately related to the consequences of human embodiment (Turner, 1987, 1992a). This is also the case with those studies that have at their centre an interest in consciousness, knowledge and ideology (e.g. Mannheim, 1991). The location of consciousness in the body, and the relationship between ideology, knowledge and the body, is rarely explored (Lakoff, 1987). However, this does not negate the fact that sociological studies are inevitably related, if sometimes only implicitly, to certain dimensions of human embodiment.

The dual status of the body in sociology is not something that has arisen and developed by accident. Instead, the position of the body as an absent presence is part of a legacy which can be traced back to the foundation and development of the discipline. It is worth examining this in a little more detail here as it helps reveal why the initial development of sociology displayed something of a schizophrenic attitude towards the body; failing to provide explicit theories on which a sociology of the body could be built, yet having much of value to say about the embodiment of social existence. Looking at the early development of the discipline also helps illustrate why the absence of a sustained, and explicit focus on the body did not prevent later sociologists from drawing on key dimensions of the sociological tradition in order to frame their own studies of the body in society.

The body in classical sociology

The dual status of the body in sociology is clearly apparent in the concerns and work of the 'founding fathers' of the discipline. On the one hand, Karl Marx, Max Weber, Emile Durkheim, and other classical sociologists such as Georg Simmel, Ferdinand Tönnies and Karl Mannheim rarely focused on the body in its entirety as a subject of investigation. Turner (1991a: 7) has even gone so far as to argue that 'The question of the ontological status of social actors remained submerged, and in so far as classical social theorists turned to such issues, they defined the human actor in terms of agency, which in practice meant the rational choice of ends' (Turner, 1991a: 7). On the other hand, though, the body was just too important to be excluded completely from the writings of these sociologists. As well as being concerned with aspects of embodiment, such as language and consciousness, the body as a physical component of social control had a habit of appearing in some of their most important writings on methodo-logy, the constitution of social systems, and modernity. This is particularly evident in Marx's analysis of how the development of capitalist technology linked and subordinated working class bodies to machinery, Durkheim's theory of the elementary processes underpinning the constitution of moral orders, and Weber's writings on the rationalization of the body within bureaucracy.

To begin with, then, there are good reasons why the body in its entirety did not occupy a central place in the foundation of sociology. Sociologists such as Durkheim were concerned with identifying and establishing a disciplinary field which was distinct from and irreducible to the natural sciences. In proclaiming sociology as an independent science, Durkheim (1938: xlix) also defined its interests and methods as opposed to those of psychology. Psychology was concerned with the individual as opposed to the social, and psychological explanation was seen by Durkheim to be based on what he called 'organico-psychic' factors. These are the supposedly pre-social features of the individual organism which are given at birth and are independent of social influences (Lukes, 1973: 17). Humans, then, were marked by a nature/society dualism, and the biological body for Durkheim was placed firmly in the sphere of nature.

This view had an enduring effect on sociology and meant that the natural and biological were frequently ruled outside of, and unimportant to, the sociologist's legitimate sphere of investigation (Newby, 1991). Consequently, there was an inevitable reluctance for sociologists to incorporate in their studies aspects of human embodment which it was thought could be explained by the disciplines of biology or psychology. The foundation and early development of sociology, then, were both social and epistemological projects which had detrimental implications for the body as subject matter.

Bryan Turner (1991a) has identified four specific reasons for the failure of classical sociology to generate an overt sociology of the body, and these can all be related to the disciplinary project undertaken by the 'founding fathers'. First, sociologists such as Durkheim, Weber, Simmel and Mannheim were generally concerned not with the historical evolution of human beings, but with similarities between industrial capitalist societies and how these contrasted with traditional societies. This involved attempting to make sense of the industrial, political and ideological revolutions occurring in Europe during the late eighteenth and early nineteenth centuries. Classical sociologists were concerned with the growth in wage labour, urban centres and mechanization; the rise of political democracy and citizenship; and the waning power of religion and the gradual secularization of values and beliefs. The very scale of these changes appeared to necessitate explanations based on changes in such societal factors as the social division of labour (Durkheim), class struggle and the forces of production (Marx), or processes of rationalization and intellectualization (Simmel and Weber).

Second, sociology has tended to concentrate on the conditions required for order and control or social change in society. The complexity of industrial capitalism generated an interest in its functioning which focused on society as a social system. As the work of Simmel and Weber demonstrated, this did not rule out a concern with individuals. However, it did encompass a commitment to the construction of theories based on interrelationships with a social rather than biological basis. Unfortunately, the body was often conceptualized as a 'natural', pre-social phenomenon, which did not warrant serious sociological analysis.

Third, the capabilities required for human agency became equated with consciousness and the mind, rather than with the management of the body as a whole. Bodies came to be seen, at best, as an uninteresting condition of social action. This is exemplified by Weber's typology of social action which associated truly human action with intellectually-processed, rational action. The body was usually considered as a passive container which acted as a shell to the active mind (which was identified as distinguishing humans from animals). This point is linked to the more general orientation that classical sociology assumed towards the conceptual dichotomies considered to be at the centre of sociological explanation. The structure/agency dilemma (with Durkheim's concentration on social facts as 'things' and Weber's emphasis on *verstehen* resolving this problem in very different ways) has usually taken precedence over issues concerned with the mind/body relationship, which has all too frequently been left to the province of philosophy.

Fourth, a theoretical consequence of these epistemological and onto-logical commitments was that sociology did not show much interest in the anthropological view of the body as a classification system. It was the mind, rather than the body, which served as the receptor and organizer of images concerned with, and deriving from, social stratification. As Turner (1991a) notes, in its most enduring form, this approach is evident in the Marxist tradition's focus on ideology, false consciousness and reification.

Turner's list of reasons why the 'founding fathers' failed to develop a sociology of the body may provide an overly harsh assessment of some of their contributions (Shilling and Mellor, 2001), as my discussion below will illustrate, but it reflects much of how their work has been received by body theorists. In addition to Turner's reasons, furthermore, two additional points help us understand further why there was no explicit sociology of the body within the classical tradition. The first concerns the methodo-logical approaches promoted by the discipline. These laid great emphasis on abstract cognitive inquiry which was somehow meant to operate as if it was located outside of, and was entirely separate from, the body. For example, Durkheim argued that it was the open and empty mind of the professional sociologist, rid of bodily impurities such as emotional preju-dices, which was able to apprehend the reality of social facts. Conceptual thought was provided by society, and concepts were defined in opposition to 'sensations' which were organically based in the body. Not only did this emphasis tend to relegate the role of bodily experience in the accumulation of knowledge, it also threw into doubt the validity of lay actors' knowledge precisely because it was likely to be infected by corporeal existence (Bauman, 1992b). As Durkheim (1938) argued, events in our daily lives gave us only confused, fleeting and subjective impressions, but nothing in the way of scientific notions or explanatory concepts.

Finally, perhaps one of the major reasons why the 'founding fathers' failed to develop a sociology of the body concerns their embodiment as men. As I stressed at the beginning of this section, the founding of sociology was a social as well as an epistemological project, and it was a project carried out by men. The risks women faced during pregnancy, the high numbers who died during childbirth, and the rates of infant mortality which characterized the industrial revolution may possibly have been reflected through a greater consideration of the body if Marx, Simmel, Weber and Durkheim had been women. This point is not meant to suggest that knowledge is entirely reducible to immediate bodily experience, but it is to acknowledge an integral connection between knowledge and embodiment. The sociologies of the 'founding fathers' were profoundly influenced by the intersection of their personal biographies with the social issues dominating the societies in which they lived, and if they had been faced at first hand with the corporeal dangers associated with being a woman at that point in history it is arguable that their writings may have been concerned to a much greater degree with such features of embodiment.

It would be inaccurate, though, to argue that classical sociology completely ignored the body. While the body was frequently ruled out of court as the primary object of legitimate sociological concern, its essential importance in understanding social life meant that classical sociologists were unable to ignore it completely. As Turner (1991a) puts it, there has been a marginalized, almost 'secret' history of the body which has included the work of Marx, Engels and Weber, and developed later through the writings of Nietzsche, Elias, Marcuse and Foucault. For example, Marx and Engels were concerned with the corporeal conditions surrounding consciousness, the condition of the English working class and the detrimental consequences of the division of labour under capitalism, which deformed the bodies of workers and made them fit only for limited and repetitive activities in the workplace. Similarly, *The German Ideology* (1970 [1846]) was concerned with the relationship between the material existence of humans, labour and the development of consciousness. Marx and Engels argued that human development occurred as the result of a dialectical relation between nature as determined by the conditions of human life, and the practical transformation of those conditions. The body was simultaneously a social and biological entity which was in a constant state of becoming, and possessed transcendent potentialities which could only be fully realized within a future communist state.

Emile Durkheim may have viewed sociology as involving the study of 'social facts', but he was also concerned with how these facts became incorporated into the bodily dispositions of individuals. In totemic societies, the identity of the collectivity was often inscribed quite literally on the bodies of its members. It is because bodies 'share in a common life, [that] they are often led, almost instinctively, to paint themselves or to imprint images on their bodies that remind them' of this life (Durkheim, 1995 [1912]: 233). Tattooing, 'the most direct and expressive means by which the communion of minds can be affirmed', exemplifies this 'instinct' and occurs within clans or tribes 'apart from any reflection or calculation' (Durkheim, 1995 [1912]: 233–4).

The writings of Georg Simmel can be interpreted as displaying a consistent interest in the relationship between embodied life and social and cultural forms (Shilling, 2001). This was associated with his argument that those forms through which the bodily dispositions of individuals were able to express themselves initially constituted a product of life's expression, but soon became stabilized, developing into fixed traditions or institutions which paid no attention to *newly emerging* bodily needs (Simmel, 1971 [1918]). The development of the money economy had a particularly deleterious effect on people's bodily character. By treating everything in terms of its exchange value, the money economy promotes the dominion of means over ends and, in so doing, distances people from the sensory gratifications associated with attaining particular ends or interacting with particular others (Simmel, 1990 [1907: 429–30]: 444). Associated with a city life in which the gaps between work and rest have shortened, the money economy is also associated with a decline of energy and an erosion of those emotions which helped bind people together into stable relationships.

Weber was also concerned with the body in his writings on the protestant ethic, social action, rationalization, the 'iron cage' of bureaucracy, charisma and eroticism. For example, in the *Protestant Ethic and the Spirit of Capitalism* (1985 [1904–5]), Weber examines the Calvinist idea of the calling as a way of ascertaining the psychological conditions which accompanied modern capitalism. According to Weber, the Calvinist view of predestination produced in people a deep insecurity which manifested itself in a motivation to lead a wholly disciplined and dedicated life on earth. This especially directed puritans into business, in which endless hours could be dedicated to the accumulation of money. Central to this 'spirit of modern economic life' was the voluntary subjugation of the body to strict routine. Hard work and effort in the sphere of production was coupled with frugality and denial of the sensuous in the sphere of consumption. Indeed, Turner (1992b) has argued that implicit within Weber's work was a concern with the relationship between modernity and the body.

The dual status of the body in sociology was, then, firmly established in the work of the 'founding fathers'. The physical, material body was evident in some of their writings, and these analyses retain an influence on contemporary studies on the exploitation and rationalization of the body. However, the *overall* orientation of the sociological project they established mitigated against locating the embodied human as the central area of investigation. This is symbolized by Durkheim's *Suicide* (1951 [1897]), a study which was implicitly all about the effects of different forms of religious community on the body, but which did not formulate explicitly the theory of embodiment which can be viewed as lying at its core.

The development of the discipline in the twentieth century continued to exhibit something of a schizophrenic attitude to the body. For example, in its continuing eagerness to maintain itself as a separate field of study, sociology reacted against variants of biological reductionism – which account for human behaviour, social institutions and social inequalities with reference to their 'natural' biological basis. As a consequence of this reaction, while structuralist and interpretive sociologies were concerned with ideologies which impacted on the mind, and questions of language, meaning and understanding, they remained uninterested in explaining the significance of those features of the body usually thought to be explicable in terms of the biological. The effect of this was that neither structuralist nor interpretive sociologies took adequate note of human embodiment in its entirety. Instead, they developed through a rather one-sided focus on those features of human embodiment which could most easily be claimed as belonging to the sphere of the social (language and consciousness). For example, structuralism tended to conceptualize structure as equivalent to the cognitive internalization of dominant value systems, and dissolved the causal significance of other features of the body by making individuals the products of forces over which they had no control (e.g. Althusser, 1971). In contrast, much interpretive work viewed agency as bound up with the mental and linguistic abilities of individuals to make and re-make their daily lives. While consciousness and language are embodied, this feature of their existence has usually been ignored. Instead, the fully corporeal agent tended to disappear in a nexus of 'projects', 'intentions', 'perspectives' and 'coping strategies' (Schutz, 1970; Woods, 1980a, 1980b), as the body was portrayed as a passive shell activated by the creative minds of subjects.

The rise of the body in sociology

Despite the limited concerns of classical sociology, the importance of the body has been highlighted by a growing number of sociologists since the 1980s. They have focused on and made explicit the 'hidden' importance accorded to the body in traditional sociology, and have sought to begin the process of integrating the body fully into the discipline. This work has resulted in a steady growth of empirical and theoretical studies. Among the most important of these, Turner's (1984) text, O'Neill's (1985) *Five Bodies*, reviews by Freund (1988) and Frank (1990), the three (1989) volumes on the history of the body edited by Feher, Naddaff and Tazi, and the collection edited by Featherstone et al. (1991) have helped to make the body a respectable and thriving object of sociological study.

This work has sought to improve the status of the body in sociology – moving it away from being an absent presence towards becoming a central object of study – and has identified the potential benefits that studying the body might bring to the discipline. For example, a focus on bodies and embodiment can shed new light on many of the problems which have traditionally preoccupied sociologists such as the structure/agency and macro/micro divisions. Furthermore, as the body is located at the very centre of the nature/culture and biology/society divisions – which have historically served to delineate and limit the scope of the discipline – taking the body seriously can be seen as central to widening the scope of the discipline to such areas as the environment.

Why was it that the body emerged as a phenomenon considered worthy of detailed study in its own right in the late twentieth century? The answer to this question involves examining some of the social and academic changes which have had the effect of highlighting the importance of the body in society during this time. This is not to imply that the body has been unimportant in previous historical periods. Indeed, the body has tradi-tionally been an object of concern for national governments at times of economic and military crises, and at times of rapid social change. For example, fears were expressed in the United States and Britain during the nineteenth century about over-indulgence and fatness among the rich, and malnutrition among the poor. Both these issues were related to worries about racial degeneration and the degenerating stock of society (Searle, 1971), and intensified when recruitment to the armed forces was perceived as a problem. In Britain, for instance, the army rejected 408 per 1,000 recruits on physical grounds between 1864–67, while the Navy rejected 4,410 out of 5,567 boys applying for naval service in 1869 (McIntosh, 1952). These themes were continued following the Boer War when the Committee on the Physical Deterioration of the Race led to a number of social reforms concerned with the threat to the race of physical, bodily deterioration. This committee was part of the wider 'national efficiency' movement which was concerned much more with the body than with the mind.

Similar worries were expressed in the United States about the fitness of youth when the draft statistics for the First World War were published. During this war, the bodily shape of American society as a whole became a concern. A professor of physiology at Cornell estimated that New Yorkers alone carried ten million pounds of excess fat that would have been better used as rations for soldiers, and stated that the most patriotic act for millions of Americans would be to get thin. Others suggested that the money saved from overeating should be invested in Liberty Bonds (Green, 1986; Schwartz, 1986). The body had become, and not for the first time, a metaphor for the fitness and health of the nation.

The body was also taken up in a more radical way, as an image and ideal, by twentieth-century totalitarian societies. Fascism, and particularly National Socialism, revolved around a cult of the 'mindless body' which was reflected in its art and derived from a clearly articulated view of the desirable social body.

The current interest by sociologists in the body, then, cannot be explained with reference purely to its emergence as a social problem. It can be argued, however, that the precise social significance of the body has begun to change. Whereas the body used to be given meaning by national governments, there has in recent years been an increased concern on the part of women to 'reclaim' their bodies, and from people in general to define their bodies as *individual* possessions which are integrally related to their self-identities. This has been accompanied by the tendencies mentioned in the introduction; that our ability to control our bodies has been accompanied by a questioning of their meaning. In this context, the modern emergence of the body as an important social issue has coincided with the interests of sociologists in a way that was not previously apparent. Furthermore, once the body was recognized as a valid object of study, there was a growing recognition among interested sociologists that those issues which had traditionally concerned the discipline were also concerned implicitly with the body.

More specifically, the social and academic changes which have formed the context for the current concern with the body involve the rise of 'second wave' feminism; demographic changes which have focused atten-tion on the needs of the elderly in Western societies; the rise of consumer culture linked to the changing structure of modern capitalism; and the previously mentioned 'crisis' in our certainty about what bodies are.

First, the rise of 'second wave' feminism in the 1960s and its subsequent development placed on the political agenda issues related to the control of fertility and abortion rights. They also formed the context for a more general project among women to 'reclaim' their bodies from male control and abuse. As Gill Kirkup and Laurie Smith Keller (1992) note, self-help groups were important parts of the women's movement in this respect, and they incorporated attempts to further women's knowledge and control over their bodies (e.g. Boston Women's Health Collective, 1971). This is linked to a strong tradition in which women have placed their bodies at risk during political struggles, for example, in the suffragette and nuclear peace move-ments. Such methods of protest, though not entirely novel, have also been drawn on by new social movements; members of Greenpeace, for example, have put themselves at considerable physical risk in order to increase public awareness of the bodily dangers of pollution.

As well as using the body as a vehicle of political action and protest, feminist analyses of women's oppression brought the body into academic conceptualizations of patriarchy. In contrast to those theories which identify the family as the basis of women's position in society, a number of feminists gave primacy to the biological body as the source of patriarchy. The best known example of this is Shulamith Firestone's *The Dialectic of Sex* (1971). Firestone's book has been much criticized for containing an analysis based upon biological reductionism: its central thesis being that an unequal sex class system emerged directly from the different reproductive functions of female and male bodies. However, one of the great merits of this early feminist text was that it addressed directly the body's implication in systems of domination and subordination. Later, more sophisticated discussions of patriarchy built on Firestone's work by incorporating the body into frameworks which sought to integrate analyses of production with reproduction. For example, McDonough and Harrison (1978) viewed patriarchy in terms of the control of fertility together with the sexual division of labour; Heidi Hartmann (1979) sought to define patriarchy by considering men's control of women's sexuality and their access to economically productive services; while Sylvia Walby's model of patriarchy (1989) as six partially independent structures explored the importance of human embodiment in her discussions of male violence and sexuality. Radical feminists have also placed great importance on the body as a basis of female oppression through, for example, its location as a site for the construction of 'compulsory heterosexuality' (Rich, 1980).

In addition to the appearance of the body in general discussions of patriarchy, feminists also undertook more specific studies of the com-modification of women's bodies in pornography, prostitution and surrogate motherhood (Singer, 1989). They have also done much to highlight both the differential socialization to which girls' and boys' bodies are subject (Lees, 1984), and the male-orientated knowledge which has informed the development of the medical services and the treatment of women's bodies during pregnancy and childbirth (Greer, 1971; Martin, 1989 [1987]; Miles, 1991; Oakley, 1984). Debates about the role of reproduction and house-work in the economy also highlighted the position of women as the prime servicers of men's and children's bodies (Oakley, 1974). For example, Nickie Charles and Marion Kerr (1988) suggested that wives are materially and symbolically responsible for the family's main meal of the day, and explored how these women sacrificed their own bodily needs for rest, recreation and nutrition to ensure their children and husbands were adequately fed and cared for during illness (see also David, 1980; Murcott, 1983).

In sum, feminist work highlighted the fact that women frequently have to learn to live with what can be termed 'over-burdened bodies'. As Rosen (1989: 213) puts it, women who are wives, mothers and paid employees 'often experience intense emotional and physical stress: there are simply too many conflicting demands, too many things to do, too little time to do them'. Building on such insights, feminist theory has also highlighted the general importance of the body in legal and gender systems of oppression, examining what it is about the embodied existence of people that has maintained men's domination over women (Eisenstein, 1988; Griffin, 1978; Heritier-Auge, 1989).

This feminist focus on the embodied existence of women did more than simply highlight the multiple ways in which bodies were implicated in social relations of inequality and oppression. Analysis of the sex/gender, nature/culture and biology/society divisions began to break down, or at least reduce the strength of, some of the corporeal boundaries which popular and academic thought had posited between women and men (e.g. Oakley, 1972). Indeed, feminist scholarship has helped to problematize the very nature of the terms 'woman' and 'man', 'female' and 'male', and 'femininity' and 'masculinity' by questioning the ontological bases of sexual difference.

This touches on a further important point which is worth emphasizing here. Feminist thought did not always concentrate on women's bodies to the exclusion of men's bodies (even though the literature has sometimes given the impression that women are somehow 'more embodied' than men). These bodies of men and women needed to be seen as inextricably related subjects, as it was the power and force exercised by male bodies which was instrumental in controlling the bodies of women. Furthermore, the development of 'men's studies' in North America and the UK gave an added impetus to the study of the embodiment of masculinity. Despite the fact that much of this work has been criticized for being rather static in its concern with what men *are*, rather than what they *do* (Maynard, 1990), it has given a further impetus to the study of the body as a valid object of sociological concern. The number of courses that came under the umbrella of men's studies grew significantly throughout the 1970s and 1980s and were accompanied by such landmark texts as Pleck and Sawyers's 1974 edited collection in the United States and Tolson's 1977 book on post-war masculinities in the UK (see Kimmel, 1987). This tradition has also included important works on the social construction of the 'male homosexual' (Bray, 1982; Weeks, 1977). As Jeff Hearn and David Morgan (1990) point out, the focus on sexuality within men's studies did not automatically entail an examination of the body. In practice, however, the two subjects have become related. This situation has been reinforced by recent studies on men, sexuality and the transmission of HIV, which include a concern with the cultural meanings given to specific sexual acts involving penetration and the exchange of sexual fluids (Connell and Kippax, 1990).

One aspect of men's studies which is particularly relevant to this discussion is the examination of male body images which has been undertaken by several writers. For example, Mishkind argues that men have become increasingly preoccupied with male body images and maintain an idealized image of the perfect body type to which they aspire: the 'muscular mesomorph'. In summarizing Mishkind's work, Kimmel (1987) identifies three social trends which have led to this preoccupation. First, the decreasing stigmatization of gay men as 'failed men' – the replacement of the old stereotype of the limp-wristed 'sissy' with the new stereotype of the gay macho bodybuilder – has increased men's overall concerns with body image and also legitimized these concerns. Second, women's increased participation in the public sphere has led to a kind of 'muscular backlash' given that cognitive, occupational and lifestyle differences between men and women are decreasing. In this context, body image emerges as one of the few areas in which men can differentiate themselves from women. The third related trend concerns the decreasing importance that the 'breadwinning' role assumes in the formation of men's self-identity. In its place, there has been an increasing emphasis on consumption and self-identity which has at its centre a concern with the surface territories of the body (Bourdieu, 1984; Ehrenreich, 1983; Featherstone, 1987). The argument that men have become increasingly preoccupied with certain types of male body images is supported by Jeffords's book *The Remasculinization of America* (1989), which examines how and why such imagery has arisen and become available. Jeffords addresses the explosion of muscular body imagery in culture and the media in the context of the increasing social and political gains which have been made by women in recent decades. These images, which are especially prevalent in the 1980s spate of Vietnam war films, promote masculinity as a set of prized qualities which are under threat and which should be defended by 'the exclusion of women and the feminine' from public life.

If the rise of feminism was the first factor to highlight the importance of the body, the second factor concerns the growth in the number of the aged in Western societies. This has become a matter of international concern largely because of the economic implications of this demographic trend. Increasing elderly populations have serious implications for social policy and state expenditure in the areas of pensions, medical provision, caring services and accommodation (Turner, 1991a). An increased focus on human bodies has come about both as a cause and a consequence of these changes. Medical advances have helped create much greater life expectancy rates in comparison with the last century. At the same time, the medical services have been faced with more problems concerning the health and well-being of the elderly. In a very real sense, they have become victims of their own success. This situation has been made more visible with the rise to power of governments in both the United States and the UK during the 1970s and 1980s that were influenced by the ideas of the 'new right' and were concerned not to increase but to reduce public expenditure commitments.

A related, if less important, reason for the rising academic concern with the body can be seen in the ageing of the sociology profession. While in the early 1980s the life experiences and reflexivity of sociologists fed into a growing interest in the sociology of ageing, this developed into a more general concern with the sociology of the body and how social definitions of bodies have entered into general conceptions of 'youth' and 'aged' which have attached to them different symbolic values. The young, slim and sexual body is highly prized in contemporary consumer culture, whereas ageing bodies tend to be sequestrated from public attention (we rarely, for example, see them engaged in sexual activities in movies).

The third factor which has increased the focus on the body in contemporary society concerns a shift in the structure of advanced capitalist societies in the second half of the twentieth century. Broadly speaking, there has been a shift in emphasis from a focus on hard work in the sphere of production coupled with frugality and denial in the sphere of consumption. Instead, the decline of competitive capitalism based on a labour force inclined to save and invest, the historical shortening of the working week, and the proliferation of production orientated towards leisure, encourages the modern individual to work hard at *consuming* as well as producing goods and services. Related to this, the body in consumer culture has become increasingly central and has helped promote the 'performing self' which treats the body as a machine to be finely tuned, cared for, reconstructed and carefully presented through such measures as regular physical exercise, personal health programmes, high-fibre diets and colour-coded dressing. As Featherstone (1982: 22) argues, within consumer culture the body ceases to be a vessel of sin and presents itself instead as an object for display both inside and outside of the bedroom.

Placed in a broader historical context, these events can also be seen to be outgrowths of changes initiated in the nineteenth century when clothes and the presentation of the body shifted from being instant signs of social place to become manifestations of personality (Sennett, 1974). Whereas flamboyant clothes, hats, make-up and wigs were once seen as objects of interest in their own right, inextricably bound to and expressive of social position, the 'presentation of self' (Goffman, 1969) is now seen as signifying the real character of individuals. In contemporary consumer culture this has helped promote among people the experience of both *becoming* their bodies, in the sense of identifying themselves either negatively or positively with the 'exterior' of the body, and of being regularly *anxious* about the possibility that their body will let them down or 'fall apart' if they withdraw from it constant work and scrutiny. This notion of body anxiety is central to the way many people perceive their bodies as projects and is also linked to the experience of the environment as dangerous and out of control, and the fear of ageing, illness and death. As Zygmunt Bauman notes, in view of 'the centrality of body-cultivation in the activity of self-constitution, the damage most feared is one that can result in poisoning or maiming the body through penetration or contact with the skin' (Bauman, 1992b: 199). Recent panics have focused on incidents like mad cow disease, salmonella in eggs, shrimps fed on poisonous algae, the dumping of toxic waste, and the levels of the carcinogen acryamide in food that has been fried, baked or microwaved.

The fourth factor behind the rise of interest in the body is concerned with the tendency mentioned in the introduction for an increase in the potential to control our bodies to be accompanied by a crisis in their meaning. In discussing the increased control that modernity exerted over the body, Turner (1992b) has pointed out that diet was central to the early rationalization of the body. Whereas early dietary schemes were connected to religious values, the nineteenth century saw an increasing scientific literature of diet emerge with the establishment of nutritional sciences. These knowledges were first applied in the realm of social policy to measure the food required by various populations such as prisoners and army recruits, and were applied by the social reformers Charles Booth and Seebohm Rowntree as measurements of poverty levels in the larger British cities. Furthermore, the rationalization of the body was intimately connected to the 'sciences of man' which sought in such places as prisons, armies and workplaces to 're-educate the mind via the discipline and organization of bodies in a regime that sought to maximize efficiency and surveillance' (Turner, 1992b: 123, 126).

Our ability to control the body has continued apace as a result of advances in transplant surgery, artificial insemination, *in vitro* fertilization and plastic surgery. As John O'Neill (1985) demonstrates, there are now few parts of our body which technology cannot restructure in some way or other. Hair implants can rid the appearance of baldness, false teeth are common and there are a growing number of organs that can be transplanted into the human body. Heart transplant surgery is no longer newsworthy (unless carried out on very young children and even here much of the newsworthiness concerns the ability of science to intervene in the infant body) and eye transplants can restore the ability to see. Pacemakers allow people with defective hearts to function normally, various parts of the body can be restructured using artificial materials, and increasingly sophisticated artificial limbs have become available in recent years.

One of the images which is frequently employed in describing such developments is the 'body as machine', and it is pertinent to this discussion to note the increasing appearance of this metaphor in lay perceptions of health and illness (Rogers, 1991). At first sight this image may appear to contradict the idea that individuals have, in the late twentieth century, sought to define their bodies as individual possessions integrally related to their self-identities. The 'body as machine' is a metaphor which might suggest the body as radically 'other' to the self. However, there is nothing to stop individuals feeling that the body is *their* machine which can be maintained and fine-tuned through diet, regular exercise and health check-ups. Nonetheless, the 'body as machine' metaphor has at the very least provided national governments with opportunities for linking the idea of the body as an individual project, with the body as an entity amenable to social control.

An interesting example of this was provided by the British government's 1992 White Paper *The Health of the Nation*. Launched in conjunction with a series of national newspaper advertisements, depicting images of machinery underneath the flesh of women's and men's bodies, the White Paper was accompanied by a campaign designed to 'improve the health of everyone in England, helping people to live longer, healthier lives'. Integral to this campaign was an attempt to get people to care for their own bodies as resources that could be maintained and fine-tuned in order to reduce the risk of heart disease, strokes, lung cancer and accidents.

The 'body as machine' is not merely a medical image, however; one of the areas in which the body is most commonly perceived and treated in this way is in the sphere of sport. Radical critics of sport have noted that the vocabulary of the machine dominates the language of sport and have argued that it is through the practice of sport that the body has come to be understood as 'a technical means to an end, a reified factor of output and production . . . as a machine with the job of producing the maximum work and energy' (Brohm, 1978). In sport, the body is seen as a complex machine whose performance can be enhanced, and which can break down and be repaired, just like any other machine. In this context, sports science is well on the way to perfecting equipment and training techniques which specify, isolate and transform those parts of the body that are of most importance for competitive performance, and it has long been recognized that success in athletics tends to be dominated by those countries whose scientific knowledge is best applied to the 'raw material' of athletes' bodies.

In discussing the rationalization of the body, it is important to recognize that this is a deeply gendered phenomenon. One of the ways in which the body has been subjected to increased discipline and control is through bureaucratic regimes which specify when particular quantities and qualities of work must be carried out irrespective of the bodily needs of workers. Productivity schemes sometimes fall into this category and, by failing to allow for adequate rest and relaxation during the working day, can lead to stress-related illness among both women and men (Hochschild, 1983). However, as Emily Martin (1989 [1987]) and Sophie Laws (1990) argue, bureaucratic regimes frequently subject women's bodies to more control than men's bodies. This is because women are expected to manage and conceal menstruation, pregnancy and menopause 'in institutions whose organization of time and space takes little cognizance of them' (Martin, 1989 [1987]: 94).

So far I have concentrated on the vast increase in control over the body that has accompanied processes of rationalization in modernity. However, while rationalization may have provided us with the potential to control our bodies more than ever before, and have them controlled by others, its double-edged nature has also reduced our certainty over what constitutes a body, and where one body finishes and another starts.

Two manifestations of this uncertainty can be seen in recent developments in electronic media and film. 'Virtual reality', for example, promises to collapse boundaries between technology and the body. One possible development is associated with the concept of 'teledildonics' which involves the user dressing in a bodysuit lined with tiny vibrators. Telephone connections would 'bring together' others similarly outfitted, and their telephone conversations would be accompanied by artificially-induced bodily sensations and computerized visual representations in their headsets of their bodies engaged in sexual encounters (Rheingold, 1991; Springer, 1991). Teledildonics promises the ultimate in safe sex through an encounter with 'intimacy' which is both disembodied and sanitized.

Horror films provide another example of instabilities in the meaning and boundaries of the body. Here, the threat to the body used to come from an exterior source, whereas it now frequently comes from the interior of the body as a result of its inherent instability. The dominant trend in the 1950s and 1960s was to portray victims as vulnerable to attack from external foes such as aliens from outer space. In the 1970s, though, the body was under threat from demonic *possession*, as in the case of *The Exorcist*. The *Alien* trilogy had both John Hurt and Sigourney Weaver 'giving birth' to monsters, and the threat to the body's interior stability continued to grow in the 1980s with the *Nightmare on Elm Street* series. The ghastly 'Freddy' would emerge from deep within the recesses of the mind, while his victims were dreaming, to mutilate and destroy the powerless body. The *Terminator* films have continued to reflect the instability of what bodies are, with machines becoming increasingly human and humans becoming increasingly machine-like.

An additional manifestation of this crisis in our knowledge of bodies can be found in the difficulties sociologists have had in pinning down precisely what is meant by the body. As Bryan Turner says in his 1984 text, 'In writing this study of the body, I have become increasingly less sure of what the body is' (Turner, 1984: 7). In this respect, we now have discursive and material bodies (Turner, 1984); physical, communicative, consumer and medical bodies (O'Neill, 1985); individual and social bodies (O'Neill, 1985; Turner, 1992b); and medicalized, sexualized, disciplined and talking bodies. We also have distinctions in German between *Leib* (the lived body) and *Körper* (the fleshy shell) (Ots, 1990); and the elaboration of this distinction into the body-incarnate, and the somatic and corporeal aspects of the body (Frankenberg, 1990). These distinctions give an idea of the rich variety of themes that have been explored in writings concerned with the body and human embodiment. They are also indicative of the uncertainty that sociologists have in identifying what the body is. These uncertainties have been reflected most clearly in post-modernist writings which have abandoned the modernist project of 'knowing' what the body is. Instead, the body is viewed simply as a 'blank screen' or 'sign receiving system', ever open to being constructed and reconstructed by external texts or discourses (e.g. Kroker and Kroker, 1988).

Four major social factors, then, have formed the context for the relatively recent rise of the body in sociology. These are the growth of 'second wave' feminism; demographic changes which have focused attention on the needs of the elderly in Western societies; the rise of consumer culture linked to the changing structure of modern capitalism; and a growing crisis in our knowledge of what the body is. The diversity of these factors is important in illuminating why it is that the body has risen as an object of academic inquiry, not just in sociology but *across* the social sciences. Given the variety of social factors which have drawn attention to the importance of the body in contemporary society, it is understandable that separate disciplines should view the body as significant to their own specific concerns. The variety of these factors also helps to explain why there has not been much in the way of common approaches to the body in society. As the reviews by Freund (1988) and Frank (1990) illustrate, there is typically little which unites the diversity of studies which have been produced on the body and embodiment.

Drawing the body in sociology

Earlier in this chapter I spoke of the dual status of the body in sociology, and sought to illustrate this status by referring to the precarious place of the body in much contemporary and classical sociology. I then described some of the social and academic factors which have highlighted the importance of the body in contemporary society. The range of these factors suggests that there are many books which could be written on the body in sociology. For example, the social construction of gendered bodies, body images, the body in medicine, the ways in which biology and culture interrelate in the reproduction and development of human bodies, and the body in consumer culture, all warrant major studies in their own right. My aim in the next few chapters of this book though, is to provide a fairly broad, critical overview of some of the most important and interesting approaches which are relevant to the sociological study of the body. I hope this will provide a number of contexts in which the recent proliferation of studies on this subject can be located, and a basis on which we can develop a more adequate approach towards conceptualizing the body and its position within, and relationship to, society.

3
The Naturalistic Body

The body may have been something of an absent presence in sociology, but it has occupied a position of far greater centrality in other traditions of social and popular thought. In this respect, *naturalistic* views of the body have, since the eighteenth century, exerted a considerable influence on how people have perceived the relationship between the body, self-identity and society. Naturalistic views are not identical, but they deserve to be seen as a coherent approach as they share an analysis of the body which views it as the pre-social, biological basis on which the superstructures of the self and society are founded.

Naturalistic views hold that the capabilities and constraints of human bodies define individuals, and generate the social, political and economic relations which characterize national and international patterns of living. Inequalities in material wealth, legal rights and political power are not socially constructed, contingent and reversible, but are given, or at the very least legitimized, by the determining power of the biological body.

The naturalistic approach continues to shape popular contemporary conceptions of the body and this is especially apparent in the view that gender inequalities are the direct result of women's 'weak' and 'unstable' bodies. Naturalistic views have also influenced how sociologists have conceptualized and analysed the human body. This has mainly been a negative influence, as sociologists have tended to react against the methods adopted by naturalistic views. However, one influential strand of contemporary feminism has forged its own radically innovative view of the origin and maintenance of patriarchy by maintaining the methodological orientation of the naturalistic approach (O'Brien, 1981). In the introduction to this book I stated that as well as describing and assessing different perspectives on the body, I would be taking from each what I considered to be most useful in building towards the outlines of a distinctive approach to the body. Now, an approach that reduces the complexities of social relationships and inequalities to an unchanging, pre-social body seems hardly to be fruitful ground from a sociological viewpoint. However, naturalistic views at least take seriously the idea that human bodies form a basis for, and contribute towards, social relationships. This is especially the case for the feminist variants I shall be examining later on in this chapter. Naturalistic views undoubtedly overstate the importance of, and draw all sorts of unwarranted conclusions from, what they hold to be 'natural' in the human body. Nonetheless, if sociology is to grasp the full importance of the body

Critique of post-structuralism

Sociology

Physl biolgral

for social systems, it does need to take into account the contribution that bodies make to social relations.

In what follows I shall look at several examples of the naturalistic approach and will pay particular attention to how sex differences have been justified with reference to the body. Before describing and assessing specific examples of this approach, though, it is important to trace the emergence of naturalistic views of the body. The view that the biological body constitutes the basis of society, and social inequalities, emerged at a particular historical period and was associated with specific social interests. Historians of the body have illustrated this particularly well in relation to the subject of sex differences.

notion of body naturalistic > emerged in C18th

The emergence of natural bodies

Thomas Laqueur (1987, 1990) has argued that the human body tended until the eighteenth century to be perceived as an ungendered, generic body. The male body was considered the norm, but the female body had all the parts of the male; they were simply arranged in a different and inferior pattern (Duroche, 1990). For hundreds of years it had been generally accepted that women had the same genitals as men, except that theirs were inside the body and not outside it. The vagina was imagined to be an interior penis, the labia a foreskin, the uterus a scrotum, and the ovaries were seen as interior testicles. It was also believed that women emitted sperm (Laqueur, 1990).

This 'one sex/one flesh' model dominated thinking about sexual differences from classical antiquity to the end of the seventeenth century. Women were considered to be the inferior of men, but their inferiorities did not inhere in any specific, permanent or stable way within their bodies. Bodies were important but, unlike their portrayal in later, naturalistic views, they were seen as receptors as much as generators of social meanings:

> the paradox of the one sex model is that pairs of ordered contrarieties played off a single flesh in which they did not themselves inhere. Fatherhood/ motherhood, male/female, culture/nature, masculine/feminine, honorable/ dishonorable, legitimate/illegitimate, hot/cold, right/left, and many other pairs were read into a body that did not itself mark these distinctions clearly. Order and hierarchy were imposed upon it from the outside. The one sex body, because it was concerned as illustrative rather than determinant, could therefore register and absorb any number of shifts in the axes and valuations of difference. Historically, differentiations of gender preceded differentiations of sex. (Lagueur, 1990: 601)

As Ludmilla Jordanova (1989) argues, it is commonly supposed that the distinction between culture and nature is a straightforward and stable division which has been used to define the separate identities and roles of male and female bodies. The conditions of women's embodiment were ruled by natural cycles associated with pregnancy, childbirth and menstruation. In contrast, men's embodiment allowed their minds a greater degree of freedom. This permitted them to engage in the sphere of culture. However, as the quotation illustrates, the scope and precise meaning of the culture/nature divide has, in fact, been historically dynamic. While gender divisions were perceived as natural before the eighteenth century, neither the content nor the boundaries of these divisions were wholly stable and did not correspond to simple biological correlates.

Laqueur (1990) illustrates this situation by looking at sex differences during the Renaissance. While there were at least two 'social sexes' during the Renaissance, with radically different rights and obligations, the human body was insufficiently demarcated to act as an exclusive ontological support for these divisions. In the usual course of events these social sexes were maintained by the unproblematic process of identifying a baby as a female or male. Humans with an external penis were declared to be boys and were allowed the privileges of that status, while those with only an internal penis were assigned to the inferior category of girl. However, changes in corporeal structures could push a body from one juridical category (female) to another (male). This was because these categories 'were based on gender distinctions – active/passive, hot/cold, formed/unformed, informing/formable – of which an external or an internal penis *was only the diagnostic sign* (Laqueur, 1990: 135, emphasis added).

Naturalistic views were not, then, dominant in the period prior to the eighteenth century. Instead of the social position of women and men being determined by their respective biologies, whatever one thought about women and their rightful place in the world could, apparently, be understood in terms of bodies permanently open to the 'interpretive demands of culture' (Laqueur, 1990). However, a revolutionary shift took place sometime during the eighteenth century which substituted 'an anatomy and physiology of incommensurability' for the existing model of social difference based on homologies between male and female reproductive systems (Duroche, 1990; Laqueur, 1987). During the eighteenth century, science began to flesh out the categories of 'male' and 'female' and base them upon biological differences. This was accompanied by the development in the late eighteenth century of the notion of 'sexuality' as a singular and all-important human attribute which gave one a self-identity which was firmly contrasted with the *opposite* sex (Laqueur, 1990: 13).

As Laqueur (1987) and other historians of the body have noted, this radical shift in the conceptualization of women's and men's bodies had much to do with one of the great dilemmas of Enlightenment egalitarianism. The model of the human body the Enlightenment had inherited from antiquity caused the problem of how – given Enlightenment beliefs in universal, inalienable and equal rights – the real world of male domination over women could be derived from an original state of genderless bodies. The dilemma 'at least for theorists interested in the subordination of women, is resolved by grounding the social and cultural differentiation of the sexes in a biology of incommensurability' (Laqueur, 1987: 19). In short, a naturalistic reinterpretation of women's bodies was made to solve some of the ideological problems involved in justifying inequality in eighteenth- and nineteenth-century gender relations (Gallagher and Laqueur, 1987).

The geography of bodies and their precise composition became increasingly important with the progress of science in the eighteenth and nineteenth centuries. Furthermore, from being a *manifestation* of self-identity and difference, the body was viewed increasingly as the very *basis* of human identity and social divisions. During the eighteenth century, it gradually became taken for granted that the body provided access to uncontestable knowledge about both individuals and society. There was in particular an obsession with the female body, as a living, fleshy phenomenon, as a corpse and as a skeleton (Jordanova, 1989; Schiebinger, 1987). The results of this obsession were used to provide a biological basis for women's social inferiority.

'Women's troubles'

Historically, the position of women in society has been undermined repeatedly by attempts to define their 'unstable' bodies as both dominating and threatening their 'fragile' minds. The seventeenth-century claims of Hobbes and Locke, and the French revolution, questioned the certainty of the natural, male-dominated, social order. However, the development of the social and natural sciences in the eighteenth and nineteenth centuries was employed to reassert the superiority of men and the inevitability of female subordination in public and private life (Martin, 1989 [1987]: 32). In short, to be embodied as a woman was to have a body and mind which were unable to withstand the rigours of physical and mental exertion.

These arguments about the physical frailty of women were brought together and crystallized into a model of health and illness in the eighteenth century which held that lifestyle and social position were closely related to a person's bodily capacities. The lesson drawn from this model was that women's bodies made them fit only for the production and care of children and the 'creation of a natural morality through family life' (Jordanova, 1989: 26).

At the onset of the nineteenth century an increased division was made between the structure and functioning of women's and men's bodies. This involved a characterization of women's bodies as pathological. For example, from being a natural and healthy process with analogues in men (in the form of blood letting), menstruation became something likely to cause disease among women. Women's behaviour was also seen to be governed by menstruation, a view which was incorporated into the very functioning of the state. For example, in 1896 an American woman was released from the charge of shop-lifting on the grounds that she was suffering from kleptomania, a condition later traced back to the effects of 'suppressed menstruation' (Shuttleworth, 1990).

Historically there have been clear links between women's attempts to gain civil, political and social rights on the one hand, and renewed interest in theories that confirm women's embodiment as biologically inferior on the other. Susan Barrows (1981) has illustrated how fears related to the Paris Commune and the political possibilities opened up by the Third Republic stimulated an elaborate physical anthropology of sexual difference which was used to legitimize the status quo. Similar responses came from those opposing the women's suffrage movement in Britain. Furthermore, when women began to campaign for entrance rights to universities, attempts to exclude them focused around the Darwinian theory of the evolution of sex differences (Fedigan, 1992; Kaplan and Rogers, 1990: 206). One of the issues raised by opponents of women's entry concerned the size and capacity of female brains. In France, Gustave Le Bon (a founder of psychology and an exponent of craniometry) measured thirteen skulls in total in order to feel able to conclude in 1879 that women:

> represent the most inferior forms of human evolution and that they are closer to children and savages than to an adult, civilized man. . . . A desire to give them the same education, and, as a consequence to propose the same goals for them, is a dangerous chimera. (Gustave Le Bon, quoted in Gould, 1981: 104–5)

A related argument concerned the damaging consequences that overtaxing the brain would have on women's reproductive ability. Writers on education during the nineteenth century were frequently concerned to promote the view that intense or prolonged intellectual activity among women would lead to specific gynaecological disorders and the general deterioration of health. As women's natural vocation involved bearing children, it followed that the world of academia should remain a male preserve. John Richardson (1991) points out that this view continued to inform educational reports in the twentieth century. For example, a 1923 report from the Board of Education in England made the following claim:

> The periodic disturbances, to which girls and women are constitutionally subject, condemn many of them to a recurring, if temporary, diminution of general mental efficiency. Moreover, it is during the most important years of school life that these disturbances are most intense and pervasive, and whenever one of them coincides with some emergency, for example, an examination, girls are heavily handicapped as compared with boys. (Board of Education, 1923: 86)

It would be wrong to give the impression that attempts to define women's bodies as inferior to men's were without opposition. For example, there were some positive views of women's menstruation in the nineteenth century which portrayed it as a healthy process (Martin, 1989 [1987]). It is also the case that not all attempts to define women's bodies as inferior relied on a simple opposition between male and female. Anthropologists have identified a long tradition of men *appropriating* women's energy and fertility, rather than defining themselves in opposition to it, and these practices continued in Western scientific and medical discourse of the nineteenth century (Heritier-Auge, 1989). For example, in 1823 Julien Virey wrote that it is the energy of sperm which *activates* women's functions and provides married women with their self-assurance and boldness (Virey, 1823). Women's natural sensitivity makes them both biologically suited to the care of children but also subject to dangerous passions which overrule the reason of the mind. Both of these states are governed by men, as sperm is seen to be responsible for the production of children and the stimulation of 'immoral desires'. Consequently, women's proper place is one of submission within the family.

Despite the inconsistencies in this argument, women's fragility and instability are viewed as both activated and safeguarded by men. It is not that women's and men's bodies simply occupy opposite poles in nature but, in a theory which both echoes and expands on the biblical tale of Adam and Eve, that men are instrumental in allowing women to lead an embodied life.

As the nineteenth century progressed, the medical profession presided over an increasing medicalization of women's bodies which established ever stronger boundaries between the bodies of men and women in the sphere of waged work, sexuality, leisure and sport (Mangan and Park, 1987). The practical effects of this medicalization were, though, largely confined to the middle classes. Men, women and children of the working classes often laboured together in similar circumstances with no regard being paid to the 'special' corporeal needs of women for rest and relaxation.

Two related features tend to be prominent in explanations of why theories equating women's bodies with 'pathological nature' and the private sphere of life became increasingly popular in the nineteenth century. These concern the growing impact of industrial change on middle class men's positions of privilege and security, and the increasing influence of economic metaphors in understanding social and natural life.

First, the rapid economic changes of the nineteenth century gave rise to fears among men that they were no longer in control of their own destiny (Shuttleworth, 1990). The growing scale of industrial operations and the pace of economic change appeared to threaten the stability of social life and reduce the importance of the individual in the productive process. Naturalistic views of the human body, bolted on to existing gender divisions in society, served to transplant fears of economic chaos away from the minds of men and on to the biological bodies of women:

Notions of gender differentiation fulfilled the ideological role of allowing the male sex to renew their faith in personal autonomy and control. Unlike women, men were not prey to the forces of the body, the unsteady oscillations of which mirrored the uncertain flux of social circulation; rather, they were their own masters – not automatons or mindless parts of the social machinery, but self-willed individuals, living incarnations of the rational individualists and self-made men of economic theory. The disruptive social forces that had to be so decisively channelled and regulated to ensure mastery and controlled circulation in the economic sphere were metonymically represented, however, in the domestic realm, in the internal bodily processes of the women in the home. (Shuttleworth, 1990: 55)

Second, the scope and pace of economic change in the nineteenth century also provided an increasing stock of metaphors which were used by the dominant in society to understand and explain social and natural life. For example, Susan Sontag (1979) has argued that medical ideas about illnesses such as tuberculosis were informed by attitudes associated with early capitalist accumulation. Energy, like savings, could be depleted through reckless and non-productive expenditure. In the case of gender differences, menstruation came to be seen as 'production gone awry', which was a threat to the 'natural' gender order. As Emily Martin (1989 [1987]: 47) suggests, women can be seen as dangerous and threatening to men when they menstruate. They are 'not reproducing, not continuing the species, not preparing to stay at home with the baby, not preparing a safe, warm womb to nurture a man's sperm'.

The practice of defining women's bodies as different from, and inferior to, the bodies of men as a result of their reproductive functions was still common in the second half of the twentieth century. The 1960s was a period when women increasingly demanded the opportunity to enter leadership positions in the business world. At the same time, medical and lay theories built on their nineteenth-century antecedents by arguing that women's behaviour was controlled by their hormones and that during periods of pre-menstrual tension they became emotionally and intellectually erratic, unreliable and 'out of control' (Dalton, 1979). Such arguments were used to safeguard men's occupational privileges. For example, they were employed in Australia by airline companies to prevent women becoming pilots, and also prevented women becoming bank managers in the United States (Kaplan and Rogers, 1990).

Sociobiology

A number of contemporary explanations of gender inequalities still argue that women's social position is derived from the reproductive functions of their bodies. Since the nineteenth-century elaboration of sexual difference, however, genetic theories have provided an additional method of defining the embodiment of women as inferior to that of men.

The development of genetic theories of women's inferiority coincided with the economic crisis of the early 1970s, and the rise of the women's movement in the late 1960s and 1970s. The most influential theories of women's inferiority around this time came collectively to be known as sociobiology. Sociobiology was initially developed at Harvard University in the 1970s and tried to establish a biological basis for human behaviour. However, it quickly became an influential contemporary version of Darwinian evolutionism regarding sex differences (Grosz and Lepervanche, 1988). Part of the reason for its rapid growth in popularity was that by explaining social inequalities as an inevitable consequence of natural, genetic foundations, sociobiology not only justified the status quo but lent itself to being incorporated within conservative ideologies (Rogers, 1988).

Conservative ideologies were opposed to the growth of state intervention and welfare services which had taken place since the Second World War, and became increasingly popular as economic crisis in the early 1970s suggested that such interventionism was ineffective. As the 1970s progressed, elements of sociobiology were used by the neo-conservative and neo-liberal strands of the 'new right' in both the United States and the UK. They helped these rising political groupings – later to find power through the leadership of Ronald Reagan and Margaret Thatcher – to justify competition, patriarchy, heterosexuality and the nuclear family as both natural and desirable. In justifying the status quo, sociobiology proved especially flexible. Genes were 'found' for aggression, territoriality, intelligence and male dominance. It was now the genetic constitution of bodies which acted as the base on which the market and patriarchal order arose as the natural and unchangeable superstructure.

The basic unit of explanation in sociobiology is the gene. Genes, the hereditary material inside the nucleus of each cell, determine simple physical traits such as an individual's hair colour and blood group. More complex characteristics, such as the 'personality' of an individual, do not rely on the action of single genes and cannot be explained merely with reference to them. However, the logic of sociobiology does precisely this. The effect of sociobiological argument is to justify simplistic social categories on the basis that they are both natural and desirable. They are natural because the determinants of social behaviour are traced to the structure of genes. As such, unitary natural causes are found for highly complex social events. Genes are posited as the ultimate causal factor for any pattern of behaviour or social event in the world (Kaplan and Rogers, 1990). So, sociobiologists have argued that there are genes for homosexuality, conformity and even, perhaps, for upward mobility. It has also been argued that genes affect the timing of such events as someone's first sexual experience (Gregory, 1978; Wilson, 1975).

As well as being natural, dominant social categories and relations are seen as desirable. Sociobiologists adapt Darwin's theory of natural selection to argue that those genes which produce individual features and social structures best suited for survival live on in subsequent generations. Consequently, the dominant features of society are desirable *irrespective* of whether they are characterized by gross inequalities and the oppression of minority groups. Furthermore, political attempts to alter these structures are deeply misguided and dangerous. By working against human nature they are both harmful and doomed to fail. As Connell (1987) notes, society is epiphenomenal to nature. It either registers what nature decrees or 'gets sick' in the process.

In the specific case of sex differences, genes are said to cause male/female differences through their impact on the sex hormones which act on the brain (Bleier, 1984; Caplan, 1978; Rogers, 1988). As sex differences are determined by genes, sociobiologists question the validity of feminist demands for change (Buffery and Gray, 1972; Tiger and Fox, 1978; Trivers, 1978; Wilson, 1975). For example, according to Wilson (1975), divisions between the sexes are determined by biology and are great enough to cause a substantial division of labour even in the most egalitarian of societies. Consequently, there is no logical basis on which these differences can be opposed or resisted (Kaplan and Rogers, 1990).

This focus on genes serves to dissolve both human behaviour and social structures as emergent *social* phenomena. It also makes the social sciences entirely dependent on and subservient to the natural sciences. Perhaps the best example of this can be found in Richard Dawkins's *The Selfish Gene*. According to Dawkins, 'individuals are not stable things; they are fleeting' phenomena whose main purpose is to act as 'survival machines' for genes. Human beings and their behaviour have been described in various ways by the social sciences, but such theories hide from view, and neglect the importance of, the real *genetic* motor force of history.

> [The gene] leaps from body to body down the generations, manipulating body after body in its own way and for its own ends, abandoning a succession of mortal bodies before they sink in senility and death. . . . The genes are the immortals . . . individuals and groups are like clouds in the sky or dust-storms in the desert. (Dawkins, 1976: 36)

Individuals are like robots controlled by forces beyond their reach. Human behaviour and social interaction are explained in terms of the costs, benefits and even strategies of genes engaged in a competitive struggle for survival. Put simply, there is no need to look to social structures as determinants of human behaviour as there is no such thing as emergent *social* structures. For example, sex differences in human mating behaviour can be explained solely in terms of the interests genes have in maximizing their chances of survival. In humans and animals the female is said to invest a greater biological cost in reproduction than does the male. She must bear and nurture the offspring and these costs are best safeguarded by finding a reliable male partner to assist in raising the offspring. However, reproduction has little cost for the male and he has 'everything to gain from as many promiscuous matings as he can snatch' (Dawkins, 1976: 176). Sociobiologists argue that these very different strategies are adopted as they maximize the chances of genes being passed on in future generations.

This view of natural selection has been used to explain an increasing number of human traits. For example, Ardrey (1976) argues that the female orgasm developed as a way of stimulating female desire in order to guarantee that men would return from hunting trips. Alexander (1974) suggests that the menopause may have evolved because women reach an age at which it is more efficient for them to stop reproducing and concentrate on caring for existing children. Morris (1969) has argued that the reason women have 'permanently enlarged breasts' is as a signal of sexual attractiveness. Gallup (1982) argues that breasts developed as an advertisement for ovulatory potential and to compensate for the fact that ovulation is concealed in humans (Kaplan and Rogers, 1990). If successful, these corporeal advertisements increase the chances of females finding a mate and improve the possibilities of her genes living on in another body.

Having briefly described the main features of sociobiological explanations, it is important to examine the flaws in this influential approach to the significance of the body in society. Critics of sociobiology sometimes take for granted that this form of explanation adopts *biological* methods which, they argue, are unsuitable for the investigation of *social* phenomena. However, as Connell (1987) points out, this credits sociobiology with an unwarranted scientific status. Sociobiology is pseudo-biological as it does not rest on serious biological investigation of human social life (see also Benton, 1991).

Despite its claim to scientific explanation, sociobiology cannot produce for inspection the mechanisms of biological causation on which its theories rest (Connell, 1987: 69). When sociobiology does deal in quantifiable phenomena, it makes unjustified generalizations and unwarranted leaps between levels of analysis. For example, in *The Inevitability of Patriarchy* (1973), Goldberg slides from using findings which identify *average* differences in hormonal levels between men and women, to statements about *categorical* differences in social behaviour between the sexes. This approach exaggerates differences and downplays the common capacities, such as language, shared by the sexes. As Connell (1987: 71) argues, the idea that 'differences in hormone levels reach out through the complex situational, personal and collective determinants of individual behaviour to remain the ultimate determinants of its social consequences, supposes a mechanism of hormonal control far more powerful than physiological research has actually found'.

Instead of resting on serious scientific explanation, sociobiology begins with an interpretation of current social life – which is often sexist, ethnocentric and factually wrong in other ways – and projects this back on to a mythical history of human societies. Processes of natural selection are then posited in order to justify these social arrangements as both natural and desirable (Connell, 1987: 68).

Sociology may traditionally have adopted a partial view of human agents by focusing on the cognitive aspects of embodiment. However, while sociobiology has refocused on the body, or certain components of the body, it also provides a partial view of human beings by reducing us to our genes. Furthermore, while sociobiology makes assumptions about the relationship between the body and society, it is unable to provide any mechanisms which would account for the collective structuring of human life and social institutions, or the likely direction of social change. As Washburn (1978) argues, by 'investigating human behaviour with the questions and techniques suitable for animals with very simple nervous systems, the whole nature of human behaviour is lost'.

In terms of sex differences in behaviour, sociobiology faces an additional criticism which calls into question its efforts to explain the biological constitution of social life. This concerns the validity of the categories 'male' and 'female' on which sociobiological explanations are based. Kaplan and Rogers (1990), Stanley (1984) and Birke (1992) all provide useful summaries of the problems involved in dividing people permanently into the two mutually exclusive categories of male and female.

Newly-born children are usually assigned to one sex or another on the basis of whether a penis is present at birth. A penis is usually present when the genetic material is XY (male) and absent when it is XX (female). In adolescence, primary and secondary sexual characteristics develop in response to hormonal changes which are governed by the XY or XX genotype. However, sexual characteristics can also be influenced by environmental factors such as nutrition and stress. Moreover, the genetic make-up of individuals is not exclusively divided into XY and XX as a range of other genetic varieties exist. For example, XO is characterized as an underdeveloped female as no sex hormones are produced. XYY and XXY are two further genetic types labelled as males. Other considerations, such as testicular feminizing syndrome, add further complications to the picture. In testicular feminizing syndrome the cells of the body fail to respond to testosterone and do not differentiate into a male pattern even though the genotype is XY and male sex hormones are released. Such individuals are genetically male but appear to be female even though they cannot reproduce (Kaplan and Rogers, 1990: 212–13).

Sex hormones are also categorized as male and female. Oestrogen and progesterone are referred to as 'female' sex hormones and testosterone as the 'male' sex hormone. However, females also release testosterone from the adrenal gland, and males also release oestrogen from the testes. So, there is a considerable overlap between the sexes, and environmental factors can also alter the degree of this overlap.

Differences between the sexes become even more minimal in the case of brain functioning. There is no direct one-way influence of the hormones on the brain and environmental factors have again been shown to have an important influence on its operation (Kaplan and Rogers, 1990: 213–17). As Lynda Birke (1992: 99) concludes, when it comes to sex differences in brain functioning, 'the mass of inferences and assumptions far outweighs that of clear evidence'.

Given the great variety of genetic types and hormonal conditions which characterize individuals, it is impossible to classify accurately all humans into the restrictive categories of male or female. Indeed, Gisela Kaplan and Lesley Rogers argue that there are no biological phenomena which can properly be organized according to this bipolar dichotomy, and conclude that the 'rigid either/or assignment of the sexes is only a convenient social construct, not a biological reality' (1990: 214). Birke (1992) supplements this conclusion by demonstrating how certain sex differences change over the human life course, and how others are culturally specific and can be eliminated even within a culture by physical and mental training.

Kaplan and Rogers's discussion is extended by Liz Stanley (1984) who, as well as providing an interesting discussion of intersexuality (cases where someone's assumed sex and one or more of their biological sex characteristics do not match), highlights anthropological data which attest to the seemingly endless variety of ways in which societies classify people as women and men. In relation to this, she cites Margaret Mead's *Sex and Temperament in Three Primitive Societies* (1963 [1935]), which describes three cultures existing in close proximity to each other, but each having very different ideas of what it is to be a woman or a man.

One particularly interesting discussion of anthropological work, which reveals the inadequacy of conventional definitions of sex which posit universal and unchanging divisions between women and men, is Françoise Heritier-Auge's (1989) article on male domination and the appropriation of women's fertility. It is worth quoting from at length:

> among the Nuer of East Africa, a woman recognized as sterile, which is to say one who has married and remained childless a certain number of years (until menopause, perhaps?), returns to her own family, where from then on she is considered as a man – 'brother' to her brothers, paternal 'uncle' to her brothers' children. As an 'uncle' she will be in a position to build up a herd, just like a man, from her share of the cattle paid as a bride price on her nieces. With the herd and the fruits of her personal industry, she will in turn be able to pay the bride price for one of several wives. She enters into these institutionalized matrimonial relations as the 'husband'. Her wives wait on her, work for her, honor her, show her the courtesies due a husband. She hires a servant of another ethnic group, usually a Dinka, of whom she demands services including sexual services for her wife or wives. (Heritier-Auge, 1989: 294)

Heritier-Auge argues that among the Nuer it is evident that the sterile woman is not or is no longer a 'woman' properly speaking. She is clearly considered more of a man than a woman. Consequently, in this society it is purely the capacity for fertility that constitutes the difference between male and female.

Despite such biological and anthropological evidence, the simplistic once and for all either/or consignment of individuals to the categories of male/female continues to influence biological and medical thinking. For example, medical models of appropriate behaviour patterns often differ for women and men. While a man may be described as angry or aggressive, the same behaviour in women may be redefined as hysteria or 'nervous disorder' and be seen as in need of correction. This explanation is certainly consistent with the much higher number of prescriptions women receive for drugs in comparison with men (Miles, 1987).

Grosz and Lepervanche (1988) argue that the biological and medical sciences still frequently compare women to male norms which are taken as universal. Some texts, such as Gray's *Anatomy*, unselfconsciously represent the general case of every feature as male. The female body is illustrated only to show how it differs from the male. As Grosz and Lepervanche note: 'Judged in these terms, women's bodies can only be regarded as anomolous, imperfect and in need of explanation whereas men's bodies are taken for granted as adequate representatives of "human" attributes' (1988: 12).

There have been repeated attempts to limit women's civil, social and political rights by taking the male body, however defined, as 'complete' and the norm and by defining women as different and inferior as a result of their unstable bodies. Women were supposedly confined by their biological limitations to the private sphere, while only men were corporeally fit for participating in public life. However, it is not only gender that has served as a principal means of differentiating bodies and limiting women to the pre-social sphere of nature. The naturalistic view of the body has also made frequent appearances in attempts to legitimize the subordination and oppression of black peoples.

Dangerous 'others'

The historical construction of masculinity and femininity in the West has been intimately bound up not only with the body, but with *Christian* notions of the body. In Christianity, the body is seen as weak and sinful and in need of strict control and regulation by the mind (Brown, 1988). Flesh, sexuality and emotionality are all seen as potentially uncontrollable forces which are a source of great anxiety.

These attitudes were especially prominent during the Protestant Reformation in England. During the sixteenth and early seventeenth centuries, English Christianity focused on personal piety, individual judgement, self-control and self-scrutiny. Winthrop Jordan (1982: 56) argues that it was in this context of self-discovery that Englishmen used peoples from overseas as 'social mirrors', and were inclined to discover attributes in 'savages which they found first, but could not speak of, in themselves'.

Instead of individualizing and internalizing their fears of the flesh, Englishmen have historically dealt with this anxiety by projecting it on to the bodies not only of black men, but of womenkind as a whole (Rutherford, 1988). As well as being unstable, women's bodies have been seen as a source of temptation which has threatened to corrupt the rationality of white men's existence. However, white women did at least have a rightful place in reproducing a healthy race fit for domestic and colonial rule (Searle, 1971). In contrast, black peoples represented 'dangerous others' and were viewed as uncivilized, uncontrollable sexual and physical beings who constituted a threat to the moral order of Western civilization (Mercer and Race, 1988). This was supposedly clear to see as a result of the sexual appetites of black men and the size of the African penis (Walvin, 1982). During the sixteenth to eighteenth centuries, European notions about the possibility of an evolutionary relationship between the African and the ape *dichotomy of*

reinforced this view. James Walvin (1982) describes how it was widely believed at the time that sexual relations took place between Africans and apes.

Explanations of why black peoples were defined through their bodies in this way usually go back to the social relations existing under colonization and slavery. However, there is evidence to suggest that in certain countries, such as England, strong notions of 'black' and 'white' existed long before there was any contact with Africans. As Jordan (1982: 44) notes, 'White and black connoted purity and filthiness, virginity and sin, virtue and baseness, beauty and ugliness, beneficence and evil, God and the devil'. Instead of being formulated as a way of legitimizing already existing white domination, these images may have been used as a way of bringing a stock of ready 'knowledge' to bear on early meetings with Africans.

It is undoubtedly the case, though, that where such images existed they were massively reinforced and supplemented by the establishment of colonization and slavery. As Frantz Fanon (1984 [1952]) argues, myths about animalistic black sexuality were self-consciously fabricated by white slave owners as a way of reducing their fears and providing an ideological justification for the brutal practices which supported colonization. These myths were incorporated into a literature which portrayed the atrocities of slavery as beneficial to its victims. For example, the beginnings of the European slave trade in Africa in the 1560s, which continued in British territories up to abolition in 1833, produced a literature which illustrated African men and women as savages who were ugly, violent and lascivious. Ethnology further justified slavery by referring to the innate capacity of blacks for knee bending, and even talked of the inherited disease of drapetomania (the tendency to run away) (Rose, 1976).

As slavery came under increased attack in the eighteenth century, the descriptions of Africans by slave traders grew increasingly derogatory. Africans were defined purely in terms of their differences from British culture. Whereas Britain was civilized and rational, Africa represented a 'pre-social' order governed by the unrestrained biological drives of primitive peoples.

Primitive

Images of the dangers and mysteries of Africa lived on, and in the late Victorian period, it was common for English upper and middle class men to undertake travels in Africa in order to prove their 'manhood' (Segal, 1990). Social Darwinism was also employed to justify the establishment and maintenance of English colonies. As Steven Rose (1976) notes, as the English were the fittest, their civilizing mission abroad was supported by a biological imperative. Other 'scientific evidence' was also marshalled to prove the 'otherness' and inferiority of black peoples. For example, Paul Broca, a leading exponent of craniometry, argued that:

science lent itself to the ideological justification of racism colonisation & slavery

A prognathous [forward-jutting] face, more or less black color of the skin, woolly hair and intellectual and social inferiority are often associated, while more or less white skin, straight hair and an orthognathous [straight] face are the ordinary equipment of the highest groups in the human series. . . . A

white supremacy is relational highly dependent on black

[handwritten: naturalistic body generates social meaning.]

group with black skin . . . has never been able to raise itself spontaneously to civilization. (Quoted in Gould, 1981: 834)

In America, defining the worth of black people through their bodies was also used to justify the treatment of blacks as commodities (more than one million blacks were sold from 1820 to 1860), and the use of black women for slave breeding (Marable, 1983). Fear of black sexuality also permeated the punishments inflicted on black people. For example, in the lynching of blacks between 1885 and 1900, the accusation of rape was made only in a third of all cases. However, the *justification* given for these lynchings always referred to the protection of white women from the bestial black man (Carby, 1987). This fear of black sexuality was also reflected in the final act of many lynchings, which involved the castration of victims, and lives on in contemporary American society. For example, with a few exceptions that are the responsibility of black film makers such as Spike Lee, Hollywood's portrayal of black sexuality has been confined to images of rape or as 'mere animal capacity incapable of producing civilization' (Dyer, 1986: 139; Lyman, 1990). Alternatively, a safer approach has been simply to deny black actors a strong sexual identity and confine them to roles updating the theme of the 'loyal black servant' (Lyman, 1990). *[handwritten: ← mammy]*

In artistic forms which have traditionally allowed for a greater range of expression than the cinema, the black body tends to be constructed as an object of dread and fascination by white men. For example, in the photography of Robert Maplethorpe, black men are both allowed and *reduced to* their sexuality. Gay pornography also tends to have a limited range of representations for black men who tend to appear either as sexual studs or as 'exotic orientals' (Mercer and Race, 1988).

The oppression of black men and women in contemporary America continues to be reinforced through social practices which appear to reflect a deep dread of the black body. In the legal system, for example, although 50 per cent of men convicted of murder involving rape in the Southern states are white, over 90 per cent of men executed for this offence are black. Most of these are accused of raping white women while, according to Staples (1982), by the beginning of the 1980s no white man had ever been executed for raping a black woman.[1] *[handwritten: Why!? Cos can't be raped]*

It is important to stress that the images of black people that have justified slavery, colonization and other forms of oppression were not uniform, but varied widely in their typifications and possessed their own specific trajectories. However, they have tended to focus on the body. An interesting example is provided by Mrinalini Sinha's (1987) research into the British ideology of moral imperialism in late nineteenth-century Bengal. Britain justified its rule in Bengal through a Victorian gender ideology which framed the stereotype of 'effeminate' Bengali men, and identified defects in Indian society which made it unfit for self-rule. Bengali men were not fit to share political and administrative power because of their questionable masculinity. Victorian ideology held that early sexual experience was meant to corrupt the moral fibre of men, and Bengali men were suspect because of their inability to exercise sexual restraint. This was exhibited through the practice of child marriage. The Bengali male's physique was also constructed as 'puny' and 'diminutive' by the colonial authorities who used these images as sources of mirth and derision (Sinha, 1987: 218, 227). Bengali bodies were still viewed as 'other' in comparison with those of their white British rulers, but their detailed construction varied widely when compared to images of the African body.

Historically, the negative construction of black bodies has made them targets for a variety of moral panics surrounding health and disease. Under slavery, black Africans were seen as diseased and dirty. Fears of unclean 'foreign bodies' were later transported into immigration law. For example, restrictive health criteria were first introduced into British immigration law in 1905 in the context of a major panic about the 'degeneration' of the British race. In the 1960s, a minor outbreak of smallpox among Pakistanis in Bradford caused a moral panic on the part of the British Medical Association who demanded the medical surveillance of black immigrants. This was subsequently put into practice in the 1970s through the 'virginity testing' of Asian women (Jones, 1977; Mercer and Race, 1988). The latest and most widespread association of black bodies with disease has come as a result of AIDS, which has scapegoated black Africans as being both the possible cause and carriers of this syndrome (Alcorn, 1988). As well as being known as the 'gay plague', AIDS has been reported as the 'African plague', and has led to suggestions in Britain that even greater immigration and travel controls were needed over black Africans (Frankenberg, 1990; Watney, 1988).

Racism has been characterized by repeated attempts to impute negative characteristics to the bodies and general corporeal existence of various peoples. Indeed, the very construction of 'race' (a social category with no scientific basis in nature) has been dependent on the efforts of dominant nations and peoples classifying humans on the basis of corporeal characteristics such as skin colour. As Philip Cohen (1988) makes clear, there is nothing natural about categorizing people on the basis of particular bodily characteristics (such as colour) rather than others (height, for example). Social factors enter into the construction of certain peoples as 'visible', and the characteristics which define visibility can change over time. For example, in Britain in the 1850s Irish immigrants were singled out as 'dangerous' whereas in the 1950s their arrival was officially hardly noticed, despite the fact that they outnumbered immigrants from the New Commonwealth (Cohen, 1988).

In the 1870s and 1880s Jewish refugees were portrayed as 'less-civilized', 'unclean' and 'immoral', while in the 1950s the corporeal lives of other groups were stigmatized. West Indians, arriving as 'cheap casual labour', were viewed as carefree, low-living, immoral, disorderly colonial subjects. Sikhs, Moslems and Hindus on the other hand, seem to have been characterized as poor yet ambitious populations, set apart from their neighbours not only by language but by alien religions and customs and a tendency toward insularity (Jones, 1977). In the 1970s, black youth were further criminalized in Britain through the social construction of mugging; a process which involved a prolonged and intense campaign on the part of the British media (Hall et al., 1978).

Sociologically, naturalistic views of the body are important because of the repeated attempts that have been made by the dominant in society to justify their position with reference to the supposedly inferior biological make-up of the dominated. The precise content of these views has varied historically, but they continue to play an influential role in contemporary society. Defining people's worth exclusively through their fleshy bodies is still common, even though the mind has come to constitute a more central part in these definitions of superiority and inferiority (Birke, 1986; Gould, 1981; Lewontin et al., 1984; Rose, 1984). However, while naturalistic views have most frequently been employed by the dominant sections of society, it is also important to examine some of the attempts that have been made to invert the arguments of these groups.

The privileged body

Historically, the practice of equating an individual's worth with their body has favoured dominant groups in society. Locating the causes of social inequalities in the unchanging, natural, biological body serves to make protests against the status quo appear both futile and misguided. However, it has not always been the dominant who have sought to equate individual identity with the biological body. The black power movement of the 1960s and 1970s sought to invert racist forms of the naturalistic body by celebrating black corporeality as privileged (Segal, 1990). Feminists have also appropriated a naturalistic approach to the body by drawing on an epistemology grounded in biological essentialism: 'a feminist version of the eternal female' (Barrett, 1987; Eisenstein, 1984: 106).

Shulamith Firestone formulated an early feminist version of the naturalistic approach, but her analysis retained many similarities to previous writings which portrayed women's bodies as inherently limiting. Firestone's argument (1971) is based on the premiss that the sexual division of labour has a biological basis. Human reproductive biology is seen as the fundamental basis for the universality of 'the biological family'; a unit characterized by children's dependence on a mother who is, in turn, dependent on a man. Although Firestone recognizes the importance of social institutions in maintaining male dominance, these have their ultimate foundations in human reproductive biology which makes women weaker than men and dependent on them. Consequently, women can break out of their subordination only by conquering the 'tyranny of their reproductive biology' through reliable contraceptive technology and methods of childbirth which minimize the use of the female body.

53

Alison Jaggar (1984) has pointed out that while Firestone's analysis was not widely adopted by the feminist movement, this did not prevent other feminists from constructing alternative accounts of patriarchy which continued to view the unchanging, pre-social biological body as the base on which self-identity and society is constructed. These accounts differed from Firestone's in seeing the female body in a far more positive light. As Jaggar (1984) notes, contemporary radical feminist writings abound with references to 'the power inherent in female biology', 'the creative power that is associated with female biology', and the 'native talent and superiority of women'. In these accounts, there is the repeated suggestion that women's special powers lie in their closeness to nature, which exists by virtue of their power to give birth. For example, Susan Griffin suggests that women and non-human nature are inseparable from each other (Griffin, 1978; Jaggar, 1984).

This feminist version of the naturalistic body involves celebrating the 'virtues' given to women by nature. Kaplan and Rogers (1990) have provided a useful summary of the social policy implications of such an approach. Feminists in the late 1970s argued that biologically innate 'talents', such as the ability to give birth and rear children, needed to be fully recognized and rewarded in order for women to reach a position of social equality. Here, social equality refers to women's *different role* being of *equal worth* to men's work. As Kaplan and Adams (1989) point out, this argument is not new and Fascist ideologies contained similar principles of equality in the 1920s even before Hitler came to power. As they say, 'Feminine virtues have been celebrated by men for thousands of years – without much evidence of gaining women any more rights or freedoms' (Kaplan and Rogers, 1990: 209).

Mary O'Brien's work (1979, 1981, 1989) constitutes what is probably the most sophisticated contemporary feminist version of a naturalistic approach to the body. Central to her analysis is the notion that reproduction is a material and historical process which has given rise to a reproductive consciousness that is 'generically differentiated in significant and identifiable ways which stand in opposition to each other' (O'Brien, 1979: 235). Childbirth, and its associated 'moments', give women a connection to and knowledge of the world through experience which is fundamentally different from that to which men have access. These differences are represented by the examples of maternity and paternity.

> For women, giving birth is a unity of knowing and doing, of consciousness and creative activity, of temporality and continuity. Paternity is a quite different phenomenon. The essential moment of paternity . . . is abstract and involuntary, it must be given meaning by abstract knowledge rather than by experience. (O'Brien, 1989: 14)

To simplify, the gendered character of reproductive consciousness develops from the fact that men's relationship to nature is characterized by alienation (of their seed in copulation), whereas women's relation to nature is marked by continuity. Jeff Hearn (1987: 79) summarizes O'Brien's argument by noting that, 'Whereas maternity and maternal reproductive consciousness involve a unity of consciousness and involuntary reproductive labour, paternity and paternal reproductive consciousness are a process in which ideas (principles) dominate materiality' (for example, the *idea* of being a father prior to the birth of a child). In order to overcome this alienation, men seek to appropriate the child through fatherhood in marriage. Furthermore, fatherhood and marriage are merely the social beginning of the 'development of human institutions' and 'ideologies of male supremacy' which find their culmination in the separation of the public and private realms over which men exert control (O'Brien, 1981: 49).

In short, patriarchy has given primacy to men's definition of life and value which is grounded in their existential separation from species continuity. This has taken place as a result of men asserting control over the product of women's labour, children, and in their 'endless preoccupation' with 'death and destruction' (O'Brien, 1989:15–16).

O'Brien's analysis traces the existence and development of patriarchy to the attempts by men to reintegrate what she terms the 'abstracted father' into the process of childbirth. Despite her critical analysis of male domination, though, this argument shares certain features with naturalistic views of the body which have historically served to oppress women. Through the biological process of birth, women are meant to have a different relation to knowledge from men. However, their world view is unable to inform the structure of society. This is because patriarchy – itself based on the *biological* separation of men from processes of birth – appropriates and devalues this experience. O'Brien's analysis implies that the forms of knowledge possessed by men and women which lead to patriarchy are both *natural* and *inevitable* as they are located in biology and nature.

As Michele Barrett (1987) argues, the danger with such analysis is that it comes close to abandoning the project of transforming the world into a place less dominated by traditional 'masculine' values. Furthermore, arguments based on the view that experience provides a privileged view of knowledge can lead to a situation in which simply to 'name yourself as part of a given group is to *claim* a moral backing for your words and actions' (Ardill and O'Sullivan, 1986: 33). As Barrett (1987) argues, the values attached to specific experiences become taken for granted in this moralistic political discourse, and the identities that people construct from their experiences are seen as unproblematic.

O'Brien's analysis also tends to presuppose a humanistic model of the subject which has complete control over access to knowledge of experience. Given the extent to which men and male-controlled technological equipment have informed the definition and experience of childbirth, though, this would seem an overly optimistic view of the knowledge which stems from such experience. A further problem with O'Brien's analysis is that it marginalizes women who are unable or unwilling to have children. Such women are still subject to a range of corporeal oppressions in

y society such as rape or the threat of rape, but these cannot be
or by an analysis of the body which concentrates exclusively on
ence of childbirth.

criticisms are not meant to dispute the very real advances that
O'Br. s analysis makes in relating bodily experience to knowledge.
Sociological accounts of knowledge and consciousness have all too often
neglected the relationship between the mind and the body, yet this is a
theme which lies at the very centre of O'Brien's work and needs to be taken
very seriously in any adequate sociological account of the body. The problems with her analysis do not stem from its recognition of this important
link, but from the overriding importance given to one set of bodily experiences attached to reproduction, and the relative neglect of other ways in
which corporeal existence affects consciousness. For example, as Hearn
(1987: 83) points out, sexuality affects male consciousness not just in terms
of genetic discontinuity, but in relation to bodily contact, pleasure and pain
in their own right.

The distorted body

An alternative feminist development of the naturalistic view focuses on
how women's experiences of their bodies are distorted by dominant social
forces. This is slightly different from the previous views of the body we
have examined in this chapter, and it can be seen as an improvement upon
them. Although the body provides a basis for the construction of patriarchal social relations, these relations are *themselves seen as shaping the bodies
of women*. Naturalistic views tend only to see the body as a pre-social
unchanging phenomenon, whereas this analysis of the distorted body allows
for the body to be affected by social relations.

Susie Orbach (1988) and Kim Chernin (1983) provide good analyses of
the 'distorted body', and represent an approach which has become increasingly popular in feminist literature concerned with eating disorders (e.g.
Lawrence, 1987). It has also been popularized, and a growing number of
magazines and newspapers now carry regular features which are concerned
with women's relations with their bodies. Both Orbach and Chernin argue
that women's bodies have *natural* sizes and shapes which are disrupted by
patriarchal forces.

Orbach (1988) focuses on 'compulsive eating', a self-perpetuating cycle
of overeating and starvation. Women engage in compulsive eating because
natural hunger mechanisms are distorted, and because women's conscious
desires to be 'thin' are undermined by an unconscious desire to be fat.
Compulsive eating occurs as a result of women's social oppression. The
pressures placed on women by the media and diet industries, and the
restricted roles available to women at work and home are the two major
sets of forces which distort their bodily development.

First, in order to become a wife and mother, a woman has to have a man; a goal represented to teenagers as essential yet almost unattainable. To get a man, a woman has to regard herself as a commodity whose value is based on her appearance and presentation (1988: 29–30). The stress placed on appearance means that women become vulnerable to the huge fashion and diet industries that put forward strong and limited images of what women should look like. The one constant in these images is that women should be thin, or at least totally free of excess fat. For Orbach, many women become seduced by these images and trapped in a circle of destructive and unhealthy diets. However, women do not always accept these pressures but, instead, often react against them. Indeed, for many women becoming fat has served as a way to avoid being marketed or seen as the ideal woman (1988: 31). As Orbach argues, these women tend to become *unnaturally* fat as this 'serves the symbolic function of rejecting the way . . . society distorts [them] and their relationships with others' (1988: 44).

The second stage to Orbach's analysis of how women's development becomes distorted involves the processes by which women treat food as a solution to other problems. For example, Orbach argues that over a period of years mothers come to subjugate and misrecognize their own needs as a result of putting first the needs of their children and husband. In these cases, eating often serves as a convenient substitute for their real emotional and intellectual needs (see also James, 1990). In the case of women who work outside the home, many remain fat as a way of neutralizing their sexual identity in the eyes of others who are important to them. As Orbach (1988: 35) argues, in this way women 'can hope to be taken seriously in their working lives outside the home' and not be treated 'frivolously' as sex objects by their male colleagues. Here again, the real needs of these women for respect are met indirectly, and inadequately, through food.

It should be clear by now that Orbach treats compulsive eating as an expression of other needs and frustrations. The relationship between unmet needs and food has its original base in the fraught mother–daughter relationship. This is distorted as a result of the patriarchal context which denies mothers status and equal opportunities to men outside the home, and becomes exacerbated when food becomes the object of struggle and conflict between mothers and daughters (1988: 36–45). *Natural* hunger mechanisms become submerged and eating becomes a response not to *biological need* but to social pressures.

For Orbach (1988: 118) compulsive eating means 'eating without regard to the physiological cues which signal hunger. . . . For the compulsive eater, food has taken on such additional significance that it has long since lost its obvious biological connection'. Orbach's work is not simply an analysis of why women eat compulsively and get fat, though, it is also a 'self-help guide' for losing *unnatural* weight. The key to weight loss is in uncoupling acts of compulsive eating from the feelings, and conflicts they express. Expressing these emotions in more productive ways and learning to listen to natural hunger mechanisms is the way to return to a *natural* and balanced size.

Kim Chernin (1983) also analyses compulsive eating and asks why women in the West are faced with a 'tyranny of slenderness' which restricts their social and physical growth and expression. In contrast to men, who are brought up to take pride in their bodies, women are socialized to dislike theirs and frequently become obsessed in the quest for reduction (Bovey, 1989: 48, 229; Chernin, 1983: 62, 92). The damaging results of this quest have become increasingly public and range from the increased use of cosmetic surgery and liposuction, to an increase in anorexia nervosa. The growing number of fatalities which stem from the pressure women face to lose weight illustrates the point that 'women suffer more from living in the body than do men' (Chernin, 1983: 62; see also Bovey, 1989: 48, 224–9).

In explaining women's bodily oppression, Chernin draws on sociology, psychology and history. First, women are seen as too powerful for the male-dominated spheres of culture, politics and finance (1983: 96, 129). To maintain their power, men make women feel inadequate; feelings which are *turned against the body* (1983: 87, 190). Second, women are *initially* viewed as dangerous by men as a result of their experience of their mother's bodies as children. From their subsequent position of social power, men convert their fear and mistrust of the female body into attempts to control and reduce the physical space women occupy in society. Third, these pressures have increased in recent years, especially since the women's movement has threatened men's dominance. As Chernin argues:

> The requirement that women remain arrested in development becomes more visible and more severe. From Mae West to Marilyn [Monroe] to Twiggy to Christine Olman there is a definite progression. . . . In this age of feminist assertion men are drawn to women of childish body and mind because there is something less disturbing about the vulnerability and helplessness of a small child – and something truly disturbing about the body and mind of a mature woman. (1983: 95, 110)

Orbach and Chernin's analyses have much to say at a substantive level about how women's bodies become damaged in patriarchal society. They reveal how social pressures can be internalized, find expression in eating and distort women's bodies. Cross-class, gender-specific processes are important to both explanations. First, Orbach and Chernin's work suggests that girls are subject to a socialization process geared to achieving success in marriage markets. Similarly, this tends to generate lifestyles which serve to set women apart from men. This involves the denial of bodily and other needs in order to serve others (Charles and Kerr, 1988; Murcott, 1983), and does not help girls appropriate leisure choices as their *own* (Griffin et al., 1982: 93).

Second, the importance of the shape of girls' bodies in society can influence attitudes to physical activity. Despite the rise of the athletic body in consumer culture (Featherstone, 1982), a clear division remains between acceptable and unacceptable forms of the female body. Large muscles remain unacceptable and the fear of developing them puts many girls off PE (Bryson, 1987; Willis, 1974, 1985). Further, PE dress is often seen by girls as an unacceptable way of displaying their bodies at school as it is opposed to their sense of self-identity as adult women (Griffin et al., 1982). Now, Orbach and Chernin make clear that not all girls follow the path of seeking to develop their bodies in line with male ideals. However, this rejection also alienates women from their bodies (for example, through compulsive eating). So, women tend either to conform to traditional socialization and seek to develop the ideal body, or, in rejecting these processes, risk damaging their bodies through eating disorders.

Third, most sporting activities occur in the public sphere of life. However, women face pressures to construct their main role in the *private* sphere of the household. For example, Griffin's findings (1985) of how girls drop their girlfriends in favour of spending evenings in with boyfriends as a way of saving money for their future is hardly compatible with them developing independent sporting interests which they may carry on in married life.

Fourth, Orbach and Chernin highlight the role of male-dominated institutions in restricting bodily development. For example, sport for boys has historically been organized to reflect the development of muscular versions of masculinity (Graydon, 1983; Simon and Bradley, 1975). PE is still the most segregated subject in schools and its organization remains embedded within gender ideologies of (male) bodily expansion and (female) bodily restriction.

In summary, this feminist development of the naturalistic approach highlights how women can become alienated from their physicality. In contrast to men, women tend to be restricted from embodying power in their physical selves (Gilroy, 1989). This view of the distorted body also represents a considerable advance in certain respects over other naturalistic views of the body in that it recognizes that women's bodies are actually *affected by* social relations and institutions. Naturalistic views tend to be too busy stressing the ways in which the body gives rise to particular patterns of social relations to recognize how these relations themselves impinge upon the shape and development of bodies. The body is not simply a basis on which society arises, *but is itself affected by society.*

However, despite the contributions made by this analysis of the 'distorted body', it is problematic methodologically. For Orbach, *thin* is natural while fat is distortion. These bodily states encompass inherent attributes. As Nicky Diamond (1985: 54) argues, '"fat, thin" appear as pregiven oppositions in nature, "thin" as a natural state and goal, "fat" as pathological and a problem'. Seeing fat as the problem 'reproduces those cultural ideals of femininity which define "thin" as the ideal' (1985: 47). Despite encouraging women to 'accept themselves', Orbach argues that 'every woman [really] wants to be thin' (Bovey, 1989).

In contrast to Orbach, Chernin sees *fat* women's bodies as positive and natural. Women who slim are caught up in a struggle against what is *natural*

(1983: 9), and the reason the vast majority put back on the weight they lose is because weight belongs to them 'by nature' (1983: 30, 54). While this analysis disputes the prevelant stereotypes of women's bodies, it suffers, along with Orbach, from essentialism. Both Orbach and Chernin have made improvements to existing naturalistic views of the body. However, neither of their writings manage to escape completely from the basic assumptions of the naturalistic approach.

Orbach and Chernin are not the only writers to view women's bodies as having natural shapes and sizes which are distorted by society. For example, Epstein (1987) and Dana (1987) both see women as naturally thin and view excess eating as a substitute for other needs and activities, while Mitchell (1987) argues that women's bodies can be distorted by vigorous exercise. However, all these writers posit the existence of an unchanging natural body, an ontological stance which has affinities with sexist views of women's bodies as inferior to men's because of their 'natural' functions (Connell, 1987), and racist views of Afro-Caribbean bodies as naturally more powerful and sexual than white bodies.

The overburdened body

In this chapter I have sought to provide a brief description of the emergence of naturalistic views of the body during the eighteenth century, and critically examine several naturalistic views which have been influential since that time.

One of the remarkable features of naturalistic views is that, with the exception of Chernin's and Orbach's analyses of the distorted body, the basic principles underlying them have remained unchanged. First, they are *reductionist*. The structure of society is explained not only on the basis of the individuals within it, but the intentions, actions and potential of individuals are explained as a result of some aspect of their physical or genetic constitution. For example, in the case of sociobiology 'a causal chain is said to begin at the level of the genetic units and run through the society as a whole' (Rose, 1984: 44). Second, having established the essential features of people's corporeality, these are then classified into simplistic *social* categories (for example, male/female, black/white, upper/middle/working class) which ignore overlaps in, and stress the differences between, human bodies (Birke, 1986, 1992). These social categories are then reified as natural phenomena.

One way to illustrate further the inadequacies of these basic principles is to describe one of the early antecedents of the naturalistic view of the body. In Plato's tale, the division of Citizens of The Republic into three classes was justified on the basis of the different metals from which God had crafted them. Those made of silver were destined to be auxiliaries, and those of brass and iron to be husbandmen and craftsmen. Furthermore, if people sought to rise above their pre-destined station in life, the State stood to be destroyed. Centuries later, sociobiologists reproduced the logic, if not the content, of this argument by justifying the status quo on the basis of its genetic foundations. Genes determine individual features and social structures which are best suited for survival. Attempts to alter social structures are ill-fated and could destroy society. In both cases, a highly limited and inaccurate definition of the significance of people's bodies is taken as definitive of their self-identity and constitutive of society. They are equally narrow and unconvincing accounts of the social importance of the human body.

The naturalistic focus on the body has proved unsatisfactory for most sociologists. In this respect, historians of the body have provided an important service by identifying a period prior to the eighteenth century when the body was seen as a receptor, rather than a generator, of social meanings and relationships. Indeed, the view of the body as open to seemingly constant reinterpretation appeared to provide a much more plausible starting point for sociologists interested in the body than did the naturalistic approach. For sociologists, naturalistic views of the bodies of women and black peoples tended to say much less about what might be termed 'corporeal reality', than about the enormous utility of the body as a highly malleable ideological resource. In rejecting the negative aspects of naturalistic views, however, sociologists have tended to neglect how the body forms a basis for, and contributes towards, social life. It is this aspect of the naturalistic view which I feel is worth developing, and which tends to get lost in social constructionist accounts of the body.

Note

1. In relation to the death penalty, it is worth noting that David Gaskins, who was executed in South Carolina in 1991, was the first white man to be killed by the state for the murder of one black victim since 1944.

4

The Socially Constructed Body

[handwritten: at odds with the notion that the "Body = only biological"]

The naturalistic approach continues to exert a considerable influence on popular images of the human body. However, contemporary social theorists have generally found more attractive ideas and theories that are based on the premiss that the body is a receptor, rather than a generator, of social meanings. In this respect, *social constructionism* has been used as an umbrella term to denote those views which suggest that the body is somehow shaped, constrained and even invented by society.

Social constructionist views are united in their opposition to the notion that the body can be analysed adequately purely as a biological phenomenon. They also share an approach which holds that instead of being the foundation of society, the character and meanings attributed to the body, and the boundaries which exist between the bodies of different groups of people, are social products. However, this basic consensus should not obscure the fact that there are a variety of social constructionist views of the body which incorporate a number of distinct, and not always complementary, propositions about the relationship between the body and society. For example, post-structuralists tend to argue that linguistic categories determine our experience of embodiment, while symbolic interactionists place more emphasis on the view that the management and control of bodies is dependent on the actions of relatively autonomous human agents. *[handwritten: agency]* Both approaches have something to say about how social forces impinge upon the body, but they disagree when it comes to identifying what these forces are and how they affect the body. More generally, social constructionist views differ according to how much of a social product the body is, and whether it is even possible to speak of the body as a biological phenomenon (Vance, 1989).

Four major influences have informed views of the body as socially constructed: the anthropology of Mary Douglas; recent work on the history of the human body; the writings of Michel Foucault; and the studies of Erving Goffman. After briefly summarizing these four influences, I shall then focus on the work of Foucault and Goffman, as they have been extraordinarily influential in shaping social constructionist views of the body. They also provide an interesting comparative example of social constructionist views as they appear initially to be radically different from each other. This is partly because the form and style of their writings differ greatly. It is also because Foucault is usually categorized as a post-structuralist (concerned with how bodies are *controlled* by discourses), while

autonomy
agency!

Goffman has been seen as a symbolic interactionist (interested in the body as a component of *action*). However, I shall argue that Foucault's and Goffman's views of the body have more in common with each other than is immediately apparent. This is because they both seek to hold on to a view of the body as central to the lives of embodied subjects, while also maintaining that the significance of the body is determined ultimately by social 'structures' which exist beyond the reach of individuals. *racism, capit, alism*

In the final sections of this chapter I shall concentrate on Bryan Turner's (1984) theory of the body in society, and Arthur Frank's (1991) 'action problems' analysis of the body. In certain respects these two theorists can be seen as building respectively on the insights of Foucault and Goffman. Turner has assembled together the work of a diverse range of theorists and has developed them into a general theory of 'bodily order'. Turner follows Hobbes and Parsons in the form of his argument, but not in its content. Instead, there is a general concern with *Foucauldian* issues related to the production and control of bodies. Other theorists are incorporated into Turner's theory (including Goffman) but they are used to facilitate this Foucauldian analysis of the monitoring and domination of bodies. In providing us with a theory of the body, Turner argues that governments do not deal with economic and political issues in the abstract, but with problems of the body which are given by society. In contrast, Frank is concerned with action as embodiment, and focuses more directly on styles of body usage and issues related to the lived body. As a result, his work can be seen in part as a radical development of Goffman's analysis of body management.

A general theme of this book is that sociologists have traditionally adopted a dual approach to the body, and have rarely focused explicitly on the body's social importance. Social constructionist views challenge this tendency by bringing society into the body. Consequently, they have done much within sociology to make the body a respectable focus of investigation. If the body is indeed shaped by society, then its study can no longer be left entirely in the hands of other disciplines. Furthermore, by highlighting the ways in which social roles, meanings and resources can be seen as determining the body and how it becomes important in society, social constructionist views have much to offer a distinctive approach to the body in sociology. However, there are problems with social constructionism. While we are told much about the social significance of the body by these views, we tend to learn far less about what is meant by the body. We hear about the social forces which are constructing something called the 'body', but we know less about what is actually being constructed. This means that while the body may be named as a theoretical space, it is all too frequently left uninvestigated. It is as if the body itself either does not exist *not* or is constantly pushed to one side by this perspective in its focus on other *enough* phenomena. Consequently, we learn little about why it is that the body, *attention* whatever it is, is able to assume such importance. *paid to*

Bryan Turner (1992a) raises a related point which represents something *how* of a departure from his 1984 theory of bodily order, when he suggests that

& experience of the body

social constructionist approaches tend not to explore the possibility that the body may be more or less easily constructed than other phenomena. Furthermore, certain dimensions of the body may be more or less open to social factors than others. For example, while sociologists have argued that health and illness can be analysed as social constructs, they have rarely focused on the possibility that judgements about human height might be similarly conceptualized (Turner, 1992a: 106–7). Turner's recent work also links up with debates within medical sociology which have questioned the explanatory power of social constructionism (e.g. Bury, 1986, 1987; King, 1987; Nicholson and McLaughlin, 1987).

The potential danger with social constructionist approaches, then, is that they may serve to reproduce in a different form, rather than overcome, sociology's dual approach to the body. The body is placed in various social contexts, but many of its dimensions are left unexplored. In what follows, I shall argue that the work of Foucault suffers from this problem, while that of Goffman and Turner remains less than fully satisfactory. However, by placing at the centre of his analysis a view of the *corporeal* body, Frank points to one possible way in which this problem might be overcome.

Constructing the human body

Of the four main influences which have informed views of the body as socially constructed, the anthropology of Mary Douglas (1966, 1970) has developed the idea of the body as a receptor of social meaning and a symbol of society. In *Natural Symbols*, Douglas argued that the human body is the most readily available image of a social system, and suggested that ideas about the human body correspond closely to prevalent ideas about society (Douglas, 1970). Moreover, particular groups within society will tend to adopt approaches to the body which correspond to their social location. For example, artists and academics who adopt a critical stance towards society are likely to display a certain bodily abandon and 'a carefully modulated shagginess according to the responsibilities they carry' (Douglas, 1970: 72). Nonetheless, the body is above all a metaphor of society as a whole. This means that in times of social crisis, when national borders and identities are threatened, there is likely to be a concern with the maintenance of existing bodily boundaries and the purity of bodies.

As Turner (1992a) notes, in this specific sense Douglas's anthropology is not an anthropology of the body, but an anthropology of the symbolism of risk and, we might add, of social location and stratification. Our anxieties about risks and uncertainties in social relations and social environments are projected on to a concern with the body. Consequently, it is hardly surprising that the body has become a project for increasing numbers of people living in what Ulrich Beck has referred to as 'risk societies'. In high modernity, social systems expose individuals, irrespective of their social location, to an increasing number of environmental and technological risks (Beck, 1992). In this situation, there is a tendency for concern about the body to be globalized.

The general theme in Douglas's work is that the social body constrains how the physical body is perceived and experienced. These perceptions and experiences themselves sustain a particular view of society. Douglas's work contains many valuable insights about the relationship between the social body and the individual body. However, at times it threatens to collapse these two bodies together by reducing the phenomenology of the individual body – the ways in which people live, experience and perceive their bodies – into the positions and categories made available by the social body.

Mary Douglas has exerted a considerable impact on anthropological analyses of the body as socially constructed. Despite the influence of Durkheim on her work, though, sociologists have tended to look elsewhere for resources to assist their investigations of the body as a socially constructed entity. As mentioned previously, Turner (1991a) has argued that sociologists have not shown much interest in the body as a classification system. However, Pierre Bourdieu is a major exception to this – Bourdieu's view of the body as a bearer of symbolic value is integrated into an analysis of the body as a material phenomenon which both constitutes, and is constituted by, society. His work represents one of the most important contemporary theoretical approaches towards the body and is examined in detail in Chapter 6.

The work of such writers as Thomas Laqueur and Ludmilla Jordanova on the history of the human body, and images of the body, has exerted an important influence on sociological research. A small selection of this work has already been examined briefly in Chapter 3 and, to reiterate, it has proved an invaluable resource for sociologists by demonstrating that human bodies have been invested with a wide range of shifting and unstable meanings. These historical studies have provided a mine of information which has been used to facilitate the analysis of such areas as the social bases of perception and smell (Duroche, 1990). They have also been used in a more general sense to legitimize the efforts of sociologists concerned to investigate the body as a social, rather than a biological, phenomenon.

Michel Foucault's work is, in many ways, the most radical and influential social constructionist approach and it goes well beyond seeing the body as a receptor of social meanings. For Foucault, the body is not only given meaning by discourse, but is wholly constituted by discourse. In effect, the body vanishes as a biological entity and becomes instead a socially con-structed product which is infinitely malleable and highly unstable. The influence of Foucault's work is such that it is now justifiable to talk of a Foucauldian approach to the body. For example, the pioneering work of Bryan Turner (1983, 1984, 1987) on the body in social theory, religion and medical sociology, draws heavily on Foucault's work. Many other studies on the socially constructed body, concerned with such issues as medical knowledge, desire, dentistry and the Welfare State, also owe a great debt to

65

Foucault (e.g. Armstrong, 1983, 1987; Davies, 1990; Hewitt, 1983; Lash, 1984; Nettleton, 1991, 1992).

The work of Erving Goffman is the fourth major influence on social constructionist views of the body. Goffman has examined the position of the body in social interaction through his work on behaviour in public and private places, the presentation of the self and the management of stigma. In Goffman's work, the management of the body is central to the maintenance of encounters, social roles and social relations, and also mediates the relationship between an individual's self-identity and their social identity. Here, the body assumes the status of a resource which can be managed in a variety of ways in order to construct a particular version of the self. The influence of Goffman's work is apparent in recent sociological studies on the relationship between the body and self-identity (e.g. Featherstone, 1982; Giddens, 1991), and in Giddens's (1984, 1988) analyses of the status of the embodied agent in structuration theory.

Power, discourse and the body

The Foucauldian approach to the body is characterized, first, by a substantive preoccupation with the body and those institutions which govern the body and, second, by an epistemological view of the body as produced by and existing in discourse. Discourse is the most important concept in Foucault's work and it is centrally concerned with, although irreducible to, language (Foucault, 1974; Poster, 1984). Discourses can be seen as sets of deep principles incorporating specific grids of meaning which underpin, generate and establish relations between all that can be seen, thought and said (Dreyfus and Rabinow, 1982; Foucault, 1974).

The importance of the body to Foucault is such that he has described his work as constituting a '"history of bodies" and the manner in which what is most material and most vital in them has been invested' (Foucault, 1981: 152). Central to this history is a concern with mapping the relations which exist between 'the body and the effects of power on it' (Foucault, 1980: 58). This includes an examination of how the 'micro-physics' of power operates in modern institutional formations 'through progressively finer channels, gaining access to individuals themselves, to their bodies, their gestures and all their daily actions' (1980: 151).

The body for Foucault is not simply a focus of discourse, but constitutes the link between daily practices on the one hand and the large scale organization of power on the other (Dreyfus and Rabinow, 1982). In describing the forms some of these linkages take, it is worth illustrating them with examples drawn from Foucault's work on disciplinary systems and the history of sexuality. At their most general level, these studies analyse a period of change, concerned predominantly with the transition from traditional to modern societies, in the modes by which individuals are produced as embodied subjects and connected to institutions.

The development of modernity brought with it a transition in the social spaces occupied by discourses, which had a profound effect on the construction of individuals. This transition involved a change in the target, the object and the scope of discourse. There was a shift in the target of discourse, as the fleshy body gave way to the mind as a focus of concern; a change in the object of discourse, as a preoccupation with matters of death was replaced by interest in the structuring of life; and a change in the scope of discourse, as concern moved away from the control of anonymous individuals to the management of differentiated populations.

To start with, there was a shift in the target of discourse. Subjects were no longer formed by discourses which directly constituted the body as flesh but, increasingly, by discourses which indirectly controlled the body by constructing it as a 'mindful body'. In contrast to its antecedent, the mindful body is not just a fleshy object, but is defined through its possession of consciousness, intentions and language. It is controlled less by brute force, as in traditional societies, and more by surveillance and stimulation.

This transition in the target of discourse from the 'body as flesh' to the 'mindful body' is evident in Foucault's 1979 study of contrasting systems of punishment. Under monarchical law the most serious categories of punishment took place in public where the criminal was ritually burned, assaulted and dismembered in a symbolic display of the sovereign's authority. The body was a highly visible target of penal repression (Foucault, 1979a: 8), and offenders had their penalties inscribed in detail on their bodies. In contrast, the prison system of the nineteenth century placed the bodies of offenders in a scientifically managed institutional space as a way of gaining access to their *minds*. This was epitomized by the Panopticon, a prison design advocated by Jeremy Bentham. The Panopticon was a circular building of cells where prisoners were always available for surveillance from a central watch-tower. Being under the constant gaze of an overseer, this disciplinary technique was meant to encourage prisoners to monitor themselves and exert self-control over their behaviour.

The body undergoes a similar transformation in Foucault's analysis of sexuality. In the Middle Ages, the Christian confession was the site in which sex was formulated. The priest was concerned with people's sexual *activities* and the dominant discourses on sex were concerned with the body as flesh. However, the Reformation and Counter-Reformation introduced processes which remain influential today. Priests started to inquire about people's *intentions*, as well as their actions, and the locus of sexuality began to shift from the body to the mind of subjects. As Foucault argues, sex was 'driven out of hiding and constrained to lead a discursive existence' (1981: 33). Its links with the fleshy, physical body faded and its location in the mind was explored through language.

This shift in the target of discourse from the body to the mind was accompanied by a change in the *object* of discourse, as governments displayed a growing concern with power over the life and welfare of people, instead of with their death. This included a preoccupation with the fertility of populations, health and illness, patterns of diet and habitation, and a general concern with people's corporeal habits and customs (Foucault, 1981: 25). For example, while punishment under monarchical law was a negative affair concerned with repression and the ultimate annihilation of the body, the modern prison system was occupied by more productive concerns and sought to stimulate among inmates 'useful' and 'productive' forms of living. Similarly, in the case of sexuality, the focus of the early confessional was to ascertain the fitness of people's actions for the afterlife following their corporeal death. However, the eighteenth and nineteenth centuries brought with them a concern with governmentally-approved forms of sexuality which would produce *life*. Furthermore, the twentieth century has seen a partial development of this trend as sexuality has become harnessed to expressions of self-identity and lifestyle.

Finally, the transition from traditional to modern societies was accompanied by a change in the *scope* of discourse. The attention of governments shifted from a concern with controlling relatively anonymous individual bodies, to regulating the *population* as a whole. The modern prison system became increasingly concerned with the behaviour of the social body, and the model of control provided by the Panopticon was extended into schools, army barracks, hospitals and other institutions (Ball, 1990; Honneth and Joas, 1988: 144). This provided a context in which detailed control could be exerted over much larger areas of society, and knowledge gained about the population for use in policy and planning decisions (for example, schools enabled governments to monitor the health of children).

Changes in the scope of discourse were also evident in the realm of sexuality. Discourses on sex moved away from the individual body, and focused instead on the reproductive fitness of the *social body*. For example, from the eighteenth century there was a large increase in discourses on sexuality which linked the sex of individual bodies to the management of national populations. This happened through the creation of four major discursive figures: the 'hysterical woman' (limited and defined by her sexuality); the 'masturbating child' (prone to engage in immoral behaviour which, through the depletion of vital energies, posed dangers to the future health of the race); the 'Malthusian couple' (socialized into bearing children according to the needs of society); and the 'perverse adult' (whose sexual instincts deviated from the legitimate norm). The dominance of these discursive figures meant that the 'legitimate heterosexual couple' tended to function as a norm, classifying other people's and other forms of sexuality as deviant (Foucault, 1981: 105; see also Connell and Dowsett, 1992).

Taken together, these changes in the social spaces occupied by discourses had two major related consequences which are relevant to the connection of embodied individuals to large-scale systems of power. First, they allowed governments to exert a far greater degree of control over individuals than had previously been the case. As discourse moved away from the relatively limited space encompassing the individual, the body and death, to the much broader space incorporating the mind, the population and life, people could be made more separate and different and, hence, more controllable. Turner (1983) describes such processes as leading to the *individuation* of people. Individuation is a set of practices by which individuals are identified and separated by marks, numbers, signs and codes which are derived from knowledge of the population and related to the establishment of norms. Individuation also facilitated the control and surveillance of people. For example, the role played by the teaching hospitals in monitoring the health of the nation made possible the development of medical norms against which individuals could be compared and classified (Armstrong, 1983; Foucault, 1973). Similarly, in plotting the relationship between individual and aggregate productivity, individuals could be compared and differentiated, rewarded or punished.

Second, these changes brought with them a change in the means by which control was accomplished. There was a reduction in the achievement of control through repression, and an increased focus on maintaining control through the stimulation of desires. Foucault argues that this has become increasingly apparent with the development of capitalism (Hewitt, 1983). For example, economic development initially brought with it great concentrations of bodies in cities that needed to be made serviceable and safe as a precondition of commercial success. In this context, from the eighteenth to the early twentieth century, power constituted bodies through what would now be considered to be 'heavy, ponderous, meticulous and constant' disciplinary regimes in schools, hospitals, barracks, factories and families (Foucault, 1979a, 1979b; Gordon, 1980). In the twentieth century, though, more discriminatory forms of control over the body became widespread which were more productive in their social and economic effects. As Foucault argues, with reference to the representation of the body in consumer culture, 'we find a new mode of investment which presents itself no longer in the form of control by repression but that of control by stimulation. "Get undressed – but be slim, good looking, tanned!"' (Foucault, 1980: 57).

Foucault's vanishing body

Foucault's analysis of the discursive body has provided an important resource for sociologists interested in examining the body as a socially constructed phenomenon. In contrast to the naturalistic approaches examined in the previous chapter, Foucault does not view bodies as naturally different entities whose biological constitution determines and limits permanently the capabilities of human subjects. Instead, bodies are highly malleable phenomena which can be invested with various and changing forms of power.

This approach has proved especially popular with feminist scholars who have used Foucault's work to argue against the notion that the natural body is the basis on which individual identities and social inequalities are built, and to support the argument that gendered identities are fractured, shifting and unstable. In a related vein, feminists have also used Foucault to challenge the 'sex-gender' division common to social science. This accepts that while many of the properties that characterize women and men are the result of gendered patterns of socialization, other differences are natural and predicated on biology. Instead, Foucault's approach has been used to argue that those biological features usually thought of as differentiating between the 'sexes' are themselves socially constructed, and that power is invested in and exercised through bodies in ways which produce gendered forms of embodiment (Brown and Adams, 1979; Diamond and Quinby, 1988; Morris and Patton, 1979; Sawicki, 1991). These Foucauldian analyses build on a tradition of feminist work, including the writings of Christine Delphy (1984) and Monique Wittig (1982) which have argued that the biological is simply a manifestation of the social and, as such, does not require theorizing as a sphere in its own right (Fuss, 1990).

There is, however, a fundamental tension in Foucault's approach to the body which means that his work is unable to overcome the dual approach sociology has traditionally adopted to the body. On the one hand, there is a real substantive concern with the body as an actual *product* of constructing discourses. For example, Foucault is often concerned with the body as a real entity, as when he examines the effects of scientific thought and disciplinary technologies on the body. Somewhat ironically, given the emphasis Foucault places on historical discontinuity in his work, this leads him to treat the body as a trans-historical and cross-cultural unified phenomenon. What I mean by this is that the body is *always already* there to be constructed by discourse. Irrespective of the time or the place, the body is equally available as a site which receives meaning from, and is constituted by, external forces. This view provides no room for recognizing that different aspects of human embodiment may be more or less open to reconstruction depending upon specific historical circumstances. It also makes highly questionable the claims of those like Jeffrey Weeks who argue that Foucault allows us to historicize the body (Weeks, 1992).

On the other hand, Foucault's epistemological view of the body means that it *disappears* as a material or biological phenomenon. The biological, physical or material body can never be grasped by the Foucauldian approach as its existence is permanently deferred behind the grids of meaning imposed by discourse. For me, this is why one gets a sense when reading Foucault that his analyses are somewhat disembodied. The body is present as a topic of discussion, but is absent as a focus of investigation. He is deeply concerned with disciplinary systems and sexuality, for example, but the body tends to become lost in his discussions as a real, material object of analysis. One manifestation of this is Foucault's view of the mind/body relationship. Once the body is contained within modern disciplinary systems, it is the mind which takes over as the location for discursive power. Consequently, the body tends to be reduced to an inert mass which is controlled by discourses centred on the mind. However, this mind is itself disembodied; we get no sense of the mind's location within an active human body.

To put it bluntly, the bodies that appear in Foucault's work do not enjoy a prolonged visibility as corporeal entities. Bodies are produced, but their own powers of production, where they have any, are limited to those invested in them by discourse. As such, the body is dissolved as a causal phenomenon into the determining power of discourse, and it becomes extremely difficult to conceive of the body as a material component of social action. Furthermore, Foucault is insufficiently concerned with lived experience. As Turner notes, despite all his references to pleasure and desire, Foucault ignores the *phenomenology* of embodiment. The 'immediacy of personal sensuous experience of embodiment which is involved in the notion of *my* body receives scant attention. My authority, possession and occupation of a personalized body through sensuous experience are minimized in favour of an emphasis on the regulatory controls which are exercised from outside' (Turner, 1984: 245). As Peter Dews argues, this neglect has serious implications for Foucault's analysis as 'Without some theory which makes the corporeal more than a *tabula rasa*, it is impossible to reckon the costs imposed by "an infinitesimal power over the active body"' (Dews, 1987: 163).

Instead of overcoming the dual approach that sociology has adopted towards the body, then, Foucault's work serves to reproduce it in a different form. The body is affected by discourse, but we get little sense of the body reacting back and affecting discourse. Even when Foucault makes the occasional reference to the body putting up resistances to power and dominant discourses, he cannot say what it is about the body that resists. This feature of Foucault's work can be highlighted further by comparing his view of the body with naturalistic approaches.

Naturalistic and Foucauldian views of the body are most polarized around the issue of the relation between the natural and the social. Naturalistic approaches posit the natural as the 'raw material' of social life, and sexual or racial difference is taken as prior to social differences when it comes to analysing the embodiment of humans. For example, 'woman' and 'man' are ontologically stable objects which make no allowance for cross-cultural or trans-historical change. For Foucault, however, the natural is a construction of the social. As Fuss (1990: 6) puts it, the body is always already 'culturally mapped; it never exists in a pure or uncoded state'. While the strength of this view is its recognition of the production of social categories and its analysis of systems of representation, this is not built on the grounds of the demise of essentialism. Instead, natural essentialism is displaced by *discursive essentialism*, a situation which leaves Foucault without the means of examining the mutual development of biology (or anything that is material about the body) and society. Society is brought so far into the body that the body disappears as a phenomenon that requires detailed historical investigation in its own right. It is present as an item of

[handwritten margin note: too much emphasis on discourse as opposed to lived body]

discussion, but absent as an object of analysis. As the body is whatever discourse constructs it as being, it is discourse rather than the body that needs examining in Foucault's work.

Ultimately, the determining power of discourse means that Foucault's work goes no further than naturalistic accounts in allowing for a theoretically adequate view of the body. The body may be surrounded by and perceived through discourses, but it is *irreducible* to discourse. Foucauldians might argue that this is irrelevant as the body cannot be known apart from specific systems of knowledge. However, if we take the view that knowledge is in some sense actually *grounded in* and *shaped by* the body, rather than separate from it, then this objection appears irrelevant. I shall develop this argument in the next chapter.

Presenting the body in everyday life

In comparison with Foucault, who focuses on how the body is invested with powers that *control* individuals, Erving Goffman's writings appear to place more emphasis on the body as integral to human *agency*. Goffman is centrally interested in how the body enables people to intervene in, and make a difference to, the flow of daily life. However, embodied individuals are not autonomous in Goffman's work. His analysis of the 'shared vocabularies of body idiom' (or conventional forms of non-verbal language) which guide people's perceptions of bodily appearances and performances, provides a sense of the social constraints under which body management occurs.

Goffman's approach to the body is characterized by three main features. First, there is a view of the body as a material property of individuals. In contrast to naturalistic views, which portray people's actions and identities as determined by their biological bodies, Goffman argues that individuals usually have the ability to control and monitor their bodily performances in order to facilitate social interaction. Here, the body is associated with the exercise of human agency, and it appears in Goffman's work as a resource which both requires and enables people to manage their movements and appearances.

Second, while the body is not actually *produced* by social forces, as in Foucault's work, the meanings attributed to it are determined by 'shared vocabularies of body idiom' which are not under the immediate control of individuals (Goffman, 1963: 35). Body idiom is a conventionalized form of non-verbal communication which is by far the most important component of behaviour in public. It is used by Goffman in a general sense to refer to 'dress, bearing, movements and position, sound level, physical gestures such as waving or saluting, facial decorations, and broad emotional expressions' (Goffman, 1963: 33). As well as allowing us to classify information given off by bodies, shared vocabularies of body idiom provide categories which label and *grade hierarchically* people according to this information. Consequently, these classifications exert a profound influence over the ways in which individuals seek to manage and present their bodies.

These first two features of Goffman's approach suggest that human bodies have a dual location. Bodies are the property of individuals, yet are defined as significant and meaningful by society. This formulation lies at the core of the third main feature of Goffman's approach to the body. In Goffman's work, the body plays an important role in mediating the relationship between people's self-identity and their social identity. The social meanings which are attached to particular bodily forms and performances tend to become internalized and exert a powerful influence on an individual's sense of self and feelings of inner worth.

Goffman's general approach to the body is revealed through his more specific analyses of the procedures involved in maintaining what he terms the 'interaction order'. Goffman conceptualizes the interaction order as a somehow autonomous sphere of social life (others include the economic sphere) which should not be seen as 'somehow prior, fundamental, or constitutive of the shape of macroscopic phenomena' (Goffman, 1983: 4; see also Burns, 1992: 17–47). His analysis of this sphere of life demonstrates that intervening successfully in daily life, and maintaining a single definition of a situation in the face of possible disruptions, requires a high degree of competence in controlling the expressions, movements and communications of the body (e.g. Goffman, 1963, 1969). After looking briefly at the importance of the body in Goffman's analysis of encounters, social positions and social relationships, I shall describe his view of the connection between the body, social identity and self-identity.

The body and social interaction

The body is central to the most basic units of the interaction order in Goffman's work, the structuring of encounters. The vast bulk of daily life consists of established routines in work, leisure and family life where individuals frequently initiate, enter and leave encounters with others. At every stage of these focused or unfocused meetings, the movements and appearances of the body send messages of intent between people. For example, in our culture regular eye contact is an integral part of maintaining focused encounters, while frequent glances at the watch signal a desire to leave.

Encounters are also important to social life as they are occasions in which people are concerned to act out specific social roles (for example, the concerned mother, the angry teacher, the sympathetic social worker). Goffman argues that if people are to appear convincing in these roles, they need to observe the corporeal rules which govern particular encounters. For example, a business meeting might be experienced as boring by an aspiring manager but, in order to maintain an image of authority, that person may seek to convey the appearance of interest. A similar approach is adopted by shopfloor workers who have become adept at 'make work', that is, at appearing to be busy when in visual range of supervisors while actually being engrossed in private discussion (Goffman, 1969). Face work and body work are, then, critical to maintaining the smooth flow of encounters and the integrity of social roles.

The body also enters into the maintenance of social relations of dominance and subordination in ways which are far removed from the brute force of physical violence. For example, bodily expressions of deference, such as when men open doors for women, can be seen as not merely *symbolic* but as *constitutive* of gender inequalities (Goffman, 1979: 6). As Goffman argues, 'Men often treat women as faulted actors with respect to "normal" capacity for various forms of physical exertion' (1974: 196–7).

Susan Bartky, quoting from Nancy Henley's (1977) analysis of body politics, elaborates on this point in her analysis of power and the gendered body. Bartky argues that the body enters into the reproduction of gender relations in ways which normally go unnoticed. A man

> may literally steer a woman everywhere she goes: down the street, around corners, into elevators, through doorways, into her chair at the dinner table, around the dance floor. The man's movement 'is not necessarily heavy and pushy or physical in an ugly way; it is light and gentle but firm in the way of the most confident equestrians with the best trained horses'. (Bartky, 1988: 68)

For Goffman, the form these relations of inequality take are carried via the positioning of the body even 'into the gentlest, most loving moments without apparently causing strain' (Goffman, 1979: 9).

The management of the body also enters into what Goffman describes as the morally 'neutral' act of *civil inattention*, the basic and most frequent type of face work involved among strangers in contemporary societies. Civil inattention involves not simply the use of the face but the careful positioning of the entire body on the street, in large gatherings or on ceremonial occasions to signify a non-threatening presence. For example, when passing each other on the street strangers will usually glance at each other before looking away, indicating recognition of each other's presence but avoiding any gesture that might be taken as implying a threat.

The widespread importance of managing the body in contemporary social life can lead to what Goffman (1969) has termed 'bureaucratization of the spirit'. This results from the amount of time individuals are required to be 'on stage', producing consistent performances during encounters (Featherstone, 1982), and suggests that individuals have a need for relaxation within 'back-regions' where they can indulge in 'creature releases' such as yawning, belching, scratching and nose picking which 'appear to provide a brief release from the tension experienced by the individual in keeping himself steadily and entirely draped in social clothing' (Goffman, 1963: 68).

At this stage in the discussion, it might be useful to reiterate the two main factors which contextualize the body's importance in the interaction order. First, individuals within a society attach similar meanings, and frequently a great deal of importance, to bodily appearances and physical actions such as facial expressions and gestures. As mentioned previously, Goffman argues that we possess shared vocabularies of body idiom which provide us with a common means of classifying embodied information (Goffman, 1963: 35).

The second major factor which contextualizes the body's importance in the interaction order concerns the body as a generator of meaning. Individuals engaged in encounters constantly display information as a consequence of their embodiment even if they are not speaking. Visible bodies are caught in webs of communication *irrespective* of individual intentions and this can exert a considerable influence on behaviour (Burns, 1992: 38). This means that certain professionals, such as teachers, diplomats and confidence tricksters, are required to be experts in body management.

Social identity, the body and self-identity

As we have seen, body management is central to the smooth flow of encounters, the acting out of roles and, more generally, to a person's acceptance as a full member of the interaction order. In Goffman's work, this acceptance is also vital to a person's self-identity as a competent and worthwhile human being. This is because the vocabularies of body idiom used by people to classify others are also used for the purposes of *self-classification*. It is generally the case that if a person's bodily appearance and management categorizes them as a 'failed' member of society by others, they will internalize that label and incorporate it into what becomes a 'spoiled' self-identity. As Goffman's analysis (1990 [1963]) of stigma suggests, we tend to perceive our bodies as if looking into a mirror which offers a reflection framed in terms of society's views and prejudices.

Goffman's analysis of embarrassment and stigma provides specific examples of how the body mediates the relationship between self-identity and social identity. Embarrassment tends to be caused when people display inconsistencies in their character (when they fail to enact their social roles with poise), or when individuals fail to maintain the smooth flow of interaction (when the rules governing encounters are broken) (Schudson, 1984: 636). The body is central to these failures of interaction, and also communicates these failures to the 'offender' as embarrassment, which is usually experienced as highly uncomfortable. Its bodily manifestations include stuttering, blushing, tremoring and making awkward gestures (Goffman, 1963, 1990 [1963]; Kuzmics, 1991).

Embarrassment signifies a threat to a person's social identity and their self-identity as a full and competent member of society as it reveals a gap between what Goffman terms their *virtual social identity* and their *actual social identity*. An individual's virtual identity refers to how they see themselves and their own identity, while their actual social identity refers to how others see them (Goffman, 1990 [1963]: 12). Our virtual social identities tend to be governed by a general desire to present ourselves as 'normal' people worthy of playing a full part in society. However, it is usually the case that over time our actual social identities impinge upon our virtual social identities. Gaps that arise between virtual and actual social identities and lead to occasional episodes of embarrassment are usually repairable. The divergence between these identities is not significant enough to spoil our self-identity as full and competent members of society. However, as Burns notes (1992: 217), if our virtual social identity is found to contain features significantly less approved than first appearances suggested, then our social identity is likely to undergo a dramatic shift. From being a whole and usual person, we will become a 'tainted, discounted one' (Goffman, 1990 [1963]: 12) in the eyes of both ourselves and society.

People with stigmas (attributes which have been labelled as deeply discrediting) confront problems in social interaction with 'normals' which can have especially damaging consequences for their self-identity. If stigmatized individuals attempt to pass as 'normal', they risk having discovered a 'special discrepancy between virtual and actual social identity' which can have the effect of spoiling their social identity and cutting them off from society and themselves so that they stand alone as 'a discredited person facing an unaccepting world' (Goffman, 1990 [1963]: 12–13, 31). As Goffman argues, (1990 [1963]: 17–18) the 'stigmatized individual tends to hold the same beliefs about identity that we do . . . the standards he has incorporated from the wider society equip him to be intimately alive to what others see as his failing, inevitably causing him, if only for moments, to agree that he does indeed fall short of what he really ought to be'. Goffman's analysis of stigma displays a particular interest in the problems of the disabled because of the amount of work they have to do in order to be accepted as full members of society (Campling, 1981).

I shall deal shortly with criticisms of Goffman's general approach to the body. It is worth stating here, however, that Goffman tends to posit too close a link between people's virtual social identity and their actual social identity. This has been highlighted by Mike Featherstone and Mike Hepworth's analysis (1991) of 'the mask of ageing'. Far from approximating more closely to other people's views of them as 'old' and 'past it', Featherstone and Hepworth argue that the elderly view the ageing process as a mask or disguise which conceals beneath it what they continue to perceive as an essentially youthful self.

Goffman's manageable body?

Goffman's analysis of the interaction order is of great importance for an understanding of the manageable body, for the insights it provides into how individuals control and monitor their bodies. He also has much of value to say about the relationship between the body, self-identity and social identity. In this respect, Goffman takes much more seriously than Foucault the idea that the body is a physical component of human agents. There is a major problem with Goffman's work, however, which concerns the absence of mechanisms which would link the body management of individuals within the bounded sphere of the interaction order to wider social norms of body idiom. For example, in his analysis of stigma Goffman implies that the classifications which categorize people's bodily performances exist prior to and are independent of social encounters. Indeed, Goffman (1983: 26) recognizes the problem this approach causes in his work when he acknowledges the difficulties of explaining how his account of interaction connects to the more general view of social order on which it rests.

This dualism which characterizes Goffman's view of the body leaves his work open to two major criticisms. The first takes as its target Goffman's substantive focus on the individual body within the interaction order. As a result of his interest in the interaction order as a clearly separable domain, it can be argued that Goffman is led to underestimate the importance of his view of the body for the more macro-structural problems of sociology. As Giddens (1988) implies, the sociological importance of Goffman's insights on the body in the interaction order is ultimately dependent on their *general* applicability. Given that economic, political and military decisions which have crucial implications for huge numbers of people are made as much in circumstances of bodily co-presence as are more mundane forms of interaction, Goffman's work should inform our understanding of structural concerns. Despite this, though, Goffman does not provide the *theoretical* means for connecting his insights to analyses of social reproduction across extended spans of time and space. Where his work has been interpreted as doing this, it has been by those who read Goffman through the work of Durkheim or other theorists (e.g. Collins, 1988). The notions of social classifications and shared vocabularies of body idiom are simply too vague and abstract to serve this purpose as we have little idea about how they originated and how they are sustained or challenged.

The second main criticism takes as its target the significance Goffman attaches to social classifications in labelling and grading the body. It also reveals certain affinities which exist between the work of Goffman and Foucault. For both these writers, the significance of the body is determined by sources (either shared vocabularies of body idiom or discourses) located *outside* of the body which are out of reach of the individuals subject to them. Furthermore, their explanatory importance means that we hear less than we might otherwise do about what the body is, or about how it facilitates human agency. We may hear of the body belching, farting, slipping and tripping in Goffman's work, but we get less of an idea of how it is a really *integral* component of agency. The body is significant for individuals but it becomes so mainly because of the classifications through which people categorize each other as competent or incompetent members

...mately, the significance of the body is determined by the ...tiveness to shared vocabularies of body idiom. As with ...e mind becomes the site in which the meaning of the body is

...g Goffman and Michel Foucault provide us with contrasting views of t.. body. However, neither writer is concerned with providing an explicit theory of the body in society. In this respect, it is worth looking at the work of Bryan Turner (1984) and Arthur Frank (1991). As I mentioned in the introduction to this chapter, the form of Turner's theory of 'bodily order' is taken from Hobbes and Parsons. However, its content, and its concern with the need social systems have to control the body, is clearly influenced by Foucault.

The body and social order

The starting point for Turner's theory of 'bodily order' (1984) is an attempt to reconceptualize the classical Hobbesian problem of order as the problem of the government of the body. He does this by incorporating Hobbes's concern with the geometry of bodies and their motion into a Parsonian analysis of the 'core problems' that social systems face in reproducing themselves. Turner's analysis is informed by structuralist and functionalist concerns: the body is viewed from the perspective of the structural problems which it poses for the government of stable social systems. However, there is also critical intent to his work and Turner is centrally concerned with issues of gender, power and oppression. As he argues:

> any sociology of the body will hinge ultimately on the nature of the sexual and emotional division of labour. The sociology of the body turns out to be crucially a sociological study of the control of sexuality, specifically female sexuality by men exercising patriarchal power. (Turner, 1984: 114)

Turner argues that all social systems must solve 'the problem of the body' which has four related dimensions. These are:

1   The reproduction of populations through time.
2   The restraint of desire as an interior body problem.
3   The regulation of populations in space.
4   The representation of bodies in social space as a task facing the surface or 'exterior' of bodies.

Although (2) and (4) may appear to be tasks facing the individual, Turner argues that the *source* of these tasks is societal and that they are intrinsic to the adequate functioning and reproduction of social systems.

Having established this typology of dimensions to the problem of the body in society, Turner goes on to identify an institutional sub-system or *mode of control* by which society has sought to manage each dimension of the government of the body, a dominant *theorist* of each of these dimensions and a paradigmatic *disease* that is liable to 'break down' bodies as a

Populations		Bodies	
Time	Reproduction Malthus Onanism	Restraint Weber Hysteria	Internal
Space	Regulation Rousseau Phobia	Representation Goffman Anorexia	External

Figure 4.1   *Turner's theory of bodily order*

Reprinted from B.S. Turner (1984) *The Body and Society*. Basil Blackwell: Oxford.
(2nd edn, published in 1996 by Sage)

result of society's imposition of these tasks (Turner, 1984: 91–114). This
analysis of disease reflects Turner's Parsonian view (1987) that sickness is a
social condition as it involves the entry of individuals into social roles.

The components to the problem of the body are illustrated in Figure 4.1.
Moving through each of the quadrants of Figure 4.1, the problem of
population reproduction has traditionally been managed by a system of
delayed marriage and **patriarchal households** in order to control fertility.
Malthus, seen as the eighteenth-century theorist of reproduction, argued
that people were dominated by the need to eat and satisfy their sexual
drives. Unfortunately, these two 'laws of nature' were contradictory as
reproductive capacity easily exceeded a population's capacity to produce
food. Apart from starvation, the other checks to population control were
either immoral (for example, prostitution, abortion), or involved celibacy
and delayed marriage. Malthus argued that delayed marriage would provide
the most rational mode of population restraint and would also serve to
inculcate positive moral virtues of sobriety and industry (Turner, 1984:
95). These, in turn, would serve to assist the health of the economy.
Masturbation came to be seen as the 'disease' which signalled the breakdown of the body under the demands of moral purity during the period
before marriage and for this reason came to be seen as wasteful, immoral
and in need of control.

The **restraint of desire** has traditionally been concerned with the
regulation of female sexuality by systems of patriarchal power. The mode
by which society has attempted to control desire has involved an **ideology
of asceticism** as a way of delaying sexual gratification. **Weber** is regarded
as the theorist of asceticism, especially in terms of his analysis of the
Protestant ethnic. Here, Weber argued that there was a close affinity
between the rise of industrial capitalism in Europe and Protestantism's
stress on the idea of a 'calling', self-denial and hard work. Consequently,
Protestantism brought about a 'rational ordering of the body which was
thus protected from the disruptions of desire in the interests of continuous
factory production' (Turner, 1984: 100). The consequences of this ideology

of asceticism were very different for men and women, as women were caught within a set of contradictory pressures. In the Victorian period in particular, women were seen as governed by their sexuality and reproductive functions, and properly confined to marriage and the domestic sphere. However, early marriage was often delayed within the European marriage pattern and this was seen as exposing women to the danger of hysterical breakdowns. Women could only lead healthy lives if they were sexually engaged with a man in a marriage which had the aim of reproduction. This view served both to reinforce the superiority of men over women and expose any deviant women to the threat of **hysteria** (Turner, 1987: 88–93).

The **regulation of populations in space** has been accomplished by what Foucault termed **'panopticism'**, defined by Turner (1984: 92) as a mode of control involving a general increase in surveillance, record keeping and population control which has entailed the bureaucratic registration of populations and the 'elimination of vagabondism'. Populations came to be regulated in social space with the developing view of urbanism as a threat to the dominant culture of the élite from the eighteenth century. **Rousseau**, viewed as the theorist of this problem of the body, argued that urbanization had a deleterious consequence on morality as the population concentrations it brought about served to undermine people's natural compassion. The anxieties of urban life were focused on middle class women who were seen as especially vulnerable to the sexual dangers of urban space. When the policing and regulation of cities had reached the point where women's travel within cities was safer, male anxiety about women's independence increased and the first coherent medical descriptions of **agoraphobia** started to appear. Agoraphobia refers to anxiety about leaving the home, travelling alone and even visiting shops. As Turner explains, in Freudian terms the agoraphobic fears sexual seduction and represses sexual interest in strangers. Agoraphobia in wives expresses the anxiety of husbands over their control of the domestic household, but is also a manifestation of the wife's dependence on the security and status of the bourgeois family setting. Fear of urban areas and the market place became converted into a medical condition which legitimated the power of the husbands over wives (Turner, 1984: 107–8). However, as middle class women increasingly entered the market place in the twentieth century as a result of the growing demand for labour in war time, agoraphobia increasingly gave way as the paradigmatic illness of the regulation of populations to **presentational concerns** about the surface of the body (for example, dress, make-up, size of body).

Finally, Turner argues that societies presuppose a certain stability in how **people represent themselves** in social space. In pre-modern societies, the representation of individuals was objectified through external marks of status and insignia. In feudal society, representation resided in a man's shield which indicated a privileged class position. However, with the development of capitalism the representation of the individual became progressively detached from institutional roles. As Turner notes, this places a great weight on face work and impression management:

> The self is no longer located in heraldry, but has to be constantly constituted in face-to-face interactions, because consumerism and the mass market have liquidated, or at least blurred, the exterior marks of social and personal difference. (1984: 109)

Commodification is the mode through which contemporary Western societies seek to ensure a minimal continuity in how people present themselves. That is, the means for managing the self have become increasingly tied up with consumer goods, and the achievement of social and economic success hinges crucially on the presentation of an acceptable self-image. **Goffman** is the major theorist concerned with how people present themselves (although it is again necessary to stress that Turner sees the problem of body management as given by the need society has to reproduce itself). In *The Presentation of Self in Everyday Life* (1969), Goffman paints a picture of individuals as actors seeking to advance their own interests by staging appropriate performances which are threatened constantly by the possibility of embarrassment or failure. The management and moulding of the body has become increasingly central to the presentation of self-image, and this has been backed up by a growing industry catering for keep-fit, dieting and general body care (Featherstone, 1987; Wolf, 1991). **Anorexia nervosa** is the paradigmatic illness which expresses the breakdown of the body under the competitive pressures of self-presentation. Anorexia mainly affects women and is, nowadays, closely connected with the association between beauty and slimness (Chernin, 1983; Lawrence, 1987).

Turner's theory of bodily order has the considerable advantage of providing a typology which can organize, classify and make sociological sense of existing writings on the body. It also provides an account of the minimal bodily tasks societies must fulfil in order to reproduce themselves. This reveals how the dual approach sociology has traditionally adopted towards the body neglects the corporeal dimensions of social structures by failing to take into account the problems of bodily order which confront social systems.

Turner's work has been extremely important in influencing subsequent formulations of, and investigations into, the problem of the body in society (e.g. Frank, 1991; Therberge, 1991). However, there are several problems with, and gaps in, Turner's approach which suggest the need to look to theorists other than Parsons, Hobbes and Foucault in establishing a theory that overcomes fully sociology's dual approach to the body.

Turner's theory of bodily order has the merit of displaying a greater concern with the material, physical body than is the case with Foucault, while maintaining a concern with such issues as order, control and sexuality. Turner illustrates how the body may break down and become ill as a result of the modes of control imposed on it by society, and provides a clear sense of how the material body is implicated in structures of sexuality and socially acceptable modes of presentation. However, this is still a partial view of the material body as we get little *theoretical* sense of the body as a thinking, acting phenomenon. This is because the body is important only in so far as it presents a problem to be managed by social systems. Furthermore, while Turner's theory tends to be strong on structure, there is much less sense of the body as an *enabling property* of individuals. We are told much more about the constraints that bodies are likely to be placed under and how this may affect their capabilities, than we are about the ways in which the body is related to and facilitative of human agency. This leaves Turner open to the accusation that his theory provides a relatively *disembodied* view of the individual in society (T. Turner, 1986).

There are other difficulties with Turner's theory which stem, in part, from its scope. The core problems approach may establish the basic bodily parameters social systems have to manage but it tells us little about why certain systems are more successful in meeting these problems than others. Neither is this approach concerned with specifying the historical mechanisms by which change comes about in how social systems seek to solve the problem of the body. Indeed, despite the depth of historical data which inform the core problems approach, it is ultimately a diachronically static theory which leaves analysis of historical change up to empirical investigation. This is a notable silence in Turner's theory.

These criticisms are not meant to dispute the value of Turner's approach to the body. They do suggest, however, that its utility may be confined to stipulating the outer parameters of the problems posed to social systems by the body.

The body and human action

Arthur Frank (1991) provides an alternative to Turner's approach by examining the relationship between the body and human action. The starting point for Frank is a consideration of the 'action problems' faced by the individual body, rather than the 'bodily order' tasks which confront social systems. As he argues, 'Theorizing about society may culminate in Turner's categories, but these categories must first be postulated not as abstract needs of a "society", but rather as deriving from the body's own problems of its embodiment within a social context' (Frank, 1991: 48). In this respect, Frank is more concerned than Turner with extending some of Goffman's insights into the body as a component of human agency.

Frank adopts a social constructionist approach to the body in so far as he views the significance and development of bodies as inextricably related to social forces and social relationships. However, his 'action problems' analysis goes beyond the limitations which characterize many social constructionist views. This is because he takes seriously the existence of the body as a *corporeal* phenomenon which itself affects how people experience their bodies. As Frank recognizes, bodies 'do not emerge out of discourses and institutions; they emerge out of other bodies, specifically women's bodies'. Bodies provide people with the means of acting, but they also place constraints on action. The corporeal character of bodies 'remains an obdurate fact. There is a flesh which is formed in the womb, transfigured (for better or worse) in its life, dies and decomposes' (1991: 49).

The recognition of bodies as corporeal phenomena provides a general introduction to Frank's analysis. More specifically, he argues that bodies are the medium and outcome of social 'body techniques' (combinations of discourse, institutions and the corporeality of bodies), and that society is also the medium and outcome of these body techniques. Discourses do not have the determining power they possess in Foucault's work but refer to ideas of the body's abilities and constraints which are experienced by bodies as already there for their self-understanding. In contrast, institutions are physical places which are located in time and space. Body techniques are usually experienced as socially given, but are only instantiated in their practical use by bodies on other bodies. Moreover, body techniques are simultaneously constraining and enabling.

Frank illustrates what he means by the body in this formulation by using the example of the ascetic practice of fasting among medieval holy women. He locates these fasting bodies within the institution of the church, as it existed at that time, and within the discourses which stemmed from the doctrines of the church (concerned with the boundary between fasting as a holy act and an act of self-indulgence), medieval marriage and the place of women within society. The final dimension of corporeality in this example poses the question of how much self-punishment and deprivation the body will bear. As Caroline Bynum (1987) suggests, the amount of punishment actually inflicted by the body on itself suggests that it is not only institutions and discourses which are in flux, but that corporeality itself is flexible and has its own history.

Up to this point in his argument, Frank has drawn selectively on the work of Turner and Giddens to set some highly suggestive parameters to his theory of the body. Much of this is very condensed and in need of elaboration but it provides a context for him to isolate 'four questions [or action problems] which the body must ask itself as it undertakes action in relationship to some object' (1991: 51). Adapted from Turner's theory of bodily order, these questions concern **control** (involving the predictability of performance); **desire** (whether the body is lacking or producing desires); the body's **relation to others** (whether the body is monadic and closed in on itself or dyadic and constituted through either communicative or dominating relations with others); and the **self-relatedness of the body** (whether the body associates and 'feels at home' in itself, or dissociates itself from its corporeality).

As bodies respond to these four action problems, typical and discrete styles of body usage emerge. Frank identifies four ideal types of body usage, and their respective media of activity, which resolve these action problems

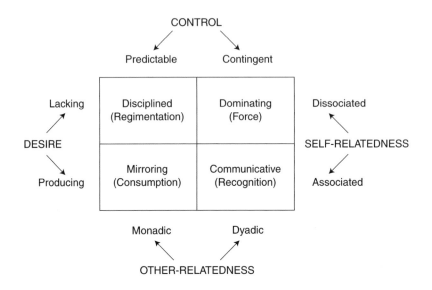

Figure 4.2   *Frank's typology of body use in action*

Reprinted from Arthur W. Frank, 'For a Sociology of the Body: an Analytical Review' in M. Featherstone et al. (eds) *The Body: Social Process and Cultural Theory.* London: Sage.

in different ways. These ideal types are not meant to encompass all possible types of body usage but serve as heuristic guides through which bodily behaviour can be understood. For the **disciplined** body the medium is **regimentation**, the model of which is the rationalization of the monastic order. For the **mirroring** body the medium is **consumption**, the model of which is the department store. For the **dominating** body the medium is **force**, the model of which is war; and for the **communicative** body the medium is **recognition**, the model of which could be shared narratives, communal rituals and caring relationships. The problems which face the acting body, the ideal types of bodily use, and the typical media of their activity are illustrated in Figure 4.2.

In attempting to clarify Frank's theory of the body as represented in Figure 4.2, I shall briefly describe his account of how the disciplined, mirroring, dominating and communicative types of body usage resolve – through their respective media of activity – the action problems of control, desire, other-relatedness and self-relatedness.

The disciplined body makes itself predictable and seeks to hide a sense of its own contingency through programmes of regimentation. It regards itself as lacking in desire but uses regimentation as a way of recognizing its own existence. The disciplined body is monadic and isolated, and is dissociated both from its own surface and from any empathy with other bodies. In sum, the disciplined body becomes a 'tool' fitted for instrumental uses which is unable to give or receive affection. Examples of disciplined bodies can be seen in contexts of military training (Foucault, 1979a), and in the case of women who fasted as a result of divine inspiration in medieval times.

The mirroring body also makes itself predictable but this time through reflecting what is available to be consumed. In order to keep its own lack of desire unconscious, the mirroring body is endlessly producing superficial desires through consumption. It adopts a monadic style of other-relatedness, as external objects are viewed purely in terms of their use for the mirroring body. Nothing in the world challenges the body's limited consciousness of itself. Indeed, the institutional structures of consumer capitalism are designed to facilitate the mutual assimilation of external objects to the body and the body to external objects. Finally, the mirroring body is associated with its own surface. It seeks connection with and absorption in its own surface which exists in order to be decorated. In contrast, the 'interior' of the body is a hidden phenomenon available only to specialist 'authorized personnel' (Frank, 1991: 61). Examples of the mirroring body include the narcissistic individual who disavows personal or political commitment, treats the body as an instrument of sensual gratification, rather than relating sensuality to communication with others, and who pursues artificially-framed styles of life (Giddens, 1991: 170–1, 198; Sennett, 1974).

The dominating body is constantly aware of its own contingency. Its world is warfare, and the dominating body is perpetually threatened by new situations and the unknown. The essential quality of these bodies is their construction of desire as *lack*, a lack which demands compensation. Combined with the body's dyadic other-relatedness, the dominating body's lack produces a fear which is turned outwards on others who are exterminated in order to combat that fear. In the context of war, others must die in order for the dominating body to live with itself. Finally, the dominating body must be dissociated from itself in order to punish and absorb punishment. Dominating bodies are overwhelmingly *male* bodies and examples can be seen in Theweleit's analysis of the German Freikorps. The Freikorps were an army unit formed at the end of the First World War to fight 'Bolsheviks' and trade unionists. When their official mandate ended, many continued as a vigilante force and eventually ended up in the SA and SS, with some of the latter becoming concentration camp commandants during the Second World War. According to Theweleit, the Freikorps were motivated partly by a fear of their own death which could be made tolerable only by destroying anything seen as a threat to their lives (Frank, 1991: 69; Theweleit, 1987, 1989).

Frank's fourth type of body usage is the communicative body, which is less a reality than a future possibility. The communicative body's contingency is no longer a problem but a series of possibilities, and its essential quality is that it is a body in the process of creating itself through constructive interaction with others. The communicative body produces desire but, unlike the mirroring body, it is a desire for dyadic expression rather than monadic consumption. The communicative body is also related to itself, being comfortable in rather than alienated from itself. In sum, communicative bodies are about the 'capacity for recognition which is enhanced through the sharing of narratives which are fully embodied' (Frank, 1991: 89). Frank suggests that communicative bodies may begin to be found among care-givers and care-receivers, and among those engaged in postmodern dance.

Each of these types of body usages draws on and contributes to the perpetuation of body techniques. Moreover, social systems grow up from the media through which these body tasks are undertaken. As Frank notes, this 'allows us to understand how bodies can experience their tasks as imposed by a system' (1991: 48).

Frank's theory intends to focus on the embodiment of agency and his analysis can be seen as stronger in its treatment of agency than it is in analysing the corporeal dimensions of social structures. However, the kernel of Frank's argument revolves around the 'action *problems*' bodies have to overcome. Consequently, there is not as much sense as one would expect of the body as a resource which is both central to and facilitative of human agency. There are also other difficulties and gaps in the 'action problems' approach. Despite the useful typologies provided, it gives us little explanation as to *why* people should choose to adopt particular relations to their bodies, *how* individuals are able to change between styles of body usage, or what wider *historical conditions* could influence their adoption of certain styles rather than others. This is left to empirical examination. Further, despite the promising selective adaptation of Giddens's structuration theory, Frank's analysis of how the embodiment of structure and agency are mutually constitutive is seriously underdeveloped.

By focusing on the embodiment of agency, Frank's theoretical approach can be seen as complementing Turner's structuralist model. Indeed, combining their theories offers the possibility of deriving the principal problems facing social systems from the action problems facing individual bodies. However, similar criticisms can be made of both these approaches and these derive from the similarities between the theories themselves. Despite Frank's criticisms of Turner, both adopt a 'core problems' approach to the body which is functionalist in its essentials. Merely transferring the level at which these core problems are addressed (from society to the individual body) does nothing to overcome the deficiencies of this approach in terms of its diachronic underdevelopment, and its difficulty in conceptualizing adequately human agency.

Bridging the gap

In this chapter I have examined some of the most important influences on social constructionist views of the body and examined two of the most recent attempts to develop explicit theories of the body. In their different ways, social constructionists all bring society into the body as a way of investigating its significance for sociology. This is most evident in the case of Foucault, who views the body as produced and constituted by discourse. However, while both Goffman and Turner show a greater concern with the material body, their work displays a number of similarities to Foucault. For all of these writers, the body becomes significant only in so far as it is deemed to be by factors external to the body, be they social systems (Turner), discourse (Foucault), or shared vocabularies of body idiom (Goffman). Consequently, there is much less sense of the body as an *integral* component of human agency.

The other problem common to social constructionist views concerns the body as an absent presence in sociology. Foucault, Goffman and Turner have all helped to reinstate the notion of the body as a topic of discussion in sociology. However, by viewing the body as significant purely in terms of society (however defined), they reproduce this dual approach in a different form. The body is present as an item for discussion, but absent as an object of investigation. At most, we sometimes get a sense that there is an absent 'other' lurking behind social constructions. Even then, however, we receive little idea about what this bodily 'other' actually is.

I have already noted that despite Frank's intention to examine the acting body, his focus on the problems facing bodies engaged in action does not provide us with a fully developed view of the body as integral to human agency. However, Frank's approach does have the considerable merit of incorporating a view of the body as a corporeal phenomenon. This corporeality does not disappear simply because it is located in society, but becomes taken up and transformed as a result of its engagement with social relations. This is a promising basis on which to develop what is positive about social constructionist views of the body.

Social constructionist views provide important insights into how bodies may be affected by power relations, how the body enters into social definitions of the self, and how the body can function as a social symbol. They also highlight how the body can be used to legitimize social inequalities, and it seems to me that these insights need to be utilized by any new approach to the body in society. However, they need to do this in a context where the corporeality of the body is taken seriously.

As Chapter 5 reveals, Frank is not the only writer to have explored the body's simultaneous status as a social and corporeal phenomenon. Indeed, a number of sociologists have expanded this view of the body in ways which begin to overcome the dual approach sociology has traditionally adopted to the body.

5

The Body and Social Inequalities

After reviewing the dual approach that sociology has traditionally adopted towards the body in Chapter 2, I concentrated in Chapters 3 and 4 on two sets of approaches which have been influential in shaping contemporary sociological accounts of the body. Naturalistic and social constructionist approaches focus respectively on the pre-social, biological location of the body, and on the social character of the body. However, there is a tendency for these perspectives to adopt reductionist views of the body, and neither of them is able to grasp fully the importance of human embodiment to the constitution of social systems. In particular, they are unable to help our understanding of why the body has become increasingly important to modern people. Bryan Turner (1984) is something of an exception here as he implies that presentational concerns have accompanied an increasing commodification of the body in capitalism. However, Turner does not elaborate on this point and he is concerned primarily with the importance of the body from the standpoint of society, rather than with the problems of embodied individuals.

In contrast to these perspectives, there is a tendency within several recent sociological analyses to focus more on what it is about the body that allows it both to be affected by society, and to become a project for modern people. These studies have begun to produce something of a realignment between naturalistic and social constructionist approaches by taking seriously the body as a phenomenon that is simultaneously biological and social. In so doing, they have sought to utilize the insights of social constructionism, but have held on to the view that the body is a corporeal phenomenon which is not only affected by social systems, but which forms a basis for and shapes social relations. The body is seen as 'unfinished' at birth, an entity which changes and develops throughout an individual's life. Like social constructionist views, this approach focuses on how the body is affected by social factors. It does not, however, allow the body to be reduced to these factors.

Restructuring the body

Bryan Turner has formulated what will probably become one of the best known attempts to go beyond the limitations of naturalistic and social constructionist views of the body (Turner, 1992a). Although my discussions in this chapter will focus on what I consider to be more productive analyses of the problem, it is appropriate at this stage to say something about this methodological approach to the body.

In his *Regulating Bodies*, Turner seeks to move beyond what he calls the 'somewhat rigid discussion of the Hobbesian problem of order' contained in his 1984 theory of bodily order (Turner, 1992a: 10). Instead, Turner is concerned with promoting an approach to the body which avoids the division between what he terms foundationalist and anti-foundationalist frameworks towards the body (terms which have similarities to, but which are somewhat more inclusive than, the naturalistic and social construc-tionist categories I have used). So, Turner wants to combine a view of the body as a biological organism and as 'lived experience', which contributes towards social relations, with an analysis of the body as a system of representation. Foucault and Weber remain central to Turner's concerns, but he also wants to integrate philosophical anthropology into his new approach.

Philosophical anthropology starts out from the premiss that something meaningful can be said about the 'unchanging preconditions of human changeableness', and has attempted to incorporate the discoveries of bio-logy and zoology into the social sciences (Honneth and Joas, 1988 [1980]: 7). This is evident in its analysis of the relationship that animals and humans have with their environment, an analysis which identifies import-ant differences between the bodies of animals and humans.

Animals enter the world with highly specialized and firmly directed drives. As a result, they are born into a world whose possibilities are more or less completely determined by their instincts. In other words, animals have a species-specific world whose territories and dangers are mapped out from the very beginning of their lives. The bodies of animals are pro-grammed to exist and survive within their environment.

In contrast, the instinctual structure of humans at birth is not as special-ized as that of animals, nor is it directed in the same way towards a species-specific environment. Consequently, the world for humans is a relatively open world, a world whose content and meaning must be fashioned from human action. The structures of the human world can never have the stability that marks the structures for the animal world, and the bodies and identities of humans are only very loosely pre-set for survival in their environment. Humans must make a world in order to survive.

Philosophical anthropology's view of the relationship between humans and their environment has specific implications for the study of the body. It implies that human embodiment is an unfinished state which compels people to act on themselves, others and the world around them. Humans must free themselves in action from the dangers to their survival which are inherent in the unfinishedness of their embodiment. This action consists of both physical intervention *and* investments of meaning. Because the world is not pre-set for humans, as it is for animals, humans need to manage the superabundance of data that threatens to overwhelm their senses. In effect, humans must create a meaningful world for themselves, by saturating their environment with meaning and shape. They must do this in order for there to be a world they can physically act on, in order to survive in.

These same conditions govern an individual's sense of self and the relation they have with their body. Because human bodies are unfinished entities, they too must be invested with work and meaning. The absence of a meaningful and ordered self, body and world for humans would make impossible effective physical intervention in the world.

Turner (1992a) provides a fascinating example of how philosophical anthropology can be applied to sociological studies of the human body by focusing on the hand. The hand allows humans to complete their own and each other's bodies by feeding and caring for their young, and by providing for their sustenance and shelter. In working on their environment with their hands, humans also develop particular orientations to their bodies. The hand also allows humans to create their world. For example, the manipulative skills of the human hand are integral to the construction and use of tools, and for the exploration of the environment. In short, the hand 'is an important aspect of human world openness' (Turner, 1992a: 114).

As well as helping humans to survive and impose meaning on the world, the hand has served as an object for classificatory systems which provide people with self-identities and specified places within the world. The hand has long served as a bearer of meaning, and Robert Hertz's *Death and the Right Hand* (1960 [1909]) argues that the historical pre-eminence of the right hand over the left is a social institution which has expressed the religious dualism between the sacred and profane. This religious dualism affected how social groups regarded the body; the right hand represented the sacred side, whereas the left side represented evil. Residues of this view continue to be found in contemporary societies: 'Right-handedness is associated with worthiness, dexterity, rectitude and beauty', and it is still a custom for a deal to be sealed not only with a signature, but with a handshake (Turner, 1992a: 109–10).

Turner's analysis of the hand can be seen as having a far wider applicability to the human body as a forward-orientated entity. Furthermore, Turner's application of philosophical anthropology to the sociology of the body allows him to retain a commitment to a view of the body as an organic object, while accepting that the social meanings attached to the body vary widely. The source of people's ability to intervene in the world comes not from prevailing forms of discourse or social classifications, as social constructionists would have it, but from the body's own material relationship to its environment. Furthermore, while the human body is integral to the formation of societies, it does not act as a base that determines the exact form of social relationships, as naturalistic views tend to argue. Instead, the body is an unfinished resource which requires humans to invest themselves, and the world they inhabit, with work and meaning.

There are, however, methodological problems with Turner's espousal of what he terms 'epistemological pragmatism'. These stem from his attempt to combine foundationalist and anti-foundationalist frameworks without altering any of their basic parameters. Turner argues that there are clearly organic foundations to the human body and to human activity, yet sees 'no reason to doubt the proposition that the body is socially constructed' (Turner, 1992a: 16, 26). These two statements appear contradictory, but we can reconcile them if we accept the proposition that Turner is talking about different things. If we confine the first statement to the actual, fleshy body and the second to classifications which concern the body, then Turner's stance makes sense. However, it is clear that Turner does not want to maintain such a degree of separation in his approach. Instead, he wants to bring about a degree of *reintegration* between foundationalist and anti-foundationalist frameworks. Now, what Turner does accomplish is to suggest that the examination of different bodily issues requires different methodological approaches. Nonetheless, he does not provide the means for actually going beyond this and reconciling foundationalist and anti-foundationalist frameworks. In fact, his 1992 approach to the body is marked by a dualism which frequently seeks to combine both frameworks without actually providing any adequate means to accomplish this task.

Part of the source of this problem can be located in the categories Turner uses to describe the major approaches which have been adopted towards the body. Despite Turner's claim that these approaches rest on different ontological views of the body, Turner actually treats foundationalist approaches as concerned with what the body *is*, while anti-foundationalist approaches are predominantly concerned with how the body has been *represented*. This division between ontology and representation is clearly apparent in Turner's discussion of the hand. It seems to me, though, that we cannot adequately discuss the question of what the body is unless we look at the ways in which social representations and classifications of the body both shape, and are shaped by, the organic body. By not focusing on this relationship, Turner underestimates the dynamic nature of the body. Our current state of embodiment derives from evolutionary processes which incorporate *social* as well as biological factors. The organic body changes historically, and over the course of an individual's life, because of its biological and social constitution.

In contrast to Turner's approach, I prefer to address the need to develop a view of the body which goes beyond the limitations of naturalistic and social constructionist approaches in the context of more general discussions on the possibility of a realignment between sociology and biology. This does not abandon the very important insights of philosophical anthropology, but it does seek to incorporate them within a different view of the body.

In his recent work on biology and social science, Ted Benton (1991, 1992) has suggested that the basic structures of sociological thought need to be revised if the discipline is to be able to analyse a range of subjects and processes which cannot be located unambiguously in either the 'social' or the 'natural' world. This involves taking the biological sciences seriously, ualities

ntail accepting the theories and methods of vulgar forms of For example, in discussing the evolution of humans and cul- rejects the view that 'natural selection' can be seen in terms of iological processes, and that every characteristic of humans mus. contributed positively to their net survival and reproductive chances. Instead, he makes a strong case for understanding natural selection as *including* patterns of social life which are adopted by evolving populations (Benton, 1991, 1992; see also Sharp, 1992).

This approach has important implications for sociological conceptualizations of the body. Although Benton is not concerned explicitly with the sociology of the body, the human body represents an excellent example of a phenomenon that cannot be located exclusively in the social or the natural world. In this respect, Benton's analysis suggests that if we are to understand the historical factors which have contributed to our current state of embodiment, we need to examine the interrelationship between biological and social processes. This holds for the historical evolution of the body, and for the development of the body over the course of an individual's life span. As the body has evolved through the centuries, it has provided different bases on which social relations were established which, in turn, contributed to its further evolutionary development. It follows from this that it would be just as much a mistake to view the body as a pre-social, biological phenomenon, as it would be to regard it as a post-biological, social entity.

Sociological studies of the body have tended to treat nature and culture as if they were separate spheres whose analysis was the responsibility of different disciplines. However, the 'natural' properties of human bodies, developed as a result of the biological *and* social processes involved in evolution, are inseparable from the cultural achievements of humans. The development of bipedalism (the capacity for upright posture and two-legged walking), and tool use, eventually shaped the human body in ways that formed a corporeal context for modern culture. Without the corporeal ability to stand upright and use tools, human societies would never have been able to develop the ways of life and physical artefacts which characterize their present existence.

Another dimension of the link which exists between the 'natural' and cultural constitution of humans is to be found in the individual human body. Writers as diverse as Mary Midgely (1979), Norbert Elias (1991) and Paul Hirst and Penny Woolley (1982) have all pointed out that the newly-born body is not infinitely malleable and cannot be shaped at will. Babies start life with a species-specific nervous system which is connected to a determinate brain and to specific organs, muscles and expressive devices. These dispose them, in all manner of ways, towards society. Indeed, as Midgley (1979: 167) argues, 'It is not clear how a species could evolve which did what Hobbes supposed and became calculating before becoming social'. Rather than being radically divorced from society, then, the 'natural' properties of humans are prerequisites for social relations and cultural activities.

Norbert Elias's *The Symbol Theory* (1991) explores these issues in greater depth and provides specific examples of how natural and social processes intertwine in the development of human bodies through the learned and unlearned capacities of humans. A child's learning of language, for instance, is made possible only by the closely-related processes of biological maturation and social learning. No human being could learn the immensely intricate sound patterns of a language without being biologically equipped for the task. Before spoken language, it was the *face* which became a major instrument of communication. The face evolved into a 'signalling board' and while face-to-face communication is genetically fixed, or unlearned, to a much higher degree than language, it can be greatly modified through culturally-acquired facial signals. For example, Elias argues that in the case of the young baby, the smile is wholly innate. As humans grow older, though, the smile becomes much more malleable and more of an expression of culture (Elias, 1991).

Elias's analysis is predicated on the assumption that humans represented an evolutionary breakthrough in being the first and only species for whom learned ways of steering behaviour became dominant in relation to unlearned ways. Another way of putting this is that cultural processes and social relations have increasingly come to shape the body. However, this does not negate the fact that the body itself *continues to provide a basis for these social relations and cannot be reduced to an expression of them.*

Analysing the body as simultaneously biological and social provides a starting point, and no more than that, for going beyond the limitations of naturalistic and social constructionist views of the body, while retaining some of their insights. For example, recognizing that social forces and biological processes are inextricably linked provides for the possibility that while social relations, actions and classifications do not create the body in a Foucauldian sense, they do contribute to its development and can become *embodied.* One example of this, which will serve to illustrate this point for now, is provided by W.B. Cannon's analysis of 'Voodoo death' (1942). Cannon argues that belief in evil spirits can have extreme physiological consequences. If a 'believer' considers himself or herself to have been cursed and doomed to death, a state of fear and terror can follow. If deep and prolonged enough, this state leads to physiological changes which are equivalent to severe wound shock. The ultimate consequence of this condition is an irreversible decline in the functioning of the circulatory system and death as a result of oxygen starvation (Cannon, 1942; Hirst and Woolley, 1982).

These comments do no more than indicate in the broadest and briefest of terms the type of approach which might serve to build a bridge between naturalistic and social constructionist views of the body. As yet, there are no fully developed perspectives on the body which seek to combine the biological and social sciences in the manner suggested by Benton. However, I shall examine the work of Bob Connell and Peter Freund in some detail. These writers have produced important analyses which, although selective in their focus on embodiment, take seriously the proposition that the body is a social and biological entity. They also have something to say about the sociological consequences of the mind's location within the body (Connell, 1983, 1987; Freund, 1982, 1988, 1990). In so doing, they suggest a promising methodological approach which could be developed by the sociology of the body.

In this chapter I shall describe Connell's work on the gendered body, and Freund's writings on the emotional body. I will then illustrate some of the implications of their analyses by looking at a small selection of studies which suggest that the body can be affected by work. The focus of my discussion here will be Arlie Hochschild's analysis of the commercialization of human feeling. *The Managed Heart* (1983) has been an extremely influential book which has been at the centre of important debates about emotion work in high modern societies.

Constructing the gendered body

Connell's analysis (1983, 1987) of gender focuses on what can loosely be termed the 'exterior' of the body; on its shapes, sizes and musculature. Connell's argument divides into three stages. After acknowledging the importance of evolutionary processes, he first examines how women's and men's bodies are defined as different through social practices such as categorization which contradict or *negate* the contemporary realities of human embodiment. In other words, social categories give a qualitatively new meaning to bodies which cannot be justified with reference to their biological constitution.

Second, Connell argues that while social categories define people's bodies as different, other social practices exert a much more direct impact on the body. Gendered social practices do not simply negate the body but *transcend* and transform it. They change the meaning and character of people's bodies by actually altering them physically. Third, processes of negation and transcendence interact. Gendered categories and practices operate as material forces which help to shape and form women's and men's bodies in ways that reinforce particular images of femininity and masculinity. The mind's conceptualization of bodies is closely related to people's experiences of bodies.

Connell starts by rejecting radical social constructionist approaches to the body. He does this by recognizing that human evolution, affected as it is by both biological and social forces, has provided us with the 'species' capacities for such phenomena as language, intellect and imagination, upright stance, tool making and manipulation, and extended childhood and parenting. Like Norbert Elias's argument in *The Symbol Theory*, Connell suggests that these common capacities and characteristics make us unique from other species and illustrate the importance of the biological dimensions to social life.

Evolutionary processes have, then, been important in providing humans with the capability of learning, and of producing and sustaining social life. In a very few instances, they have also provided groups of people with different capacities. For example, we have yet to reach the stage where someone who is chromosomally male is able to give birth to a child. However, what is remarkable about the species of humans is not the few biological differences that exist between them, but their *shared* capacities for action. Indeed, the few differences that exist between humans pale into insignificance beside the common abilities they possess in comparison with other species.

Negating the body

Having established the importance of biology to the human species, Connell argues that the major inequalities within society are based on socially-determined criteria *without* permanent foundation in the body. However, this has not prevented biology serving as an ideological justification for these divisions. In such cases – ranging from the reasons men give for their privileged position over women, to the justifications given by Hitler for the segregation and extermination of Jews – biological differences are either fabricated or exaggerated.

Connell terms this contradiction between social processes of categorization and the bodily bases on which they rest, the *negation* of biology. It is important to note that by negation Connell does not always mean the complete neglect of biology, but is often referring to its distortion. For example, far from being an expression of natural difference, exclusive gender identities are based on the suppression of bodily similarities and the exaggeration of bodily differences. Indeed, the early gender identities given to biologically male and female bodies actually contradict their physiological development in certain respects.

The suppression of bodily similarities is most obvious in the case of young children who have gender identities imposed on them long before they are capable of reproducing, asserting dominance over each other, or even understanding the processes involved in reproduction (Connell, 1983: 28; 1987: 81). The popularity of baby clothes which are pink for girls and blue for boys illustrates the continuing importance attached to highlighting differences between bodies when there are none of any significance. Babies are all usually capable of feeding, urinating, defecating, vomiting and keeping their parents awake at night. They are not, though, capable of significant social tasks which can in any simple sense be attributed to the 'sex' of their bodies. Other examples of the negation of biology include situations where young girls are defined as 'weak' and 'fragile' even though they may be taller and stronger than their male counterparts, and when a young boy cries in response to pain, yet is reprimanded and told to 'act like a man'.

In short, if the difference between girls and boys and women and men is so natural, it would not have to be marked so heavily and persistently by such practices as the sex-typing of clothes. Instead, such practices should more accurately be seen as:

> part of a continuing effort to sustain the social definition of gender, an effort that is necessary precisely *because the biological logic*, and the inert practice that responds to it, *cannot sustain the gender categories*. (Connell, 1987: 81)

Women and men differ enormously in their height, weight, strength, endurance etc., and the distribution of these features overlaps between the sexes (Birke, 1992). The production of 'women' and 'men' as separate and unequal categories, though, operates by converting *average* differences into *absolute* differences. Statements such as 'men are physically stronger than women' neglect the large numbers of women who are in fact stronger than many men. So, social categories which focus on the body and negate biology are central to the ideological construction of differences between women and men. Similarities between their bodies are neglected, differences are fabricated or exaggerated, and the meanings of biological features are changed into new sets of categories and oppositions.

Connell's analysis of negation is concerned with the production of gender differences. However, negation is also a process which acts to produce other social divisions. In the case of biological racism, for instance, the physical features of a group are evaluated according to their supposed social and cultural superiority or inferiority (Cohen, 1988). Biological similarities are suppressed, and physical differences are highlighted and used to support racist classificatory systems. Negation has also been used historically to differentiate between the bodies of children belonging to separate social class backgrounds as fit and suitable for unequal social positions. In nineteenth-century English schools, for instance, the bodies of children from the aristocracy and working classes were defined as different and treated accordingly in separate institutions (Simon and Bradley, 1975).

Transforming the body

The first part of Connell's argument analyses how social categories define people as different by negating the similarities which exist between their bodies. However, as Connell notes, this can only be an initial stage in examining the social significance of the body. To speak of a simple contradiction between biology and social practices is insufficient as it presupposes that biology is fixed – being the focus of social practices without being altered by them. One implication of such a view would be to set up a dualism between biology and society such that the two were entirely separate. Another would be to establish a dualism between the mind and body, whereby gendered images and social practices operated only on the mind by affecting people's perceptions of female and male bodies. In order to avoid these problems, Connell uses the term transcendence to signify how biology (in the form of the body) is actually *transformed* by social practices.

Transcendence recognizes that the body is an object of labour which is worked on by people just as are other aspects of the natural and social world. For example, gymnastics and weight training can build up the physical body, while solitary confinement in prison or too much time spent sitting in front of a word processor can lead to its deterioration. Technological advances can also alter the size, shape and composition of bodies. This happens directly, through such factors as advances in transplant surgery, and indirectly, by changing the quality and quantity of physical effort required to travel and work.

In the construction of gendered bodies, processes of transcendence create corporeal differences where none existed previously. The physical sense of maleness experienced by many men comes not just from the symbolic significance of the phallus, or even simply from the images of power frequently attached to the male body by popular culture. It also derives from the *transformation* of the body through social practices (Connell, 1983, 1987).

This can happen in a variety of ways and includes the greater encouragement boys usually receive in comparison with girls to engage in strenuous physical exercise and 'cults of physicality', such as football and weight training, which focus on the disciplined management of the body and the occupation of space. These differences tend to grow during adolescence when girls are encouraged by the media to focus more exclusively on the relatively passive decoration of their bodies (for example, through make-up and jewellery), while boys are meant to concentrate on the more active building up of their bodies.

Such practices have very real effects on the body and these are not simply confined to muscle size and strength. Lowe (1983) has shown how different patterns of physical activity and muscle use can affect the size and shape of skeletal development and stature. This may work partly as a result of hormone production, itself influenced by patterns of physical activity and social stress, affecting a person's height. It also occurs in more straightforward ways through work and sports activities. So, the different opportunities girls and boys have to engage in muscle-building work and leisure activities can play an important part in developing and transforming their bodies.

There are many oppressive aspects to the construction of bodies in line with gender stereotypes. For example, the social desirability of slimness for women and muscularity for men adds to the pressures which create eating disorders (Turner, 1987), and the increased use of illegal drugs such as anabolic steroids by American males in their teens. Indeed, in 1992 it was estimated that some 500,000 school children were taking stimulants and steroids to improve their sporting prowess (Wearne and Jones, 1992). As well as being physically dangerous to the user, the side effects of drugs such as anabolic steroids include increasing aggression and a propensity to engage in violent acts.

Gendered practices and images of the body exert an influence which does not remain at the level of consciousness or discourse. The ways in which we perceive, categorize and value women's and men's bodies are undoubtedly important in legitimizing and reproducing social inequalities. However, gendered images and practices can also become embodied. While the processes of embodiment involved in transcendence are not always irreversible, they can often be relatively enduring and are sometimes permanent in their effects.

The reproduction of gendered bodies

The third part of Connell's argument concerns the interrelationship between negation and transcendence. In the case of gender, we have seen how dominant conceptualizations of masculinity and femininity can become embodied through social practices. However, this embodiment can itself serve to *justify and legitimize the original social categories* in ways which oppress women as 'the weaker sex'.

There is a self-fulfilling prophecy at work here as bodies can sometimes change in ways that support the validity of original images and practices. It is important to emphasize, though, that these changes are not usually programmed from birth, but are contingent on social practices and are potentially reversible. *Potentially* is the key word here. Women may develop a taste for sport, for example, after their teenage years. By this time, however, the development of their bodies may already have placed restrictions on their participation and the degree of expertise they are able to display. So, gender 'training' means that many women do become weaker than many men and less expert at managing their bodies in sporting contexts, thus helping to legitimize existing conceptions of women as weak and those social relations and practices which are predicated on women's physical inferiority.

Writing from a historical perspective, Jennifer Hargreaves illustrates how the dominant image of women possessing frail bodies was internalized among middle class women in Victorian times:

> Middle class women fulfilled their own stereotype of the 'delicate' females who took to their beds with consistent regularity and thus provided confirmation of the dominant medical account that this should be so. Women 'were' manifestly physically and biologically inferior because they actually 'did' swoon, 'were' unable to eat, suffered continual maladies, and consistently expressed passivity and submissiveness in various forms. The acceptance by women of their 'incapacitation' gave both a humane and moral weighting to the established so-called 'facts'. (Hargreaves, 1987: 134)

This situation was exacerbated both by expert advice handed out to Victorian women (Ehrenreich and English, 1988), and by the widespread prescription of opiates by medical practitioners (Berridge and Edwards, 1987 [1981]). In short, processes of negation and transcendence have been vital in helping to provide an ideological justification for gender differences and in sustaining the myth that men are biologically superior to women:

> The social definition of men as holders of power is translated not only into mental body-images and fantasies, but into muscle tensions, postures, the feel and texture of the body. This is one of the main ways in which the power of men becomes 'naturalized', i.e. seen as part of the order of nature. It is very important in allowing belief in the superiority of men, and the oppressive practices that flow from it, to be sustained by men who in other respects have very little power. (Connell, 1987: 85)

This argument can be seen as complementing Mark Johnson's (1987) and George Lakoff's (1987, 1991) work on the bodily basis of meaning, imagination and reason. Johnson and Lakoff investigate the close inter-relationship that exists between the mind and the body as a result of the mind's location within the body. The body has traditionally been ignored by objectivist theories of knowledge because it has been thought to introduce subjective elements which are supposedly irrelevant to the objective nature of meaning. However, Johnson (1987) argues that any adequate account of meaning and rationality must give a central place to the embodied structures of understanding by which we grasp our world. Johnson focuses on processes of 'imagination' and 'categorization'. Imagination refers to how we abstract from certain bodily experiences and contexts to others in order to make sense of new situations. Categorization is concerned with how the classificatory schemes with which we work typically depend on the nature of the human body, especially on our perceptual capacities and motor skills. This approach towards knowledge has been termed 'experiential realism' by Lakoff, and it is based on the assumption that experience and knowledge is structured by the human body in a significant way which is prior to and independent of discourse. Far from discourse determining the body in a Foucauldian sense, then, the body is integrally involved in the construction of discourse.

The relevance of this work to our present discussion is that it implies that the concepts and classificatory schemes which inform our under-standing of women's and men's bodies do not stem purely from disembodied categories we utilize as a result of some externally located dominant ideology. Instead, they are based in a very important way upon our multiple *experiences* of embodiment. These involve seeing, experiencing and imagining our own and other people's bodies.

This analysis complements Berger's argument (1972) that a man's presence (be it fabricated or real) is dependent on the promise of power he *embodies*. This power is always an active power, a power which can be exercised on and over others. If a man's physicality is unable to convey an image of power, he is found to have little presence precisely because the social definition of men as holders of power is not reflected in his embodiment.

It is important to note that the embodiment of power does not always have to occur purely through the development of a powerful body (although this is increasingly a dominant ideal type). It has other variants which incorporate such elements as posture, height, weight, walk, dress etc. The fat businessman may not have a muscular body but his size, dress, demeanour and bodily attitude can still embody the promise of power.

Berger's recognition that a man's physical presence may not convey the embodiment of power illustrates the important point that processes of negation and transcendence are neither universal nor inevitable. If our embodied experiences negate dominant conceptions of gender roles, for example, there is a basis for the creation or support of alternative views about women and men. Furthermore, not every social inequality is embodied and certain parts and layers of the body are more malleable or intransigent than others (Kelleman, 1985). It is also important to note that not all bodies are changed in accordance with dominant images of masculinity and femininity, and there is much that individuals can do to develop their bodies in different directions. Connell is not concerned with the mechanisms involved in such resistance, but he is keen to point out that resistance occurs. Female athletes are a good case in point; a group which has often provided both exceptions to dominant images of femininity and alternatives which can be drawn on by girls seeking to develop their bodies in non-traditional ways.

At this point it may be useful to summarize the argument so far. Connell's approach to the negation and transcendence of biology concentrates on the 'exterior' of the body. His focus on the shapes, sizes, textures and muscularity of bodies has been supported by additional arguments which highlight how common it can be for our bodies to be given meaning and changed by social practices. This is a dynamic relationship which involves the body both affecting and being affected by social relationships. Connell's work also illuminates what it is about the body which enables it to become a project. Because of its unfinishedness at birth, the body is caught up in an ongoing process of being formed after it enters into social life. While Connell is not concerned with the implications of the reflexive recognition by individuals of these processes, he at least lays the basis for recognizing the body as a project.

Having said this, however, Connell does tend to equate biology with what can very roughly be termed the 'exterior' of the body. Despite the value of his approach, little is revealed about how other dimensions of embodiment are taken up and transformed in society. For example, while Connell concentrates on the size, shape and strength of bodies, he has little to say about their experience of disease or discomfort. In this respect, Peter Freund's work on health and illness, which is concerned with the body's experience of 'well-being', can be seen as a useful addition to Connell's work.

The emotional body

Peter Freund's work (1982, 1988, 1990) has at its centre a focus on how people's experiences of health and illness are shaped and transformed by social relations of domination and subordination. Freund's argument is developed in three stages. First, he identifies some general conditions which are prerequisites for the individual achievement of what he terms 'bodily well-being', an holistic view of health concerned with the relationship between the body and the mind. He then argues that the achievement of these conditions is intimately related to our social existence via 'emotional modes of being', before investigating how these modes of being are socially differentiated.

At the centre of Freund's work (1982: 40) is a concern with people's experiences of health, illness and disease (with illness referring to social constructions and subjective experiences, and disease referring to physiological processes). It is in this context that he identifies two interrelated conditions which constitute 'bodily well-being'. In the first place, the body must be able to regulate and maintain such features as its blood pressure, body temperature, hormonal levels and electrolyte balance within 'parameters that demarcate conditions of excess or deficiency'. While Freund is interested in the body as a system, the body is not viewed as a closed, self-regulating system. Indeed, his second condition for 'well-being' requires that individuals have a sufficient degree of control over the close integration which exists between the body and mind. He refers to this control as 'being in touch', a condition which requires awareness of the linked nature of the mind/body relationship, a capacity to monitor and interpret messages that come from within (for example, pain), and the ability to mobilize the body's resources in a manner which allows it to deal with such messages. For example, the body usually lets us know when we are hungry and our interpretation of that message can allow us to prepare and consume food to satisfy our need. However, if we are not 'in touch' with our body we can ignore these hunger signals and eat irrespective of them, or starve our body of nutrition.[1] One outcome of the decision to ignore such signals can be seen in the case of those with eating disorders, such as anorexics, who lose touch with their body's needs (Lawrence, 1987).

The second stage of Freund's argument illustrates how the achievement of bodily well-being is intimately related to our social existence via 'emotional modes of being', the mind/body experience of being obstructed or assisted in achieving our aims. Following Buytendijk (1950, 1974), Freund argues that being emotional is fundamental to human life and that emotions arise out of interaction with others. For example, modes of feeling unpleasant can stem from the experience of encountering resistance in one's meetings with others, being subdued, and being injured (Freund, 1990: 461). All of these are ways of being *disempowered*, a situation which can impinge upon the 'interior' of our bodies (by, for example, affecting our neuro-hormonal system) and affect detrimentally our ability to achieve bodily well-being.

According to Freund, then, emotional modes of being connect our embodied selves to social relationships in ways which fundamentally shape our ability to achieve bodily well-being. For example, there is evidence to suggest, although it is not yet conclusive, that being in stressful social situations can have neuro-hormonal consequences that may adversely affect blood pressure (Lynch, 1985), and our immune systems (Oruchow, 1979; Locke et al., 1985; Moss, 1973; Pettingale, 1985; Solomon, 1985; Suter, 1986). Overwhelming emotional episodes such as loneliness and isolation (Lynch, 1979, 1985), grief and bereavement (Bartrop et al., 1977; Engel, 1971), anger and hostility (Friedman and Rosenman, 1974; Harburg et al., 1973, 1979; MacDougall et al., 1985), anxiety and depression (Johnson and Sarason, 1978; Kelly, 1980; Lauer, 1973) and feelings of hopelessness and helplessness (Antonovsky, 1979, 1984, 1987; Lennerlof, 1988; Seligman, 1975) have also been linked to damaging physiological changes – primarily concerned with our nervous and endocrine systems (the latter referring to glands that secrete hormones directly into the bloodstream). For example, Kushner's study (1989) of suicide suggests that adverse social conditions can affect moods such as depression by changing levels of serotonin metabolism. His biocultural study combines the concerns of sociological studies such as Durkheim's with a biochemistry of mood, suggesting that social circumstances can cause biochemical changes which can make a person more vulnerable to contemplating and committing suicide (Freund, 1988; 1990: 454).

The third stage in Freund's analysis consists of an elaboration of the argument that emotional modes of being are *socially differentiated*. As a result, our ability to achieve bodily well-being varies according to our social and economic position. While neuro-hormonal reactivity varies between individuals, styles of bodily 'reactivity' can be learnt and are related to the occupation of particular social positions (McCarty et al., 1988; Miller, 1979).

In elaborating on this point, Freund argues that levels of stress (a term he uses to denote connections between emotions and social relations which impede bodily well-being) tend to be inversely related to the degree to which people are able to maintain intact their self-identities. Stress levels tend to increase when someone perceives their performance in a situation as inconsistent with their general concept of self. Furthermore, there is a possibility that stress can recur long after the original event that caused it, being triggered by situational contexts which prefigured the original episode.

People in positions of power tend to have fewer problems in this respect than others. This is related to the differential access people have to what Hochschild (1983) calls *status shields*. Status shields protect people from attacks against their self-esteem and a lack of status shields constitutes a structural source of feeling disempowered (Hochschild, 1983). Further, those in positions of subordination without access to status shields tend to be more vulnerable to being socially redefined as the kind of people those in power expect them to be. In this situation, people may find it difficult to break out of exploitative social relations. These possibilities have radically increased in the conditions of modernity as a result of increases in the amount of *emotion work* expected from employees (Hochschild, 1983).

Freund's analysis of the emotional body may only be at a preliminary stage. However, his work has provided a highly suggestive conceptualization of how our experiences of health and illness are connected to social relationships. This is an analysis which goes beyond disembodied theories of emotions which tend to be one-dimensional in their treatment of our corporeality (e.g. Collins, 1975; Della Fave, 1991). As Freund argues, sociology 'cannot afford to regard human physiology as irrelevant' (1988: 856). Furthermore, Freund's analysis not only examines some of the mechanisms by which society shapes our experiences of health and illness, but also has implications for how these experiences 'react back' upon social classifications and social relations. As Freund argues, the appearances and experiences of bodies 'act as concrete manifestations and prototypes of "ideas" about socially appropriate bodies' which can help sustain social divisions and inequalities. There is a close link between the mind/body relationship and social practices here and a simple case of this would be the development of stereotypical ideas about the emotionality of women and men which are used to sustain sexist ideas about 'men's' and 'women's' work (Collinson et al., 1990).

Connell and Freund examine how different dimensions of the human body are taken up and transformed by social relations in ways which can help reproduce positions of dominance and subordination. In doing this, they take seriously, in quite different ways, the notion that the body is a biological and social phenomenon. Human biology is itself partially formed by social factors. It is enmeshed within, is receptive to, and is affected by social relationships and events.

Connell and Freund are concerned with different aspects of human embodiment. However, they both provide interesting analyses that could be developed by future sociological studies of the body, and which contain affinities with certain other important analyses which have been assimilated to this area (e.g. Young, 1990). In the rest of this chapter, I shall explore further some of the implications of their studies by focusing on the relationship between the body and waged work.

Work, the body and emotions

Sociology has long neglected the amount of work which we conduct on our bodies. As Pasi Falk (1991) notes, this is partly because Western thought has been dominated by a reified conception of the relationship between the subject and object, 'be it in the form of "worker – raw material" or "artist and the work of art"' (Falk, 1991: 4). However, what I shall refer to as *body work* is the most immediate and most important form of labour that humans engage in. Its neglect is one of the most remarkable features of contemporary sociology.

Margaret Stacey (1988) has written of the important role that individuals have to play in the production of their own health, and we can develop her insights by looking at the numerous ways in which individuals work on their own bodies. Body work is rarely called work, but in cleaning our teeth, washing our bodies, cutting our nails, making-up, or shaving our legs or faces, we are all working on our bodies. Sociologists have talked of the work that carers do for others and, implicitly at least, the bodies of others, but have yet to look at the work the cared for do on their own bodies. Toilet training, for example, is as much work (or nearly as much work!) for the children being trained as it is for the adults doing the training.

While sociology has failed to investigate the importance of body work, it has long established that both employment and unemployment can have detrimental effects on people's physical and mental health. Nonetheless, much less importance has been attached to the specific consequences of what Arlie Hochschild terms *emotion work*. Emotion work refers to the management of feeling to create the facial and bodily displays expected from employees (Hochschild, 1983: 7). It is central to how we experience our bodies as 'lived', and can be seen as one dimension of Freund's 'emotional modes of being'. It has three components: face-to-face or voice-to-voice contact with the public; the requirement that employees should produce a particular emotional state in another person; and methods of training and supervision which allow the employer a degree of control over the emotional activities of employees. Emotion work requires employees to manage and manipulate their emotions, and can be seen as a central component of the social relations of inequality at work. The management and manipulation of emotions can be accomplished by either surface acting or deep acting. Surface acting is when we disguise what we feel, *pretending* to feel what we do not, while deep acting refers to taking over 'the levers of feeling production' and actually *altering* what we feel (for example, suppressing anger and replacing it with sympathy) (1983: 33).

The conditions and consequences of emotion work are examined in Hochschild's analysis of women flight attendants in the United States. Flight attendants have long been expected to service the needs of passengers, deal with their problems and make them feel relaxed. This requires that flight attendants pay particular attention to their appearance (as smiling, reassuring and readily available) as a way of inducing an emotional state of ease among passengers. In order to cope with this work, Hochschild argues that flight attendants are faced with the dilemma of how to feel identified with their role and the company, without becoming fused with them. This requires the ability to depersonalize situations and yet this is difficult to do in a job that lays such emphasis on emotions. One response is that of surface acting. However, this is an unsatisfactory solution for those who perceive surface acting as 'phony' and who would, by engaging in it, lose their self-esteem. Instead, experienced flight attendants tended to go in for deep acting. For example, in dealing with passengers who were rude or aggressive, these women said they thought of reasons to excuse the passengers' behaviour and make themselves feel sorry or sympathetic rather than angry.

This solution to their dilemma allowed attendants to escape the feelings of insincerity associated with surface acting, but it was not without consequences. These included feeling estranged from their bodily demeanour and emotions (as a result of constantly interrupting their usual responses to events). The personal costs of emotion work could also be high. In terms of Freund's (1990) analysis, constantly interrupting the connection between emotions and their usual responses may be deleterious for the maintenance of bodily well-being, making it difficult for flight attendants to interpret and take appropriate action in response to bodily signals.[2] Furthermore, the face work required as a flight attendant in the form of frequent smiling leaves permanent marks in the form of lines and wrinkles (themselves signs of ageing not generally valued in women by employers or by society).

These problems are exacerbated by other aspects of the work required of flight attendants. To start with, the job has long imposed restrictions on the employee's body. Attendants can be fired for being overweight and some companies subject attendants to thigh measurements, and used to include upper bust, waist and hip limits. Such measurements are totally undiscriminating, and they make no distinction between the size of bone, muscle, fat or flesh. Interestingly, while women here are subjected to regulations stipulating maximum bodily size, traditional male occupations such as the fire brigade and police have tended to stipulate *minimum* bodily size. Employment rules can, quite literally, embody gender inequalities.

Roberta Lessor's (1984) research has also uncovered a range of health problems faced by flight attendants connected to the demands of the job. For example, attendants are on their feet for long hours and engage in heavy physical labour in helping passengers with baggage and pushing large duty-free trolleys. In doing this they are not helped by aircraft flying at a constant angle or by regulations requiring them to wear shoes with leather soles and minimum sized heels. The chronic or recurring problems reported in Lessor's research included varicose veins, low backache, bunions, hearing loss, diminished pulmonary function and early menopause. Dehydration in planes led to bodily signs of premature ageing and bladder infections (exacerbated by insufficient time to drink water while flying).

In Hochschild's study, increased demand for attendants to fly reserve (being on call) made it even more difficult than usual to establish regular sleep patterns and led to drug problems among attendants who used stimulants and depressants to manage their sleeping/waking patterns. Furthermore, other studies have noted that it is not unusual for flight attendants to have eating disorders; a situation exacerbated by weight requirements and the lack of nutritious and slimming food available on flights (Pennington, 1991).

The requirements of emotion work often mean that employees have to take particular care over the management of their bodies. For instance, flight attendants often report that their work is made more onerous by the public image of their sexual availability incorporated in airline advertising (Hochschild, 1983). More generally, the stress on the body caused by the physical work involved in these jobs is deepened by the requirement that tasks are conducted in particular emotional and physical states. Rather than grunting and groaning when pushing the duty-free trolley around, they are expected to look more like models freshly made-up for a photo session.

Hochschild's book (1983) also includes a small study of debt collectors for comparative purposes. Emotion work is not exclusively carried out by women and it is not always concerned with reassuring clients. As the example of the debt collector illustrates, it is also something that men do, and it can aim to instill anxiety and fear in clients. The processes involved in debt collecting (having to work up an emotional pitch of aggression) can also affect men's relations with their bodies and may have spillover effects into their private lives. For example, the readiness with which aggression needs to be displayed and achieved in debt collecting may make it an emotion frequently felt and displayed in personal relations with wives and children.

While both men and women engage in emotion work there is a division of labour which separates their involvement. Hochschild argues that men tend to do the debt collector type of emotion work while women occupy the flight attendant side. This division is facilitated by the sex-typing of jobs, associated images of women's and men's bodies as suited for different types of work, and by the discriminatory practices which are still common in job appointments (Collinson et al., 1990). It is also implicated in the processes of negation and transcendence described by Connell in his analysis of gendered bodies. Employment discrimination draws on, and helps reproduce, the emotion work and forms of bodily development which girls and boys tend to become used to performing. It does the same with those emotional skills which wives and husbands tend to become most adept at in managing the family and paid work on the one hand and dealing more exclusively with the public sphere on the other.

The inequalities involved in this gender division of emotion labour are evident in other studies. Rosemary Pringle (1989a, 1989b) has illustrated how the emotion work and body management conducted by secretaries is symbolically related to that carried out by wives, mothers and daughters. Peta Tancred-Sheriff's analysis of gender, sexuality and the labour process (1989) provides further examples of how emotion work is utilized by employers. Tancred-Sheriff argues that women's emotionality and sexuality tend to be deployed in what she calls 'adjunct control jobs' (women occupy nearly two-thirds of these jobs). These jobs fall into two main categories: clerical workers who help exert control over producers, and sales and service staff who help control consumers. Both categories of adjunct control workers are required to engage in emotion work which involves empathy and sympathy and, at times, the regulated display of sexuality.

It is important to note that the gendered division of emotion work does not involve an absolute segregation. Neither is there any reason to suppose that the effects of emotion work should *always* be different for women and men doing similar jobs. However, the generally disadvantaged position of women in society does tend to leave them with fewer status shields at work against the aggression and arbitrary feelings of others. In this respect, they may be particularly vulnerable to being redefined in the images of others. In contrast, while men may be in subordinate positions at work, they more frequently occupy dominant positions in the family which can provide an alternative source of self-esteem. It may also be the case, though, that the emphasis on aggression and assertion in contemporary images of mas-culinity may create more stress among men than women in jobs requiring sympathy and responsiveness. These factors mean that the same job may involve quite different demands and bodily consequences for women and men.

In discussing emotion work in formal employment it is important to make several further points. First, employer control over emotion work is unlikely to be total. This is because displays of emotion remain embodied within employees. As a result, the rules of emotion work are subject to contestation and resistance. For example, in Hochschild's study increased pressure on flight attendants was met by a 'slow down' on emotion work. As she notes, attendants smiled less broadly, with a quick release and without a sparkle in their eyes (1983: 127). Indeed, if Hochschild were to repeat her study now, I suspect she would find that while first class passengers may receive first class emotion work, flight attendants are not required to perform in the same way for economy passengers.

Resistance to emotion work can also become manifest in less conscious forms. For example, sexual problems can result from having to respond to the needs of others all the time while denying one's own needs. Here, the body can be seen as making its own protest at being stretched beyond tolerable limits:

> sexual problems could be considered a pre-political form of protest against the overextension and overuse of their traditional femininity. This form of protest, this holding on to something so intimate as 'mine', suggests that vast territories of the self may have been relinquished as 'not mine'. (Hochschild, 1983: 183)

Second, neither surface nor deep acting are exclusive to waged labour. As Goffman's work so ably demonstrates, rituals in everyday life require both. For example, in ceremonies such as weddings and funerals people will often seek to make themselves feel happy or sad, or, at the very least, appear to experience those emotional states. Third, the 'feeling rules' which people respond to in and out of work are neither fixed, nor necessarily constant over time or between cultures. This also holds for the emotions people experience in response to particular events. Individuals within the same cultural setting may respond very differently to an identical situation, and the above studies of emotion work do not intend to imply that emotions are fixed or natural in terms of being entirely pre-social. Rather, they illustrate that there may be common responses for particular groups of individuals in particular situations, and that certain working conditions may have a strong tendency to produce similar responses in people.

The number of people involved in emotion work in high modernity has grown significantly with the rise of service sector jobs in such areas as banking, insurance, tourism and other sectors of the leisure industry. Furthermore, Cas Wouters (1989a, 1989b) has argued that emotion work characterizes people's public and private lives, and cannot be confined to particular categories of jobs (cf Hochschild, 1989). At home and at work, we are all required to shape and manage our emotions (ranging from boredom to anger) within certain limits (Elias, 1982 [1939]). For example, shopping expeditions with young children are frequently exercises in emotion work for hard-pressed parents, managing to smile instead of scream while waiting in the checkout queue.

Moving away from the specific examples of emotion work, Frankenhauser and Gardell (1976) argue that both overload and underload in waged work in general can lead to increased production of stress-related hormones. Assembly line workers illustrate this point as they suffer from much higher than average 'stress'-related illnesses. As Freund puts it, the body 'becomes a machine but cannot tolerate what a machine can' (1982: 101). People exposed to arbitrary authority and unable to express anger are most prone to high blood pressure across the social spectrum. In this context, it is not suprising that black males in the United States tend to have higher blood pressure than white males (Harburg et al., 1973).

Work affects people's bodies in other ways which are closely related to their social location (Freund and McGuire, 1991). Approximately 100,000 Americans die each year of occupational diseases (these figures do not include occupational accidents) and about 390,000 new cases of disabling occupational disease are diagnosed each year (Elling, 1986). Workplace accidents alone lead to a total of five million reported accidents a year (Hills, 1987). Lower status jobs generally involve more accidents (Dutton, 1986) and because many black males work in high risk jobs, with little control over their work environment, they have a 37 per cent greater likelihood than whites of suffering occupational illness or injury (Goldsmith and Kerr, 1982). With reference to rural areas, a 1984 study reported that one-fifth of US farm workers did not have access to drinking water, and one-third had no access to toilets (Weinstein, 1985).

While employment-based practices and social relations can be damaging, so can social isolation and the absence of relationships based in and facilitated by paid work. For example, the isolation and depression accompanying long-term unemployment is associated with high levels of both physical and mental illness (Warr, 1987). The role of the body in these processes is graphically illustrated by Bloch's study (1987) of thirty working class women who had recently been made unemployed having been regularly involved in waged work throughout their adult lives. These women's feelings of 'personal continuity' were challenged by redundancy and they felt uncertain about who they were and what they wanted from life. They were constantly restless and tired, and felt generally alienated from social and private life. Without being able to articulate fully what was wrong, Bloch argues that their bodies were expressing what they were not yet able to clarify through discourse. Unemployment was accompanied by 'emphatic bodily signs of mental conflict and loss' which included violent bouts of overeating, muscular tension, migraine, nausea, stomach pains and loss of appetite (Bloch, 1987: 438).[3]

The embodiment of inequality

There are as yet no fully developed sociological perspectives on the body which take into account the importance of the social and biological sciences. In their different ways, however, Connell and Freund provide the beginnings of a methodological approach which views the body as simultaneously biological and social. While their analyses may initially appear to be alternatives, it can be argued that these writers are merely focusing on distinct dimensions of our embodiment.

Connell and Freund also provide in their work an implicit ontology of the body which highlights its status as an unfinished phenomenon. The shapes, sizes and meanings of the body are not given at birth and neither is the body's future experience of well-being: the body is an entity which can be 'completed' only through human labour. The most important issue raised by Connell's and Freund's work on the negation and transcendence of biology is that social relations, inequalities and oppressions are manifest not simply in the form of differential access to economic, educational or cultural resources but are *embodied*. The experience, understanding and effects of social relations is not a disembodied cognitive phenomenon but is corporeal through and through (Finkler, 1989). The social reproduction of society also involves the *social reproduction of appropriate bodies*.

I now want to turn to the work of Pierre Bourdieu and Norbert Elias. Connell and Freund illustrate how the body can be considered a project, as a result of its unfinishedness, but they have less to say about *why* the body has actually become reflexively appropriated as a project for modern people. Furthermore, while they provide a methodological approach to analysing the body, they are not interested in providing a general theory of the body in society.

Bourdieu and Elias's writings have been interpreted in many ways, but they have yet to be seen as providing theories of the body. In contrast, I argue that specific theories of the body lie at the very heart of their respective concerns, and that these theorists have much of relevance to say about both how and why the body has become a project for increasing numbers of people in high modernity.

In particular, Bourdieu points to how the multiple commodification of our bodies is a potent source of our current concern with them. The more people attach value to how we look and what we do with our bodies, the greater are the pressures for people's self-identities to become wrapped up with their bodies. In contrast, Elias highlights the importance of the increased individualization of our bodies, and looks at how conflicts which used to occur between bodies have now moved within embodied individuals as a result of the rising demands of affect control. This situation tends to leave us alone with our bodies; investing more time and effort in their monitoring, control and appearance, and yet losing many of the sources of satisfaction we once gained from them.

Both Bourdieu's and Elias's discussions of physical capital, symbolic value, taste and violence, emotional expression and affect control can also be located within the general approach that views the body as biological and social. This is easier in the case of Elias than Bourdieu, as Elias has dealt explicitly with the relation between biology and society in *The Symbol Theory*. However, I suggest that Bourdieu's focus on the importance of taste, body management and the surfaces, textures and appearances of the body, can also be classified broadly within this approach.

Notes

1. This picture is complicated somewhat by the taboos placed on certain foods by ethnic and cultural groups.

2. Emotion work can disrupt both the body's equilibrium and our ability to interpret bodily messages and respond in the appropriate way. This happens when people experience what Freund terms *emotional false consciousness*. Emotional false consciousness is when a split occurs between bodily displays and awareness of internal psycho-physical sensations, on the one hand, and on the other, continued heightened reactivity to stressful conditions. People may have trained themselves to feel one thing, but can actually be experiencing something quite different (Freund, 1990: 469). So, a waiter dealing with rude and impatient customers, or a teacher attempting to control unruly pupils, may feel calm when dealing with the demands of their job, yet actually be suffering from the damaging physiological consequences associated with high blood pressure. In more general terms, the physiological consequence of social relations can also act indirectly to facilitate social control. For example, situations which lead to depression (unemployment, for instance) can also construct an emotional state whereby the motivation to resist is blunted.

3. Bodies are not just affected by various forms of work, though, but can act as a corporeal conscience which has the potential to affect people's willingness to engage in certain tasks. This is illustrated by Gusterson's analysis (1991) of nuclear physicists. As a physicist who refused to work on nuclear weapons explained: 'There's this thing in my stomach. My head understands the reasons to work on the weapons, for deterrence and so on, but when I think about doing this work, I feel this thing in my stomach'. Physicists who continued to work on nuclear weapons programmes did not necessarily avoid this 'rebellion of the body', but had learned to treat their bodies as machines 'prone to malfunction' (Gusterson, 1991: 48).

6

The Body and Physical Capital

Pierre Bourdieu's theory of social reproduction has at its very centre a concern with the body as a bearer of symbolic value. The body for Bourdieu, as for Elias, is an unfinished entity which develops in conjunction with various social forces and is integral to the maintenance of social inequalities. Indeed, Bourdieu's conceptualization of the body as a form of physical capital has several similarities with Elias's view of the civilized body. Both recognize that there is an interrelationship between the development of the body and people's social location, and both view the management of the body as central to the acquisition of status and distinction. There is even overlap in the conceptual apparatus used by Bourdieu and Elias to analyse the body. For example, Bourdieu appears to have taken and adapted the term 'habitus' from Elias's use of the term 'social habitus' in 1939 (Mennell, 1990). However, it would be wrong to over-emphasize the similarities between their work. Bourdieu is concerned with the body as a bearer of value in contemporary society, while Elias is more concerned to identify and trace the historical processes involved in the development of civilized bodies. As such, Bourdieu's work follows on nicely from Chapter 5 in terms of its focus on the relationship between the body and social inequalities in high modernity. In contrast, Elias is more interested in those processes which exert a *general* effect on embodied persons.

Bourdieu's analysis of the body involves an examination of the multiple ways in which the body has become commodified in modern societies. This refers not only to the body's implication in the buying and selling of labour power, but to the methods by which the body has become a more comprehensive form of *physical capital*; a possessor of power, status and distinctive symbolic forms which is integral to the accumulation of various resources. The production of physical capital refers to the development of bodies in ways which are recognized as possessing value in social fields, while the conversion of physical capital refers to the translation of bodily participation in work, leisure and other fields into different forms of capital. Physical capital is most usually converted into economic capital (money, goods and services), cultural capital (for example, education) and social capital (social networks which enable reciprocal calls to be made on the goods and services of its members) (Bourdieu, 1978, 1984, 1986).[1]

Scott Lash (1990) has argued that while Bourdieu's work has been criticized for failing to include an explicit theory of modernization, it does make a significant contribution to the study of the development of modern societies. Similarly, Bourdieu's view of physical capital has much to say about the increasing importance of the body in high modernity. In contrast to traditional societies, where power is exercised more directly by one embodied individual over another, the modern body has a far more complex role in the exercise of power and the reproduction of social inequalities. Different classes and class fractions tend to develop distinct orientations to their bodies which result in the creation of various bodily forms. In the conditions of modernity, the symbolic values attached to these forms become particularly important to many people's sense of self and there is a tendency, for those with the resources, to treat the body as a lifelong project.

This chapter is concerned with providing an interpretation and elaboration of Bourdieu's analysis of the body. Although Bourdieu has not described his work as providing a theory of the body in society, I suggest that extending his analysis of embodied and physical capital provides us with an approach to the sociology of the body which is, in many ways, compatible with the concerns central to Elias's work. After looking at Bourdieu's analysis of how bodies develop, I shall focus on the unequal opportunities people have for producing symbolically-valued bodily forms and converting them into other resources.

The social formation of bodies

Bourdieu is not concerned with examining in any detail the simultaneously biological and social nature of the body. However, he displays a clear interest in the unfinishedness of the body, and maintains a more comprehensive view of the materiality of human embodiment than those theorists who focus exclusively on language, consciousness, or even the body as flesh. Bourdieu recognizes that acts of labour are required to turn bodies into social entities and that these acts influence how people develop and hold the physical shape of their bodies, and learn how to present their bodies through styles of walk, talk and dress. Far from being natural, these represent highly skilled and socially differentiated accomplishments which start to be learnt early in childhood. As it develops, the body bears the indisputable imprint of an individual's social class (Bourdieu, 1984).

More specifically, bodies bear the imprint of social class because of three main factors: an individual's social location, the formation of their habitus, and the development of their tastes. **Social locations** refer to the class-based material circumstances which contextualize people's daily lives and contribute to the development of their bodies. These locations consist of the overall volume of capital possessed by an individual, the relative weight of their different assets, and the change in these properties over time (Bourdieu, 1984: 114; 1985: 724). Social locations can also be measured by their 'distance from necessity', or financial, cultural and social want (Bourdieu, 1985).

The *habitus* is the second main factor which contributes to the development of the body. The habitus is a 'socially constituted system of cognitive and motivating structures' which provide individuals with class-dependent, predisposed ways of relating to and categorizing both familiar and novel situations (Brubaker, 1985: 758).[2] According to Bourdieu, the habitus is formed in the context of people's social locations and inculcates in them a 'world view' based on, and reconciled to, these positions. As such, it tends towards reproducing existing social structures. The habitus is located within the body and affects every aspect of human embodiment. Indeed, the way people treat their bodies 'reveals the deepest dispositions of the habitus' (Bourdieu, 1984: 190). This is evident in 'the most automatic gestures [and] the apparently most insignificant techniques of the body – ways of walking or blowing one's nose, ways of eating or talking – and engage[s] the most fundamental principles of construction and evaluation of the social world' (1984: 466).

Bodies are also formed through the development of **taste**. 'Taste' refers to the processes whereby individuals appropriate as voluntary choices and preferences, lifestyles which are actually rooted in material constraints. In other words, taste makes a virtue out of necessity (1984: 175–7). People develop preferences for what is available to them. The development of taste, which can be seen as a conscious manifestation of habitus, is embodied and deeply affects people's orientations to their bodies. As such, Bourdieu has defined taste as 'a class culture turned into nature, that is *embodied*. . . . It is an incorporated principle of classification which governs all forms of incorporation, choosing and modifying everything that the body ingests and digests and assimilates, physiologically and psychologically'.

The consumption of food is an obvious example of how taste affects the body and develops in class-based material locations. Historically and contemporarily, people's taste for food has developed in the context of its relative scarcity or surplus and has been affected by the efforts of the dominant in society to appropriate certain foods in order to distinguish themselves from the dominated (Mennell, 1985). This distribution of foodstuffs has important consequences for bodily development. For example, in contemporary French and English society, cheaper fatty foods are consumed more by the working class which has implications not only for their body shapes, but for their relatively high incidence of coronary disease in relation to the upper classes (Bourdieu, 1984; Townsend et al., 1988). Indeed, differential rates of morbidity and mortality express in a particularly direct way one of the implications that class taste can have for the body.

To summarize, bodies are unfinished entities which are formed through their participation in social life and become imprinted with the marks of social class. Bodies develop through the interrelation between an individual's social location, habitus and taste. These factors serve to naturalize and perpetuate the different relationships that social groups have towards their bodies, and are central to the choices people make in all spheres of social life (Bourdieu, 1981).

The body and social difference

Bourdieu argues that social classes develop clearly identifiable relations to their bodies which result in the production of distinct bodily forms. These bodily forms are valued differently and are central to the formation of social inequalities in the quantities and qualities of physical capital produced by individuals. In this and the next section of this chapter, I will focus on how the formation of bodies is related to social class locations.

The working classes tend to develop an *instrumental* relation to their body as they have little time free from necessity. The body is a *means to an end* and this is evident in relation to illness and medication (for example, 'putting the body right' is primarily a means to returning to work, getting ready for a holiday, or being able to play sport); and in the choice of sports for working class men (for example, in soccer, motor-cycling and boxing the body is primarily a means for the experience of excitement even though the physical investment in these sports can involve considerable effort, risk of injury and pain). Furthermore, workers who have used their bodies all day in heavy manual labour tend to have little time for what they see as the 'pretensions' of jogging and health and fitness centres. To the extent they do engage in exercise, 'the working class are concerned to spend their efforts on weightlifting and activities directed towards strength, both fields in which manual dominance can be asserted' (Wilkes, 1990: 118).

Gender divisions within the working class, and the 'double-burden' of waged and unwaged work faced by wives and mothers, means that women tend to develop an even more instrumental relation to their body then men (e.g. Finch, 1983a). This means that working class women tend to have little time at all for sporting/leisure activities apart from those compatible with work. As Rosemary Deem and other sociologists of leisure have argued, even 'low-key' activities like watching the television tend to be accompanied by such chores as ironing and knitting (Deem, 1986; Green and Hebron, 1988).

Working class women, then, develop orientations to their bodies which are strongly marked by the need to earn money *and* service the needs of a household. According to Bourdieu (1984) this is evident in the ways wives and mothers tend to dress at home and the effort they put into preparing food (for example, at home clothes are worn to 'make do' and be functional for undertaking household chores, while the physical effort invested in preparing food is designed to produce cheap, filling meals which will stretch the household budget). It is also evident in the tendency for working class wives and mothers to sacrifice their own bodily needs (for rest, recreation and even food) in order to fulfil those of their husbands and children. These sacrifices are evident in the value many of these women place on their health as being important primarily in terms of fulfilling their family responsibilities or in helping with the family economy in other ways (Calnan, 1987; Cornwell, 1984). Such attitudes have very real effects on the bodily development of women, as evidenced, for instance, by the disproportionately high incidence of physical (as well as mental) illness among mothers with children (Graham, 1984; see also Miles, 1987).

In general, then, the working classes develop bodies marked both by the immediate demands of 'getting by' in life and the forms of temporary 'release' they seek from these demands (Crawford, 1984). In this respect, it is interesting to note the common metaphor of the 'body as machine' used by working class women and men in analyses of lay perceptions of health and illness (Rogers, 1991). Here, the body becomes a project in the rather limited sense of it being something which may need servicing from medical experts in order to keep it working efficiently.

In contrast, the dominant classes have the time and resources to treat the body as a project 'with variants according to whether the emphasis is placed on the intrinsic functioning of the body as an organism, which leads to the macrobiotic cult of health, or on the appearance as a perceptible configuration, the "physique", i.e. the body for others' (Bourdieu, 1978: 838; 1984: 212–13). The dominant classes tend not to be overly concerned with producing a large, strong body, but with a slim body better 'suited to a world in which economic practice is constituted more strongly by the presentation of the self' (Wilkes, 1990: 118). The bourgeois development of the body for others is manifest, for instance, in a deportment characterized by 'a certain breadth of gesture, posture and gait, which manifests [itself] by the amount of physical space that is occupied . . . and above all by a restrained, measured, self-assured tempo' (Bourdieu, 1984: 218). This confidence is also evident in the perceptions of health and illness held by the bourgeoisie. In contrast to the working class, there is evidence to suggest that members of the middle class believe they have more control over their own health; control which can be exercised by choosing an appropriate 'lifestyle' (Calnan, 1987: 83).

Orientations to the body become more finely differentiated *within* the dominant classes. For example, fitness training for its own sake is often engaged in by the upwardly mobile middle classes who 'find their satisfaction in effort itself and . . . accept – such is the meaning of their existence – the deferred satisfactions which will reward their present sacrifice' (Bourdieu, 1978: 839). In contrast, professionals in the field of cultural production such as university teachers, tend towards activities which combine the health-orientated function of maintaining the body with 'the symbolic gratifications associated with practising a highly distinctive activity' such as mountaineering or walking in remote places. As Bourdieu notes (1978: 839), this combines the 'sense of mastery of one's own body' with the 'exclusive appropriation of scenery inaccessible to the vulgar' (an element of consumption developed in Urry's (1990) analysis of the middle class 'romantic tourist gaze'). Such activities can be 'performed in solitude, at times and in places beyond the reach of the many' (Bourdieu, 1984: 214). Another distinction in physical activity is made for the élite, well established bourgeoisie, who tend to combine the health-giving aspect of sporting activities with the social functions involved in such sports as golf, dance, shooting and polo (Bourdieu, 1978: 839–40).

Although Bourdieu does not provide a detailed account of gendered orientations to the body, we can extend his insights in that direction and suggest that women tend to be encouraged more than men to develop their bodies as objects of perception for others. Nonetheless, Bourdieu does show very clearly how different social classes produce distinct bodily forms. This is important to his theory of social reproduction as there are *substantial inequalities in the symbolic values accorded to particular bodily forms*. The instrumental relation commonly adopted to the body does not mean that working class bodies are without symbolic value. For example, the muscular male body carries particular symbolic weight in certain contexts where strength is valued. However, the overall character of working class bodies (for example, their accent, posture and dress) is not generally valued as highly as are the bodily forms produced by other social classes.

The dominant classes are more willing and most able to produce the bodily forms of highest value as their formation requires investments of spare time and money (Bourdieu, 1986: 246). It is the dominant classes who are financially able to keep their children in (élite) education for the longest time, release them from the need to work full- or part-time, and encourage them to engage in activities likely to increase their acquisition of a socially valued body. One of the most obvious examples of this is those parents who send their daughters to 'finishing schools' to complete not only their mental education but to polish up their dress, deportment and speech in ways which express, quite literally, a sense of class. However, many other examples could be cited such as the encouragement and financial help given to young girls and boys to participate in pre- and extra-school activities such as ballet, tennis or horse riding.

Changing bodies

The interrelationship between social location, habitus and taste produces distinct and relatively stable bodily forms and orientations. Indeed, Bourdieu's use of the term 'body hexus', closely related to his concept habitus, is used to signify the relative intractability of corporeal habits and customs. However, it is important to note that these orientations are not always static. This is because an individual's body is never 'fully finished'. While the body is implicated in society, it is constantly affected by social, cultural and economic processes (Bourdieu, 1985).

For example, economic, cultural and other forms of capital have a permanent influence on participation in sporting activities which affect the development of the body. Yachting and flying usually involve participants in hefty financial outlays which tend to confine them to the wealthiest sections of society. Similarly, sports and social activities organized around élite clubs often require entrants to have acquired certain social or cultural capital before they join (for example, applicants to prestigious golf or tennis clubs may require social contacts within the club and a suitable standing within the local community). In these examples, if an individual's stock of capitals has declined, both options may be ruled out and a taste for other activities and a new orientation to one's body may, eventually, be developed.[3]

The body remains central, though, and is sometimes *the* most important factor in determining the distribution of physical activities. In the case of exclusive sports, for example:

> It can be seen that economic barriers – however great they may be . . . – are not sufficient to explain the class distribution of these activities. There are more hidden entry requirements, such as family tradition and early training, or the obligatory manner (of dress and behaviour), and socializing techniques, which keep these sports closed to the working class . . . and which maintain them . . . amongst the surest indicators of bourgeois pedigree. . . . *We can hypothesize as a general law that a sport is more likely to be adopted by a social class if it does not contradict that class'[s] relation to the body at its deepest and most unconscious level, i.e. the body schema, which is the depository of a whole world view and a whole philosophy of the person and the body.* (Bourdieu, 1984: 217–18, emphasis added)

The relation between a social class and its body schema does not mean that the dominant classes across societies will always pursue similar physical activities. In order to understand the social composition of a sport, it is important to locate that sport within the entire field of sports, *and* examine the structure of sports in relation to other social fields within a nation (Bourdieu, 1988a). First, the field of sports is constituted by such features as the orientation sports require towards the body, their relative prestige, rate of growth and their distance from the 'national sport' (Bourdieu, 1988a). Second, the relation between sports and other social fields can affect the social composition of its participants. For example, boxing was popular among the English aristocracy in the nineteenth century and was common in private schools. Learning how to box was one of the accomplishments which went to make the 'English gentleman'. Later in the century, however, it was students from élite private schools who spread boxing among working class youths in boys clubs, ostensibly as a way of building character and learning self-control. As the twentieth century wore on, boxing became increasingly popular among the working classes (in its amateur and professional guises) and a decreasing activity among the dominant classes in society. Though still retained in some private schools, it has lost its visibility and compulsory position.

If there is no simple correspondence between social groups and sporting practices, neither is there a straight match for other aspects of our embodiment. Be these concerned with food and drink, cinema and television viewing, dress and make-up, styles of speech and mannerisms, Bourdieu argues that the relationship between someone's class location and these practices may change between societies and over time. For example, the reason a social group adopts a particular style of dress or diet is connected to the distribution and meanings given to *alternative* styles of dress or diet, the *orientation to the body* a style of dress or diet encourages, and to the relationship between the fields of fashion and diet and other *social fields*. In French society, the relationship between these factors in the case of diet have led to radically contrasting attitudes and habits towards the consumption of food. As one goes down the social hierarchy

> the food consumed is increasingly rich (both in cost and in calories) and increasingly heavy (game, foie gras). By contrast, the taste of the professionals or senior executives defines the popular taste, by negation, as the taste for the heavy, the fat and the coarse, by tending toward the light, the refined and the delicate. . . . The disappearance of economic constraints is accompanied by a strengthening of the social censorships which forbid coarseness and fatness, in favour of slimness and distinction. . . . Finally, the teachers, richer in cultural capital than in economic capital, and therefore inclined to ascetic consumption in all areas, pursue originality at the lowest economic cost and go in for exoticism (Italian, Chinese cooking etc.) and culinary populism (peasant dishes). (Bourdieu, 1984: 185)

Bourdieu's examples of food focus on contemporary relationships in France. However, his analysis can be applied to other sectors of social life. Davis's fascinating article (1989) on status ambivalences in clothing and fashion provides an example of how orientations to the body can change over time in response to the field of fashion and its relation to other fields.

To summarize, social class exerts a profound influence on the ways in which people develop their bodies and on the symbolic values attached to particular bodily forms. This is the production of physical capital. However, the significance of this is not simply that the lifestyles of women and men from different social classes become *inscribed* within their bodies, but that these bodies 'fit' people for different activities. Change is not ruled out, but Bourdieu (1981) argues that there is frequently a close match between social positions and human dispositions. Paul Willis (1977) provides one example of this in his study of how working class 'lads' rejected mental labour at school and embraced manual work. Social differences become incorporated as 'natural' differences, and are misrecognized as such, and it becomes more or less automatic for people to participate in different forms of physical activity which are themselves invested with unequal social value.

The conversion of physical capital

Bourdieu argues that the bodily forms produced by the working classes constitute a form of physical capital that has less exchange value than that developed by the dominant classes (Bourdieu, 1978). This does not mean, of course, that the working class completely lacks opportunities for converting physical capital into other forms of capital. For example, the training of the body for manual work can provide for a direct wage and equip individuals with the skills required to undertake tasks outside of the formal workplace in the 'hidden economy'. Furthermore, the instrumental approach towards sports as a means to particular ends provides the working class with the potential to convert physical capital into economic capital via entry into sporting careers. Here, the power, speed and agility invested in the body becomes the object of exchange value. However, this form of capital is limiting to the working class in several respects.

First, only a very small percentage of its members can hope to earn a living through sport. Second, this form of convertibility is usually partial and transient. It is partial because of its less frequent availability to working class women than to working class men, and is transient as the capacity of the body is an important limiting factor even for those who do become professionals. It only takes one injury to end a soccer player's, an American Footballer's or track athlete's career and the average length of many sporting lives is low, leaving most ex-professionals needing to find work for the rest of their lives. Indeed, the type of severe injuries sustained in particularly high risk sports such as American Football or boxing can have the effect of both finishing an individual's sporting career, and of ending their chances of entering *any* other career. Third, the time working class children spend on sports may affect detrimentally their acquisition of academic qualifications at school. Bruce Carrington (1982) suggests this may be particularly true for working class black pupils who get directed towards sports because of the racist views of teachers who feel blacks are 'naturally' gifted at sports yet not suited to mental labour. Finally, this instrumental approach to their bodies can also steer working class children away from activities engaged in by the dominant classes, and hence reinforce their class distinctiveness.

If there are limitations involved in the working class converting their bodily forms into economic capital, this is also true for cultural and social capital. In respect of cultural capital, Bernstein (1970), Keddie (1971) and Bourdieu and Passeron (1990 [1977]) have all argued that working class speech and bodily demeanour tends to be interpreted negatively by teachers. In the case of social capital, the aggressive management of their bodies may lead to admiration among peer groups at school in terms of a prowess at fighting (Willis, 1977), or an ability to appear as adult and feminine as possible (McRobbie, 1978), but it does little to gain the support of teachers in helping with academic work. Similarly, the public expression of male violence in such settings as pubs and soccer grounds may gain prestige among peers (Clarke, 1990; Marsh et al., 1978), but it does little to impress the courts and has no economic value.

In sum, there tend to be high risks and opportunity costs associated with working class efforts to convert physical capital into other resources. Educational, sporting and other fields in society are generally not structured in ways that provide frequent opportunities for value to be bestowed on working class bodies.

In contrast, the dominant classes in society tend to have more valuable opportunities to convert physical capital into other material resources without the risks or opportunity costs faced by the working class. While sport does not carry the same means or meanings of upward mobility for the children of dominant classes, they have access to alternative sources of economic capital (Bourdieu, 1978: 832). Consequently, children from these classes tend to engage in socially élite sporting activities which stress manners and deportment and hence facilitate the future acquisition of social and cultural capital. This is reflected in the PE curricula of élite private schools which contrast greatly to the activities available to pupils in state schools (Salter and Tapper, 1981). For example, while polo and golf may be available to pupils in élite private schools in England, those in state schools are more usually channelled into playing soccer or netball. Further, developing a taste for élite sporting and leisure activities is important as while these activities may not always represent a *direct* route to a career for the dominant classes, they can lead to social situations which indirectly facilitate entry into a profession or allow business contacts to be forged.

Élite sporting activities can also serve the purpose of finding 'appropriate' marriage partners for their offspring, hence safeguarding the transmission of their own economic capital (Bourdieu, 1986). As Douglas and Isherwood (1979: 85) note, such groups can be seen as 'closed and stable . . . holding to their privileges, and jealously guarding their women'. The prominence of élite sporting venues focused around such activities as equestrianism and polo in England is, perhaps, an important factor in the high incidence of intra-class marriages among the dominant class.

The symbolic value of upper class bodies can also be converted into social and cultural capital. Socially élite sporting/leisure occasions often encompass strict rules of etiquette and allow for the demonstration of bodily competence in formal contexts which allow members of élite groups to recognize the body as a sign signifying that the bearer shares a certain set of values (for example, through modes of dress, ways of speaking, managing the face and general 'body language'). Friendships amid informal contacts are made at these occasions which can be of great value in acquiring the services of others in such areas as the legal and financial professions (Allan, 1989). Physical capital can also be converted into opportunities to acquire cultural capital. For example, while qualifications serve as an initial screening device, the interview, in which the management of speech and the body is central, is still an integral part of the selection process for, for example, élite jobs, private schools and entrance to Oxford and Cambridge Universities in England (Dale and Pires, 1984; Moore, 1989).

All of these situations share in common the placement and management of the body by the dominant classes in exclusive social occasions where contacts can be forged leading to the future accumulation of resources.

The changing value of physical capital

Bourdieu's theory of social reproduction highlights the importance of the body in the formation of inequalities. However, it is important to note that the symbolic value attached to specific bodily forms is changeable. Just as forms of economic or cultural capital may fluctuate in value (for example, stocks and shares can fall in price, and the value of educational certificates may decrease because of qualification inflation; Collins, 1981; Dore, 1976), so may the convertibility of physical capital.

In order to understand the reasons for these fluctuations, it is necessary to examine Bourdieu's concept of social field. Social field is a term which has been used several times, but has yet to be fully explained. Lash (1990: 261) describes social fields as Bourdieu's structures. More specifically, a social field refers to a set of *dynamic organizing principles*, ultimately maintained by social groups, which identify and structure particular categories of social practices (be they concerned with art, economics, eating, fashion, sport, sexuality, education etc.). Each field has a relative autonomy from other fields, and bestows values on social practices according to its internal organization. So, in the field of professional sports, value is placed on performance and winning over participation and effort, while in the field of art and design value may be placed on creativity and innovation.

When social fields bestow value directly on a specific bodily form, activity or performance, they are effectively creating a category of physical capital. Having recognized a particular form of physical capital, though, the dynamic principles which constitute a field are subject to change. Consequently, those bodily forms which are regarded as valuable, and the precise values attached to them, are also likely to change. For example, individual sports may rise and fall in value as may the earnings of professional sports people. Changes in the field of fashion may affect the symbolic value of certain styles of deportment, talk and dress. This means that the initial production of a valued bodily form among a group or class does not guarantee its *continued* exchange value. The value attached to particular bodies changes over time; as fields within societies change, so may the forms of physical capital they reward.

This has implications for people's experiences of ageing which go beyond the biological determinants usually associated with growing older. As people age, their capacity to produce and convert physical capital into other resources tends to decline. Again, though, social class is important in determining how specific groups experience the ageing process. Featherstone has usefully developed Bourdieu's work in this area:

> While in general terms . . . the movement into old age necessarily involves a shedding, a reduction of the capacity to accumulate economic capital and a devaluation of particular types of cultural capital (by dint of attachment to forms of knowledge and styles which have become deemed as outmoded). At the same time certain types of [physical] capital, manifest in demeanour, way

of speaking and attitude towards the body, may retain their distinction and value into deep old age, for example among the aristocracy or royalty. (1987: 125)

Not only does the capacity of social groups to convert physical capital into other resources vary with age, but the habitus tends to develop within groups different attitudes to ageing which are aligned with the extent to which their bodies still possess symbolic value. Featherstone (1987) suggests that while the working class tend to be more prepared to accept bodily decline as inevitable with age, the 'new' middle classes find the ageing body a source of anxiety. Consequently, body maintenance techniques tend to be employed as a way to combat age and its associated characteristics. In contrast, the upper classes tend to have acquired orientations to their bodies which can overlay and disguise many of the effects of ageing, 'wearing' their age unselfconsciously as a mark of status rather than decline.

These attitudes towards ageing are not solely linked to the habitus, though, they also reflect the economic fields in which people work. For the working class, resignation about bodily decline is linked to the fact that middle age brings declining living standards and a reduction in control over the future. Middle class anxiety is linked to uncertainty about work status (for example, there may be a danger of being usurped by younger rivals). In contrast, upper class ease is connected to middle age being 'truly the prime of life, they are the command generation' and can afford a more relaxed approach to ageing processes (Featherstone, 1987: 117).

Central to the value of different forms of physical capital at any one time, though, is the *ability of dominant groupings to define their bodies and lifestyle as superior, worthy of reward, and as, metaphorically and literally, the embodiment of class*. This is a process concerned with the search for *distinction* which may involve regular struggles over defining and controlling those fields in which bodily forms are defined as valuable. It may also involve conflict over the bodily forms most valued within a social group. For example, conflicts over definitions of physical capital may possess a generational basis. Certain struggles between working class males may be resolved with reference to physical strength, while age group conflicts among the middle classes may involve struggle over the power to *define* when old age begins:

To allow middle age, for example, to be redefined as middle youth from one perspective is to suggest an appropriation of youthfulness, a desired quality, from the young. Yet from the perspective of the young–old this may be a label they willingly foster on the middle aged, because youth (here associated with irresponsibility and frivolity) is a quality opposed to the maturity and wisdom necessary for power holders, which the old seek to preserve for themselves. Likewise, the middle aged may seek to send the young–old into old age as they in turn seek to maximise their choice to either retain command or retire on their own terms. At the same time, they distance themselves from the old–old, who possess few resources in the game to combat institutionalisation and the repelling properties of deep old age. (Featherstone, 1987: 120–1)

It is not simply the power to classify what is meant by ageing that can become a source of conflict between generations. The value of styles of talk and fashion, ways of behaving and managing the body, are often contested in terms of whether they are appropriate or outdated.

Featherstone argues that age is an important structuring principle in the competition between groups to define their bodies as possessing greatest symbolic value. However, the conflict between classes is of greatest importance to Bourdieu's work, and attempts by the dominant classes to define lower class body implicating activities as 'crude', or attempts on the part of the working classes to define upper class practices as 'pretentious', occupy a prominent place in his book on French life, *Distinction* (1984). This struggle is wide-ranging and includes attempts on the part of social groups to appropriate particular styles of dress or sports as their own exclusive property (Bourdieu, 1985).

The stakes in this struggle are high. As mentioned above, they include the respective abilities of social groups to define, develop and appropriate the most prestigious bodily forms. However, this is neither a 'fair' struggle in which participants have equal resources nor a stable struggle in which the 'rules of the game' are necessarily explicit or remain unchanged. This is because of the different volumes and qualities of capital possessed by social groups.

Because of their greater access to and possession of cultural and social capital, the dominant classes in society are more likely than the dominated to be in occupational or social fields invested with the power of bestowing value on bodily forms and body implicating activities. This means that even when individuals have managed to move upwards into middle class jobs, prevailing definitions of physical capital continue to mark their bodies with the stamp of their origins. As Bourdieu (1984: 338) says of the petit bourgeois, 'strict and sober, discreet and severe, in his dress, his speech, his gestures and his whole bearing, he always lacks something in stature, breadth, substance, largesse'. Furthermore, the dominant classes are also likely to be in privileged positions in terms of the value of their social capital. This can keep them informed of the opportunities in various fields for converting physical capital into other forms of capital. As Douglas and Isherwood put it:

> the homogeneous working-class social environment is never going to provide the sort of information that the middle-class family can get by its social contacts. . . . To be in control of this information may be vital for getting and keeping a high earning potential. (1979: 9–12)

Those without such contacts are, then, likely to be less aware of existing opportunities for converting physical capital into other resources. They are also likely to be less certain as to what constitutes symbolically valued bodily forms at times of change, as dominant groups in society tend also to have greater power to change those social fields which define what constitutes physical capital.

The transmission and control of physical capital

Even without the difficulties faced by the dominant class in maintaining the symbolic value of their bodies, neither the production nor the conversion of physical capital are unproblematic or without limitations. To begin with, physical capital cannot be transmitted or inherited *directly*. Unlike money, stocks and shares or property rights, it cannot be given by one generation to the next by mere gift, bequest or exchange. Instead, because of the unfinishedness of the body, its development is a complex and lengthy process which can last for years (Connell, 1983: 30–1). Furthermore, although the development of bodies is related to social class processes, it is not reducible to them. Irrespective of their class position, people can be 'gifted' or 'cursed' with bodies which cause disruptions to the intra-class transmission of economic capital. For example, Bourdieu (1984) uses the term 'fatal attraction' to refer to the physical beauty which inspires cross-class relationships and disrupts mechanisms of social class closure.

Second, physical capital cannot be accumulated beyond the appropriating capacities of an individual agent. Instead, it declines and dies with its bearer (Bourdieu, 1986: 245). Consequently, the possession of physical capital can be seen as a more *transient* resource than the possession of economic capital.

Third, physical capital cannot be *purchased* in the same sense as one can buy an economic good. Parents can buy their children time free from the necessity of waged work and an education where they will have the opportunity to develop valued styles of accent, dress and demeanour, but they cannot guarantee its acquisition. Instead, acts of labour are involved in the acquisition of symbolically valued bodies for each new generation. The habitus and tastes of individuals from different backgrounds mean that they are likely to be more or less inclined to carry out the labour required to develop prestigious bodies. However, the actual acquisition of any one type of physical capital can never be guaranteed. Just as some children fail to acquire academic qualifications despite enjoying the most expensive private schooling, so some may fail to accumulate the physical capital 'appropriate' to their élite background. It is not just because of the fear of academic failure (or failure to acquire a form of cultural capital) that middle and upper class parents worry about anti-school subcultures. Such cultures can reject the demands of mental work and the imposition of certain modes of body management and dress (Hargreaves, 1969; Lacey, 1970).

Fourth, even if certain bodily forms are developed by an individual, there are always risks that they will not be recognized as physical capital. As mentioned earlier, the value of bodily forms may rise or fall over an individual's lifetime. The recognition of élite bodies may also vary between social sites at any one time (Bourdieu, 1986). As those writers concerned with the development of a post-modern consumer culture within late capitalism have argued, multinational corporate enterprises have become involved in the *production of difference* by assisting the proliferation of clothing styles and other consumer goods which can be appropriated as signs of bodily identity by social groups (e.g. Hall and Jameson, 1990; Jameson, 1984, 1985; see also McRobbie, 1989).

These changes in production have been generated partly by segments of the middle class in design, fashion and advertising, and facilitated by global forms of industrial reorganization. However, while these changes may be in the interests of sections of economic capital in terms of its continued profitability, they may also lead to a proliferation of styles which could pose threats to the ability of the dominant class continually to legitimize their bodies as being of greatest symbolic value. As Mike Featherstone (1990) argues, the rapid internationalization and circulation of consumer and 'lifestyle' goods threatens the readability of those signs used by the dominant to signify their élite physical capital.

These issues raise doubts about the continuing management and control by the dominant class of those fields in which physical capital is recognized and valorized. If fields become saturated with increasing body images and social practices which are presented as constituting valuable forms of physical capital, then their structure may change. Unless the dominant sections of society are able to classify these styles into existing hierarchies, and have these classifications recognized as valid, then the 'logic of differences in which taste in cultural and consumer goods and lifestyle activities are held to be oppositionally structured' is threatened (Featherstone, 1990: 12). In contemporary consumer society, then, we may be witnessing processes which will make it extremely difficult for any one group to impose as hegemonic, as worthy of respect and deference across society, a single classificatory scheme of 'valuable bodies'.

A fifth problem with the conversion of physical capital is that, in contrast to certain forms of economic capital, the 'exchange rate' of physical capital is not guaranteed and there may be losses in converting physical capital into other resources. Further, there may be situations in which a disproportionate and unwarranted amount of effort has to be invested in order to convert physical capital into other resources. In sum, the development of symbolically valued bodies is subject to both a more disguised, but also a more risky, transmission process than is the case with economic capital (Bourdieu, 1986: 254).

In the context of these problems, it becomes pertinent to ask why individuals from the dominant classes should invest time and resources in the development of the body when they could use their material wealth to invest in other, potentially safer, forms of capital acquisition. One answer to this would be that not all of these people do invest such effort. Depending on their holding of other forms of capital, individuals may choose to maximize their investments in economic or cultural capital. For example, those fractions of the dominant class most rich in economic capital may place most of their efforts in continuing to maximize their own, and their children's possession of financial resources.

There are good reasons, however, for why those in the dominant classes continue to make substantial investments in the body. This has much to do with the natural and biological *appearance* of physical capital. As a consequence of the naturalized appearance of physical capital, the *attempts* of one generation to cultivate it in the next are often heavily disguised, invisible or at least *misrecognized*. The social conditions of the (indirect) intergenerational transmission of physical capital are much less visible than the (direct) transmission of economic capital. Consequently, while governments may attempt to control the intergenerational transmission of economic capital (through taxes), the development of physical capital is a hidden form of privilege which can nonetheless be reconverted into economic capital. As such, the dominant classes are likely to invest a considerable amount of time and money in élite activities for themselves and their children designed to maximize the potential production and conversion of physical capital. Indeed, the more the state is able to prevent or hinder the official transmission of economic capital, the more the effects of the clandestine circulation of physical capital are likely to affect the reproduction of the social structure (Bourdieu, 1986: 254).

The legitimate body

Much of this chapter has been concerned with struggles over the power to develop, define and appropriate bodily forms which are of most value in society at a given time. However, struggles over the corporeal have an added importance when they include definitions as to what counts as a legitimate body, and the legitimate use of the body in society. These struggles are related to the production and realization of physical capital, but they also go beyond matters of resources. They concern the very structure of fields (for example, education, health) which pass judgements on whether certain bodies or bodily practices should even exist. Those with particular power over fields that concern themselves with the body include:

> moralists and especially the clergy, doctors (especially health specialists), educators in the broadest sense (marriage guidance counsellors, etc.), pacemakers in matters of fashion and taste . . . (Bourdieu, 1978: 826–7)

These groups of what could loosely be termed 'body experts' are all involved in educating bodies and labelling as legitimate or deviant particular ways of managing and experiencing our bodies. This affects the recognition we have of our own body practices, and the body practices of others, as 'right' and proper or in need of control and correction.

Definitions of the legitimate body and legitimate bodily activities are to be found across many social fields. For example, in contributing to the structure of the field of sexuality, the state has historically, ideologically and materially privileged a particular form of heterosexuality (that is, the monogomous, married relationship). It has also acted to penalize and define as 'unnatural' homosexuality (Walby, 1989).

Conclusion

Bourdieu's work has developed as a result of a creative engagement with classical sociology. His conceptual scheme has been forged through a Marxian concern with social reproduction, a Weberian concern with the particular styles of life and attributions of honour or dishonour that define status groups, and a Durkheimian concern with the social origin and function of symbolic forms, classifications and representations. They have been central to Bourdieu's development of what has been called the 'sociology of interest' – a mode of thought which conceives of all social practices (even those which may appear to be disinterested such as the pursuit of education) as 'economic', as directed towards the maximization of material and symbolic profit (Brubaker, 1985). In this sense, Bourdieu's work provides us with an example of how contemporary sociological studies of the body have been able to draw productively on the legacy of classical sociology. However, Bourdieu's work has also developed beyond the concerns of classical sociology, most notably in his insistence on the central importance of the body in the formation of physical capital, as constitutive of society and the maintenance of social inequalities.

Bourdieu's general theory of social reproduction has been subject to a number of criticisms and it is worth looking at some of these here as they relate to his analysis of the body. While providing an analysis which is synchronically dynamic, Bourdieu's work is diachronically underdeveloped. Historical change enters into Bourdieu's analysis, but only at a descriptive level. While regularly *asserting* that his theoretical formulations allow for change, the mutually determining power of social fields on the one hand, and social location, habitus and taste on the other, disallow for mechanisms that would accomplish this at a theoretical level. The exception to this is Bourdieu's analysis of distinction, which appears to imply that historical change occurs as a result of the unremitting struggle for resources in which social classes engage.

In his defence, Bourdieu has claimed that social stasis is in fact more prevalant than social change and that this justifies the focus of his work (Lash, 1990). However, while providing us with a detailed view of the bodily forms, appearances and consumptions of the body in particular societies, Bourdieu is unable to account fully for the sort of historical changes which occur in the body and which have been examined elsewhere by Norbert Elias.

The emphasis on social reproduction in Bourdieu's work also affects the degree to which people are able to exercise agency. It is difficult to see at a theoretical level how people are able to 'break out' of the corporeal trajectories assigned to them by their social location, habitus and taste. This is because habitus operates at the level of the subconscious 'beyond the reach of introspective scrutiny or control by the will' (Bourdieu, 1984: 466) and occurs outside the control of each successive generation, and taste functions by making choice out of necessity. Consequently, although Bourdieu frequently asserts the facts of changing bodily dispositions, it is difficult in the extreme for his formulations to account for forms of embodiment and taste which do not correspond to their pre-assigned class bases. Furthermore, this focus on reproduction means that the body is primarily a bearer of external structures or cultural codes. As Turner (1992a) notes, this means that there is little room in Bourdieu's work for a phenomenological understanding of the 'lived body'.

Bourdieu's treatment of social class makes it difficult to focus on *cross-class* factors of importance to the formation of bodies and the conversion of physical capital. For example, in Bourdieu's work it is difficult to find a methodological justification for focusing on the bodies of women or ethnic minorities as they are affected by a society that is *patriarchal* or *racist*, as well as capitalist, in its central features. Bourdieu's notion of class is very broad and it becomes a 'metaphor for the total set of social determinants' (Brubaker, 1985). Gender and ethnicity are not hidden within this formulation and Bourdieu has much of value to say, for example, about the situation of working and middle class women and the physical capital which can be converted by working in or making use of the beauty industry. However, women are analysed in terms of belonging to class categories defined *in opposition* to other class categories. This means that Bourdieu tends to underestimate the extent to which gendered processes affect bodily orientations, and is relatively weak when it comes to analysing the different forms of physical capital that can be acquired by women and men (Shilling, 1991).

Despite the varied groups which make up a class (or class fraction), Bourdieu's conceptualization of social class also makes it difficult to identify features of gender oppression which influence orientations to the body and confront women to some extent *across* class categories (Walby, 1989). Rape, or the fear of rape, for instance, is something which impinges far more on the lives of women than it does men across the social class scale. Its experience or threat can have a devastating effect on the ability of women to continue producing valued forms of physical capital irrespective of their class position. There are also a number of gender-specific issues surrounding the convertibility of symbolically valued bodies into other resources. Irrespective of their class location, many women have far fewer opportunities than men to turn any participation they may have in physical

ties into social, cultural or economic capital. The obvious exception to
when social and sporting settings act as 'marriage markets'. However,
onversion carries its own costs in patriarchal society (Finch, 1983b).
onversion of physical capital into other resources tends also to be

limited for women in that its benefits are frequently mediated through their husbands (Wright, 1989).

Similar points can be made with reference to the experiences of people belonging to ethnic minorities. Individual prejudices and institutionalized racism means that the colour of an individual's skin enters into the value placed on their bodies. For example, in contemporary American and British society racism has effects across class categories and influences the ability of individuals to produce symbolically valued bodily forms. This does not exclude the possibility of a substantial black bourgeoisie in the United States, for instance, but it does make the process of capital accumulation far more difficult for some groups than others. This is graphically illustrated by Verna Keith and Cedric Herring's analysis (1991) of skin tone and stratification in the black community. Citing several studies which suggest that, in past generations, higher status blacks tended to have lighter skin tones than lower status blacks, Keith and Herring go on to argue that complexion continues to have significant net effects on stratification outcomes.

Bourdieu's analysis of the body as a bearer of symbolic value, and a form of physical capital, can be seen as implicitly containing a view of the body as a biological and social phenomenon. However, he is not concerned with examining in any detail the importance of biological processes to human embodiment. In this respect, his work does contain an under-developed view of the biological dimensions of human embodiment. By placing the material body at the very centre of his theory of social reproduction, however, Bourdieu manages to overcome certain dimensions of the dual approach that sociology has traditionally adopted to the body – in naming the body as a theoretical space but failing to examine that space. Indeed, the depth and scope of Bourdieu's work can be seen as offering one of the more promising bases for the sociology of the body to develop.

Bourdieu's analysis of the physical bases of social inequalities provides us with a view of the body as an unfinished phenomenon which is in a constant process of becoming while living within society. His work also has much to tell us about the growing importance of the body to indi-viduals in high modernity. Bourdieu suggests that there has been a multiple commodification of the body in modernity. For Bourdieu, the body has become a bearer of value to the degree that it constantly enters into cultural and social markets which bestow value on prestigious bodily forms irrespective of whether people are engaged in formal work. In this situation, there is every reason why the body should become increasingly important to the modern person's sense of self-identity. The body may not become a project for everyone in the same way, as bodily orientations vary across the social classes. However, Bourdieu illustrates the general import-ance of the body to people, be they concerned only with its immediate functioning or, alternatively, with cultivating the body as an expression of élite status.

Notes

1. Bourdieu's concern with the body derives from his treatment of a particular form of capital: cultural capital (Bourdieu, 1973; Bourdieu and Passeron, 1990 [1977]). The notion of cultural capital enabled Bourdieu to explain why different classes and class fractions invested unequal proportions of their resources in the field of education, and why they could expect different returns on their investment (Bourdieu, 1986; Bourdieu and Passeron, 1990 [1977]). Bourdieu did not, however, confine the notion of cultural capital to its institutionalized state via education. Instead, he argued that cultural capital existed in three irreducible forms: in the **objectified** state (for example, pictures, books which are the trace or realization of theories and bodies of knowledge); in the **institutionalized** state, where original properties are conferred on the cultural capital which institutions are presumed to guarantee (for example, as academic qualifications are conferred on those who reach a certain level of education); and in the **embodied** state (in the form of long-lasting dispositions of the body and mind) (Bourdieu, 1986: 243). Bourdieu (1978) has also referred to this form of cultural capital as *physical capital* and has treated it as a form of capital in its own right. This is a more useful conceptualization of the physical, as it allows one to examine the forms of embodiment which create the basis of all other varieties of capital, and is the one I shall develop in this chapter.

2. The concept of habitus is central to Bourdieu's attempts to mediate between the determining power of social fields and the creativity of individual action. So, the habitus does not correspond to any single cultural or economic field, but mediates between the structures of co-existing fields and individual action. The concept of habitus also seeks to overcome the opposition between mind and body characteristic of much social theory. So, the body itself enters into the production of habitus, both shaping and being shaped by the structure of social fields. The concept of habitus has a lot of work to do in Bourdieu's conceptual scheme. It is something of an overburdened concept whose meaning tends to slip, slide and even occasionally disappear, as it is deployed in different contexts.

3. Another, perhaps more likely, possibility is for such individuals simply to reduce their involvement in sports and leisure activities. It can take a long time for the habitus of an individual to change and, for Bourdieu, changes in the habitus characteristic of classes are more likely over generations than within the lifetime of an individual. This means that there is every possibility of a mismatch between a person's orientation to their body and a related taste for sport on the one hand, and the available capital required to turn such preferences into actual participation on the other.

7

The Civilized Body

The human body may not be *the* central focus of Norbert Elias's theory of the civilizing process (1978a [1939], 1982 [1939]), but it is of great importance to his work. In this chapter I argue that Elias's writings contain within them an implicit theory of the development of what I shall refer to as 'civilized bodies'. This underpins his more general concern with civilizing processes. Elias is mostly interested in the body in terms of its relevance to historical transformations in behavioural codes and forms of affect control. More specifically, he examines the body as a bearer of value in court societies. However, his work also provides us with a long-term view of the individualization, rationalization and socialization of the body which addresses how people relate to their bodies, and helps explain what it is to be an embodied individual living in a particular historical epoch. In this respect, Elias is a notable exception to those who have traditionally adopted a dual approach to the body in sociology. As well as incorporating the body as a subject of discussion into his writings, Elias explores the historically changing character and capabilities of human bodies.[1]

In contrast to social constructionists, who tend to see the body as a product whose meaning is determined by external social classifications, the body for Elias is an unfinished biological and social entity which requires a lengthy process of education before it is accepted fully into society. Consequently, Elias's analysis of the civilizing process can be seen as a development of some of the methods and themes examined in Chapters 5 and 6. Despite the fact that most of Elias's work was published before that of Bob Connell and Peter Freund, his analyses can be read as incorporating many of the insights of these writers into a comprehensive theory of the body in social formations.

In accounting for the formation of civilized bodies, Elias adopts an evolutionary and developmental view of the body which holds that there has been a shift in emotional and physical expression as a result of long-term civilizing processes in the individual and society. To simplify, the civilized body characteristic of modern Western societies is highly individualized in that it is strongly demarcated from its social and natural environments. The civilized body also has the ability to rationalize and exert a high degree of control over its emotions, to monitor its own actions and those of others, and to internalize a finely demarcated set of rules about what constitutes appropriate behaviour in various situations. The civilized body can be contrasted with the 'uncivilized' body of early medieval times which was only weakly demarcated from its social and natural environment. The uncivilized body was constrained by few behavioural norms, gave immediate physical expression to emotions, and sought to satisfy bodily desires without restraint or regard for the welfare of others.

The gradual civilizing of the body has taken place in the context of changes in the major *fears* facing individuals and the dominant mode of *social control* characteristic of societies. Fears of attack in relatively unregulated societies are increasingly replaced by social 'fears' of shame and embarrassment in modern societies, and from being forced on people externally, control comes to be self-imposed.

Before examining more closely Elias's view of the body, it is important to clarify his use of the term 'civilization', and the methodological approach he adopts in examining civilizing processes. 'Civilization' has traditionally been used in evaluative contexts as a way of describing and ranking hierarchically the economic, moral and political progress of societies. However, by examining the changing historical uses of terms for civilization, and the forms of behaviour underlying them, Elias (1978a) attaches a different meaning to the term.

Instead of referring to the relative merits of different societies, Elias is more concerned with civilization as a set of processes which encompass the degree of internal pacification in a society; the refinement of customs; the amount of self-restraint and reflexivity involved in social relations; and the experiences of growing up in a society (Kuzmics, 1988). Thus, although certain societies and bodily forms may be considered more civilized than others (Elias, 1983), this is not a simple value-judgement on their comparative worth. Furthermore, in describing individuals and societies as 'civilized', Elias is not using this term to denote a static pinnacle of achievement. Instead, 'civilized' is a *relational* term which, while providing a means of comparison, always refers to *ongoing* processes of change. According to Elias, there is no beginning and no end to civilizing processes. The same holds for the development of civilized bodies.

The methodological approach adopted by Elias is informed by the central idea that bodies are unfinished entities which develop in social contexts, are mutually interdependent and, historically speaking, are in a constant state of flux and change. This approach is manifest in Elias's work in three major ways. First, the social contexts in which bodies develop are determined neither by isolated individuals nor by social facts operating entirely beyond the reach of people. Instead, social figurations are the basic unit of Elias's work. Figurations have a relative independence of particular individuals but not of individuals as such. Their shape is constantly changing as a result of the fluctuating relations of interdependence entered into by humans. As social figurations change, so too do the influences which are brought to bear on the development of human bodies.

Second, in examining the development of civilized bodies, Elias's approach is both sociogenetic and psychogenetic as it encompasses the broadest of long-term processes underlying society's development, and the specific personality and drive structures of individuals (Elias, 1978a [1939]: xv, 222; 1982 [1939]: 284). This involves the study of such features as historical transformations in the social division of labour on the one hand, and the minutiae of people's behaviour on the other.

Third, Elias's conceptualization of corporeal and societal change is based on a view of the body as simultaneously social and biological. Neither human bodies nor human history could exist without the interlocking of biological and social factors in evolutionary processes. While human bodies remain irreducibly biological, however, evolution has equipped them with capacities (for example, of speech and thought) which release them from dependence on further biological change (Elias, 1987a, 1991).

Evolutionary processes provided humans with the biological facilities to communicate, think and orientate themselves towards reality via symbols. This gave humans the ability to act in the light of learned knowledge and provided them with an evolutionary advantage over other species. Elias (1991: 53) refers to this as *symbol emancipation*. Humans have a unique ability to learn and synthesize symbols, to develop these into a language marked by reflexivity, variability, precision, flexibility and a high degree of reality congruence, and to transmit accumulated knowledge between generations in the form of symbols (1991: 93–6). Symbol emancipation enabled humans to adapt to new circumstances independently of biological changes and represented a breakthrough of the evolutionary process to a new, 'post-animalistic' level (1991: 31–2, 43). Symbol emancipation has also enabled humans to reflexively monitor and control their own behaviour and, as such, is a crucial prerequisite for the development of civilized bodies. In sum, evolutionary processes and the advantage of symbol emancipation made possible both the dominance of human bodies over those of other species, and the development of civilized bodies.

In the introduction to this book I suggested that Elias's work can do much to illuminate the increasing importance of the body in modernity. This statement is problematic in several respects, not least because the central part of his theory was written in the mid-1930s and published in 1939 and is, therefore, unfinished with regard to civilizing processes in the industrial capitalist era. However, Arthur Bogner has addressed the relation between Elias's work and theories of modernization and has suggested that the former has much to offer the latter in relation to the analysis of inter-state relations, and monopolies of physical force and taxation. Elias identi-fied and examined processes which are still with us today (Bogner, 1992). In what follows, I want to extend Bogner's observations by arguing that Elias has identified processes occurring in and around bodies which remain relevant to, and have sometimes intensified within, contemporary society. These arguments become particularly significant for the penultimate chapter of this book where I suggest that the processes identified by Elias have become central to people's sense of self in the conditions of high modernity.

The historical development of bodies

The development of the civilized body in Europe is not determined by the rise of modern capitalism, as a response to the demands of production and accumulation, but is related to the transformation of the warrior nobility of the early Middle Ages into a court aristocracy. After summarizing the changes associated with the rise of civilized bodies in this section, I shall then examine the major 'local' and systemic causes behind these changes.

As Elias makes clear, there is no absolute starting point in the development of civilized bodies. However, the era between the medieval period and court absolutism in particular witnessed long-term changes in the modes of bodily expression and personality structure which are still continuing today (Elias, 1978a [1939], 1978b, 1982 [1939]). In early medieval times, the personality structure was volatile, behaviour was unpredictable and frequently fluctuated between extremes for apparently minor reasons. Life was short, food was often in irregular supply (Mennell, 1987), and violence was part of everyday life and was not seen as exceptional or even undesirable. Pleasure was taken in torture, mutilation and killing, and people had to be ready to defend themselves and be prepared to give free reign to their emotions in order to safeguard their lives, property and possessions (Elias, 1982 [1939]: 192, 233–6).[2]

In this context, a strong and continuous moderation of drives and physical acts was not necessary, feasible or useful. Where possible, people satiated themselves without moderation, and pleasures focused on the immediate desires of the flesh. The existence of extreme forms of asceticism and renunciation in medieval society does not contradict this general picture. Such 'restraint' was also a flight into physicality, as Bynum (1987) and Mellor (1990: 56–8) make abundantly clear, and 'is no less intense and one-sided, no less radical and passionate than its counterpart, the fight against others and the maximum enjoyment of pleasures' (Elias, 1982 [1939]: 240).

With all the wars, killing and destruction of the recent past, it is not surprising that Elias has been criticized for exaggerating the differences between medieval and contemporary societies. However, it is not the aggregate *outcome* of violence, but its nature and occurrence in everyday life that is of importance to Elias and lies behind his (1978a [1939]) statement that we are like choir boys compared to our ancestors. Furthermore, war has become rationalized in the modern world, and compared to the battle fury of Abyssinian warriors or the frenzy of the tribes at the time of the Great Migrations, 'the aggressiveness of even the most warlike nations of the civilized world appears subdued' (Elias, 1978a [1939]: 192, 202; see also Sica, 1984). In comparison with high modernity, more individuals of previous eras were much more directly implicated in acts of violence, body against body, such as killing and mutilation.

In contrast to the violence and lack of prohibitions on behaviour which characterized the Middle Ages, the Renaissance onwards witnessed a long-term trend towards greater demands on emotional control and the rise of differentiated codes of body management. These trends were very much associated with the development of court societies. Courts gained increasing importance in almost every European country from the Renaissance onwards and had a representative and central significance for most Western European countries in the seventeenth and eighteenth centuries (Elias, 1983: 35–6).

Court societies institutionalized highly detailed codes of body management which were used to differentiate between people on the basis of their relative worth. Sanctions were invoked against those who refused to follow court etiquette and there was a heightened tendency among people to observe and seek to mould themselves and others (Elias, 1978a [1939], 1983). In this context, bodies were placed at the very centre of the value system within court etiquette. A clear example of this is found in the most important figure of all within court society, the king. From being woken each morning, the king's dressing was broken down into a series of acts which involved important others and had a prestige value which symbolized the distribution of power at the time (1983: 83–4).

These developments were assisted by the changing social contexts in which people lived. In contrast to medieval times, court societies did not require individuals to be constantly ready to display a high level of aggression. Instead, physical battles were frequently replaced by courtly intrigues, and survival depended less on bodily strength than on adherence to behavioural codes and the skills of impression management (Kuzmics, 1988). The presentation of the body was more important for success than overcoming other bodies by force, and it became a necessity for court people to develop 'an extraordinarily sensitive feeling for the status and importance that should be attributed to a person in society on the basis of his bearing, speech, manner or appearance' (Elias, 1983: 55).

This increase in the monitoring and controlling of the body spread both inside and outside of court societies. Some of the general changes which have occurred over the centuries include the rationalization of sleeping cycles and stricter taboos concerning where to sleep. It became increasingly embarrassing to share a bed with strangers, bodily functions such as defecating became subject to greater taboos, and sexuality was moved to the back-regions of social life (treatises on manners once included advice on how to act if sharing a bed at an inn with a stranger and what to do if one passed a couple copulating in the street). Before this time, neither the body nor its functions were felt to be disgusting. For example, Elias (1978a [1939]) cites a treatise on good manners from the mid-sixteenth century which was addressed to the aristocracy and felt the need to devote an entire chapter to the satisfaction of bodily necessities. It included the following guidance:

> When you come across something distasteful lying in the road, it is improper to turn toward company and show them this filth. Still less is it permissible to

present foul-smelling things to others, as some are accustomed to doing who lower their nose and say, 'Do take a sniff; it really stinks'.

As Elias notes, if this treatise takes pains to emphasize this practice in order to condemn it, it is likely to be evidence of its existence.

These changes in body management did not occur in a vacuum but were accompanied by a gradual decline in people's propensity for obtaining pleasure directly from violence, a lowering of the threshold of moral repugnance concerning violent acts, and a decrease in the swings and fluctuations in people's behaviour. Society, which is beginning to limit the physical dangers faced by people, also begins to place restrictions on the symbols of danger. One example of this is the gradual increase in prohibitions surrounding use of the knife (Elias, 1978a [1939]: 124–5). Long used as a weapon and the only eating utensil, the knife became a symbol of danger and death. It generated feelings of unease that led to its restriction and suppression from general use in society (Elias, 1978a [1939]).

Underlying these changes in manners, we can see an attempt by people to define their embodiment in opposition to everything they feel is animal or natural. Humans increasingly define themselves in opposition to nature or biology, and reminders of the body's 'natural functions' are frequently hidden away in back-regions. Even the 'animal' in food is suppressed:

> From a standard of feeling by which the sight and carving of a dead animal on the table are actually pleasurable, or at least not at all unpleasant, the development leads to another standard by which reminders that the meat dish has something to do with the killing of an animal are avoided to the utmost. In many of our meat dishes the animal form is so concealed and changed by the art of its preparation and carving that while eating one is scarcely reminded of its origin. (Elias, 1978a [1939]: 120)

Another way of describing this general trend is that the development of civilized bodies involves a progressive *socialization* of the body. As used here, the socialization of bodies involves two main features. First, from being closely associated with the rhythms and dictates of nature, natural functions are socially managed and organized. This is facilitated by technical advances, such as the design and construction of the toilet as an enclosed unit, which 'solved fairly satisfactorily the problem of eliminating these functions from social life and displacing them behind the scenes' (1978a [1939]: 139). Second, as the body becomes subject to ever expanding taboos, it is transformed into a location for and an expression of codes of behaviour. This 'separation' of the body from nature helped provide the basis for differentiating between individuals on the basis of their bodily worth. With the bodily functions which people *shared* increasingly hidden from view, the manners and dispositions which *separated* individuals could increasingly be taken as markers of their value and self-identity.

Bodies and the search for distinction

Having described some of the major features involved in the development of civilized bodies, I shall now identify more precisely the major factors which contributed to these changes. In the case of bodily manners, it is possible to trace a number of medical justifications for changing customs. However, medical justifications could not have caused these developments as it was mostly *after* manners had changed that they came to be seen as unhealthy and socially unacceptable (e.g. Elias, 1978a [1939]: 114–16, 126). Instead, Elias identifies two main systemic and one major 'localized' cause – the search for distinction – which had important consequences for the history of body management.

The main local cause of these changes concerns the *search for distinction* among individuals in court society which helped facilitate the internalization of behavioural codes. In medieval times, free knights had little to worry about concerning threats to their social position from below. Consequently, there was little psychological pressure on them to censor behaviour which resembled that of the lower classes. However, the development of court societies changed that situation. A person's rank within court society was determined first of all by their house, their official title. However, permeating and altering this hierarchy was an order of rank which depended on the favour a courtier enjoyed with the king. This was dependent on the power and importance an individual enjoyed within the field of court tensions, and involved a significant degree of social mobility. As Elias notes:

> The position a person held in the court hierarchy was . . . extremely unstable. The actual esteem he had achieved forced him to aspire to improve his official rank. Any such improvement necessarily meant a demotion of others, so that such aspirations unleashed the only kind of conflict – apart from warlike deeds in the king's service – which was still open to the court nobility, the struggle for position within the court hierarchy. (1983: 90–1)

This search for distinction placed great demands on the management of the body. As displays of 'bad manners' were seen as distasteful and likely to bring the offender into disrepute, behavioural codes exerted a compelling influence on people's behaviour. Actions at any time could decide a person's place in society and success in this status competition demanded a finely honed set of impression management skills. People had to 'meticulously weigh the gestures and expressions of everyone else', carefully fathoming 'the intention and meaning of each of their utterances' (1983: 104). For example, the 'degree of aloofness or familiarity with everyone must be carefully measured; each greeting, each conversation has a significance over and above what is actually said or done. They indicate the standing of the person; and they contribute to the formation of court opinion on his standing' (Elias, 1982 [1939]: 271). It was dangerous both to be 'discourteous to a person whose stock was rising' and to be 'unduly amiable to a person who was sinking in the hierarchy' (Elias, 1983: 91). In

The Body and Social Theory

this context, affective outbursts were damaging as they revealed the true feelings of a person, and signified a loss of control.

Elias argues that the status competition of court life 'enforces a curbing of the affects in favour of calculated and finely shaded behaviour in dealing with people' (1983: 111). The fear of loss of face in the eyes of others instilled in individuals an habitual reproduction of distinctive conduct and the strict drive control underlying it (Elias, 1982 [1939]: 254–5). The preservation of high status and prestigious personality characteristics requires foresight, self-restraint and 'prudence beset by anxieties' (1982 [1939]: 311):

> To keep one's place in the intense competition for importance at court, to avoid being exposed to scorn, contempt, loss of prestige, one must sub-ordinate one's appearance and gestures, in short oneself, to the fluctuating norms of court society that increasingly emphasize the difference, the distinction of the people belonging to it. One *must* wear certain materials and certain shoes. One *must* move in certain ways characteristic of people belonging to court society. Even smiling is shaped by court custom. (1983: 231–2)

As a result of this situation, body management norms became *internalized*. Instead of being imposed from outside, through the threat of sanctions, codes of behaviour became adopted partly at a subconscious level to the point where they were followed irrespective of the presence of others (a situation which still pertains today – people will usually dress in the mornings even if they are spending the day at home with no intention of seeing anyone).

The struggle for status which existed in court societies was 'no less strong than competition for capital and economic power in industrial societies' (Elias, 1983: 73). However, rather than being decided in the economic market place, competition in court society was mediated through an individual's control over, and position within, the demands of court etiquette. This situation led to social superiors attempting to distinguish themselves through manners and deportment, and establish their standards as norms which others were obliged to follow.

The 'rules' of competition had been shifted in court society in com-parison with earlier times. Victories and defeats were no longer decided by physical battles, but by status competition which attached a 'fetish char-acter' to every act of etiquette. Consequently, the constant pressure from 'below' in court societies for recognition, reward and status, and the fear this competition induced in those 'above' is 'one of the strongest forces of the specifically civilized refinement by which the people of the upper class distinguish themselves from others' (Mennell, 1989: 107). For example, in the latter half of the seventeenth century in France:

> customs, behaviour, and fashion from the court are continuously penetrating the upper middle classes, where they are imitated and more or less altered in accordance with the different social situation. They thereby lose, to some extent, their character as a means of distinguishing the upper class. They are

somewhat devalued. This compels those above to further refinement and development of behaviour. And from this mechanism – the development of courtly customs, their dissemination downward, their slight social deformation, their devaluation as marks of distinction – the constant movement in behaviour patterns through the upper class receives part of its motivation. (Elias, 1978a [1939]: 102)

Historically, status competition is manifest in two major forms. The first is characterized by individualistic attempts at social mobility when members of the lower class imitate the upper class, yet tend to be left with marks in their behaviour which reveal 'the immense effort which individual social advancement requires' (Elias, 1983: 186). Second, when the social power of the lower group is rising at the expense of the upper, there is a tendency for groups to exaggerate their differences and each claim them as models of superiority (Elias, 1982 [1939]: 311–12).

The search for distinction within court society, then, was a major motor force behind the internalization of codes of behaviour, and the increased attention given to the monitoring and control of the body. However, court competition had three further unintended consequences in addition to the internalization of behavioural norms. First, the amount and frequency of **mutual identification** between people increased. As Elias demonstrated in *The Court Society* (1983), preserving or improving one's social position within a competitive situation necessitated a more 'psychological' view of people which involved precise observations of both one's own and others' actions and expressions. Taking more conscious account of how one's behaviour will be interpreted by others can also be seen as constituting a higher level of identification with others. People are forced to pay more attention to more people than was previously the case (Goudsblom, 1987). One implication of this is that mutual identification is conducive to promoting both a greater degree of sympathy and empathy with others.

As Bourdieu (1984) and Goffman (1969) illustrate, the search for distinction remains a major motor force behind impression management in contemporary society and, in Elias's terms, can be seen as promoting levels of mutual identification between people which are far higher than in previous historical eras. Accompanying this process of mutual identification was an advance in thresholds of shame and embarrassment; shame being experienced when emotions overcome emotion controls and transgress internalized codes of behaviour, and embarrassment when others break societal conventions (Elias, 1982 [1939]: 296). Treatises on manners even sought to cultivate shame and embarrassment among individuals (Elias, 1978a [1939]: 134).

Second, taking more notice of others necessitated not just a more psychological view of people, but involved the ability to **plan ahead** and anticipate actions in light of their future consequences. When opinions counted for so much, the consequences of actions were no longer limited to their immediate effects but had to be considered in relation to their subsequent implications. In comparison with contemporary business life, where contacts are often temporary and quickly terminated, every relationship in court society is 'necessarily permanent' and 'a single unconsidered utterance can have a permanent effect' (Elias, 1983: 110). Furthermore, the lack of a split between public and private life in court society meant that the body was more permanently on display and required constant vigilance and management.

The third consequence of this search for distinction within court society concerns the creation of an increasing **bodily and psychological distance between adults and children**. According to Elias (1978a [1939]: xiii), the process of 'growing up' in Western societies is nothing other than 'the individual civilizing process to which each young person, as a result of the social civilizing process over many centuries, is automatically subject from earliest childhood'. As the degree of self-control exercised by adults increased, so did the amount of learning children had to do in order to develop civilized bodies and become full and acceptable members of society. In modern times, there is a 'profound discrepancy' between the behaviour, language and thought of adults and children, and children have only a few years to attain the advanced level of 'shame, revulsion and knowledge that has developed over many centuries' (1978a [1939]: 140; 1991). Consequently, their instinctual life must very rapidly be subject to strict control and this includes an ever increasing moulding of the sexual drive (1978a [1939]: 140, 182). The importance of developing civilized bodies is indicated by the fact that children who don't acquire the level of control of emotions demanded by society are regarded as 'ill', 'criminal' or simply 'impossible' (1978a [1939]: 141; Elias and Scotson, 1965).

It is parents (and more particularly mothers) who are the prime agents involved in educating and developing children's bodies in line with the standards of civilized bodies. For example, parents are responsible for toilet training their children, teaching them to blow their noses without messing their hands, tying their shoe laces and generally managing their bodies in public without screaming or crying or bumping into people or other obstacles. Indeed, Elias (1978a [1939]: 140, 189) argues that the greater the demands of the civilizing process, the more pressure falls on parents in the nuclear family to accomplish this task. However, parents are only the (often inadequate) instruments of this conditioning as it is always 'society as a whole, the entire configuration of human beings, that exerts its pressure on the new generation'. From this analysis, it is clear that Elias rejects the historical analyses of childhood put forward by many psychologists. The problems involved in the 'socialization' of children cannot be understood if the individual is regarded as developing uniformly across historical epochs. Instead, problems relating to children's consciousness and instinctual urges vary with the amount and quality of distance incorporated in the relationship of children to adults (Elias, 1978a [1939]: 182).

The civilizing process, then, involves an increase in both the psychological and bodily distance between the bodies of adults and children. This occurs in terms of the range of expression, predictability and control adults are able to exhibit, and the degree to which they are able to plan ahead and identify with others. The further the adult body becomes subject to the monitoring and control of self and others, the greater the work which has to be invested in the child's body before it is accepted into adulthood. From expressing instantaneously a link between drives and physical expressions, children's bodies are transformed into adulthood where affective impulses can only rarely be lived out as before.

In accounting for these differences it is important to keep in mind that the gap between adults and children is made possible by the simultaneously social and biological status of the body. It is the evolutionary development of symbol emancipation which lies at the root of the ability of humans to monitor, control and develop their bodily actions apart from immediate biological change and in accordance with socially accepted norms of behaviour.

The social interdependence of bodies

The local and immediate motor force behind the changes associated with the civilized body concerned the search for distinction initially pursued by members of court society. However, there were broader systemic processes underlying these changes which constituted pre-conditions for their occurrence. The first concerns the progressive increase in the **social division of labour** which led to lengthening chains of interdependence between people. As the density of individuals and the frequency of their interactions increased, people had to take greater account of the present and future effects of their own actions and the actions of others. Success no longer depended on the ability to fight, but on continuous reflection, foresight and the increased acquisition of knowledge.

The second systemic factor underlying changes in bodily control and expression concerns the formation of increasingly effective **monopolies of violence**. In feudal times, population growth and a rapidly exhausting supply of available land created a situation where territorial owners were forced into fighting and competing for land. As Elias (1982 [1939]: 43) argues, anyone refusing to participate in this struggle 'merely conserving his property while others strive for increase, necessarily ends up "smaller" and weaker than the others, and is in ever increasing danger of succumbing to them'. However, as competition progressively eliminated the numbers participating in this struggle, the power of central authorities began to grow with the effect that people in those areas came under greater pressure to live in peace with each other. As the means of legitimate violence become steadily more concentrated into the hands of the court or state, the threat represented by particular individuals becomes more calculable. The costs of violent behaviour also rise steeply and affective outbursts are liable to harsh punishment by central authorities. In such a situation, 'the moulding of affects and the standards of the economy of instincts' are very gradually changed as well (Elias, 1978a [1939]: 201). This means that the dangers of daily life are both reduced and become more predictable. Insecurity declines and the possibility of planning becomes both realistic and necessary.

The establishment of monopolies of violence, and the development of lengthening chains of interdependence and civilized bodies are related phenomena. On the one hand, taboos against acts of violence are closely linked to the growing effectiveness of state monopolies of violence. As people realize that violent acts are punished by government, there is a gradual tendency for them to monitor and control aggressive impulses. Indeed, in the long run state monopolies cannot be maintained merely by force and the growth of drive control is an important condition of their success. Bodies not only have to be controlled, they have to be made relatively docile. Furthermore, growing relations of interdependence among people makes violence less appropriate and its effects less predictable. On the other hand, state forms that incorporate monopolies of violence inter-weave in a spiralling process with the growing division of labour to assist the growth of towns and administrative apparatuses, the use of money and an increasing population (Mennell, 1990: 208).

The social interdependence facilitated by a complex social division of labour also encourages something of an 'equalizing' effect between indi-viduals as a result of what Elias terms 'functional democratization'. This is because the further interdependence advances, the more dependent the dominant classes become for their position on the dominated classes and the greater becomes the potential strength of these classes (Elias, 1978a [1939]: 210; Elias and Dunning, 1986). Established groups struggling among themselves for status and other rewards are obliged to take into account the demands of the mass of outsiders. Such a situation also facilitates 'exchanges' in behavioural codes characteristic of different groups. This becomes true not only for social classes, but in the case of relations between the sexes (Elias, 1987b). For example, Elias argues that the complete dominance of the husband over the wife is broken for the first time in absolutist court societies of the seventeenth and eighteenth centuries (1987b: 184). During this time, the power of the wife rises sharply as social opinion, central to success in the status market, is determined to a high degree by women.

In sum, with the advance of the social division of labour and monopolies of violence, competition for rewards moves increasingly away from the unpredictabilities of force, towards the regulated realms of trade and impression management. Within this context, the controlled and calculated management of the body becomes increasingly necessary and important for success, and a prerequisite for the development of civilized bodies.

Civilized bodies

We are now in a position to summarize the major characteristics of civilized bodies, and to clarify how Elias's work helps inform our understanding of the body in modernity. The development of civilized bodies involves a progressive socialization, rationalization and individualization of the body. As mentioned earlier, I refer to the **socialization** of bodies as involving the hiding away of natural functions and the transformation of bodies into a location for and an expression of codes of behaviour. The body is perceived and managed as increasingly social, and more of its dimensions and functions are defined in opposition to the biological or natural spheres of life.

This is accompanied by the **rationalization** of the body. In medieval times, impulses were manifest instantaneously in consciousness and actions. However, in the development of civilized bodies, the boundaries between consciousness and drives strengthen. The civilized body possesses self-controls manifest in 'morals' or 'rational thought' which interpose themselves between 'spontaneous and emotional impulses, on the one hand, and the skeletal muscles, on the other', and which allow for the deferral of satisfaction. This prevents impulses from expressing themselves in action 'without the permission of these control mechanisms' (Elias, 1978a: 257; 1983: 243). The rationalization of the body also involves the progressive differentiation of the body: it is seen as less of a 'whole' and more as a phenomenon whose separate parts are amenable to control.

Elias's analysis of the socialization and rationalization of the body provides a historical basis, which is otherwise absent, for Goffman's analysis of the presentation of self and shared vocabularies of body idiom, Freund's examination of the emotional body, and Hochschild's study of the social norms which envelop the bodies of flight attendants. The more civilizing processes socialize the body, the more the body becomes a location for and an expression of codes of behaviour which people find hard to resist. Similarly, the more civilizing processes rationalize the body, the greater capacity people have to control their bodies, and the greater the demands they may face to control their bodies.

Furthermore, Elias's analysis of the rationalization of the body, like Weber's analysis of social rationalization, shows that this is a double-edged phenomenon. With the progression of the civilization process, life becomes less dangerous but also less exciting. As strategic thinking replaces immediacy of expression there is a trade-off between spontaneous pleasure and the security of controlled planning (Kuzmics, 1988: 155). One effect of this is that the drives and passions that can no longer be displayed directly between people, often struggle just as violently *within* individuals against the supervising part of themselves. The strict moulding of children often leads to interpersonal conflicts which serve to pattern their personality structure and can have a detrimental effect on their relationships as adults (Elias, 1978c: 242; 1982 [1939]: 245). The amount of violence in everyday life may have been reduced, but 'the battlefield is . . . moved within . . . the drives, the passionate affects, that can no longer directly manifest themselves in the relationships *between* people, often struggle no less violently *within* the individual against this supervising part of himself' (1982 [1939]: 242).

Indeed, there is often no complete resolution between the supervising consciousness and the supervised drives of individuals. The balance between these is frequently subject to disturbances which range from 'revolts of one part of the person against the other, or a permanent atrophy, which makes the performance of social functions even more difficult', to feelings of boredom, perpetual restlessness and dissatisfaction. The external and internal attempt to achieve complete control over the body and its drives can also lead to compulsive actions and other symptoms of disturbance (1982 [1939]: 243). In short, the 'learning of self-controls . . . the civilizing of the human young, is never a process entirely without pain; it always leaves scars' (1982 [1939]: 244).

The costs involved in the rationalization of bodies informs Elias's and Elias and Dunning's (1986) work on the rise and place of sports and leisure activities in society. To start with, Elias (1978a [1939]: 202) argues that the carefully regulated deployment of passions and emotions in spectating or merely listening to an event is a particular feature of civilized society, and has affected the development of books, theatre and the cinema. Historically, individuals have been educated from an early age away from aggressive expressions of pleasure, into the ordered, mediated, cerebral and relatively passive pleasures of spectating. As Pasi Falk notes (1985: 115), there has been a clear shift of emphasis from 'the expressive aspect to the experience aspect of corporeality'. This has been accompanied by a shift in the senses with which it is acceptable for individuals to gain excitement in public. Here, Elias (1978a [1939]: 203) quotes from the 1774 edition of La Salle's *Civilité* which reads: 'Children like to touch clothes and other things that please them with their hands. This urge must be corrected, and they must be taught to touch all they see only with their eyes'. Nowadays, this precept is taken almost for granted among adults who tend to be denied, by socially instilled self-controls, from spontaneously touching what they desire. It is now the eye and the ear that have become the dominant mediators of experience for people in public.

Historically, the emergence of sport as a form of physical contest of a relatively non-violent type was associated with the reduction of violence in society at large and the resolution of conflicts by non-violent means. The violence into which uninhibited drives were channelled in past eras has now been replaced by individuals watching 'mock' contests in which rules are carefully established to maintain an appropriate 'tension equilibrium' (Elias and Dunning, 1986). The emotional restraints required by occupational work have tended to reach far into the non-occupational lives of people and can lead to individuals experiencing themselves as 'dry', 'dull' or 'stale'. Sport has become one of the main ways in which people are able to experience excitement (Goodger and Goodger, 1989). Spectating at events such as baseball, American Football or soccer, provides individuals with the opportunity to experience a 'controlled decontrolling of emotions' which is rarely available to them in other public spheres of life such as work (Wouters, 1986, 1987). These opportunities also make more tolerable the internal self-restraints brought about by civilizing processes. They provide the civilized body with release, with a 'recharging' which helps it return to the highly controlled behavioural norms which dominate society.

If the socialization of the body is the first, and the rationalization of the body is the second, main characteristic of civilized bodies, the progressive **individualization** of the body and self is the third. As Elias notes (1978a [1939]: 253), the idea of the 'self in a case' is one of the recurrent themes of Western philosophy and is actually experienced by people as real. Individuals tend to conceptualize themselves as separate from others, with the body acting as the container for the self or, as Wittgenstein puts it, 'an empty tube which is simply inflated by a mind' (Wright, 1980: 11). According to Elias, this idea is so self-evident that it is rarely questioned, and this is not surprising given the stress placed on self-control in contemporary society. The nature of this boundary separating individuals is, though, 'never properly explained' (Elias, 1978a [1939]: 249). In contrast to these assumptions, Elias has no ontological commitment to the idea of a body and self which is completely separate and isolated. Instead, the body, emotions and physical expressions are themselves formed by civilizing processes made possible by symbol emancipation and forged out of social figurations. In particular, with the increased capacity for self-detachment and affect control which humans possess from the end of the Middle Ages, people come to perceive themselves more as individuals who are separate and detached from others. Objects also take on an appearance of externality and begin to possess meanings which are separate from the immediate use to which they are put by people (Elias, 1983: 252).

The individualization of bodies has important consequences for the advance of manners as it encourages among people a greater degree of reflexivity about their bodies, and a perception of themselves as different from others. As a result, Elias argues that people come to construct an 'affective wall between their bodies and those of others'. For example, the handkerchief and nightshirt arise as symbols of the transformation at work in people, as they create an emotional wall between themselves and their bodies (Elias, 1978a [1939]). Smells, sounds and actions come to be associated more and more with specific individuals rather than with the species in general (Duroche, 1990). Distance came to be created between bodies, and the flesh of humans became a source of embarrassment. Consequently, bodies have increasingly to be managed with reference to social norms of behaviour.

In civilizing processes, individuals change by becoming more aware of themselves and others as separate entities, and exerting more control over their bodies. The experience of being 'separate' and 'isolated' from others is, though, the result of civilizing processes, not a pre-social state universally experienced by individuals. This is why Elias (1978a [1939]: 261; 1983: 209) argues that people should not be conceived of as 'isolated, hermetically closed individuals, but as mutually interdependent individuals who form figurations of the most diverse kinds with each other'.

Furthermore, civilized bodies are social phenomena which are able to develop as they do only as the result of the interlocking of biological and social processes.

The three main characteristics of civilized bodies involve the progressive socialization, rationalization and individualization of the body. Although the historical period of Elias's analysis of civilized bodies is of limited relevance to the study of the body in modernity, we could argue that the processes he identifies are still occurring and highlight the growing importance of the body to the modern person's sense of self-identity. The development of civilized bodies tends to leave people alone with their bodies acting as barriers to contact and meaningful communication with other people. Standards of body management demand that people monitor and control their bodies, yet the implication of this affect control is that they become stale in and with their bodies. The existence of strong, trans-personal social and religious meaning systems, provided people in court society with a rationale for these actions. In contemporary society, how-ever, individuals are increasingly left alone with a heightened reflexivity about the limitations of their civilized bodies, yet are without meaningful socially legitimated resources for justifying this situation.

The breakdown of civilized bodies

Although there is an overall direction to the development of civilized bodies in Elias's work, civilizing processes are uneven and can go into periods of reversal. While evolutionary processes provided humans with the biological equipment necessary for the development of civilized bodies, their realization remains contingent on the actions of people. This contin-gency is made clear by the effects on the body of different levels of civil-ization on inter- and intra-state levels, periods of reversal when decivilizing processes occur within social systems, and in the existence of relatively 'uncivilized' outsider groups in societies.

First, civilizing processes at the levels of inter-state and intra-state relations have reached different levels and this has important implications for the maintenance of civilized bodies. International controls and mono-polies of violence are frequently much weaker than those which exist nationally. As Elias argues: 'If the reduction of mutual physical danger or increased pacification is considered a decisive criterion for determining the degree of civilization, then humankind can be said to have reached a higher level of civilization within domestic affairs than on the international plane' (1988: 181). When antagonistic relations between countries end in war, physical conflict results in the breakdown of certain features of the civilized body, a situation which finds one manifestation in the difficulties many soldiers face in readjusting to civilian life.

Second, expectations and reversals to the development of civilized bodies can occur within a state when groups are threatened with the loss of their existing social position. For example, while sections of the old warrior class in Western Europe were being 'tamed' and transformed into courtiers, others not involved in courts actually became more violent and aggressive in the late Middle Ages as a result of the erosion of their social base (Mennell, 1990). A similar process was at work in the case of atrocities carried out by the German Freikorps. As Elias (1988: 197) explains, these soldiers opposed the peace which threatened their position within society and 'set out to destroy a world which refused them fulfillment and purpose and which therefore seemed meaningless' (see also Theweleit, 1989). Indeed, at times of war in general, civilizing processes are subject to weakening as a result of the engagement of state-sponsored violence.

Third, the development of civilized bodies can reach different levels among established and outsider groups in society. The existence of strong established–outsider boundaries between peoples who are included and excluded from full membership of a society can lead to the regular use of violence as a means of expression on the part of the outsiders. While the established are usually committed to using dominant codes of behaviour in conflicts to safeguard their privileges, this is not always the case with outsiders. For example, Dunning, Murphy and Williams (1988) speculated that Britain may be experiencing a decivilizing surge in violence. While functional democratization has allowed for the demands of outsider groups to be expressed strongly, it has not proceeded far enough to break down the obstacles that prevent their social and political demands from being met.

Elias and Scotson's community study of established and outsider groups in 'Winston Pravda' illustrates some of the processes involved in established–outsider relations which can lead to these differentials. Shared definitions of low worth were attached to families living on an estate which were 'almost automatically extended from the parents to the children and affected the latter's personality development, particularly their self-image and their self-respect' (Elias and Scotson, 1965: 144). Consequently, while 'outsider youth' wanted to attain a self-identity which would provide them with respect, they could achieve this only by 'attacking and, as far as they could, destroying the orderly world from which they were excluded without quite understanding why' (1965: 120).

Elias and Scotson make clear that this study is not without wider ramifications for the civilizing process. The self-concepts of people are integrally related to their position as established or outsiders within a society (Van Stolk and Wouters, 1987) and differentially affect their ability to establish effective and constant drive control. Indeed, Elias (1982 [1939]) argues that for people to install and maintain a stable drive controlling super-ego agency, a relatively high standard of living and a fairly high degree of security are necessary. This is as true for established–outsider groups in contemporary society, as it was for aristocratic and dispossessed groups centuries ago (Kuzmics, 1988: 173).

Waves of formalization and informalization also complicate the development of civilized bodies. For example, the 1960s has often been seen as a period when emotional restraints were cast off in favour of spontaneous self-expression. However, Wouters (1986, 1987) argues that this and comparable periods can more accurately be seen as a time when a highly controlled decontrolling of emotions took place. For the social informalities and personal experimentation of the period to work, a high degree of self-restraint was required. The same conditions can be traced back to earlier periods, as in the 1930s when taboos relaxed surrounding such facets of life as bathing, dancing and talk of natural functions. Again, these events were only possible 'because the level of habitual, technically and institutionally consolidated self-control . . . [had] been on the whole secured. It is a relaxation within the framework of an already established standard' (Elias, 1978a [1939]: 140). If this view is accepted, it becomes very difficult to specify what precisely constitutes decivilizing processes: a period when standards of self-control were apparently relaxed may be only a movement *within* a tightening period of civilization (for an attempt to specify these conditions, see Mennell, 1990).

The historical body

Elias's theory of the civilizing process contains within it what I have referred to as a theory of the civilized body which is concerned primarily with the historical development of human bodies. In contrast to naturalistic views, the body and society do not wholly stem from a pre-social sphere of biology or nature. Instead, Elias is concerned with humans whose embodiment is the product of the biological and *social* processes involved in evolutionary development. It is in this context that Elias is concerned to examine the interrelation between 'the structure of psychological functions, the particular standard of behavioural controls at a given period' and 'the structure of social functions and the change in relationships between people' (1982 [1939]: 324). So, changes in individual bodies and social figurations are integrally related.

If Elias's view of the body is different from that adopted by naturalistic approaches, it also contrasts with that held by social constructionists. Bodies become increasingly socialized in Elias's work, but this process is itself facilitated by those biological characteristics of humans which make history possible. As already noted, Elias (1991) argues that evolutionary processes equipped humans with a biological capacity for learning which released them from dependence on further biological change. It is the exceptional ability of humans to learn and their unique capacities for synthesis – for making connections through the use of symbols – and transmitting accumulated knowledge in the form of symbols between generations which makes possible 'rapid social differentiation and adaptation to new circumstances independently of biological change' (Mennell, 1989: 204). The biological equipment which enabled humans to shape their action mainly by means of learnt experience conferred on humans a unique capacity for making their own history and moulding their 'own' bodies which was not shared by other species. In contrast to most socio-logists, who view social and cultural processes as having made biology all but irrelevant to history, Elias argues that it is evolutionary processes which have helped to reduce massively the importance of biology.

Elias's work takes seriously the history of the body and provides a promising basis for the development of a sociology of the body. I shall return to the importance of his work in the next chapter of this book. However, several criticisms can be levelled at his analysis of the civilized body. The first is that in contrast to court society, capitalism cannot be understood with reference to the conditions surrounding face-to-face inter-action (Honneth and Joas, 1988 [1980]; Kuzmics, 1991). Now, Elias (1982 [1939]) is well aware of the vastly increased demands which have been placed on individuals as a result of the development of capitalism and points out the importance of individual management of the body in the increased commodification of time and space that has characterized capitalism. While this does not directly address the criticism, there is a strong case to be made for such face work and body work being the very stuff of capitalism; a case which has been made in part by Anthony Giddens (1988, 1990).

It might be more appropriate to criticize Elias for his overly selective focus on certain dimensions of the body. Elias's stress on the decreased significance of biology as a result of symbol emancipation is important but simply goes too far. Post symbol emancipation, the biological constitution of humans tends to be relegated to a mere bearer of civilizing processes. This could be described as an example of 'human exceptionalism' (Benton, 1992: 229). Human exceptionalism holds that at a certain stage of human evolution, cultural and social capacities emerge which displace the import-ance of biological mechanisms. Now, as Elias himself recognizes, capitalism has a profound effect on the body in terms of the demands it places on people to subordinate 'momentary inclinations to the overriding necessities of interdependence' and eliminate all irregularities from behaviour and achieve permanent self-control (Elias, 1982 [1939]: 248). However, while Elias identifies the double-edged nature of this corporeal rationalization, he fails to explore fully the effects such processes have on the health and illness or, in Freund's terms, the bodily well-being of people. This is sup-rising given Elias's (1985) interests in death and dying. Biology does not stop being a constraint on human action simply because of the increased sophistication of society, and differential rates of mortality and morbidity in contemporary societies suggest the continuing centrality of social *and* biological processes to the constitution of human subjects.

Second, Elias's concept of civilization can be seen as too undifferentiated a mechanism to deal with certain corporeal changes. For example, contem-porary capitalism has placed an increasing discipline on individuals which has forced them to regulate their behaviour at work. In contrast, it might be argued that home life has become more private and less subject to behavioural codes than was the case in court societies. Elias (1978a [1939]) recognizes this in part when he talks about a decline in the 'intensive elaboration of consumption techniques', but does not fully explore the implications of these changes. In contemporary society, private life may well have become more of a 'back-region' where people escape from the demands of waged work (Goffman, 1969). Television dinners and fast food have replaced formal sit-down meals and while farting, belching and nose picking may be socially unacceptable in many public spheres of waged work, they are often carried out unselfconsciously in the privacy of the home. Far from completely internalizing behavioural codes, it could be argued that individuals *selectively apply* standards depending upon the shifting contexts they inhabit.

These codes may also, as Bourdieu (1984) suggests, be adhered to differentially according to a person's social location. Crawford's research (1987) on self-control and health supports this point. He found that demands for bodily control during time-off from waged labour among the working class were likely to be regarded as an invasion of time reserved for 'letting go' and therefore rejected. Similarly, despite the fact that inequalities between women and men may have declined, many would question the suitability of the concept civilization to describe the widespread incidence of rape and sexual harassment that women are still subjected to by men. At the very least, women have borne a disproportionate share of the costs attached to civilizing processes. While both men and women may have increased the monitoring and control of their emotions, behavioural codes are still gendered in important ways. For example, behaviour and talk which pass as 'assertive' for men is often classified as 'aggressive' for women. Indeed, the consequences of attempting to keep a consistently tight reign on their emotions at home and at work may well help explain why far more women than men are diagnosed as suffering from neurotic disorders (Miles, 1988). Gender differences may also be observed in the opportunities which exist for a controlled decontrolling of the emotions in contemporary society. Indeed, the numbers of ways in which women's bodies have been presented and made available for men to consume may be taken to suggest that while men 'let go', women work.

These criticisms may simply be dismissed as signalling a misinterpretation of Elias's use of the term 'civilization'. More generally though, Bauman's analysis (1989) of the relationship between modernity, rationalization and the Holocaust suggests that instead of being its antithesis, mechanisms allowing for genocide and mass destruction may be integrally related to some of the chief characteristics of civilizing processes.

An associated point concerns the discrepancy in time periods concerning the building up and the breaking down of civilizing processes and civilized bodies. As Mennell (1990) points out, civilizing processes take centuries to achieve solidity yet only moments to break down. Why should this be? It sometimes appears as if Elias is having to alter his overall theory to account for the empirical evidence that does not fit it. Elias can be defended against this criticism in so far as he makes clear that the civilization of each new generation is dependent upon the actions of human subjects. In this context, a period of social disorder, which interrupts the usual patterns of socialization, can quickly disrupt long-term civilizing processes. However, there is a problem with this defence. Elias places great emphasis on the internalization of drive control among individuals. This appears to exert an enduring effect on individual behaviour, and assumes a stability that approximates to Pierre Bourdieu's notion of the embodied habitus. Nonetheless, decivilizing processes necessitate that these controls break down rapidly within individuals, a situation which sits uneasily beside their stable internalization.[3]

A third criticism is that Elias allows little room for embodied action resulting in *intended* outcomes. The sum total of individuals' actions creates civilizing processes, but they do not intend their actions to have these effects. The institutions and bodily changes brought about by civilizing processes are neither intended nor planned by individuals (Elias, 1978a [1939]: xvi; 1982 [1939]: 232). The increasingly complex and stable control of conduct is instilled in the individual from his or her earliest years 'as an automaton'. The civilizing process is a compulsion which cannot be resisted even if people consciously wish to oppose it (1982 [1939]: 233). In sum, the intended is dominated by the unintended in the historical process and the creation of civilized bodies, and the civilizing process is an order 'more compelling and stronger than the will and reason of the individual people composing it' (1982 [1939]: 230). Haferkamp (1987) has criticized the a priori weighting given by Elias to unforeseen developments in the historical process and argues that a greater emphasis should be placed on the possibilities of intended outcomes. A similar point can be made with regard to the body. For Elias, bodies themselves become structures which affect the ability of humans to exercise intentional agency (Honneth and Joas, 1988).

Despite these criticisms, Elias's approach to the civilized body is a clear improvement on naturalistic or social constructionist views and represents, in many ways, an exception to the dual approach that sociology has traditionally adopted to the body. His identification of those processes concerned with the socialization, rationalization and individualization of the body is particularly relevant to the growing importance of the body in high modernity.

Notes

1. Elias is careful not to overgeneralize from his study of civilizing processes in European societies. In this respect, the processes leading to the development of civilized bodies in North America may possibly be different to those investigated in this chapter.

2. While Elias tends to talk about the lack of restraints placed on behaviour in medieval times, it could be argued that people were merely following different behavioural codes.

3. It might be argued that this is not a problem in Elias's work as the rapid breakdown of behaviour is dependent on social conditions. However, this still leaves us with the problem of explaining how decivilizing processes occur.

8

The Body, Self-Identity and Death

Over the course of this study I have examined the changing status of the body in sociology, and have assessed the relative merits of different theories of the body. It has been my intention throughout this book to demonstrate the importance for sociology of taking the body seriously. In the previous chapters I have also been concerned to build on the work of several writers who adopt a view of the body as an unfinished, biological and social phenomenon. This view of the body provides us with the outlines of an approach which goes beyond the reductionist tendencies of naturalistic and social constructionist perspectives, and helps explain why the body has become particularly important to modern people. In this chapter, I shall develop the major themes which have informed this book by looking at the relationship between the body, self-identity and death.

Sociological studies of the body have generally been concerned with the living body and have only rarely addressed the demise and death of the embodied individual (Mellor and Shilling, 1993). However, if we take seriously Peter Berger's point that death is an essential feature of the human condition that requires people to develop means of coping with it, then to neglect death is to ignore one of the few universal parameters which impinge upon the body in social systems (Berger, 1990 [1967]). Indeed, it is only in the context of the body's inevitable death that we can understand its full social importance.

In this chapter, I shall examine three ways of locating people within their environment which enable us to take seriously the importance of death to an analysis of the human body and self-identity. Each of these provides distinct, if limited, insights into the body's biological and social constitution. The latter two also suggest why it is that the body has become increasingly important, and the confrontation with death a particular problem, to modern people. Irrespective of modern technological advances, death remains a biological inevitability which is ultimately outside of human control. This fact can pose particular problems to people whose self-identity has at its centre a concern with the body as a project.

The first approach towards death and the body can be derived from the links which exist between philosophical anthropology and Peter Berger's *The Sacred Canopy*, first published in 1967. What Berger conceptualizes as the problem of death can be traced, via philosophical anthropology, to the evolutionary status of humans. The argument here is that humans are a species whose very conditions of embodiment force them to *act*, and to invest themselves and their actions with *meaning*, in order to survive. In this context, the prospect of death constitutes a threat to people's 'world-building' and 'self-building' activities which needs to be dealt with by society through the provision of shared meaning systems. The provision of such systems has become increasingly problematic in modernity, especially in the context of the shrinkage of space occupied by religion.

Berger's work builds sociologically on the insights of philosophical anthropology, and it has been criticized precisely because of the anthropological constancies imputed to humans. Irrespective of their cultural or historical location, humans are seen as having a psychological need for meaning which compels them to act (Abercrombie, 1986; Beckford, 1989). As Turner puts it, Berger's social actors are 'burdened creatures who require the relief (*Entlastung*) of culture' (1992a: 117).

Anthony Giddens (1991) provides a second approach to the relationship between death and the body by examining how the conditions of high modernity have made the modern individual's confrontation with death especially difficult. The radical discontinuity of modernity sweeps away the traditional certainties which characterized pre-modern societies and which provided people with a stable sense of self-identity. It is in this context that Giddens suggests there is a tendency for modern people to become increasingly associated with their bodies, and that the prospect of death poses specific existential problems for these people in high modernity. However, despite the fact that the burden of Giddens's explanation is concerned with the conditions of high modernity, he does not escape completely from the criticisms which have been levelled against Berger's work. In particular, Giddens's analysis of ontological security implies that humans have a fundamental and unchanging need to feel secure about the basic parameters of themselves and the world around them.

I derive the third approach to the relationship between the body and death from the previously examined work of Norbert Elias and Pierre Bourdieu. This is easiest in the case of Elias as he has written explicitly about death in *The Loneliness of the Dying* (1985). However, I build on the work of both of these theorists by locating the contemporary 'problem' of death within the historically developed orientations that people have adopted towards their bodies. Consequently, I view death as having become a particular existential problem for people as a result of modern forms of embodiment, rather than being a universal problem for human beings which assumes the same form irrespective of time or place.

These three approaches have not been chosen arbitrarily. They are included here and are examined in this particular order, as I shall be developing their insights within my own analysis of the relationship between the body, self-identity and death. This suggests that the individualization and rationalization of the body has been accentuated by the organization of death within high modernity.

Paradoxes of the body

The influence of philosophical anthropology on Peter Berger is evident from the very beginning of *The Sacred Canopy*. Citing Gehlen and Plessner, Berger (1990 [1967]: 5) argues that the biological constitution of humans means that they must both construct their world and give meaning to those constructions. However, Berger takes this insight a step further by identifying a central paradox within these world-building and meaning-giving activities of humans which has important implications for the relationship between the body and death. Turner summarizes Berger's argument as follows:

> all reality is socially constructed, as a consequence of Man's incompleteness, but human beings require stable meanings and cannot live in permanent awareness of the socially constructed and precarious nature of everyday reality, and they are forced to clothe these certainties with permanent significance. (Turner, 1992a: 117)

Crucially, this paradox holds for the relationship people have with their bodies and self-identities, as well as for the relationship they have with the world. As Berger (1990 [1967]: 5–6) argues, people must invest their embodied selves with meaning, but these meanings must assume the appearance of an objective reality. Otherwise, existential problems can arise for humans which disrupt their sense of self. In this context, *shared meaning systems* become essential for human beings as a way of hiding them from the contingency of their world-building actions and the uncertainty and fragility of their embodied self-identities.

Thus far, Berger has built sociologically on the insights of philosophical anthropology by suggesting that humans require meaning systems as a result of the paradox which stems from their biological constitution. Traditionally, these meaning systems have taken a number of forms. For example, humans have constructed social positions such as 'mother' and 'father' which act as relatively solid and reliable sources of self-identity. These social positions allow people to order and make sense of their bodily experience of the world. They also become internalized by successive generations and provide people with relatively set ways of relating to themselves and the world (Berger, 1990 [1967]: 14).

More generally, social institutions, such as schools and the military, provide firmly established interpretations of the world and generalized rules for body management, behaviour and appearance, which combat the dangers of people's openness to the world (Gehlen, 1969: 97; Honneth and Joas, 1988: 57). At the widest level, however, it has been *religion* which has traditionally provided humans with the 'sacred canopy' which sustains a shared vision of the world, the body and self-identity.

The importance of death to Berger's analysis becomes clear through his analysis of how these shared meaning systems work and, more specifically, how they can be disrupted. Social positions, institutions and religions are all initially the products of human activity or *externalization*. However, they become *objectivated* for successive generations and assume the status of a reality that confronts individuals as 'social facts'. Finally, humans come to *internalize* these meanings and transform them 'from structures of the objective world into structures of the subjective consciousness' (Berger, 1990 [1967]: 4). Nonetheless, individuals cannot be completely socialized into shared meanings. As Berger argues, 'Consciousness precedes social-ization. What is more, it can never be *totally* socialized – if nothing else the ongoing consciousness of one's own bodily processes ensures this. Socializa-tion, then, is always partial' (1990 [1967]: 83). This means that there is always the possibility for humans to become aware of the contingency of their world-building and self-building activities.

Berger, adapting Karl Jaspers's use of the term, refers to moments when this occurs as 'marginal situations'. Marginal situations push us to the borders of our existence; they force into our consciousness knowledge that the human world is open-ended and unstable, and that the meanings we attribute to our bodies and our world are based on nothing more solid than human activity. The major marginal situation is the individual confronta-tion with death, because this can radically undermine and call into question the 'cognitive and normative operating procedures' of day-to-day life (Berger, 1990 [1967]: 23). In other words, death can threaten the basic assumptions upon which society is organized, as well as open up the indi-vidual to the dread of personal meaninglessness. Death radically questions the taken-for-granted, 'business as usual' attitude which is usually adopted in everyday life (Berger, 1990 [1967]: 43).

Death, then, is an acute social problem for Berger because of its potential to challenge people's sense of what is real and meaningful about their embodied selves and the world around them. The status of the problem of death is also related to the unfinishedness of the human body. We have bodies which are forward orientated in relation to survival and meaning, and which provide the 'foundational potentialities' on which all manner of *future* cultural practices can be constructed (Turner, 1992a: 118). How-ever, while death is an inevitability, the open-endedness of our bodies means that death becomes an existential problem for humans. Zygmunt Bauman (1992a, 1992c) sums up this problem by referring to what he terms the 'ultimate failure of rationality': the human inability to reconcile the 'transcending power of *time-binding* mind and the transience of its *time-bound* fleshy casing'. While Bauman locates this problem in human ration-ality, Berger suggests that it exists more generally as a result of the total conditions of human embodiment. The unfinishedness of human embodi-ment means that the death of the self is presented to the mind as a particular problem.

Shared meaning systems in the face of death assume a particular importance for Berger's analysis. As he puts it, 'In so far as the knowledge of death cannot be avoided in any society, legitimations of the reality of the social world *in the face of death* are decisive requirements in any society'

(1969: 43–4). Furthermore, Berger (1969: 51) argues that religion, or 'the establishment, through human activity, of an all-embracing sacred order', has a particular role to play in providing and sustaining such legitimations. Religion legitimates the world-building activities of people because the cosmos posited by religion both transcends and includes the individual. It appears to the individual as an immensely powerful reality which locates life in an ultimately meaningful order. The individual who internalizes these meanings transcends the contingencies of their own life. As such, religion even allows for the possibility of having a 'good death', that is, a death in which the individual retains to the end a sense of the meaningfulness of their body, their self-identity and the social world (Berger, 1990 [1967]: 26, 32, 44).

Religion, then, has traditionally provided a potent source of self-identity enabling individuals to locate themselves and their bodies within trans-personal meaning structures. For example, dieting in the Christian Middle Ages was related to spiritual purification and the domination and denial of the flesh (Miles, 1992). The unpredictable, sexual impulses of the body were implicated in the adoption of ascetic regimes which glorified the soul and released the spirit (Turner, 1982, 1984). However, there has been a massive shrinkage of space occupied by religious authorities in the modern West. This has undermined the ability of societies to provide people with meaning systems which allow them to deal with death. In this context, the prospect of death can serve to radically undermine people's sense of reality, calling into question and revealing the 'innate precariousness' of even the most fundamental assumptions on which our relation to our bodies and our world are based (Berger 1990 [1967]: 23).

By building on the insights of philosophical anthropology, Berger has much to say about the importance of the individual's confrontation with death which stems from the embodied constitution of humans as an 'open-ended' species. His work also has important implications for how the mind/body relationship is conceptualized as it suggests that the mind's search for meaning is driven by its location within an unfinished body. However, Berger has been criticized repeatedly for the anthropological constancies which inform his analysis. Humans are forced to act, and require a shield from the terror of death, because of the universal biological conditions of their embodiment. Berger also assumes that humans are a meaning-seeking species incapable of sustaining a stable existence apart from the nomic constructions of society (Abercrombie, 1986; Beckford, 1989). As Philip Mellor (1993) points out, a difficulty apparent with such analysis is that if we question the fundamental assumption that humans crave meaning, then Berger's entire theoretical edifice appears highly questionable.

An additional problem with the assumptions that underpin Berger's work is that they do not allow for the possibility that the need humans have for trans-personal meaning structures might vary through time or cross-culturally. This has some peculiarly unsociological consequences. Mellor (1993) identifies one of these by pointing out that although Berger is concerned primarily with the secularization of modern societies, and the consequences of this for the continued legitimation of socially constructed realities, his analysis is meant to apply to all societies. In other words, Berger sees no *essential* difference between the mechanisms by which modern or pre-modern societies are justified and maintained.

Modernity and self-identity

The second approach that locates humans within their environment, in a manner which allows us to take seriously the importance of death to the relationship between the body and self-identity, is provided by the work of Anthony Giddens. In contrast to the highly general concerns of Peter Berger, Giddens is interested much more in how the *distinctiveness* of modern societies presents people with death as a particular existential problem.

In locating people within their contemporary environment, Giddens (1990, 1991) argues that modernity has swept away '*all* traditional types of social order, in quite unprecedented fashion' (1990: 4). High modernity has radicalized these changes even further in terms of the sheer pace of change, the scope of change and the nature of modern institutions. By undermining traditional meaning systems, the conditions of high modernity stimulate within people a heightened reflexivity about life, meaning and death. In this context, the formation and maintenance of self-identity becomes particular problem for modern people.[1]

In traditional societies, identities were received automatically throug ritual practices which connected people and their bodies to the repr duction of long established social positions. High modernity, though, makes self-identity *deliberative* (Lyotard, 1988). The self is no longer seen as a homogeneous, stable core which resides within the individual (Shils, 1981). Instead, identities are formed reflexively through the asking of questions and the continual reordering of self-narratives which have at their centre a concern with the body (Giddens, 1991). Self-identity and the body become 'reflexively organized projects' which have to be sculpted from the complex plurality of choices offered by high modernity without moral guidance as to which should be selected.

The concept of 'lifestyle' is used by Giddens in order to illuminate how individuals seek to establish a meaningful and reliable sense of self-identity in the conditions of high modernity. Lifestyle refers to a relatively inte-grated set of practices chosen by an individual in order to give material form to a particular narrative of self-identity. The more tradition loses its ability to provide people with a secure and stable sense of self, the more indi-viduals have to negotiate lifestyle choices, and attach importance to these choices (Giddens, 1991: 2, 5, 80–1).

The concept of lifestyle dovetails nicely with Giddens's view of the self as a project. Lifestyles always occur within the constraints and opportunities provided by an individual's social location, but in the conditions of high modernity we are all to some extent 'forced' into adopting reflexively constructed lifestyles in order to sustain our self-identities. Lifestyles affect the body as well as the mind, partly because individuals adopt particular *body regimes* as part of their lifestyles. Body regimes are programmes of behaviour relevant to the cultivation of body traits and their adoption has become widespread in the West. For example, in the United States the adoption of health and fitness regimes has reached the stage among sections of the professional middle classes where those who reject them are regarded as deviants (Crawford, 1987).

Philosophical anthropology suggests that the body is always a project for individuals, in that humans are a peculiarly 'world open' species which requires for its survival that they complete themselves and their own environment. Building on Giddens's work, however, I suggest that in high modernity people have become unusually aware of their own unfinishedness. Furthermore, the emphasis that many modern individuals place on their bodies as constitutive of the self can be seen in many respects as a *retreat* from the world-building activity that is imperative to meaningful participation in social systems.

If the experience of living in high modernity is like riding a juggernaut which is out of control (Giddens, 1990), then at least the body provides individuals with a 'last retreat', an entity which *appears* to be a solid basis on which a reliable sense of self can be built. The problem with such investment is that the body has become an increasingly inadequate basis on which this project of the self can be built. This is because the body is itself implicated in technological developments, or 'abstract systems', which have called into question our sense of what the body is.[2]

As Erving Goffman has demonstrated, regularized control of the body is fundamental to the maintenance of self-identity and the appraisal of others. Nevertheless, the control which can be exerted over the body in high modernity has grown. In this respect, Giddens argues that it is increasingly difficult to maintain a view of the body as a 'given', an aspect of nature governed by processes only marginally subject to human intervention. Technological advances and expert knowledge have invaded the body and made it available to be worked on and reconstructed. The growing number of self-help books in the areas of diet, exercise, sex, relaxation, posture and skin care programmes are all illustrations of the body's 'emancipation' from nature. They also aim 'to provide a way of steering between reliance on pre-established bodily habits and the barrage of new information developed within abstract systems (emanating from doctors . . . holistic health practitioners, dieticians, and so forth)' (Giddens, 1991: 100).

The boundaries of the body have shifted away from the natural and on to the social, and the body now has 'a thoroughly permeable "outer layer" through which the reflexive project of the self and externally formed abstract systems enter' (1991: 218). While the human body may have been an unfinished entity from a very early stage in our evolutionary development, affluent societies nowadays have an unprecedented degree of control over how the body is to be 'finished'.

The increased focus which many modern individuals place on the body as constitutive of the self, and the greater degree of control that affluent Western societies can exert over the body, contains a paradox first raised in the introduction to this book. We now have the means to exert an unprecedented degree of control over our bodies, yet we are also living in an age which has thrown into doubt our certainty of what bodies are and how we should control them. The basic dynamic working behind this paradox can be traced to the reflexivity of modernity: the greater the knowledge we gain about our bodies and how to control them, the more is our certainty undermined about what the body is and how it should be controlled. In the conditions of high modernity, our notion of the body is regularly re-examined and reformed in light of new and incoming information that is gained about the body and its changing limits and boundaries. Knowledge about the body rejoins its subject matter, having the effect, in principle, of altering the body (Giddens, 1990).

These circumstances help us account for what has been described as a crisis in our knowledge of what bodies are. Adapting Frank's argument (1991: 39–40), we can view modernity as characterized by a confidence that our knowledge of and control over our bodies was gradually increasing. With advances in our knowledge of medicine, nutrition and the effects of the environment on morbidity and mortality, the body was seen as a knowable object which provided something of a foundation for both the natural and some of the social sciences. However, high modernity has seen the dissolution of much of this certainty. The boundaries which traditionally made secure our knowledge of what the body is have begun to shift as we gain increased power over the construction and control of bodies.

Furthermore, if the 'successes' of modernity have diminished the body's status as a natural and reliable foundation of life, so have its limitations. Despite existing achievements, our ability to exert control over our bodies has been thrown into doubt with the development and rapid spread of AIDS, and with the present failure of the medical community to find a cure for, or prevention against, HIV infection. This is just one instance of the increasingly recognized limitations of medical knowledge – which may eventually be reduced to the fact that it has yet to conquer death – and the inescapable bodily dangers posed by the 'natural' and social environments characteristic of contemporary society.

Giddens's analysis suggests that high modernity places individuals in an environment which constructs death as a particular problem. The prospect of death may always have been disturbing, but the reflexivity of high modernity confronts people with this prospect in a manner which can throw into radical doubt their concern with lifestyle and body regime. Another way of putting this is to note that modern individuals have become increasingly aware that they live in circumstances of 'existential contradiction'; being of the inanimate world, yet set off against it (Giddens, 1984, 1991). In this context, Giddens reminds us of Kierkegaard's point (1941: 147) that the death of our own subjective selves is an 'absolute uncertainty' – something of which we can have no intrinsic understanding.

This situation is especially disturbing to modern individuals as death represents the precise point where human control ends in a world which is orientated to the successful achievement of control. The ability to construct a reliable self-identity through the adoption of lifestyles, which have at their centre a concern with body regimes, is inextricably concerned with control. However, death remains 'the great extrinsic factor to human existence', the point zero at which individuals lose control over themselves and their bodies (Giddens, 1991: 162, 203).

Giddens's analysis of high modernity has at its core a concern with the relation between self-identity and the body which allows us to take seriously the sociological importance of death. Furthermore, this is an analysis which refuses to adopt all of the anthropological constancies that are evident in the work of Peter Berger. However, it is something of an exaggeration on the part of those who have claimed that Giddens makes no assumptions about essential psychological needs. Indeed, Giddens's analysis of ontological security seems to be based squarely upon a view that humans have a fundamental and unchanging need for a secure sense of themselves and the world around them.

Ontological security refers to an individual's 'confidence and trust that the natural and social worlds are as they appear to be, including the basic existential parameters of self and social identity' (Giddens, 1984: 375). To be ontologically secure, is to possess ' "answers" to fundamental existential questions which all human life in some way addresses' (Giddens, 1991: 47). Ontological security allows people to adopt a 'business as usual' approach to social life (Giddens, 1984: 123), yet the meaningfulness provided by ontological security is always threatened by the possibility of disorder or chaos.

Drawing on Kierkegaard's (1944) concept of 'dread', Giddens argues that humans face the prospect of being overwhelmed during 'fateful moments' by anxieties concerning the meaningfulness and reality of themselves and the world around them. Like Berger, Giddens argues that death is the most threatening factor individuals can face in fateful moments as its inevitability, and its status as unknowable and uncontrollable, can radically undermine all that we hold to be real and of value. As Giddens notes (1991: 50) human consciousness of death is 'associated with anxieties of an utterly fundamental sort'.

If Giddens's examination of ontological security is less than ideal – because of its assumptions concerning essential psychological needs – then so is his analysis of the nature/culture relationship (Burkitt, 1992). For Giddens, the human body has moved away from the sphere of nature into the sphere of culture. Nature still intrudes, but tends to do so only in the border areas of birth and death which have been sequestrated from the public gaze and taken over by experts. There is a dualism here which separates out 'culture' from 'nature' in a way which neglects how the evolution of the body has always combined biological *and* social processes (Benton, 1991). The body is increasingly open to reconstruction in high modernity, but it still provides a basis for the social relations and technological advances which facilitate that reconstruction. Indeed, the resistance of the flesh still places very real limits on the degree to which the body can be reconstructed in line with the self-identity of its owner.

These criticisms are not meant to detract from the importance of Giddens's work. Giddens is much more concerned than Berger with the problems of meaning with which modernity confronts people, rather than with the problems of meaning with which people universally confront themselves. In this respect, his analysis of death, self-identity and the body is able to capture much of what is novel about this relationship in high modernity.

The death of the body

The third approach that allows us to take seriously the importance of death to the relationship between self-identity and the human body can be derived from the previously examined work of Norbert Elias and Pierre Bourdieu. In what follows, I shall briefly summarize the implications of their work for an analysis of death before exploring these in more detail through an examination of the sequestration of death in modern societies.[3]

The work of Elias and Bourdieu adds to Berger's and Giddens's analyses of death by providing a deeper and more rounded *corporeal* basis which shapes the individual's existential confrontation with death. This is because the emphases of their analyses have much to say about the historical and the contemporary orientations that individuals have adopted to their bodies. Consequently, we can argue that the existential problem of death identified by Berger has much less to do with the *universal* status of humans as a meaning-seeking species, and much more to do with the psychological problems generated by the orientations that we have adopted towards our bodies in the conditions of high modernity.

Pierre Bourdieu has highlighted the multiple commodification of the body in modernity. Social systems incorporate within them a variety of social fields which attach values to different types of bodies. In these conditions, there is a tendency for people's self-identity to become increasingly tied to their bodies. In this respect, although he overstates his case, Goffman's analysis of stigma is relevant as it suggests that an individual's sense of self is likely to be affected by judgements made about the worth of their body. Furthermore, as Mike Featherstone (1987) argues, the values attached to particular bodily forms can change rapidly within contemporary consumer culture and induce uncertainty about the body. These developments can serve to heighten an individual's reflexivity about their body and make people feel fundamentally uneasy about their embodied self.

Nonetheless, in all of these contexts, value is attached to the *living*, acting body, and old age brings with it for most social classes a decline in the symbolic value of the body. Consequently, it should not be surprising if the prospect of dying makes modern individuals particularly anxious. For the individual whose self-identity has become closely connected to their body, death is disturbing partly because it represents an end to value in a world geared towards the accumulation of value. Death represents the ultimate end of the self and, once it has been buried or burnt, places severe limits on the body as a bearer of value. An individual may struggle to secure selective treatment for their corpse, but their efforts remain ultimately dependent on the actions of others (Bendann, 1969). In the case of cryonics, for instance, the frozen corpse is dependent on living scientists to find a cure for death (Kamerman, 1988).

Bourdieu's analysis also provides us with the means to differentiate between how various people confront the prospect of death. Berger and Giddens stress the *general* existential problems which death poses to humans and are much less concerned with how this confrontation can vary between people. Giddens analyses the differences between modern and pre-modern societies, but has little to say about variations among modern people. However, Bourdieu's analysis suggests that the modern confrontation with death is likely to differ depending upon an individual's habitus. For example, we might expect the prospect of bodily demise and death to vary for people as a consequence of the time and effort they have invested in their bodies as a source of symbolic capital.

As well as being concerned with the body as a bearer of value, Norbert Elias's writings analyse the historical socialization, rationalization and individualization of the body. The socialization of the body refers to the way in which we have become associated with our bodies as social phenomena and have sought to hide away from view any traces of their natural functions. However, irrespective of the technological advances made in modernity, we cannot escape from the fact that our bodies are biological as well as social entities. In particular, we cannot escape from the inevitability of their demise and death. We might speculate from Elias's work that the further we seek to define our bodies as social, and the more investment we make in body projects, the more difficult and disturbing it will be to come to terms with their end.

The rationalization of the body in Elias's work refers to the increased degree of control that modern individuals are able to exert over their emotions and bodily actions. Historically, rationalization has also involved the division of the body into progressively more detailed parts and processes. As Zygmunt Bauman (1992a, 1992c) argues, this has helped facilitate among modern people a subjective avoidance of death through a concentration on identifying and controlling the current and specific limitations of the body. Finally, the individualization of the body refers to how the body has come to be experienced in the West as a 'case' or 'barrier' separating individuals from each other and from the external world. With the rising demands of affect control in modernity, individuals invest more effort in monitoring and managing their bodies, yet tend to lose many of the satisfactions they once gained from their bodies. These processes of rationalization and individualization are related, and their effects serve increasingly to leave people alone with their bodies, reflecting more upon the character of their bodies, in the face of death.

In short, the work of Bourdieu and Elias can be read as having much to say about the modern tendency for people to adopt a heightened reflexivity towards their bodies and why, in this context, the prospect of death should appear so disturbing. The socialization, individualization and rationalization of the body in particular can also be explored further by looking at the changing organization of death in modern societies. Elias perceives the causes of our closer association with the body as bound up with the changing webs of interdependency formed by people. However, Elias is less precise when it comes to specifying exactly what types of relationships constitute these webs. In this respect we can develop Elias's work, which includes an analysis of the experience of dying, by looking at the organization of death in society. Examining the changing organization of death also highlights the relevance of Giddens's work on high modernity, and the importance of meaning systems for *modern* individuals.

The visibility of death

Those studies which have been conducted into the history of death identify several themes which are relevant to the individualization and rationalization of the body, which affect the modern person's confrontation with death. These involve a gradual privatization in the organization of death (or a decrease in the public space afforded to death); a shrinkage in the scope of the sacred in terms of the experience of death; and a fundamental shift in the corporeal boundaries, symbolic and actual, associated with the dead and the living. These developments have accompanied and accentuated shifts in the orientations individuals have adopted to their bodies and have made the prospect of death increasingly problematic for modern people.

The work of Phillipe Ariès (1974, 1981) has been particularly influential in mapping these changes. Ariès argues that death, until recently, has always been a social phenomenon, an event which produced communal responses and which was contained by collective signs and rituals. When death occurred its significance denoted a disruption to the *social body* more than it did the passing of an *individual body*. There was a resignation about one's own death, an acceptance that nothing could be done about it. Furthermore, as identity was rooted more in the group than within the individual, death did not threaten the individual in the same way as it does in the modern world (Elias, 1982 [1939]; Walter, 1991). Death meant that society had lost a part of itself, more than that an individual had lost society (Bloch and Parry, 1982).

Protestantism did not *initially* stimulate a greater fear of death, nor provoke the modern desire to sequester it away from public spaces. However, it did tend to particularize death in terms of its concern with the *individual's* confrontation with death (e.g. Douglas, 1977). The symbolic boundaries through which death was organized gradually shifted from the social body to the individual body. Focus shifted to the forms of body management that would lead to a 'good death' for the individual, and away from the social rituals which would ensure the continuation of the social body. Although death in this context remained an event of immense religious significance, the Protestant desacralization or, in Weber's term, disenchantment of much of reality, helped prepare for the eventual desacralization of death itself. In making death more of an individual phenomenon, Protestantism prefigures the eventual, more radical removal of death from public space. The privatization of death could not be complete while it retained religious significance, but with the decline of traditional religious belief, there was less of an impulse to keep death in the public domain.

These events help us understand contemporary attitudes to death. Rather than being an open, communal event, death is now a relatively hidden, private experience which is marked by increased uneasiness over the boundaries between the corporeal bodies of the living and the dead. When an individual dies it is likely that she or he will be isolated from families and friends and subjected to the professional control of medical discourse and practical expertise. As Bauman (1992c) notes, death in modern conditions has been given 'its own location in social space, a segregated location; it has been put in custody of selected specialists boasting scientific credentials'. Even the funeral service itself has been viewed as a collective 'shying away from mortality' rather than a communal attempt to deal with death in a meaningful way (Huntingdon and Metcalf, 1979: 195). Embalming, for example, can be seen as an attempt to hide the decomposition of the corpse until it has been buried or burned. As Lyndsay Prior (1989: 161–2) notes, death is only put on display when it is in accord with a socially acceptable image. The once traditional practice of keeping the body in the home for the few days preceding the funeral has also become increasingly rare.

These processes of individualization and privatization in the organization of death have important implications for the strength of boundaries between the bodies of the living and the dead. Their cumulative effect is to ˙ ˙people uncertain, socially unsupported and vulnerable when it ˙ling with death. Elias (1985) argues that this makes people ˙ome into contact with the dying. Elias tends to overgeneralize ˙ssion of death, and his comments may not be valid for every ˙ people, such as terminally ill children. However, his general point remains valid. Unable to confront the reality of the demise and death of their own bodies, the self-identities of individuals are often made insecure by the presence of death in other people's bodies. This can result in an increase in the boundaries surrounding the bodies of the living and the dying, and a consequent tendency to shun the dying:

> [We have] an inability to give dying people the help and affection they are most in need of when parting from other human beings, just because another's death is a reminder of one's own. (Elias, 1985: 10)

As Elias notes, people tend not to like touching the dying, fearing subconsciously that death is somehow contagious. The development of medicine, sanitation and improved diets has meant that death can be now pushed back into the darker corners of our minds, since the time of most people's death is likely to be fairly far off, though the phenomenon of AIDS has complicated this. The dying make death real, immediately present, so people tend to cut themselves off from the dying emotionally and spatially, locating them in hospitals away from everyday life. As Elias (1985: 85) notes, 'Never before have people died as noiselessly and hygienically as today in these societies, and never in social conditions so much fostering solitude'.

This medicalization of death is a particularly significant manifestation of the disappearance of death from the public domain. While the *discussion* of death occupies a form of public space (Walter, 1991), hospitals can be seen as the institutional expression of the modern desire to sequester *bodily* evidence of sickness and death away from the public gaze. This is reinforced by the hiding of dead bodies in hospitals and their carefully regulated transfer from hospitals. The organization of space in funeral parlours also serves to keep the recently bereaved away from any immediately visible signs of dead bodies (Illich, 1976). Locating the sick in hospitals and the dead in back-regions means that many people only have to encounter decaying bodies through choice. This organization remains even in the case of hospices, which still remove the dying from their families and local communities.

At the same time as death is hidden from the public gaze, there is a growing demand for representations of death: from war documentaries and news, to violent movies and television series based around hospital casualty departments. It is as if the growing removal of actual death from the public sphere has stimulated a demand for an anaesthetized 'knowledge' of death. Perhaps the thousands of deaths we see on television each year stand as an empty testament to our continued existence.

The deferral of death

The organization of death within modernity strengthens the boundaries between living and dying bodies and accentuates the individualization of bodies. However, the modern reluctance to come into contact with the dying, and the medicalization of death, can also be seen in terms of what Bauman (1992a) has called 'survival strategies'. Survival strategies are characterized by attempts to keep death at bay through a strategic manoeuvring between various life-options. People deny death by engrossing themselves in projects geared towards ensuring their survival which are increasingly focused upon maintaining the health of their bodies.

Traditionally, it can be argued that religion served the purpose of survival strategies. Bauman notes that religion has sought to deny the finality of death in various ways. For example, in Hinduism there is a pattern whereby death is privatized but this is compensated for by a collective immortality, the idea of the permanence of being relativizing the relationship between life and death so that they are seen as 'exchangeable forms of eternal being' (Bauman, 1992a: 2). The Christian denial has been through its insistence on personal immortality, or at least the immortality of the soul. Trust in God enables Christians to transcend their bodily limitations by believing that the death of the body is not the death of the person (Bauman, 1992a: 13) and that the resurrection of the body will occur with the Second Coming of Christ. In short, putting trust in God has been a particularly effective policy of survival. Once this belief is called into question, however, then Christianity loses its potential to reassure that death can be meaningful.

Bauman suggests that the relative absence of religious survival strategies in the face of death is now compensated for by a policy of *self-care* (Bauman, 1992a: 18). This focuses not on the ultimate mortality of the body, but on how its specific and localized limits can be overcome through what 1 have referred to earlier as body projects. A major feature of this survival strategy is the pervasive concern with issues relating to health and the body. As Bauman notes (1992c: 141), if the cancellation of death is not a realistic goal of life, lifelong health is.

Keeping the body in a healthy and shapely condition is a time consuming business – requiring constant vigilance against health risks and hours of working-out in the gym or aerobics studio – which leaves people little time to think about death itself. When Bauman comments that 'death from natural causes is diminishing' (1992a: 19), he is referring us to the fact that each death now has an individual explanation. Death has been so privatized and individualized that each death is understood to be the product of a particular cause, such as lung cancer, heart failure, a blood clot, kidney failure and so on. No death is considered to be complete without a post-mortem which has successfully identified its (theoretically *preventable*) cause.

These processes contribute towards the general rationalization of the dead body which has occurred in high modernity. As Lyndsay Prior notes, 'the nature of "mortality" was endlessly and meticulously broken down into finer and finer divisions. . . . And it was measured through ever more complex instruments, namely, crude death rates, infant death rates, occupational mortality rates, adult rates, male and female rates and standardized rates' (1989: 8). We may now hear of *categories* of dead people, but, as Bauman puts it, 'we do not hear of people dying of mortality' (1992a: 5; 1992c: 138). This attitude encourages modern persons to stop smoking, eating fatty foods and to begin taking more exercise, while diverting their attention from the fact that all of these things are ultimately futile. Death gets us all in the end.

This reduction of death to an individual event with an individual cause is therefore one more representation of the individualization and rationalization of the body and the modern sequestration of death. An 'unexplained death' is scandalous to modern sensibilities because people no longer recognize the inevitability and universality of death (Bauman, 1992a: 20), but instead seek to contain each instance of it in a specific medical explanation. Modernity has made death a radically unnatural occurrence.

It is worth recalling here Berger's and Giddens's point that the individual experience of 'marginal situations' or 'fateful moments' makes the subjective deferral of death inevitably contingent and problematic. Elias's work enables us to view this situation slightly differently: although the rationalization and individualization of the body may serve to defer the subjective confrontation with death, it also has the effect of leaving people alone with their bodies in the face of death. Body projects concerned with health and fitness require a degree of investment in the body which can help to defer thoughts about death. When these projects begin to go wrong, however, as they inevitably must, when the body refuses to be reconstructed in line with the designs of its owner, then this investment in the body can itself serve to make the prospect of death particularly real and terrifying.

Death and the narcissistic body

Arthur Frank's 'action-problems' theory of the body, which was examined in Chapter 4, includes a typology of different orientations that people adopt to their bodies. One of these orientations is referred to as the 'mirroring body', a concept which draws on Christopher Lasch's view of the narcissistic personality. Lasch argues that the narcissistic personality may be the dominant type emerging in the conditions of modernity, and it is worth briefly examining Lasch's work here. The narcissistic personality can be viewed as adopting a bodily orientation which is affected most profoundly both by the sequestration of death, and by the processes of socialization, rationalization and individualization identified by Elias.

Discussing dominant trends in the formation of self-identity in contemporary American culture, which place particular importance on the youthful body, Lasch comments that old age 'holds a special terror for people today' (Lasch, 1991: 207). While it is reasonable to assume that women and men have always feared death to some extent, this fear takes on a special intensity in societies where the space occupied by religion and the sacred has shrunk, and which are interested more in prizing youth and the future rather than in posterity. The prospect of death cannot be contained easily within such a context because it represents no future in a culture orientated to futures. Lasch identifies one possible consequence of this when he argues that the dread of old age and death can produce an almost neurotic desire to remain youthful, a refusal to accept one's own ageing. Offering a bleak vision of the relations between different generations, Lasch notes how the lack of interest in posterity produces an ambivalent attitude to youthfulness:

> Because the older generation no longer thinks of itself as living in the next, of achieving vicarious immortality in posterity, it does not give way gracefully to the young. People cling to the illusion of youth until it can no longer be maintained, at which point they must either accept their superfluous status or sink into dull despair. (Lasch, 1991: 213)

The older generation desires eternal youth but resents the embodiment of youth and vitality in the younger generation. These attitudes are expressed most fully by what Lasch sees as the dominant personality type of our time, the 'narcissistic personality'.

The narcissistic personality has a 'pervasive uneasiness about reproduction', which stems not only from the fact that having children may disrupt reflexively constructed life plans, but from the fact that producing children demands they face up to their own mortality (Featherstone and Hepworth, 1983; Hepworth and Featherstone, 1982). The narcissistic personality develops in high modernity under conditions of moral deprivation which are closely related to the shrinkage of the sacred in modern life. It seeks to shut itself off from fears of death through its refusal and inability to form deep or enduring relationships with others. When no great attachments are formed, no great losses can be experienced.

Central to the narcissistic personality is an orientation to the body as youthful, enduring and constitutive of the self. The narcissistic body is open to new experiences, but only as long as they can be easily appropriated and consumed to reinforce its own sense of self as sacred and immortal (Frank, 1991). Old relationships and responsibilities are to be replaced with new contacts and opportunities which can validate this sense of self. The narcissistic personality is not confined to the young, but is evident as a type in the therapeutic and psychological mechanisms which older people are increasingly encouraged to draw upon:

> The psychology of growth, development, and 'self-actualisation' presents survival as a spiritual progress, resignation as renewal. In a society in which most people find it difficult to store up experience and knowledge (let alone money) against old age, or to pass on accumulated experience to their descendants, the growth experts compound the problem by urging people past forty to cut their ties to the past, embark on new careers and new marriages ('creative divorce'), take up new hobbies, travel light, and keep moving. (Lasch, 1991: 214)

With Giddens we might question the unremitting bleakness of this analysis: Lasch pictures individuals as passive agents at the mercy of external social forces and modern expert systems (Giddens, 1991: 175). As Giddens notes, modern life *does* impoverish human action, but at the same time it also facilitates new possibilities and opportunities. It is also prudent to acknowledge that this cutting of ties with the past, which Lasch finds so alarming, will be experienced as profoundly liberating by many people and not just those who necessarily correspond to the narcissistic personality type (for example, women who have been trapped in oppressive and violent relationships). Nevertheless, it is generally the case that perspectives and practices focused on the cutting of social ties and the cultivation of self and the youthful body do not seem likely to be able to account for death very adequately, since death is so inherently undermining of an ethos of movement and growth. When only the self is left, no external referents remain which actually provide a justification for life. As Bauman notes (1992c: 40), the continued being of the self makes sense only in so far as there are others to give that self meaning.

In this context, the phenomenon of AIDS is likely to be particularly disturbing to the narcissistic personality. AIDS has proved fatal to the young, as well as to the old, as a result of what has long been considered a major source of personal gratification – sexual activity. This link between sexuality and death confronts the living, sensuous body with the prospect of its own demise. It exposes the intimate connection between the flesh as a source of 'ultimate' joy and the source of decay and death. It confronts even the narcissistic personality with the reality that in addition to the agentic possibilities which stem from having bodies, humans are limited by the brute fact of being bodies.

The fear associated with AIDS can also be understood partly by reference to the sequestration of death. When death is associated with old age, the narcissistic personality can put off thinking about it until that time. However, when people become aware that death may be already lurking in their bodies, and those of their sexual partners, its reality becomes more pressing. In high modernity, death is not present simply at the end of life, but can speak to us during the very moments that we affirm and create life.

Love, sex and death

Moving away from Lasch's specific analysis of the narcissistic personality, the loving, erotic relationship has come to be seen as a focus for considerable personal and emotional investment in modernity (Giddens, 1991: 205). Here, the subjective deferral of death can be sought by investing hope and meaning in a loved one. However, as Bauman argues, 'Terminal dangers surround the love relationship on both sides' (1992c: 29). The loved one is another mortal creature whose very existence provides regular reminders of bodily fragility and mortality.

The contradictions which exist in using love as a 'policy of survival' are particularly clear in the case of sexual reproduction:

> sexual procreation is a method through which the species preserves its
> immortality *at the expense of the mortality* of its individual members. The
> cunning of the species leaves its indelible stamp, and for this reason erotic
> partnership is, deep down, unfit for the role of the vehicle of individual
> transcendence of death. (Bauman, 1992c: 29)

Ageing bodies present a further problem for the love relationship as a
means of deferring the subjective confrontation with death. With their
diminutions of strength, stamina and physical attractiveness, ageing bodies
disadvantage their possessors in two major ways: first, aged bodies are
sequestrated from public attention; and second, the aged's attitude to their
own bodies is problematized by the ultimate resistance of flesh to the
reflexive constructions and demands of body projects.

If the *decline* of bodies is at odds with the prioritization of the erotic
relationship in modernity, their *demise* is even more so. In this respect, the
association, through AIDS, of death with sexuality is going to be particularly disconcerting. The destruction wrought by AIDS tells people not
only that the meaning they have invested in their sexual relationships
cannot protect them from the reality of death, but that the very focus of
this investment can be a channel through which death now enters their
lives. It may be that the paradox this situation highlights to modern
individuals at fateful moments is that *life* is the ultimate cause of death
(Bauman, 1992a).

The loneliness of the dying

Elias has written of the loneliness of people who are dying, a loneliness
represented by their removal from home to hospital, and by the increasing
emotional and bodily detachment of friends and family which they may
have to endure as soon as their condition is known. People find it difficult to
know what to say to a dying person partly because they have no further use
for the language of survival (Bauman, 1992c: 130). However, death is so
alarming in contemporary Western societies not simply because modernity
has deprived increasing numbers of people with the means of containing it
– in an overarching, existentially meaningful, ritual structure – but because
of the historically and socially developed orientations to the body that have
left people alone with their bodies in the face of death. It is in this respect
that 'our existential questions' in the face of death 'are rooted in the
biographical history of bodies – their being in and departure from the
world' (Turner, 1991a: 246).

Luckmann suggests that the dominant representations of the sacred
today originate in, and refer to, the area of individual existence (Luckmann,
1967: 107). Neither ageing nor death figure in these representations, since
the quintessentially modern individual is young and never dies (1967: 114).
The reduction of the scope of the sacred from the wider cosmos to the area
of individual existence mirrors the transference of the significance of death

from the social body to the individual body. This general privatization of meaning and experience leaves embodied individuals alone with the difficult task of constructing and maintaining values to guide them through life and death.

Notes

1. This reflexivity is bound up with the project of the Enlightenment. As Giddens notes (1990: 48–9), promoting the powers of reason as the path to knowledge contained its own paradox: 'If the sphere of reason is wholly unfettered, no knowledge can rest upon an unquestioned foundation, because even the most firmly held notions can only be regarded as valid "in principle" or "until further notice"'. In this context, high modernity replaces traditional answers about self-identity, meaning and order with questions.

2. Abstract systems consist of 'symbolic tokens' such as money, which separate transactions from their immediate context, and 'expert systems', which are systems of technical accomplishment or professional expertise that organize large areas of material and social environments. Abstract systems serve to remove social relationships from immediate contexts of co-presence and necessitate a great deal of trust from the users of these systems.

3. This analysis of the sequestration of death is concerned with *dominant tendencies within modernity* (Mellor and Shilling, 1993). This does not, of course, preclude other, minority responses to death. For example, Walter (1991: 299) notes that 'the first generation of Caribbean and Asian immigrants from the 1950s and 1960s is beginning to die. Their funerals are often much more elaborate and ritualized than white urban British funerals'. However, as he notes, this minority practice does not appear to be influencing the rituals of other groups in modernity.

9

Concluding Comments

In analysing the position of the body in sociology, I have argued that the discipline has traditionally adopted a dual approach to the body. The body has been absent from sociology in the sense that the discipline has rarely focused on the body as an area of investigation in its own right. However, while the body may seldom have been an explicit concern of sociology, its interest in the structure and organization of industrial societies inevitably led sociology to deal with aspects of human embodiment. Furthermore, classical sociology did not completely ignore the human body. As Karl Marx's analysis of the division of labour and Max Weber's work on rationalization demonstrate, the human body was just too important to neglect entirely.

More recent writers such as Erving Goffman and Michel Foucault did much to rectify certain aspects of this dual approach. While the body was named as a theoretical space in their work, however, there was a tendency for that space to remain uninvestigated and undertheorized. For example, Foucault has done much to suggest how power is invested in the body, yet we hear much more about power than we do about the body in his studies. The problem with this approach, and with social constructionist views of the body more generally, is that there is a tendency for the human body to be reduced to social forces. This is exemplified by Foucault's epistemological view of the body as existing only in discourse.

Of course, if we recognize that the body is unfinished at birth, *all* bodies are socially constructed to some degree. Social categories label bodies, socially controlled diets affect their size, health and height, and families and schools participate in the inculcation of 'body techniques'. However, merely to state that the body is socially constructed does not tell us enough about what it is that is being constructed; it fails to consider just how socially constructed the body is, and neglects the possibility that certain dimensions of our embodiment might be more amenable to social intervention than others.

Alternative traditions of social thought have focused more centrally on the body. As I argued in Chapter 2, however, these tend to be less than satisfactory. In naturalistic views, the body steps outside of society and becomes the pre-social, biological basis of social relationships and inequalities. Now, I have been concerned in this book to stress the importance of taking seriously the material, biological and physical dimensions of the body. However, naturalistic views both overstate and underestimate the importance of the biological body to society. They overstate its influence by assuming that social phenomena can be seen as direct and unmediated products of the body. They understate its importance by failing to perceive that social inequalities can themselves become embodied.

Several recent sociological studies have sought to build something of a bridge, or, perhaps more accurately, to steer a course between the reductionist tendencies apparent in social constructionist and naturalistic views of the body. The works of Bob Connell and Peter Freund recognize that while the body cannot be explained away by social factors, neither can it be analysed as something which exists beyond or outside of society. More precisely, there is a recognition of the body as a simultaneously social and biological phenomenon. I have suggested that this entails that:

1   The human body at birth is itself the product of evolutionary processes which are affected by social as well as biological processes.
2   As the body develops it is taken up and transformed, within limits, by social factors.
3   The body is not only affected by social relations but forms a basis for and enters into the construction of social relations.

This view of the body implies that sociology needs to broaden its disciplinary boundaries if it is to start appreciating the full social importance of the body.

The work of Connell, Freund and Hochschild, examined in Chapter 5, demonstrates the inadequacy of the Cartesian mind/body dualism which has traditionally characterized sociology. Each of their studies can be seen as demonstrating in different ways the important insights of Mark Johnson and George Lakoff on the bodily bases of perception and social categories. Instead of being separate from the body, the mind is located within, and is inextricably linked to, the body. The categories and images we use and build up about social and natural life are not independent of our corporeal existence but are based firmly in it.

The studies of Connell, Freund and Hochschild are also relevant to my concern with the body as a project. By examining the unfinishedness of the body, they provide grounds for accepting that the body is something which can be monitored and shaped by concerned individuals and social systems. Furthermore, they each point to inequalities in the degree to which people are able to treat their bodies as projects. Occupational position, gender and ethnicity are just three of the variables that can affect the orientations individuals adopt towards their bodies. Similarly, if people are as reflexively aware of their bodies as Giddens suggests, then we may expect those in positions of subordination, without the time or resources to nurture their bodies, to be particularly prone to feelings of alienation and disaffection. Indeed, these feelings have been documented in the case of women by the valuable work of Emily Martin (1989 [1987]).

My analysis of the body as a project in high modernity involves two initial propositions: that we now have the knowledge and the technical ability in the affluent West to intervene in, and substantially alter, the body; nd that growing numbers of people are increasingly aware of the body as n unfinished entity which is shaped and 'completed' partly as a result of festyle choices. The idea of the body as a project does not entail that veryone has the willingness or the ability radically to transform their body. does presuppose that people are generally aware of these transformative evelopments, and that there is a strong tendency in the conditions of ontemporary Western societies for people to become increasingly associated with, and concerned about, their bodies. This is not meant to imply that modern people are the first to be concerned about their bodies. As Bernard Rudofsky (1986) demonstrates, different cultural and tribal groups have long inscribed their identities on the bodies of their members. However, in contrast to pre-modern societies, where the body tended to be marked by traditional signs in ritualized settings, the body in modernity is more frequently treated as a phenomenon to be shaped, decorated and trained as an expression of an *individual's* identity.

The schizophrenic body in structuration theory

In examining the notion of body projects I have sought to develop, in a new direction, Anthony Giddens's suggestive analysis of the self as a reflexively constructed phenomenon. Giddens's work has come under detailed scrutiny in recent years and it is surprising that his view of the body has yet to be examined in any detail (e.g. Bryant and Jary, 1991; Clark, Modgil and Modgil, 1990; Cohen, 1989; Craib, 1992). As Giddens's view of the body provides a good contrast to the broad approach I have been seeking to develop in this study, and as the body constitutes something of a critical case for structuration theory, I want to begin rectifying that omission in the conclusion to this book.

Anthony Giddens's recent theoretical writings divide into two main, related, categories: an elaboration and defence of structuration theory, and the development of an original analysis of modernity. Structuration theory is designed to overcome many of the dualisms which have characterized social science and is concerned, above all, with overcoming the structure/ agency division. Giddens's solution to this problem has been to argue that, rather than constituting a dualism, 'structure' and 'agency' form a *duality*. 'Structures' are both the medium and outcome of social intercourse (Giddens, 1979: 5; 1981: 171; 1984: 26). 'Structures' are not social facts in the Durkheimian sense, but sets of 'rules' and 'resources' which actors draw on, and hence reproduce, in social interaction.

In one sense, Giddens's comments on the body complement his view of the structure/agency relationship. Human bodies are themselves the medium and outcome of human (reproductive) labour. Furthermore, as well as constraining human action, bodies provide us with the means to intervene in, and alter the flow of, daily life. However, a limitation of

174

implies agency.

Giddens's structuration theory is that it fails to specify how we go about ascertaining the conditions under which bodies constrain and enable action. Indeed, Giddens's writings alternate between presenting us with voluntaristic and deterministic views of the body.

Bryan Turner has concentrated on the deterministic tendencies of structuration theory by arguing that the body is primarily treated 'as a constraint on action and therefore in some sense "outside" the actor' (Turner, 1992a: 87). Turner's view is supported by the comments Giddens makes about the body being a 'physical constraint' which imposes 'strict limitations upon the capabilities of movement and perception of the human agent' (Giddens, 1984: 111; 1990: 258). However, Turner is wrong to argue that structuration theory relegates the body 'to a feature of the constraining environment' (Turner, 1992a: 87). As Giddens (1984) makes clear, the body is enabling as well as constraining.

I suggest that it is more accurate to view Giddens's major works on *structuration theory* as displaying what is *predominantly* a deterministic view of the body. In contrast, his analyses of *modernity* (which contain within them substantive investigations of the central theoretical concerns of structuration theory) exhibit a voluntaristic view of the body. The source of this oscillation between determinism and voluntarism can be found in Giddens's conceptualization of the relationship between nature and culture. This becomes particularly clear if we compare *The Constitution of Society* (1984) with *Modernity and Self-Identity* (1991).

Whereas *The Constitution of Society* locates the body as organism within the realm of nature, *Modernity and Self-Identity* argues that nature and the body have become colonized by society and the reflexively mobilized self. The body is 'less and less of an extrinsic "given", functioning outside the internally referential systems of modernity, but becomes itself reflexively mobilized' (1991: 7). In traditional societies, 'The body used to be one aspect of nature, governed in a fundamental way by processes only marginally subject to human intervention', It was a 'given' (1991: 218). In contrast, the body becomes increasingly malleable in high modernity and 'We become responsible for the design of our own bodies' (1991: 102).

In *Modernity and Self-Identity* Giddens effectively establishes a divide between nature and culture (Burkitt, 1992) which is both unnecessary and unhelpful to an analysis of the body. Nature tends only to intrude in high modernity at the extreme points of birth and death. However, if we want to understand the body as both forming a basis for social relations (as well as being affected by social relations) and as offering varying opportunities for human action, we need to recognize that the body has its own history as a simultaneously biological and social phenomenon. *As the human body has evolved through the centuries, through the interweaving of biological and social factors, it has provided people with different opportunities for action*. While the body is always constraining and enabling, in the very broad sense of those terms, we need to examine human embodiment at particular stages of its development if we are to ascertain the balance between these features.

for e. dis,
biological
constitution = imp

Many people in the affluent West may have an unprecedented degree of control over their bodies, but this does not mean that the body has become infinitely reconstructable. As Ulrich Beck (1992) points out, we live in a risk society where the dangers to our physical health have become, in certain respects, incalculable. Nuclear reactors, food additives, pesticides and the erosion of the ozone layer, all pose dangers to our health which pay little heed to our attempts to reconstruct our bodies. Indeed, the inconclusive nature of scientific knowledge can pose great obstacles to our successful adoption of body projects. Having taken up running over a number of years in the belief that it will make me fitter and healthier, I then learn that the wear and tear of the exercise has permanently damaged my hips. I then adopt a low fat diet in order to safeguard my health, but hear that some of the additives used in margarine may be a contributory factor to heart disease. Just because scientific knowledge and technological developments increase the degree to which we are able to alter our bodies does not mean that their biological constitution becomes unimportant.

These brief observations do not alter the fact that the body is simultaneously enabling and constraining. Indeed, this is one of the themes which I have explored throughout this book. Nevertheless, we need to examine the work of writers like Bob Connell, Peter Freund, Norbert Elias and Pierre Bourdieu if we are to examine more precisely the conditions that affect the degree to which the body is constraining and enabling for different groups of people at particular historical conjunctures.

Bringing all of the body back in

The analysis contained in Chapter 5 of this book provides insights into the body as a project, and indicates in broad terms a general sociological approach towards the body. The same can also be said of the work of Norbert Elias and Pierre Bourdieu. Both of these theorists hold on to a view of the body as a material and physical phenomenon, while exploring in detail how the body becomes enmeshed within and transformed by social relations. Elias's analysis of the historical figurations which lead to the socialization, rationalization and individualization of the body, and Bourdieu's analysis of the body as a form of physical capital, both provide insights into why it is that the body has become a project for modern people. They also allow us to differentiate between people who are more or less disposed to treat their bodies as projects. Bourdieu does this through his view of the bodily dispositions encouraged by the habitus, and Elias analyses these differences by placing a greater emphasis on historical developments and changes.

Birth and death are the two points which represent human entry into, and exit from, social life. While feminist writers have scrutinized the male-dominated processes which have historically surrounded conception, pregnancy and childbirth, much less theoretical work has been conducted into the subject of death. However, death is particularly important to the sociology of the body. As Lyndsay Prior (1989) has argued, the dead body represents a focal point for religious, medical and social discourses. My interest in Chapter 8 of this book was less on the dead body, though, and more on the embodied individual's confrontation with death. Here again, the work of Norbert Elias in particular is able to illuminate how people's orientations to the body can affect their confrontation with death. Technological interventions in the body may have thrown into doubt our ability to define the body with any certainty, but the individualized orientations we have developed towards our bodies leave us increasingly alone with our bodies in the face of death.

The sociology of the body is still in its infancy and it would have been unwise in this study to attempt to develop a comprehensive theory of the body. I have sought instead to describe and build on a range of existing work in order to suggest the outlines of an approach towards human embodiment which sociologists might productively draw on when conducting future studies on the body. The body is centrally implicated in questions of self-identity, the construction and maintenance of social inequalities, and the constitution and development of societies. It is far too important a subject for sociologists to leave to the natural sciences.

Afterword
Embodiment, Identity and Theory

I wrote *The Body and Social Theory* in the early 1990s for several reasons. At that time I thought it was important to try to map out a field of what we might now refer to as 'body studies', and to highlight existing theoretical resources that contained within them an appreciation of the social significance of the body. I also sought to develop a broad theoretical approach towards embodiment which took the materiality of human physicality seriously, and chose to do this by building on the writings of Pierre Bourdieu, Anthony Giddens and, most significantly, Norbert Elias. In this new afterword, I want to build analytically on three themes that were central to the first edition in the context of the most important recent developments in the field. These themes resonate most strongly with current debates in the area, and with my contemporary work on the subject, and highlight distinctive dimensions of the ongoing endeavour to construct a fully embodied sociology. Reflecting the order in which I deal with them in this chapter, they are the 'absent presence' of the body in social thought, the relationship between the body and self-identity, and the question of how to advance theoretically the study of the body in society.

These three themes are related in that the problems associated with conceptualizing the body as an absent presence continue to pervade dominant conceptions of self-identity in the literature and have yet to be overcome fully within general theories of the body. Such problems have contributed to the sense that there has been something of an *impasse* in theorizing the body in recent years; a situation that has been reinforced by the tendency for dominant approaches to the subject to be presented as general theories when they actually revolve around the conceptualization of completely different and often equally partial views of embodiment. If we want to improve upon this situation, I argue, we need to recognize the particularity of these approaches without throwing away the genuine gains they have made, and to acknowledge the full presence of the body in the constitution of identity and society. In this context, I introduce a broad framework for a more comprehensive theory that builds on the position I developed in the first edition (avoiding the essentialisms of naturalistic and constructionist approaches, while recognizing the body as a physical phenomena centrally grounded in social action which both shapes, and is shaped by, its social environment), and that provides the beginnings of a basis for the consolidation of body studies.

Absent-present bodies

During the 1980s a number of books prepared the way for the establishment of a field of body studies by addressing themselves to various issues concerned with the body/society relationship (e.g. Feher, Naddaff and Tazi, 1989; Freund, 1982; Hirst and Woolley, 1982; Johnson, 1983; Martin, 1989; O'Neill, 1985, 1989; Turner, 1984). These varied analyses were enormously important in establishing the body as a legitimate subject of theoretical concern. Nevertheless, they were also often characterized by agendas that ultimately subordinated the materiality and sensuality of the body to *other* factors. These included the concern to incorporate a view of the body as a governed *object* into a theory of the social system (as in Bryan Turner's [1984] ground-breaking 'core problems' theory), viewing the body from the perspective of a particular *sub-discipline* (as in Peter Freund's [1982] excellent analysis of the social implications of health and illness), and using the body as a way of establishing an interdisciplinary *dialogue* between sociology, biology and psychology (as in Paul Hirst's and Penny Woolley's underrated [1982] *Social Relations and Human Attributes*). For all the undoubted accomplishments of such writings, the body tended to be subordinated to, or restricted by, these other concerns. The 'absent presence' of the body in theoretical writings remained a real problem: while the body had become an undoubted stimulant to the sociological imagination, it still tended to fade from view in favour of a concern with more traditional analytical concerns.

This absent presence was not, of course, new. Writings on the body were struggling against the dominant philosophical approach in Western thought which had for centuries prized the thinking mind above the physical flesh. Descartes's *Cogito ergo sum* ('I think, therefore I am') involved at one level a dismissal of all the body's senses. He argued in *The Meditations* that 'I am . . . only a thing that thinks', that 'my mind . . . is entirely and truly distinct from my body and may exist without it', and that our bodies prompted us towards irrational sentiment and impulsiveness (Descartes, 1974: 105, 156). There were exceptions to this denigration of the body. Humanists like Montaigne held that 'part of our humanity is to accept responsibility for our bodies, our feelings', and sought to limit the truth claims of abstract thought (Toulmin, 1990: 40). Nevertheless, the most influential philosophical thought tended to examine the body only insofar as it interfered with the supposedly transcendent powers of the mind. Thus, Kant (1985 [1797]) viewed bodily passions and emotions as impediments to self-determining actions, and conceptualized moral orientations as deriving from the inherent human capacity to *transcend* desires and comply with the universal 'categorical imperative'. The body was not completely absent in

179

these writings, then, but it was viewed with suspicion and tended to be marginalized in relation to the allegedly self-determining powers of the mind.

Given its interest in the workings of industrial society and the lives of modern people, and the elementary processes underlying these phenomena, it is not surprising that classical sociology paid more positive attention to issues of embodiment. Emile Durkheim, for example, refers to the natural body as profane, but also argues that the ritual practices that have historically surrounded human flesh and fluids suggest that the body 'conceals in its depth a sacred principle that erupts onto the surface in particular circumstances' (Durkheim, 1912 [1995]: 138). Manifest via cutting, scarification, tattooing, painting or other forms of decoration, these eruptions affirm the communion of individuals in a shared moral whole and hence serve to bind together society (Durkheim, 1912 [1995]: 138, 233). Such direct discussions of the body can be found elsewhere in classical sociology, but they did not solve the problem of the absent presence of the body because the totality of the embodied subject frequently remains fragmented and fades from view. Comte, Durkheim, Weber and Simmel, for example, have left us with a rich variety of analyses of 'effervescent attachments', 'moral sentiments', 'vitalistic energies', 'affectual actions', 'pre-social' contents, 'psychic responses', 'passions' and related phenomena. These seek to explain how people are propelled to or alienated from particular types of social relationships, and they have clear implications for what the body is, and for the lived experience of embodiment (Shilling and Mellor, 2001). Nevertheless, such concepts also often serve as ways of leaving behind the conceptual significance of other aspects of the body, and frequently provide routes through which the body can be subsumed beneath the 'real' topics of interest such as the social system, the metropolis, or the coordination of the division of labour. This is exemplified by the work of that great visionary of the sociological tradition, Talcott Parsons. He identified the physical organism as a 'unit point of reference' for sociology that 'is never safely neglected' (Parsons, 1991 [1951]: 541–2, 1969: 13), but also insisted that the social significance of the body was given to it by society. This is the context in which Parsons could argue that health was *not* primarily a quality of the biological body but referred to the 'underlying capacity' of individuals to contribute to the productive resources of society (Parsons 1991 [1951], 1978: 21, 81).

These comments do not, of course, suggest that classical writings are of no use if we wish to understand the significance of the body to individuals, groups and nations in the contemporary era. At the very least, however, it is necessary to explicate and build on the implicit theories of embodiment contained within the works of its major representatives and this is something that has been a central aim of my ongoing work in this area (Shilling, 2001, 2002a, 2002b, 2003, 2004). It is also necessary to recognize that it is all too easy for the apparently exclusively social referents of body studies (be they concerned with cultural understandings of sexuality, élite sports or the commodification of human physicality) to tear discussion of human physicality *away* from our blood, flesh, bones and senses and *towards* a disembodied vision of organizational, technological or other factors. It is precisely this problem that continues to characterize many recent developments in the area.

Hollow bodies

If philosophy imparted the body with a good deal of negative content, and classical sociology was unable to restore human physicality fully to the conceptual landscape, this left contemporary writers seeking to invest the body with more theoretically productive meanings with a relatively high degree of latitude. By the 1990s, indeed, it became clear that the body had assumed the status of an underdetermined concept that was able to 'stand in' as a malleable signifier for things *other than itself*. Different theories proceeded to define the body in widely contrasting ways and invested it with incompatible roles. The body was a surface phenomena which had become a malleable marker of commercial value subject to the vagaries of fashion for theorists of consumer culture. It was a sexed object that had been used as a means of justifying women's subordination for feminists. It was an object that had been rendered passive by changing modes of control for analysts of governmentality. It was changed into an uncertain and even a rapidly disappearing remnant of pre-technological culture for those interested in the meeting of meat and machines which had occurred with the development of 'cyborgs'. It was defined in terms of its frailties for those interested in developing a new universal system of ethics. It was even reduced to a positive conceptual category (i.e. a category that could explain phenomena previously marginal to a theory) for those concerned with addressing problems within their own discipline.

In this context, 'the body' became one of the most unstable and contested concepts in the social sciences, with its analysis constituting something of an intellectual battleground over which the respective claims of post-structuralism and post-modernism, phenomenology, feminism, sociobiology, sociology and cultural studies have fought (e.g. Howson and Inglis, 2001). Tied to competing agendas, the body became little more than a metaphor through which particular concerns could be pursued. The body was all things to all people and there seemed to be no agreement about how it should be conceptualized. In being tied to these other agendas, however, the physical *materiality* of the body was not only subordinated to them, but often disappeared over the theoretical horizon. This is exemplified by Judith Butler's attempt to place the body at the centre of her analysis of the cultural enforcement of sexuality through the 'heterosexual matrix'. Butler develops her work through the notion of 'performativity', but concludes that the gendered body 'has no ontological status apart from the various acts which constitute its reality' (Butler, 1990: 136). Such an approach ultimately results in a loss of the fleshy physicality of our embodied being.

As Butler (1993: ix, 29, 68) admits, in seeking to consider the materiality of bodies she found herself moving to other domains and 'kept losing track of the subject'.

This fading of the body is chronic within those writings which conceptualize human physicality exclusively as a *location* on which structures, cultures or relationships 'imprint' themselves, 'inscribe' their effects, or 'hail' subjects. If the body is 'always already' invested with discourses and structured by society, an argument which remains the norm in so much body theory, then it becomes perfectly legitimate to focus on these extra-corporeal factors. However, we should not pretend that such an approach is really interested in, or can throw much positive light on, the physical materiality of the human body. If, in contrast, we wish to understand how the body can be a *source* of, as well as a location for, 'social forms' (even if some of these 'forms' may have ossified and become separated from their founding desires and dispositions) then I would want to reiterate the argument I made in the first edition of this book. In order to overcome the problem of the absent presence of the body in social thought, we need to conceptualize the body as a simultaneously biological and social phenomenon that is both shaped by but irreducible to contemporary social relations and structures. To rob the body of its *own* history and characteristics, in contrast, is to neglect how our embodied being enables us to remake ourselves by remaking the world around us.

The body and self-identity

The damaging consequences of allowing the body to become an absent presence are not confined to abstract theoretical debates about the content and viability of body studies, but are related directly to the second theme of this new afterword: the conceptualization of self-identity. The debate about the relationship between the body and self-identity is one of the most important and contentious to have stimulated writings on the body, intruding as it does on the beliefs of several academic sects, and can be illuminated through an analysis and comparison of three approaches that have informed much debate in the area.

In recent decades people have become increasingly preoccupied with the appearance, size, shape, texture and performance of their bodies. This has been encouraged by the centrality of the body in consumer culture (Featherstone, 1982) – a culture which appears to idolize as sacred the young, sculpted and sexualized body only to suggest that it is actually available to us all. Such a view of the body appears to highlight one of the problems involved in viewing human physicality as an absent presence; it simply cannot cope with any culture or identity which revolves around the flesh and its desirability. Not everyone would agree with this diagnosis of the body, however, and it is ironic that one of the most powerful studies of the phenomenology of bodily experience that has been published in recent years *embraces* the idea of the absent present body. In this respect, I want to start this section by examining Drew Leder's theory of the latent body as it reflects the traditional theoretical view that the body is, under 'normal' circumstances, marginal to our sense of self. This view has been immensely popular in Western philosophy and remains highly influential in much contemporary social thought, but a critical interrogation of Leder's book can highlight the problems associated with this approach to embodiment. I then turn to the notions of the body as a 'project', an 'option' and a 'regime' (related conceptions of identity which constitute in certain respects the opposite to Leder's analysis), before examining two contrasting visions of the 'body as a mask'. The section concludes with an analysis of the general underlying processes which can be seen as shaping the acquisition of varied embodied identities.

Self-identity and the latent body

The conception of self-identity Leder outlines in his (1990) *The Latent Body* is predicated on the argument that the body remains latent for individuals while they are engaged in that purposeful action that tends to dominate our modern lives. It is based theoretically on an unlikely combination of phenomenology and deconstructionism. Leder's starting point is Merleau-Ponty's (1962) phenomenology of perception which focuses on the foundational, lived experience of our given body: the habits and routines of our bodies provide us with our 'vehicle of being in', and our necessarily partial 'point of view' on the world. Drawing on the deconstructive argument that every presence is dependent on a corresponding absence, however, Leder (1990: 2, 62) also argues that the phenomenological body is neither 'fully fleshed out with bone and guts' (e.g. it ignores the 'recessive' features of our bodies such as our internal organs), nor does it enable us to understand the importance of *corporeal absence* to people's lived experiences. This issue of corporeal absence is particularly important to Leder's thesis.

As the modern world promotes and rewards outcome-oriented, rational action, our working lives and leisure activities immerse us in the pursuit of goals that are *external* to our bodies. We may be immersed in writing an assignment, responding to complaints in a call centre, or attempting to score a goal on the soccer field, but our bodies are rarely at the forefront of our minds when interacting unproblematically with physical objects or other people. Instead, they slip from view and disappear from consciousness:

> When reading a book or lost in thought . . . I experientially dwell in a world of ideas, paying little heed to my physical sensations or posture. Nor is this forgetfulness restricted to moments of higher-level cognition. I may be engaged in a fierce sport, muscles flexed and responsive to the slightest movements of my opponent. Yet it is precisely upon this opponent, this game, that my attention dwells, not on my own embodiment. (Leder, 1990: 1)

Several factors contribute to this corporeal absence. First, we usually have a practical command of our bodies which enables us to perform actions such as walking, talking and reading without thinking about them. Second, this taken-for-granted practical command also applies to specialist working or sporting skills (Leder, 1990: 33). A competent tennis player, for example, will move to and strike a ball travelling towards them on the court without consciously thinking through what they are doing. Third, the process of engaging in any activity, such as reading a book, requires that countless skills and motor schemas remain unused. Indeed, in the general process of sensing the world around us 'the perceptual organ remains an absence or nullity in the midst of the perceived' (Leder, 1990: 13–26). Finally, our internal visceral organs provide an example of 'depth disappearance'. We may be suffering from dangerously high hypertension or cholesterol levels, for example, without having any awareness of our condition, and without them causing any interruption to our reading a book or playing a sport. Unlike the 'view' provided to us by sight, hearing, smell, touch, and taste, then, our internal organs are phenomenologically 'marked by regional gaps, organs that although crucial for sustaining life, cannot be somesthetically perceived' (Leder, 1990: 26, 43, 53).[1] This is why doctors must be skilled at reading bodily signs that may be symptoms of deeper problems.

None of these points should be taken to suggest that our body literally disappears. It remains part of our 'corporeal background', but does ordinarily fade in the context of our lived experiences. If the properly functioning body recedes from our consciousness, however, Leder also recognizes that pain, illness or the embarassment caused by 'slips' or 'gaffes' (Goffman, 1956) can make the body *reappear* with a vengeance.

The dys- or re-appearing body

Utilizing the Greek prefix 'dys' (signifying 'bad', 'hard' or 'ill' and deployed in an adapted form in such words as 'dysfunctional'), Leder (1990: 84) employs the term *dys-appearance* to refer to when the body reappears as a thematic and sensory focus of our experience but in a biologically pathological or socially deviant form. In contrast to our normal engagement with the world, dys-appearance alienates us from the social world and throws us back onto the limited world of our bodies.

Pain provides us with the clearest example of this dys- or re-appearance. Unexpected pain can 'take our breath away' and remove us completely from the activity we were engaged in. Intense pain makes us acutely aware of our bodies as we search for its location and cause. The body is no longer a background medium of foregrounded action, and we can become lost in a world of pain whose parameters consist of a highly restricted body image shot through with stabbing, piercing, searing agony (Scarry, 1985). Our primary aim is to rid ourselves of this pain, to escape from the dys-appearance of the body and to restore ourselves to a state of normal functioning in which the body recedes from our minds and experience.

Pain is not the only sensation to effect this reappearance of the body. Our rational calculations can be completely overwhelmed by the emotional body in the face of sexual passion or in the context of other strong emotions such as fear (Smith, 1992). Unexpected sensations or bodily events can also cause us to focus on a particular aspect of our body. Leder provides as an example the actions of rubbing our eyes and squinting prior to refocusing on something we see but disbelieve. Other examples include one's first period, or the breaking of one's voice. In each of these, a particular bodily 'state' foregrounds itself within our experience and identity (e.g. Prendergast, 2000).

There is also a social equivalent to this painful or emotional dys-appearance of the body, and it concerns that bodily consciousness which can arise when there is disruption to social interaction. Goffman (1956) is particularly insightful on this point and suggests that when the orderly flow of interaction breaks down, as a result of inappropriate gestures or expressons, the offender becomes acutely conscious of their body. Embarrassment often follows and this can be accompanied by dryness of the mouth, a tenseness of the muscles, and a feeling of wobbliness which results in disruption of the social encounter (Goffman, 1956). Individuals become acutely aware of their bodily dys-appearance as the mutual attunement of people to each other is ruptured, and as the dyad is dissolved and the encounter is reduced to two isolated, awkward bodies. The effects of social dys-appearance are not confined to embarassment and disrupted inter-action, but can even lead to illness (Leder, 1990: 99). Anorexia nervosa and bulimia, for example, have been associated respectively with cultural pressures on women to achieve an 'ideal' body shape and with the tensions involved in a society which values the contrasting bodily activities involved in productive labour and hedonistic consumption (Bordo, 1993; Turner, 1984).

Leder's analysis of the latent body constitutes a radical challenge to writings that seek to make a relatively continuous sense of the body central to people's self-identity. His work can be taken to suggest that the body is relatively unimportant to people's sense of self in the contemporary era: it tends to absent itself from those external activities and social roles from which individuals acquire and develop their identity. At the very least, it provides us with a sophisticated phenomenological understanding of how it is that Western philosophy has historically prioritized the mind over the body as that which makes us distinctively human beings and moral actors. If, in deep thought, the body fades from view, it is no wonder that the abstract and speculative concerns of philosophy should relegate its signi-ficance. Despite its radical appearance, however, Leder's vision of the latent body resonates strongly with some of the most traditional figures in the sociological tradition. Leder is not the first to conceptualize illness and pain in relation to the disturbance of purposeful action. Parsons (1991 [1951]) associated sickness with a disruption in the smooth functioning of normal social roles and the expectation that individuals would seek help in order to make the dysfunctional body disappear. The effect of Leder's thesis, indeed, is to provide a corporeal rationale for classical conceptions of modernity as a system characterized by the coordination and integration of purposeful actors.

Deconstructing the latent body

Despite its subversive effects, a deconstructionist approach to the body can itself be deconstructed by uncovering the principles through which it makes (in)visible certain aspects of embodiment. The body for Leder is invisible when immersed in purposeful action, yet his argument that 'It is precisely because the normal and healthy body largely disappears that direct experience of the body is skewed toward times of dysfunction' appears to be based on the experiences of healthy heterosexual males in their mid years. Indeed, Leder (1990: 86) acknowledges this in part by drawing on Iris Young's (1990: 147–8, 163) argument that women's bodies often do not disappear in the same way that men's do. For women, tran-scendence is laden with immanence. In the case of pregnancy, for example, there is a 'doubling' of the subject: boundaries and body images shift and undergo flux yet 'awareness of my body in its bulk and weight does not impede the accomplishing of my aims' (Young, 1990: 163, 165). Never-theless, Leder's central thesis remains unchanged. There is little suggestion here that the body can become a major, prolonged focus of attention in its 'normal' state.

The problem with this thesis is that it tends to marginalize those people for whom the body is regularly foregrounded as an essential part of their identity. One central effect of racism is to make those affected feel deeply self-conscious and uneasy about their skin colour (Fanon, 1984 [1952]). In similar manner, theorists of sexuality have pointed out that individuals who do not conform to dominant norms of heterosexual identity can be made to feel alienated from their appearance and actions and must regularly censure their behaviour in order to protect their personal security (Diprose, 1994). Individuals who have experienced marked upwards or downwards mobility are also left frequently feeling ill at ease with their manners and appearance as they negotiate unfamiliar social environments and new vocabularies of bodily idiom (Goffman, 1963). Bourdieu (1984), indeed, attributes such unease as a fundamental characteristic of the petite bourgeois, a group that is filled with reverence for and striving towards a higher-status bodily demeanour that they are unable to attain with any comfort or assurance. Instead of expanding upon the implications of such cases, Leder seems to assume that there exists a fit between people's bodily *habitus* and the social fields they inhabit.

This vision of corporeal latency also disallows for the possibility that the body has become a project in recent years. The only major time the body becomes a project for Leder, in contrast, is when the imperative of pain demands the attention of the individual. This raises more questions about the cultural and historical specificity that forms a background for, yet fades away within, his analysis. Hunger, disease and fear is a chronic part of daily life for millions of people across the globe, and enters into the 'normal' state of their bodies. Here, it might be more applicable to talk of the emergence of the healthy, fully functioning body as a process of *reappearance* rather than disappearance.[2] Furthermore, early, medieval and early modern Christian regimes promoted a constant monitoring of the flesh, albeit in different ways and, again, cannot be used readily to support the notion of the normal body's absence (Mellor and Shilling, 1997). The experiences of certain people with impaired mobility may also question the assumptions underpinning Leder's analysis. Sufferers of arthritis, for example, can experience their body as chronically dys-functional, regularly having to foreground the movement of their legs and hands in relation to steps, bumps, slopes and handrails, and apparently hyperactive offspring intent on using them as a trampoline or climbing frame. On a more mundane level, the frequency with which the body intrudes into our awareness is illustrated by the cycles of feeling hungry, thirsty, tired, uncomfortable, and the need to empty the bladder and bowels that characterize our daily lives.

Despite these limitations, the notion of the latent body issues a strong challenge to the field of body studies and does much to explain a particular phenomenological experience of the body. Leder's writings have informed important work in the sociology of health and illness, and can also help explain why social theory sometimes focuses selectively on particular aspects of embodiment such as vision, a focus made possible by allowing other aspects of people's embodied identities to disappear. If we wish to examine how the body may have been more permanently prominent and foregrounded for people, however, it is useful to turn to the closely related analyses of the body as a 'project', an 'option' and a 'regime'.

The body as a project, option and regime

The idea that people are commonly involved in body projects or options, and that some were once immersed in the demands of body regimes, is in direct opposition to conceptions of our physical selves as latent. This is because each of these conceptions of bodily identity suggests that the sizes, shapes, appearances and sensual experiences of the flesh are integral to the picture we have of ourselves. In each of them, the body is treated as an enterprise to be worked on, and altered, in line with a developing conception of self. As the notion of body projects is a key theme of the original text of *The Body and Social Theory*, and I developed the notions of body options and regimes with Philip Mellor in *Re-forming the Body*, I do not want to spend much time exploring them here. For the purposes of comparison, however, it is necessary to summarize their main features and to explicate and develop their theoretical basis.

Body projects

The notion of body projects develops Anthony Giddens's (1991) suggestion that the self has become a reflexively organized construct in the contemporary era of 'high modernity', and Max Weber's (1991 [1904–05], 1948 [1919]) examination of the irrational consequences of rational action. To summarize, Giddens suggests that late modernity is characterized by a qualitative advance in technological control and an intensified concern with consumption in which the body becomes a central object of cultivation in its *own* right. The purposeful, externally directed rational action Leder discusses has turned *inwards* to encompass the body as an object of attention. Weber's concern with the irrational consequences of rational action, in contrast, alerts us to how purposeful interventions in the body can become *meaningless* in a modern world characterized by an absence of moral criteria that previously informed how people developed their embodied identities. As the body becomes a project, the limited referents for intervention identified by Leder (based, for example, on removing physical pain) undergo a massive expansion, and become dislocated from firm goals and exposed to the vagaries of fashion.

Two characteristics of the high modern world have had a particular impact on this increased prominence of the body. First, there has been a decline in those religious, political and other 'grand narratives' which attributed people's lives with meaning in relation to some transcendent totality such as an afterlife or communism. This development was accentuated by the rise of possessive individualism associated with a succession of right-wing governments that presided over North America and Britain during the 1980s. Second, the contemporary era appeared increasingly 'out of control' (Giddens, 1990). In this context, the body was seen as one last 'raw material' over which the individual could exert influence. Subject to an unprecedented degree of rationalization, bodies are now seen and subject to intervention in terms of their genes, blood pressure, cholesterol, size, shape, appearance, aerobic capacity, colour, weight, and a host of other variables. As such, they can *appear* to provide a firm foundation on which to construct a reliable and meaningful sense of self in the modern world.

This increased prominence of the body has also been affected by the irrationalities and limits of rationalized interventions into the organism. The potential for enhanced bodily control among the affluent remains compromised by the absence of ultimate guidelines concerning *how* people should treat their body as a project. Thus, while modernity provides us with unprecedented opportunities to intervene in and change our embodied selves, it also stimulates a chronic reflexivity which exacerbates the problem of finding answers to the question of whether and how we should make such changes (Weber, 1948 [1919]). The benefits of enhanced body control are also limited by those aspects of our bodily being that remain outside the reach of science. Despite advances in new reproductive technologies, for example, infertility continues to be a major and growing problem. Bodies also often refuse to be moulded in line with our intentions. Over 95% of all weight taken off during diets is put back on again, while the body can react to dieting by reducing the rate at which calories are consumed and by storing greater amounts of fat as a safeguard against future periods of 'starvation'. Thus, body projects can have the irrational consequences of making desired bodily ideals more difficult to achieve. More generally, all bodies age and decay, and the inescapable reality of death can appear particularly disturbing in a modern age obsessed with the body. As our hips give way under the pounding of running marathons, we may console ourselves with strict dietary regimens and regular gym workouts before injuries prompt us to turn to swimming and then, perhaps after muscular pulls have interrupted this particular activity, the meditative but gruelling discipline of Tai Chi Chuan. Short-term reversals apart, however, the gradual decline of the body continues and, as we get older, it becomes increasingly difficult to find ways of rejuvenating the physical flesh.

Whatever the problems associated with body projects may be, they are unlikely to 'fade into the background'. Indeed, recent technological advances may make this focus on the body even more intense through the creation of *body options*, forms of radical physical transformation that may make obsolete the 'blood, sweat and tears' involved in body projects.

Body options

Body options can be defined as technologically-informed methods of restructuring human embodiment which extend the possibilities associated with *having* a body, through a direct and radical assault on the limitations connected to *being* a body (see Mellor and Shilling, 1997). While more prosaic body projects help us explore the possibilities of living in *one* body, the options associated with virtual reality and cyber-technologies promise us the potential of exploring and even occupying bodies which differ substantially according to time and place.

Certain of these developments lie in the future, others may not be fully realized, but there exists the possibility that a body may one day be radically reconstructed several times over a single life. Nanotechnology has the potential to provide micro machines which can be injected into our veins and repair arteries or break down cholesterol deposits (Rucker et al., 1993), while the possibility of computer chip brain implants may ultimately provide us with new languages, the ability to undertake millions of mathematical operations in a split second, and the capacity to process and present large volumes of data in a flash (Tomas, 1991). Virtual reality may shortly be able to simulate this same degree of change in a single evening (Benedikt, 1991; Rheingold, 1994). Linked to others via a computer, stimulated by bodysuit responses connected to electronic graphics, one could before lunch slip into a 'virtual suit' to do battle as a Borg chasing the Starship Enterprise, participate before dinner in an orgy set in ancient

Rome, and finish the day as Marilyn Monroe enjoying a quiet drink with Fidel Castro before retiring to bed.

The social potential of body options can be explored through Jean Baudrillard's (1993) discussions of the 'code'; a term which signifies his view of technology's theoretical ability to remove finalities, absolutes and opposites. For our purposes, the code is best seen as belonging to a *possible* future scenario in which nature has been controlled by and absorbed into socio-technological procedures and institutions. Contemporary examples of what this means, however, can already be found in the DNA code of biology, the binary code of computers, and the digital code of television and sound recording. Each of these codes possesses the potential to make anachronistic our ability to simply copy or counterfeit objects through production or imitation. Instead, the code makes possible the reproduction of 'originals'.

This reproduction of originality, operating through such technologies as artificial evolution (Kelly, 1994), could ultimately make human life entirely self-referential; nothing would be outside our control because nothing would be outside our power to reproduce (Robins, 1995: 144). Even death, we are told, may one day become obsolete if science acquires the ability to regenerate life through cryogenics or a single human cell (Kimbrell, 1993). In Braudel's (1973) terms, individual time could triumph over that of the *longue durée* of evolutionary time. The spatial and temporal flexibility of body options could also challenge the conventional parameters associated with what it means to be an individual by undermining the 'singular body'. As Ian Watt (1957) notes, the principle of individuality accepted by Enlightenment thought depended on the possibility of identifying what was unique to a person across the contingencies of date and location. Developed to their logical extreme, body options may remove any such continuities. An individual may, one day, no longer resemble herself or himself from one occasion to the next in terms of size, appearance, disposition or even sex.

Before we get carried away by the novelty of body options, however, it is necessary to recognize that they may simply exacerbate the problems associated with body projects. The quantity and velocity of choices body options make available to people threatens to leave individuals uncomfortable and uneasy, as well as dissatisfied, with the choices that face them and the choices they have made. It is also important to note than even the most spectacular cases explored by sociologists (e.g. Featherstone and Burrows, 1995) build on *previous* inventions in architecture, temperature control and transport which distanced people from their climate, environment and neighbours, and increased the level of control they could exert over their bodily environment (Sennett, 1994). It may eventually become difficult to distinguish humans from machines, but people have long transformed themselves by transforming the environment in which they live (Marx and Engels, 1970). People have, indeed, long engaged in practices which bear a striking similarity to contemporary body projects, and this becomes clear if we examine the *regimes* which were popular ways of structuring self-identity in the medieval era.

Body regimes

The medieval habitus was formed in an environment characterized by violence, disease and food shortages, and was clearly unconducive to the adoption of habits designed to cultivate the 'body beautiful' (Elias, 2000 [1939]). Nevertheless, the flesh could become a site for the pursuance of religious body regimes: structured programmes of disciplining the body which had a long history within Christianity. Early Christians had 'seized upon' the body as a symbol of Christ's victory over death and the old, corrupt human order, and entry into the Christian community resided in a baptism involving fasting, sexual abstinence, vigils, prayers and exorcisms (Miles, 1992). It was medieval Christianity, however, that refined these regimes into more generalized programmes of physical discipline involving diet, prayer and a severely ascetic lifestyle.

In contrast to modern body projects, medieval body regimes often appeared to centre on a destructive hatred of the flesh. Fighting one's sins could include self-flagellation and walking around with pins stuck in the flesh constantly agitated by clothes. Comparing these behaviours with the norms of contemporary culture, Camporesi (1988: 43) argues 'No one, in these days of mass beauty culture and sublimated corporeality, would be prepared voluntarily to transform his or her body into a gruesome dummy of dead and larval matter'. In medieval Europe, though, devout penitents 'burned . . . with a desire to annihilate their physical selves in the most repugnant manner possible' (ibid.). Despite their apparent contrast with contemporary practices, however, the medieval religious focus on the sinful flesh did not occasion a flight *away* from the body, but brought about a flight *into* physicality no less intense than their modern counterparts (Bynum, 1987; Mellor, 1991). Furthermore, when we think of some of the chemical and surgical procedures people now endure for the sake of their identity, and the hours of painstaking exercise and dietary deprivation they are prepared to undergo in order to 'purify' their bodies of 'sinful' fat, alcohol and nicotine, the gap between these practices narrows further. It is not that such practices as obsessive dieting, for example, display a simple 'hatred' of the body but that they signify an involvement in restructuring the body which can be described as associated with an almost religious devotion to an ideal self.

Medieval body regimes may bear a striking resemblance to the form of body projects not only in terms of their preoccupation with the body, but in allowing certain individuals to reconstruct their self-identities. As Caroline Walker Bynum (1987) has shown, fasting, religious charity work, and the experience of bodily states of 'ecstasy', allowed a number of women to escape the role of nurturer, and bypass certain forms of clerical control. These identities were surrounded with dangers (male priests could judge religious ecstasies to be inauthentic or even demonic), but illustrate how women drew on religious traditions, and integrated them into personal biographical narratives which provided status, religious 'careers' and challenged male hierarchies. If body projects are drawn on by individuals seeking to stablilize their identities in a 'runaway world' (Giddens, 1990), moreover, body regimes were often used to combat medieval anxieties about the *instability* of the body. Worms have, for centuries, been associated with sin and decay and were, in medieval times, often thought to reside *inside* the body as manifestations of sin (Ariès, 1974: 42), and ascetic body regimes were thought to minimize their destructive effects.

The notions of the body as project/option/regime, in contrast to the conception of the latent body, do not provide us with a general theory of bodily experience. Nevertheless, they can be seen as a conceptual inversion of the latter. Instead of fading into the background of purposeful activities, the body becomes foregrounded as a purposeful activity. Certain parts and senses may still pale relative to others, but the notion of body projects/options/regimes challenges the appropriateness of 'disappearance' and 'dys-appearance' as ways of typifying contemporary bodily orientations. The idea that the body is positively central to people's identities has obvious limitations when it comes to dealing with the bodies of the poor, the homeless and the starving for whom survival is a full-time concern (though this entails its own preoccupation with the body). Nevertheless, it does seem to capture how the body can become integral to people's identities. However, the notions of the body as a project and an option are not *complete* opposites of Leder's vision of the latent body. Given the emphasis they place on the cognitive monitoring of the body (as opposed to the carnal knowledge of the flesh characteristic of body regimes), there is a sense in which conceptions of body projects and options underestimate the extent to which the body intrudes on our identities irrespective of our conscious designs (Mellor and Shilling, 1997). Some of the more futuristic visions of body options, for example, seem to ignore how our basic bodily needs and capacities have themselves shaped and limited the development of virtual environments (for more on this, see Heim, 1995; Sobchak, 1995).

There is another, perhaps more significant, concern about the adequacy of utilizing the notion of the body as a project or option as a way of conceptualizing the self in the current age. Medieval body regimes were entered into on the basis of religious criteria, and saturated with sacred meanings: their normative source was clear to those engaged in them and their pace of change was relatively slow. There were, furthermore, ready alternatives to these regimes. Carnivals, for example, may have been closely aligned to religious purposes, to a carnal indulgence leading to a purging of the body, but these festivities displayed a corporeal celebration of the grotesque and a sensual transcendence of the individual which went beyond the goals of the Church (Bakhtin, 1984). The physical ideals associated with body projects, in contrast, are increasingly pervasive and raise the issue of who is able to control 'images of the desirable'.

If social norms and classifications filter into our bodily self-image, our efforts to mould our bodies may have less to do with the exercise of creative agency, and more with seeking to live up to dominant norms of appearance: norms which may help reproduce social inequalities by implicating people within the signifying practices of others (Pfohl, 1993). In recent decades, for example, there has been a profusion of procedures to 'lighten' or 'whiten' the skin, face and features of black peoples. 'Passing' as white – or indeed as middle class or masculine – is not new. Nevertheless, these technological advances offer the means for more radical and sinister 'racialized' reconstructions of the human body, and the accentuation of a new form of corporeal imperialism. In short, the issue of who controls the norms which act as criteria against which individuals seek to mould their bodies raises the possibility that images of the body beautiful may constitute an oppressive mask forced by one group of people on another (Bartky, 1988; Bordo, 1989). Alternatively, is it just possible that there may be enough room within and outside of these norms for body images to be used as flexible 'masks', to be donned and removed by individuals as a way of exercising agency and maximizing their opportunities for self-expression?

The body as a mask

The image of the *body as a mask* is evident in those theories of gendered, racial and generational identities which suggest that visual norms of appearance contribute toward the disadvantaging or oppression of one group by another. It has also become popular in a range of writings, informed by social interactionism, that are interested in how individuals manage their bodies in order to 'give off' particular impressions to others and focus on the playful, changeable and indeterminate qualities of embodiment. Each of these approaches implies, in very different ways, that bodily appearance constitutes as a 'second skin' (Fanon, 1970), a symbolically charged mediator of our biological bodies. The former approach points to those occasions when the 'masking' of a body involves the imposition of negative stereotypes which make people acutely self-conscious about their bodies. Here the body becomes a *straitjacket* or in extreme cases a *prison*. The latter approach, in contrast, suggests that appearance is carefully constructed and managed by the presentationally skilled individual, projecting a range of identities to others according to the needs of the social situation. Here, the body becomes a *performance* and is integral to the exercise of agency (though performance must still account for situational norms).

These constrasting views of the mask as a straitjacket and a performance, then, focus on the symbolic meanings associated with bodily appearance, and on the various degrees of self-awareness, control and choice, and imposition and constraint, that individuals feel they possess over that appearance. They also suggest that appearance and vision have become *the* media through which modern social relationships are constructed, consolidated and reproduced (Evans and Hall, 1999).

The mask as a straitjacket

Frantz Fanon's (1984 [1952]) analysis of the relationship between the construction of blackness and colonialism examines how the 'body as mask' can constitute an oppressive 'second skin' imposed on one group of people by another. Fanon discusses how the white male colonial gaze helps create a social and visual space in which black peoples are equated with, and reduced to, their bodies. There is no disappearance of the body here, and no hope of treating the body as an agentic project. Instead, a negatively stereotyped 'blackness' becomes the essence of what the self is, an essence seen through a 'white mask' and filled with shame and self-contempt. Talking about his own experiences, for example, Fanon notes how the white 'generalized other' reflected his bodily being back to him in a highly oppressive manner. As he explains, 'My blackness was there, dark and unarguable. And it tormented me, disturbed me, angered me' (Fanon, 1984 [1952]: 117).

More generally, colonial associations of blackness with lasciviousness, with animality and with immorality, mean that 'the man of color encounters difficulties in the development of his bodily schema'. Consciousness of the body becomes 'solely a negating activity' which fills the body's space with uncertainty, with a 'third-person consciousness' which makes even the process of reaching for a pack of cigarettes and a box of matches an activity full of awkwardness (Fanon, 1984 [1952]: 110). The imposition of such 'white masks' on black peoples is associated with various strategies of exposure and concealment. Fanon characterizes French colonial resolve in Algeria, for example, with a determination to 'conquer the women; we must go and find them behind the veil where they hide themselves and in the houses where men keep them out of sight' (Fanon, 1970: 37–8). Here, the colonial gaze sought to penetrate all those spaces which might prevent the imposition of a white mask on black bodies. Alternatively, in many West African countries, 'the colonialist offensive against the veil is replaced by the missionary offensive against the breasts'. Here 'it is the very *exposure* of the body, its unabashed exhibition' which characterizes, 'for the Western mind, the African man's primitive promiscuity and possessiveness' (Fanon, 1970; Kanneh, 1992: 347). If there is no single colonial mask, however, the logic remains the same: to rob colonized bodies of their autonomy and to subject them to the physical and behavioural norms of the colonists.

The gendered character of the colonialisms analysed by Fanon can serve to introduce us to feminist writings that examine body masks as essentially patriarchal. Efrat Tseelon (1995: 124) argues that women have constantly to wrestle with a normative mask which reflects male notions of female essence. Women are 'trapped' in a visual space which defines them in terms of their body and appearance, yet which opposes this essence to the superior male spirit of the mind. Tracing the archetypal features of this mask back to the legends of Pandora, Eve and Lillith, Tseelon (1995: 12) suggests that the mask of womanhood is framed as a manipulative essence masquerading behind 'false decoration': its 'beauty and finery' acts as a 'vehicle to dazzle men to their destruction'. In such a context, women's 'essence' is ever present as a normative and reductionist judgment focused around the flesh.

This masking process has a major impact on women's self-identity. If the 'generalized other' which affects how women view themselves is a '*masculine* other', as feminists suggest, girls from the earliest of ages have more pressure placed on their physical appearance than do boys. Their subsequent development is caught between the cultural demand to attain a beautiful appearance and the damnation of that appearance as evidence of low moral character. In this context, it is hardly surprising that research into body image consistently finds that women are more concerned and dissatisfied about their bodily attractiveness, weight, and appearance than are males. One manifestation of this is the high numbers of teenage and even pre-teenage girls who are already caught in harmful cycles of dieting (Grogan, 2000).

Analyses of social responses to ageing provides us with another area in which this notion of the body as an oppressive mask has been developed. Of particular significance here is Mike Featherstone's and Mike Hepworth's (1991) argument that old age is frequently experienced as if it were an obdurate mask which veiled the real identity of the individual. This is exemplified in J.B. Priestley's account of what it feels like to be old:

> It is as though, walking down Shaftesbury Avenue as a fairly young man, I was suddenly kidnapped, rushed into a theatre and made to don the grey hair, the wrinkles and the other attributes of age, then wheeled on stage. Behind the appearance of age I am the same person, with the same thoughts, as when I was younger. (cited in Puner, 1978: 7)

We often hear the expression that people in their seventies and eighties are 'young at heart', but Featherstone and Hepworth highlight how ageing is also shaped by the experience of being masked in an old skin which evokes negative reactions from individuals immersed in a consumer culture which places enormous symbolic capital on the values of youth. Thus, some of us may sometimes still feel like freshers at university (and remember with increasing fondness being able to party until late before putting the world to rights with friends over a few bottles of wine and copious cups of coffee until dawn, and then watching the sun come up while jogging in the local park). Unfortunately, one look in the mirror while shaving or making-up confronts us with furrowed brow, crow's eyes, and bags under the eyes. We can reassure ourselves that a 'lived in' face is a sign of character, but it is not simply the existential sign that death is coming closer that disturbs us. Corporeal signs of ageing are saturated with negative images and these images appear to be determined to mummify our experience of ageing.

The notion of the 'mask of ageing' highlights three key issues of general relevance to this approach towards the body as a straightjacket. First, 'the image of the mask alerts us to the possibility that a distance or tension exists between the external appearance of the face and body and their functional capacities, and the internal or subjective sense or experience of personal identity which is likely to become more prominent in our consciousness as we grow older' (Featherstone and Hepworth, 1991: 382). Second, the mask that people place on ageing bodies helps 'fix' people in limited roles, such as grandparent, which allow little room for individuality and variety (ibid.; Fairhurst, 1998). Third, while the image of the mask seems accurately to capture the experience of ageing for many of the present generation, there are signs that 'a new language of ageing with a much greater expressive range has been gradually emerging' (Featherstone and Hepworth, 1991: 383).

This analysis possesses parallels with those which examine the imposition of negative 'masks' on the skins of black peoples and on women. Instead of facilitating voluntaristic performances, these studies suggest that bodies can be central to the process of *stigmatization*. Originated as a term to refer to 'bodily signs designed to expose something unusual and bad about the moral status of the signifier', to be stigmatized now tends to refer to 'the situation of the individual who is disqualified from full social acceptance' (Goffman, 1990 [1963]: 9, 11). Goffman identifies three major types of stigma (physical 'abnormalities', failings of character, and tribal stigmas such as racial identity), yet emphasizes that *social relationships* determine what is and is not stigmatized. An attribute 'that stigmatizes one type of possessor can confirm the usualness of another, and therefore is neither creditable nor discreditable as a thing in itself' (p. 13). A stigma, therefore, is a special kind of relationship between attribute and stereotype' (p. 14). Masks are not, then, necessarily permanent. Indeed, if social relationships are the crucial factor in determining which bodily identities get stigmatized, we should expect changes in the meanings of particular racial, gendered and generational masks when there is a change in the power ratios and degrees of interdependency between groups. In this respect, it is interesting that Paul Gilroy (2000: 23) argues that legions of athletes and performers have helped begin to change blackness from a 'badge of insult' into an 'increasingly powerful' signifier of prestige, while there has in recent years been a large growth in the association of 'blackness' with the most prestigious forms of popular music, street fashion and youth identity.

The mask as a performance

While writers concerned with bodily appearance as a straitjacket conceptualize the flesh in terms of 'constraint', those interested in appearance as performance focus on the agentic capabilities associated with our visual selves. This is clear in their widespread use of dramaturgical images and their interpretations of the work of Erving Goffman. Goffman's writings are characterized by a battery of concepts, such as 'make work' and 'civil inattention', which describe how individuals manage their appearances and actions in order to convey particular impressions to others. The use of props (such as a newspaper to hide an inappropriate smile), memory (fixing on a sad event from the past in order to appear sombre in the present), make-up or plastic surgery (to hide signs of ageing and promote the look of youth) are just three examples of how the body can act as a mask in projecting particular appearances (Goffman, 1969 [1959], 1990 [1963]).

In addition to the obvious significance of appearance, two contextual factors are of particular importance for the construction and display of facial and bodily masks commensurate with different performances. First, Goffman suggests there is a common *moral* understanding that we take people for what they appear to be, at least until evidence to the contrary arises, and will engage in reciprocal 'turn taking' and even interactional 'repair work' to help ease a presentational performance. Second, while an individual may construct and project a different bodily mask for different audiences, and can relax and distance themselves from all of these masks or identities in 'back-regions', performances for the same audience need to be *consistent* if they are to be regarded as authentic (Goffman, 1983, 1990 [1963]). The management of space and locale, then, as well as cooperation between embodied actor and audience, are essential to the creation and success of different masks of identity (Tseelon, 1995).

There is considerable disagreement about whether this conception of the body as a mask for the presentation of self implies that individuals seek to deceive and manipulate others. Efrat Tseelon (1992), for example, discusses the work of 'impression management researchers' who analyse the 'mask-like' properties of the body as integral to individuals's attempts to *misrepresent* themselves in order to gain benefits from others (e.g. Baumeister, 1986; Snyder, 1987). These researchers suggest that there exists a private, authentic self behind the shifting identities projected by the donning of different masks: masks designed to create false impressions of an individual's social status, economic worth, or moral trustworthiness. In contrast, postmodern views of identity suggests there is no such thing as an unchanging, authentic self, and that social life is dependent on us projecting different embodied identities to various audiences (Gergen, 1991; Tseelon, 1992). One sign of the creativity, and perhaps ambiguity, of Goffman's writings is that both approaches have employed them to support their arguments (Tseelon, 1995).

If there exists disagreement over the moral consequences of managing the body as a mask, Sennet (1992) points out that the idea that social life represents a theatre in which people stage performances is one of the oldest views of society. Plato conceived of human life as a puppet show staged by the gods, Petronius analysed society as a theater, while Christian thought held that God looked on in anguish at the masquerades of His children below. More recently, Balzac, Baudelaire, Mann, and even Freud have each made the identification between theatre and society (Sennett, 1992: 34–5). Sennett examines the processes by which people living in the eighteenth century came to see each other, rather than God, as the audience for their performances. The play acting and pretences of people's dress, appearance and social performances were there to be enjoyed, if somewhat cynically. In mid-eighteenth century Paris, for example, the body was treated as a mannequin 'on which wigs, elaborate hats, and other adornments were to be placed' in order to create a sense of character and a public face that would facilitate communication between strangers (Sennett, 1992: 40–1).

Sennett's historical perspective reveals how treating the body as a mask facilitated communication between people during the eighteenth century. Sumptuary laws sought to restrict certain fabrics and styles to the socially privileged but these were rarely enforced. The mask of the body could, then, be a flexible means of presenting different faces to different public and private audiences. If Sennett provides an historical context for Goffman's concern with the presentation of self, however, he is less sanguine about the present meanings associated with appearance. By the end of the nineteenth century, Sennett suggests that bodily masks came to be seen as fixed indicators of people's personality. Phrenology (which sought to deduce character from the shape of the head) contributed to this change of perspective, as did advances in surgery which viewed the body as a route to the essence of human being, and Darwin's suggestion that individual emotions manifested themselves directly in physical appearance. According to Sennett, these developments meant that the mask of the body no longer provided individuals with a means of communicating in public, but had become an inflexible prison revealing the deepest depths of one's soul.

The image of the bodily mask as a performance highlights the agentic potentialities of the physical self in a manner which has similarities with the idea of body projects. In both cases, the body is viewed as a relatively flexible yet central aspect of people's self-identities. In perceiving the body as significant, at least partly because of its *appearance*, however, both analyses also raise (yet do not answer fully) the question of who sets the criteria by which bodies are evaluated. It is these norms that theorists of race, gender, disability, and age (and other variables along which social inequalities are structured) take as central to their deliberations on the body as a straitjacket. With certain exceptions, however, there is a tendency for these writings to underplay the fact that bodies are irreducible to representations of them, and to overlook the physical capacities of individuals to make at least some difference to their surroundings in all but the most exceptional and oppressive of circumstances. Does this mean that we have to start afresh in considering the relationship between the body and self-identity?

Complementarities and body image

Conceptions of the body as latent, as a project/option/regime, and as a mask provide us with clear alternatives, but can also be brought into productive dialogue. Such dialogue can proceed if we recognize that there exists a partial complementarity between them which can be used to expand their explanatory power. It can be enhanced if we acknowledge that there may be certain common processes concerned with the development of any particular orientation to the body; processes which enable at least the more viable elements of these orientations to be seen as culturally and historically specific forms of embodiment.

Points of contact

In terms of their partial complementarity, while the latent body focuses somewhat unhelpfully on the normal body as a receding body, it can still help explain how certain features of embodiment escape the attention of body projects. Used creatively, a selective combination of the conception of the latent body, body projects and the body as mask can also help explain why it is that people undertake routinized physical activities without being fully committed to them. Debra Gimlin's (2002) analyses of women's involvement in different elements of the beauty industry, for example, suggests routinized work on the body (such as that accomplished by regularly attending aerobics classes) can excuse one from not meeting body norms and can allow one's body to fade into the background at least to a limited degree on some occasions. As Gimlin (2002: 6) argues, 'By engaging in body work, women are able to negotiate normative identities by diminishing their personal responsibility for a body that fails to meet cultural mandates'.

Moving to conceptions of the bodily mask as a straitjacket, such oppressive impositions can be interpreted as a social dys-appearance of the body (albeit in a form mediated by symbolic codes) and as determining the status attached to various body projects. Finally, the notion of the body as a mask can be analysed as having important implications for which aspects of the body may fade into the background during its 'normal' functioning, and as revealing the social relations and power inequalities associated with the criteria of body beauty and stigmatization informing people's motivations for embarking on particular body projects.

If these images of the body can be drawn upon selectively in order to rectify some of their individual gaps and weaknesses, this has something to do with them each being associated with analyses of modernity. They may concentrate variously on the modern age as purposeful, as reflexive, and as a stage where appearance is central to agency and oppression, yet these are each features of the *same* modern system (even if they have not been confined to this system). Modernity is an age which prioritizes purposeful and productive activity, yet has also stimulated a high degree of reflexivity, and has historically been predicated on the colonization and corporeal denigration of much of the globe by Europe and America (Connell, 1997).

The body schema

In addition to putting these conceptions of bodily identity in dialogue with each other, it is possible to examine the common basis on which each of them may develop by drawing on research that has been conducted into the issue of *body schema* or *image*. The concept of body schema was developed to address the problem of how it is we are able to coordinate our bodies to perform actions without having complete sight of them or consciously monitoring our every movement. It suggests that self-identity and social actions are dependent on us building up a non-conscious psychic picture of our corporeal appearance, size and capacities, which provides a basis on which we can coordinate our sensory and motor facilities. As Elizabeth Grosz (1994: 83) argues, our body schema 'unifies and coordinates postural, tactile, kinaesthetic, and visual sensations so that these are experienced as the sensations of a subject coordinated into a single space'.

The body schema develops from two major sources. First, it is fostered by the feelings, perceptions and movements of the physical body as it 'bumps into' and learns to deal with, and problem-solve in, the world around it. The body schema is not identical to these experiences, however, and neurophysiology has long established (through the investigation of such cases as 'phantom limbs' when amputees report pain and sensation in their missing arms or legs) that it is not a replica of the topography of the physical body.[3] This point is reinforced when we realise that physical objects, such as a stick or clothes, can also be taken into our body schema. As Simmel (1971 [1918]: 356) implies in his discussion of how technological developments can expand our sensory capacities, the formation of such a schema means that we have socially 'transcended the compass of our natural being'. The second factor associated with the development of a body schema is social interaction. This involves the elementary structures of role-taking (and the affects and expressions involved in this interaction) engaged in with early care-givers by the pre-linguistic infant (Joas, 1983, 1997; Mead, 1938; Schilder, 1935). The experience and image we have of our own bodies, then, is not wholly given by phenomenological self-experience, but is derived significantly from the experience and image we have of *other people's* bodies (and their reactions to our body).

Sociologically, these two sources of the body schema are of particular importance as they suggest that the biological body is open to cultural meanings which focus on and define symbolically particular body parts or appearances, yet which must also take account of the *physical materiality* of the body and the environment. As George Herbert Mead argues, body schemas develop on the basis of a *practical* intersubjectivity (Joas, 1997), the interactional effects of bodily selves on each other as they are engaged in the manipulation of physical things (Mead, 1932: 169).

Having drawn on Mead's writings to identify the processes involved in the formation of a body schema, his work is also useful if we wish to examine why individuals develop particular embodied identities. The practical intersubjectivity that is one central factor in the development of a body schema is governed for Mead by the need individuals have to adjust their own actions to those of the group. This adjustment stimulates a reflexive self-consciousness which enables individuals to contemplate their bodily being from the viewpoint of other people. As Mead (1934: 138) argues, 'The individual experiences himself as such . . . from the particular standpoints of other individual members of the same group, or from the general standpoint of the social group as a whole to which he belongs'. Mead refers to the subjective internalization of this group standpoint as a 'generalized other': an other which acts as a censor and filter for the development of embodied identity. The process through which an individual develops a coherent embodied self-identity is not a simple internalization of the group attitude, however, but an internal dialogue between the 'me' (the identity that others attribute to us) and the 'I' (our subjective reflection on this identity) (Mead, 1934). We must also remember that the continuity of this particular group-influenced bodily identity is also subject to its ability to facilitate successful interventions in the physical environment. Those stigmatized within a community because of a physical disability, for example, may critically reflect on their 'spoiled identity', discover that they are much more capable than society assumes, and reject their bodily identity in favour of a radical alternative.

These insights have major implications for the notions of the body as latent, as a project/option/regime, and as a mask. They suggest that the relevance and applicability of each form of embodiment will be dependent on the subjectivities forged through practical interactions and their efficacy in relation to the social *and* physical environment. If the dominant social group is a colonizer, or a patriarch, those subject to this oppression are likely to develop restricted and constraining body images which hamper their opportunities to exercise agency. It is no accident that the notion of 'generalized other' illuminates Fanon's notion of white masks imposed on black peoples in colonial spaces. The notion of body projects, in contrast, suggests the dominance of a social context in which individualism is valued to the extent that people are expected to manage and enhance the value of *themselves* as well as of the goods and services they work with, yet must do so without enduring guidelines as to how to accomplish this task. Finally, the phenomenological experiences behind the notion of the latent body (overstated as these are) can be interpreted as promoted by an interactional context in which the mind and purposeful action is valued above the body and sensual experience. Such notions as the latent body, body projects and body masks should not, therefore, be reified and treated as signifying approaches to the body that are equally relevant irrespective of historical and cultural context. The common interactional significance of the body to the sense of self an individual possesses can itself result in identities which are radically different historically and cross-culturally depending upon the practices and values considered sacred within a community (Shilling, 1999, 2003). As such, the analyses of self-identity we have examined here may more productively be seen as representing parts of a typology (although Leder's thesis gets a role not because the body is chronically absent but because it can help explain why certain aspects of the body slip into the background at certain times). That is, they may be seen as approximations to different forms of embodied identity which may become more or less relevant over time and will almost definitely need to be supplemented with additional visions of the body and identity.

New directions in body theory

This discussion of the common processes underpinning the development of a body schema highlights three dimensions of embodiment that I want to suggest are absolutely necessary to the development of new directions in body theory. In the development of a pictoral body schema the physical body is at once a *source* of self-identity (involving experiences, feelings, and perceptions), and a *location* for the effects of society (group norms permeate the individual's sense of self and their evalation of this sense of self). Given its continued engagement in practical interventions in the physical environment, that can serve as a catalyst for a changing sense of identity or commitment to that identity, the body also constitutes a medium whereby people can be *attached to* or *repelled from* their social milieu. This view of the body as a multi-dimensional phenomena provides us with the key not just to analysing the relationship between the body and identity, but to constructing a sociological vision of the constitution of society which is more fully embodied than existing perspectives in the area. This is not because it works at the level of the individual and, therefore, could and should be extrapolated to the level of the social system, but because it captures vital, irreducible and generalizable dimensions of the body's productive and receptive capacities. I begin this section by examining and critically evaluating those perspectives which remain or have become dominant in the last decade, before identifying the outlines of a more satisfactory approach to analysing the body's relationship with society.

For all the diversity and variety of body theories, three now exert most influence in the area. Over the last decade, social constructionist analyses of the ordered body, action or phenomenological approaches towards the lived body, and conceptions of the body in structuration theory have not only imparted this area with a developing identity, but have provided valuable insights into the social significance of the body and continue to set agendas which steer much writing in this area. Despite their achievements, however, each of them is characterized by serious theoretical limitations and by radically different views of the body which seem to make this subject more rather than less elusive. Having examined the first and third of these theories in the main text, I shall confine my discussion to brief analyses of their developments and continued limitations, though it is also worth noting that I adopt a more critical view of the analytical worth of structuration theory than is evident in the first edition.

Social constructionist analyses of the ordered body

Social constructionist analyses of the ordered body view human physicality as an object which is produced and regulated by political, normative and discursive regimes. Studies which developed this approach did much to initiate and consolidate the form taken by the corporeal turn in social theory. Thus, Bryan Turner's (1984) structuralist *The Body and Society*, and later post-structuralist studies such as Judith Butler's (1990) *Gender Trouble* and (1993) *Bodies that Matter*, established the *governmental management* of the body as key to the external environment in which social action occurs.

Turner's and Butler's analyses may appear to have little in common, and Turner (1996) is critical of Butler's conception of the body. Nevertheless, their analyses converge in so far as Butler (1990, 1993) focuses on two of the systemic problems identified by Turner, the restraint of desire and the presentation of self. Butler's specific interest may be the cultural enforcement of heterosexuality, but she remains, like Turner, concerned with the ordering and regulation of bodies. The influence of Michel Foucault is also readily apparent in these studies. Foucault (1977) conceives of the body as 'the inscribed surface of events' and as 'totally imprinted by history'. There are no irreducible 'essences' that define people's identity or actions for all time, just 'inscriptions' of identity which change over time.

Theorists concerned with the governmental environment in which the body is controlled have not relied exclusively on Foucault, however, but combined his insights and methods with those of other thinkers. Turner's (1984) study, for example, is heavily steered by Parsons (as well as by Hobbes and Foucault). This use of Parsons is particularly creative. Instead of being a sub-system of action as it was for Parsons, the behavioural organism becomes for Turner the model for the *overarching environment in which action occurs*. This enables Turner to draw on innovative thinkers such as Foucault, while blunting the radical consequences of their analyses by containing them within a Parsonian framework. Similarly, Butler's (1993) concern with the 'heterosexual matrix', which positioned the body as an object and target of gendered power relationships, drew on Althusser in arguing that individuals are 'hailed' to perform particular subject positions. Again, the impulse towards order for an apparently radical theory is firmly established.

These theories may have been effective at illuminating how the body was ordered and inscribed by power relations, but frequently remained silent about the 'lived experience' of embodied action. Turner, for example, condemns phenomenology for providing 'an individualistic account of embodiment from the point of view of the subject' which is 'largely devoid of historical and sociological content' (Turner, 1984: 54). Sociologically, he insists, 'the body' should be examined as 'socially constructed and socially experienced' (ibid.). The body remains an object, and one which is ultimately attached to its social milieu by the dull compulsion of structures and matrixes over which it has no control.

Phenomenological and action-oriented studies of the 'lived body'

In response to this lacunae, the 1990s witnessed a rise in studies about 'the body's own experience of its embodiment' which viewed the opportunities and constraints of action as given by the 'problems of bodies themselves' (Frank, 1991: 43). Drew Leder's (1990) focus on the lived experience of instrumentally rational action and Iris Marion Young's (1990) feminist phenomenology are important examples of this genre, as we have seen, while Arthur Frank (1995) has drawn creatively on experiential accounts of the prominence of the body during illness in analysing how a 'pedagogy of suffering' can result in a lasting new ethics of relating to others. These and other accounts of their kind drew on phenomenology, on existentialist and on interactionist resources. It is the phenomenology of Merleau-Ponty, however, that has been most influential in shaping these calls for a 'carnal sociology', the founding assumption of which was that '"self", "society" and "symbolic order" are constituted through the work of the body' (Crossley, 1995: 43). Crossley's call was timely as it coincided with a growing feeling that while theories of the body illuminated the *Körper* (the structural, objectified aspects of physical being), they had yet to come to grips fully with the *Lieb* (the living, feeling, sensing, and emotional aspects of bodily experience) (Csordas, 1994; Stoller, 1997). For Merleau-Ponty (1962: 136), embodied subjects develop direction and purpose on the basis of the *practical* engagements they have with their surroundings and through the *intentionality* they develop as a result of the situatedness of embodied existence.

This emphasis on the determining rather than determined nature of our embodiment, and on the universal bodily basis of meaning and knowledge, constitutes a major challenge to structuralist and post-structuralist theories. Part of the legacy of action-oriented and phenomenological approaches, indeed, can be seen in the growing number of empirically discrete explorations of 'bodies in a social context' which variously express a dissatisfaction with the abstract character of body theory and a desire to listen to people talking about their bodies (e.g. Evans and Lee, 2002; Gimlin, 2002; Nettleton and Watson, 1998). Despite its ostensible focus on the 'lived body', however, there is a paradox within phenomenology. Having been interpreted as analysing how people experience their bodies, this tradition is actually concerned with the bodily *basis* of experience. As Leder's (1990) study illustrates, it is quite possible for the body to fade away within a phenomenological account of people's practical experiences of the world, to neglect the importance of physical differences, and to overlook how structures sometimes shape our physical dispositions.

Structuration theories of the body

These analyses of the ordered and 'lived' bodies provided the field with alternative lines of development, but replicated what many saw as a debilitating division between theories of structure and agency that had long characterized sociology (Dawe, 1979). Structuration theories developed as a means of overcoming this opposition. Based on assumptions about the mutually constituting nature of social structures and actions, the body was central to structuration theory's vision of society. Pierre Bourdieu and Anthony Giddens are the most influential proponents of this theory of social life, while Elizabeth Grosz provides us with a quite different, feminist analysis of the mutual constitution of the body and dominant norms of sexuality. Despite their differences, each theorist claimed that the body was a recipient of social practices and an active creator of its milieu.

In Bourdieu's theory of social reproduction, the body is shaped by yet also reproduces class inequalities. The embodied dispositions that people acquire during their upbringing 'continuously transform necessities into strategies, [and] constraints into preferences' (Bourdieu, 1984: 190). Giddens's (1991) conception of 'high modernity' provides us with a different version of how the body and the major social principles characteristic of a society are mutually determining. The contingency of the contemporary social world is incorporated into and reinforced by the contingency of the body. Modernity's capacity for controlling the body provides individuals with the potential to change their bodily appearances and capacities, while modernity's demolition of certainties is associated with a 'chronic reflexivity' in individuals that stimulates the search for new biographical narratives, new relationships, and new answers to major existential issues (Shilling and Mellor, 1996). Grosz's (1994) view of how the sexual body is both constituting and constituted is again quite different. Using the Lacanian appropriation of the topographical image of the mobius strip (the inverted three-dimensional figure eight), she explores how the body provides a morphological basis for sexual difference, yet is also structured (both internally and externally) by the inscriptive powers of sexual norms.

These structuration theories provide us with a 'middle way' between social constructionist accounts of governmentality and phenomenological accounts of 'lived experience' and, in the cases of Bourdieu and Giddens, are designed to inform empirical research. Whether they provide us with *viable* alternatives, however, is another question. While Bourdieu asserts the facts of changing bodily dispositions, his argument that the *habitus* operates at the level of the subconscious (Bourdieu, 1984: 466) makes it difficult to see how individuals can escape from the dispositional trajectory assigned them. The emphasis Giddens's later writings place on changeability and reflexivity, in contrast, invests the body with an unlikely 'lightness of being'; it is a highly malleable resource rather than a frail, inescapable part of existence, and can be reinvented by individuals alongside their reflexively constituted narratives of self. Finally, despite her

205

concern to identify possibilities for change, Grosz's focus on the body's sexual specificity and the additional 'investments of difference' made by society into the interiors and exteriors of bodies seems to ensure the continuation of opposing male and female identities.

Mediating theories, mediating bodies

These three approaches may have demonstrated the ubiquity of the body as a subject, and imparted to the field a theoretical identity, while each of them adds something of enduring significance to the analysis of embodiment and society. Social constructionist theories of the ordered body draw our attention to how power is exercised on and through bodies, and have made a valuable epistemological break by distancing sociological thinking about embodiment from naturalistic, biologically reductionist analyses. The body, in short, is an important *location* on which society imprints itself and through which it is able to exercise influence and power. Action-oriented and phenomenological approaches have demonstrated the importance of the body as the basis for human agency and the lived experience of social actors. Sociology will not capture the complexity of the body by viewing it simply as a physical object, they suggest, but needs to recognise how the organism is our vehicle of being in, experiencing, and creating the world in which we live. If we combine this with an appreciation of how certain evolutionary developments and bodily capacities may be out of reach of phenomenological introspection, we can appreciate the body as a vital *source* for the creation of society. Conceptions of the body in structuration theory seek to position human physicality as a central part of a circuit connecting the individual to society. Social actors both create their social milieu, through the capacities and facilities of their bodies, and are simultaneously shaped by the impact their social location exerts on their bodies. The body, in short, is a *means* through which individuals are attached to, or ruptured from, society.

These are very real insights and it would perhaps be rash to dismiss one in favour of another of these theories, or to jettison every aspect of them. Nevertheless, we need to recognize that they are actually talking about very different dimensions of embodiment. In terms of the language I am using here, they are focused on distinctive issues concerned with the body as a source of, or a location for, or a means of attaching (or repelling) the embodied subject to society, but *none of them* recognizes adequately the body's implication in *all* of these processes. Thus, theories of the ordered body let the individual's active and experienced body fade from view. Phenomenologically-informed theories tend to occlude the effect of structures on the experiences of individuals and, ironically, sometimes converge with structuralist approaches when suggesting that the body disappears during purposeful action. Structuration theories condemn the body to a state of oscillation between the dead weight of structure and the lightness of reflexive choice.

There are several ways of responding to this situation. Firstly, it is possible to simply endorse one of these approaches as essentially 'correct', and reject the others as false, misguided attempts to apprehend the reality of social life. This would be the easiest option and there is something to be said for it. It would enable us to pursue and refine a single agenda, perhaps extending it here and there to cope with some of its residual categories, and to advance that particular theoretical paradigm. This is Crossley's (1995, 2001) strategy in representing Merleau-Ponty as a flexible theorist who can reconcile the dualisms apparent in sociological theories of the body through his treatment of the body as subject and object if only we add to his thought appropriate doses of such disparate theorists such as Habermas, Foucault and Bourdieu. Second, one could start afresh by rejecting each of these approaches and pursuing a quite separate programme based upon a different philosophical starting point, defining the body and its social consequences anew (e.g. Turner, 1999). The problem with both these responses, however, is that they would almost certainly overlook some of the advances that the major existing theories of the body have made in this area, and undermine the identity that body studies has developed.

A third way of responding to the current diversity in the field of body studies is to accept the body's elusiveness in social thought and recognise that its enigmatic character is most usefully tied to the development of diverse theoretical traditions. These traditions can be seen as providing different resources for the pursuit of different analytical tasks. Again, there is something to be said for this option. Focusing on the body has led to advances within diverse areas of study and has provided historically marginalized modes of thought, such as 'queer studies' and 'lesbian studies', with a substantive vehicle through which the importance of their endeavours has been more widely recognized. This proliferation of theories on the body also provides apparently tailor-made perspectives that can be used to interrogate a wide range of subjects. However, if we have reached a point where theoretical consolidation is needed, as I have suggested, the time for simply endorsing the sheer growth and scope of body studies has passed.

A fourth way of proceeding is to seek to incorporate the most useful features of the approaches we have examined into a more comprehensive framework which avoids their debilitating limitations. This cannot be accomplished by 'taking together' incommensurate paradigms (a problem with Turner's [1996: 33] suggestion that he incorporate a focus on the 'phenomenology of experience' as a corrective to 'the underlying structuralism' of his The Body and Society). It must also avoid the associated problems of conflating distinct capacities of the body, a step which loses the theoretical means to account for the interaction that occurs between these capacities and for historical change (Archer, 2000). Finally, it needs to refuse the theoretical excesses of dominant approaches by placing at its centre a view of the body as a socio-natural phenomenon which is an ongoing source of society as well as being a location for the structures and contours of the social environment (see Chapter 9 and Burkitt, 1999).

This fourth option is the one I favour and I believe it can be accomplished by developing a view of the body as a multi-dimensional medium for the constitution of society (a source of, a location for, and a means of positioning individuals within, society). This framework is designed to establish the fundamentals of any comprehensive theory while also providing guidelines for empirical studies of the body in society. The body's status as a source, a location for, and a means of attachment/repulsion is viewed as three key dimensions in its relationship with the social environment. While we may have to start by focusing on one or other of these elements, it is important to leave space for examining the effects over time of each of them.

This approach has not been developed in the field of body studies, but neither does it require us to start anew.[4] It is possible, indeed, to explicate its outlines through a creative engagement with the writings of Marx, Durkheim, Simmel and Elias (see Shilling, 2004). Their work derives from very different and incompatible theoretical traditions, yet it is possible to identify in their writings a *convergence* of interest in the body as a multi-dimensional medium for the constitution of society. Thus, while Durkheim is distinctive in beginning with the theoretical and moral primacy of the collectivity, and looked to the possible rise of a moral individualism that could provide a suitable framework for an advanced capitalism (Durkheim, 1984 [1893]), he also viewed the body as a source and recipient of a collective symbolism that possessed the capacity to incorporate individuals into the moral life of the group. Similarly, while Simmel is distinctive in attributing primacy in theoretical and moral matters to the (interacting) individual, he analysed the increasingly pervasive impact on embodied identity of the money economy, while also identifying the body as a source of dispositions conducive to the formation of embryonic social forms which could stimulate in individuals socially-binding emotions. Marx combines elements from different theoretical traditions in focusing on the relationship between social class, the market-place of competitive individualism, and the possibilities of collective emancipation, but he viewed the body as a source of economic relations and developed a deep concern with the destructive bodily effects of capitalism. These effects could 'fit' workers to restrictive jobs within the market-place, but could also form the basis for class struggle and social change. Finally, while Elias rejected philosophy and turned his back on much of the sociological tradition, his processual approach recognized the body as a productive hinge between nature and society, and a location for the figurations that have historically effected major alterations to people's bodily identities. He was also centrally concerned with how the successful *attachment* of individuals to peaceful social figurations in the contemporary West is dependent on an internalization of controls previously maintained by external authorities. Furthermore, Elias's suggestion that there are increasing costs associated with the body being a location for capitalist society advances a number of questions raised by Marx, Durkheim and Simmel that can usefully be explored further. In particular, it asks us to consider the possibility that the products of embodied individuals have come to dominate us and restrict the manner in which our bodies are presently shaping the social world in which we live.

The enormous theoretical differences that exist between these figures means that this convergence thesis will have to be drawn very carefully. To reiterate, the point is *not* that their general social theories are compatible, but that they share certain elements in their analysis of the body in constructing their distinctive visions of social life. In recognizing that the body constitutes a source of society, Marx, Durkheim, Simmel and Elias each invest it with *transcendent* properties that enable our physical selves to be temporarily freed from the constraints of individual existence and natural life and placed in a productive relationship vis-a-vis the formation of social relationships. In viewing the body as a location for society, they each recognise that these relations can develop in such a way as to condemn the body to a period of *immanence* in which it is confined to and shaped by the structural forces of society. In addressing the body as a means of attaching people to, or distancing them from, social milieu, each of these figures also shares a concern with social outcomes as embodied phenomena. Social outcomes cannot be conceptualized adequately as exclusively cognitive processes, but need to take into account how people's orientation to their social environment have been shaped by bodily dispositions, desires, habits and preferences.

This broad approach to the body as a multi-dimensional medium for the constitution of society remains to be explicated fully, but it seems to me that it has the advantage of identifying essential elements in any specific body theory while leaving flexible the specific political, cultural and economic directions of analysis. The limited convergence that exists in the writings of classical theorists is not a political convergence and does not prescribe how we should judge society. It does insist that we view the body as foregrounded in the constitution and maintenance of social relations and in the positioning of agentically-capable individuals within these relationships. I also see this theoretical approach as building directly upon, rather than constituting a radical departure from, the route mapped out in the first edition of this text. There, I was concerned to rescue analysis of the body from the forms of biological reductionism that characterized naturalistic approaches and the forms of discursive reductionism that characterized many sociological approaches to the subject, while also highlighting the importance of conceptualizing the body as a material phenomena that both shaped and was shaped by its social environment. The notion of the body as a multi-dimensional medium for the constitution of society takes this as its basic assumption and builds towards a theory of society as a thoroughly embodied phenomena. At the same time, it retains the very real advances made by the dominant theoretical approaches that have developed within body studies.

In conceptualizing the body as a *source* of society, it builds on the action-oriented and phenomenological insight that society is constituted through the work of the body, while adding to this other sociological analyses of the body as a socio-natural entity which shapes the contours and content of the social milieu (Benton, 1991; Burkitt, 1999; Hirst and Woolley, 1981). It does this by recognizing that the body is possessed of potentialities that enable it to transcend the natural world and individual existence. In conceptualizing the body as a *location* for the effects of society, it recognizes that once social norms and institutions are established they set the parameters in which subsequent social action occurs and have a real impact on the bodily being of those subject to them. These effects can alter people's physical dispositions and capacities for action. Placed in this context, with an ontological view of the body as a physical productive phenomena which is irreducible to discourse, it is possible to employ to good effect the useful insights from stucturalist and post-structuralist theories of governance. Each of them is possessed of a view of the body as socially immanent; it can at times become tightly constrained, shaped and limited by its social surroundings. In conceptualizing the body as a *means* of positioning individuals within their social milieu, it builds on the insight from structuration theories that the processes of social reproduction and change are mediated by bodies. Social change does not happen automatically and nor does it occur simply as a result of purely intellectually-motivated actions. Instead, people's experiences of, and responses to, social structures are shaped significantly by their sensory and sensual selves. These variables are important as they can exert an important impact on whether people feel at ease with, and tend to reproduce the 'rules', 'resources' or 'social fields' they are most familiar with, or emotionally experience these structures as unpleasant, undesirable and worthy of transformation. This recognizes a thoroughly embodied view of social outcomes which rejects the philosophical view that it is the mind, separated from any bodily tastes or dispositions, that determines how people relate to their social environment.

Conclusion

This new Afterword has been concerned to revisit and develop three themes in my original text that resonate most strongly with current debates in the area and with the ongoing endeavour to construct a fully embodied sociology. The 'absent presence' of the body in social thought, the relationship between the body and self-identity, and the question of how to advance theoretically the study of the body in society are linked issues. It seems to me that we will only be able to make substantial theoretical progress in the latter two if we reverse the current tendency of effectively absenting the material body from our considerations. Bodies constitute an irreducible source of society: it is the properties and capacities of embodied humans that provide the corporeal basis on which identities and social relations are consolidated and changed. Without ceasing to be an ongoing source of their social milieu, they are also marked and contoured by the structural effects of society. Finally, our embodied being is also implicated centrally in our positioning within the social and cultural worlds we inhabit. People's attraction to or repulsion from different elements of their environment is often a deeply sensual, visceral matter and it is these responses, and not just apparently 'disembodied' intellectual evaluations, which provide an essential motor force for the maintenance, development and transformation of social systems.

The body has served as an enormously productive focus for theoretical and, increasingly, empirical work over the last two decades, but this has resulted in not only a diverse but an increasingly fragmented field of studies. If we are to turn this explosion of creativity into something more enduring, then now is the time for theoretical consolidation. The challenge for sociological research is to demonstrate how the thoroughly bodily dimensions of societal constitution operate generally and in particular circumstances.

Notes

1. Expressed in physiological terms, our *proprioception* (the sense of balance, position, and muscular tension provided by the receptors in our muscles, joints, tendons, and the inner ear) provides us with crucial information about the world and options to utilize different modalities of engaging with the world, but fades from our phenomenological experience of living. Such absence is even more marked with regards to the information provided to us by our interoception (the sensations of our internal organs) which provide us with only general, delayed, or inaccurate pictures of our body and external world (Leder, 1990: 41–3). It may take years for an unhealthy diet to result in heart disease, for example, or for smoking to cause a blood clot or cancer which hinders our ability to engage in productive labour.

2. There is a related problem with accounts of chronic illness which employ Leder's analysis to examine the biographical narrative work involved in returning the body from a state of dys-appearance to one of re-embodiment. Sufferers often talk of reclaiming or rediscovering their bodies, yet Leder's notion of the lived body does not fully support this as it conceives of the normal lived body as a disappearing rather than a reappearing body.

3. This research originated with neurophysiology at the beginning of the twentieth century. Neurophysiology suggested that the ability of the body to coordinate its actions was dependent on a non-conscious three-dimensional postural model of the body: a model which registers past and present sensory information experienced by an individual's body and its relation to other objects (Grosz, 1994; Head, 1920). Physiological and psychological research into body schema developed by examining such issues as phantom limbs, hypochondria, hysteria, and other disturbances in how and where particular stimuli are felt in the body.

4. Arthur Frank (1991) presents his theory of the body as a medium for distinctive forms of action, but actually develops a core problems approach to embodiment which is pitched at the level of the individual instead of at the level of the social system.

References

Abercrombie, N. (1986) 'Knowledge, order and human anatomy', in J. Hunter and S. Ainley (eds), *Making Sense of Modern Times, Peter L. Berger and the Vision of Interpretive Sociology*. London: RKP.

Adams, P. and Minson, J. (1978) 'The "subject" of feminism', *m/f*, 2: 43–61.

Alcorn, K. (1988) 'Illness, metaphor and AIDS', in P. Aggleton and H. Homans (eds), *Social Aspects of AIDS*. London: Falmer.

Alexander, R. (1974) 'The evolution of social behaviour', *Annual Review of Ecology and Systematics*, 5: 325–83.

Allan, G. (1989) *Friendship, Developing a Sociological Perspective*. New York: Harvester Wheatsheaf.

Althusser, L. (1971) 'Ideology and ideological state apparatuses', in L. Althusser (ed.), *Lenin and Philosophy and Other Essays*. London: New Left Books.

Antonovsky, A. (1979) *Health, Stress and Coping*. San Francisco: Jossey Bass.

Antonovsky, A. (1984) 'The sense of coherence as a determinant of health', *Advances*, 1: 37–50.

Antonovsky, A. (1987) *Unravelling the Mystery of Health: How People Manage Stress and Stay Well*. San Francisco: Jossey Bass.

Archer, M. (2000) *Being Human: The Problem of Agency*. Cambridge: Cambridge University Press.

Ardill, S. and O'Sullivan, S. (1986) 'Upsetting an apple cart: difference, desire and lesbian sadomasochism', *Feminist Review*, 23: 31–57.

Ardrey, R. (1976) *The Hunting Hypothesis*. London: Collins.

Ariès, P. (1974) *Western Attitudes towards Death from the Middle Ages to the Present*. Baltimore, MD: Johns Hopkins University Press.

Ariès, P. (1981) *The Hour of Our Death*. London: Penguin.

Armstrong, D. (1983) *Political Anatomy of the Body: Medical Knowledge in Britain in the Twentieth Century*. Cambridge: Cambridge University Press.

Armstrong, D. (1987) 'Bodies of knowledge: Foucault and the problem of human anatomy', in G. Scambler (ed.), *Sociological Theory and Medical Sociology*. London: Tavistock.

Atkinson, P. (1987) 'The feminist physique: physical education and the medicalization of women's education', in J. Mangan and R. Park (eds), *From 'Fair Sex' to Feminism*. London: Tavistock.

Baber, Z. (1991) 'Beyond the structure/agency dualism: an evaluation of Giddens' theory of structuration', *Sociological Inquiry*, 61(2): 219–30.

Bakhtin, M. (1984 [1965]) *Rabelais and His World*. Bloomington: Indiana University Press.

Ball, S. (ed.) (1990) *Foucault and Education: Disciplines and Knowledge*. London: Routledge.

Banner, L. (1983) *American Beauty*. New York: Knopf.

Barrett, M. (1987) 'The concept of "difference"', *Feminist Review*, 26: 29–41.

Barrows, S. (1981) *Distorting Mirrors: Visions of the Crowd in Late Nineteenth Century France*. New Haven: Yale University Press.

Bartky, S. (1988) 'Foucault, feminism and patriarchal power', in I. Diamond and L. Quinby (eds), *Feminism and Foucault: Reflections on Resistance*. Boston, Mass.: Northeastern University Press.

Bartrop, R., Lazarus, W., Luckhurst, L., Kiloh, L. and Penny, R. (1977) 'Repressed Lymphocyte function after bereavement', *Lancet*, 1: 834–6.

Baudrillard, J. (1993) *Symbolic Exchange and Death*. London: Sage.

Bauman, Z. (1989) *Modernity and the Holocaust*. Cambridge: Polity Press.

Bauman, Z. (1992a) 'Survival as a social construct', *Theory, Culture and Society*, 9(1): 1–36.

Bauman, Z. (1992b) *Intimations of Modernity*. London: Routledge.

Bauman, Z. (1992c) *Mortality, Immortality and Other Life Strategies*. Cambridge: Polity Press.

Baumeister, R. (1986) *Public Self and Private Self*. New York: Springer.

Beck, U. (1992) *Risk Society: Towards a New Modernity*. London: Sage.

Beckford, J.(1989) *Religion and Advanced Industrial Society*. London: Unwin Hyman.

Bell, D. and Kennedy, B. (eds) (2000) *The Cybercultures Reader*. London: Routledge.

Bendann, E. (1969) *Death Customs*. London: Dawsons.

Benedikt, M. (1991) 'Cyberspace: some proposals', in M. Benedikt (ed.), *Cyberspace: First Steps*. London: MIT Press.

Benton, T. (1991) 'Biology and social science: why the return of the repressed should be given a (cautious) welcome', *Sociology*, 25(1): 1–29.

Benton, T. (1992) 'Why the welcome needs to be cautious: a reply to Keith Sharp', *Sociology*, 26: 225–32.

Berger, J. (1972) *Ways of Seeing*. Harmondsworth: Penguin.

Berger, P. (1990 [1967]) *The Sacred Canopy. Elements of a Sociological Theory of Religion*. New York: Anchor Books.

Berger, P. and Luckmann, T. (1967) *The Social Construction of Reality*. London: Allen Lane.

Bernstein, B. (1970) *Class, Codes and Control*, vol. 1. London: RKP.

Berridge, V. and Edwards, G. (1987 [1981]) *Opium and the People: Opiate Use in Nineteenth Century England*. New Haven: Yale University Press.

Berthelot, J. (1986) 'Sociological discourse and the body', *Theory Culture and Society*, 3: 155–64.

Birke, L. (1986) *Women, Feminism and Biology*. Brighton: Wheatsheaf.

Birke, L. (1992) 'In pursuit of difference: scientific studies of women and men', in G. Kirkup and L.S. Keller (eds), *Inventing Women, Science, Technology and Gender*. Cambridge: Polity Press.

Bleier, R. (1984) *Science and Gender: A Critique of Biology and its Theories on Women*. Oxford: Pergamon Press.

Bloch, C. (1987) 'Everyday life, sensuality, and body culture', *Women's Studies International Forum*, 10(4): 433–42.

Bloch, M. and Parry, J. (eds) (1982) *Death and the Regeneration of Life*. Cambridge: Cambridge University Press.

Board of Education (1923) *Report of the Consultative Committee on Differentiation of the Curriculum for Boys and Girls Respectively in Secondary Schools*. London: HMSO.

Bogner, A. (1992) 'The theory of the civilizing process', *Theory, Culture and Society*, 9: 23–53.

Bordo, S. (1988) 'Anorexia nervosa', in I. Diamond and L. Quinby (eds), *Feminism and Foucault: Reflections on Resistance*. Boston, MD: Northeastern University Press.

Bordo, S. (1989) 'Reading the slender body', in M. Jacubus, E. Fox Keller and S. Shuttleworth (eds), *Women, Science and the Body Politic*. New York: Methuen.

Bordo, S. (1993) *Unbearable Weight: Feminism, Western Culture and the Body*. Berkeley: University of California Press.

Boston Women's Health Collective (1971) *Our Bodies, Our Selves*. New York: Simon and Schuster.

Bourdieu, P. (1973) 'Cultural reproduction and social reproduction', in R. Brown (ed.), *Knowledge, Education and Social Change*. London: Tavistock.

Bourdieu, P. (1974) 'The school as a conservative force: scholastic and cultural inequalities', in J. Eggleton (ed.), *Contemporary Research in the Sociology of Education*. London: Methuen.

Bourdieu, P. (1978) 'Sport and social class', *Social Science Information*, 17: 819–40.

Bourdieu, P. (1981) 'Men and machines', in K. Knorr-Cetina and A.V. Cicourel (eds), *Advances in Social Theory and Methodology*. London: RKP.

Bourdieu, P. (1984) *Distinction: A Social Critique of the Judgement of Taste*. London: Routledge.

Bourdieu, P. (1985) 'The social space and the genesis of groups', *Theory and Society*, 14(6): 723–44.

Bourdieu, P. (1986) 'The forms of capital', in J. Richardson (ed.), *Handbook of Theory and Research for the Sociology of Education*. New York: Greenwood Press.

Bourdieu, P. (1988a) 'Program for a sociology of sport', *Sociology of Sport Journal*, 5: 153–61.

Bourdieu, P. (1988b) *Homo Academicus*. Cambridge: Polity Press.

Bourdieu, P. and Passeron, Jean-Claude (1990 [1977]) *Reproduction in Education, Society and Culture*, 2nd edn. London: Sage.

Bovey, S. (1989) *Being Fat is not a Sin*. London: Pandora.

Braudel, F. (1973) *Capitalism and Material Life 1400–1800*. London: Weidenfeld and Nicolson.

Bray, A. (1982) *Homosexuality in Renaissance England*. London: Gay Men's Press.

Brittan, A. (1981) *Masculinity and Power*. Oxford: Basil Blackwell.

Brohm, J.-M. (1978) *Sport: A Prison of Measured Time*. London: Ink Books.

Brown, B. and Adams, P. (1979) 'The feminine body and feminist politics', *m/f*. 3: 35–50.

Brown, P. (1988) *The Body and Society: Men, Women and Sexual Renunciation in Early Christianity*. London: Faber and Faber.

Brubaker, R. (1985) 'Rethinking classical theory', *Theory and Society*, 14(6): 745–75.

Bryant, C. and Jary, D. (1991) *Giddens' Theory of Structuration*. London: Routledge.

Bryson, L. (1987) 'Sport and the maintenance of masculine hegemony', *Women's Studies International Forum*, 10: 349–60.

Buffery, A. and Gray, J. (1972) 'Sex differences in the development of spatial and linguistic skills', in C. Ounsted and D. Taylor (eds), *Gender Differences: Their Ontogeny and Significance*. Edinburgh: Churchill Livingstone.

Burkitt, I. (1991) *Social Selves: Theories of the Social Formation of Personality*. London: Sage.

Burkitt, I.(1992) 'Beyond the "iron cage": Anthony Giddens on modernity and the self', *History of the Human Sciences*, 5: 71–9.

Burkitt, I. (1999) *Bodies of Thought*. London: Sage.

Burns, T. (1992) *Erving Goffman*. London: Routledge.

Bury, M. (1986) 'Social constructionism and the development of medical sociology', *Sociology of Health and Illness*, 8: 137–69.

Bury, M. (1987) 'Social constructionism and medical sociology: a rejoinder to Nicolson and McLaughton', *Sociology of Health and Illness*, 9: 439–41.

Butler, J. (1990) *Gender Trouble*. London: Routledge.

Butler, J. (1993) *Bodies that Matter*. London: Routledge.

Buytendijk, F. (1950) 'The phenomenological approach to the problem of feeling and emotions', in M. Reymert (ed.), *Feelings and Emotions* (The Mooseheart Symposium in Cooperation with the University of Chicago). New York: McGraw-Hill.

Buytendijk, F. (1974) *Prolegomena to an Anthropological Physiology*. Pittsburgh, PA: Duquesne University Press.

Bynum, C. (1987) *Holy Feast and the Holy Fast: The Religious Significance of Food to Medieval Women*. California: University of California Press.

Calnan, M. (1987) *Health and Illness - The Lay Perspective*. London: Tavistock.

Campling, J. (ed.) (1981) *Images of Ourselves. Women with Disabilities Talking*. London: RKP.

Camporesi, P. (1988) *The Incorruptible Flesh*. Cambridge: Cambridge University Press.

Cannon, W.B. (1942) 'Voodoo death', *American Anthropologist*, 44.

Caplan, A. (ed.) (1978) *The Sociobiology Debate: Readings on Ethical and Scientific Issues*. New York: Harper and Row.

Carby, H. (1987) '"On the threshold of women's era": lynching, empire and sexuality in black feminist theory', in H. Gates (ed.), *Figures in Black*. Oxford: Oxford University Press.

Carrington, B. (1982) 'Sport as a sidetrack', in L. Barton and S. Walker (eds), *Race, Class and Education*. London: Croom Helm.

Chapman, R. and Rutherford, J. (eds) (1988) *Male Order: Unwrapping Masculinity*. London: Lawrence and Wishart.

Charles, N. and Kerr, M. (1988) *Women, Food and Families*. Manchester: Manchester University Press.

Chernin, K. (1983) *Womansize. The Tyranny of Slenderness*. London: The Women's Press.

Clark, J., Modgil, C. and Modgil, S. (1990) (eds) *Anthony Giddens: Consensus and Controversy*. Lewes: Falmer Press.

Clarke, J. (1990) 'The skinheads and the magical recovery of working class community', in S. Hall and T. Jefferson (eds), *Resistance through Rituals*, 2nd edn. London: Hutchinson.

Cohen, I. (1989) *Structuration Theory. Anthony Giddens and the Constitution of Social Life*. London: Macmillan.

Cohen, P. (1988) 'The perversions of inheritance: studies in the making of multi-racist Britain', in P. Cohen and H.S. Bains (eds), *Multi-Racist Britain*. London: Macmillan.

Collins, R. (1975) *Conflict Sociology: Toward an Explanatory Science*. New York: Academic Press.

Collins, R. (1981) *The Credential Society*. New York: Academic Press.

Collins, R. (1988) 'Theoretical continuities in Goffman's work', in P. Drew and A. Wootton (eds), *Erving Goffman: Exploring the Interaction Order*. Cambridge: Polity Press.

Collinson, D., Knights, D. and Collinson, M. (1990) *Managing to Discriminate*. London: Routledge.

Connell, R. (1983) *Which Way Is Up?* Sydney: George Allen and Unwin.

Connell, R. (1987) *Gender and Power*. Cambridge: Polity Press.

Connell, R.W. (1997) 'Why is classical theory classical?', *American Journal of Sociology*. 102(6): 1511–1557.

Connell, R. and Dowsett, G. (1992) 'The unclean motion of the generative parts: frameworks in Western thought on sexuality', in R. Connell and G. Dowsett (eds), *Rethinking Sex: Social Theory and Sexuality Research*. Melbourne: Melbourne University Press.

Connell, R. and Kippax, S. (1990) 'Sexuality in the AIDS crisis: patterns of sexual practice and pleasure in a sample of Australian gay and bisexual men', *Journal of Sex Research*, 27(2): 167–98.

Corbin, A. (1986) *The Foul and the Fragrant, Odor and the French Social Imagination*. Cambridge, Mass: Harvard University Press.

Cornwell, J. (1984) *Hard Earned Lives - Accounts of Health and Illness from East London*. London: Tavistock.

Craib, I. (1989) *Psychoanalysis and Social Theory: The Limits of Sociology*. Brighton: Harvester Wheatsheaf.

Craib, I. (1992) *Anthony Giddens*. London: Routledge.

Crawford, R. (1977) 'You are dangerous to your health: the ideology and politics of victim blaming', *International Journal of Health Services*, 7(4): 663–80.

Crawford, R. (1984) 'A cultural account of "health": control, release, and the social body', in J. McKinlay (ed.), *Issues in the Political Economy of Health Care*. London: Tavistock.

Crawford, R. (1987) 'Cultural influences on prevention and the emergence of a new health consciousness', in N. Weinstein (ed.), *Taking Care: Understanding and Encouraging Self-Protective Behaviour*. Cambridge: Cambridge University Press.

Crossley, N. (1995) 'Merleau-Ponty, the elusive body and carnal sociology', *Body and Society*, 1(1): 43–66.

Crossley, N. (2001) *The Social Body: Habit, Identity and Desire*. London: Sage.

Csordas, T.J. (1994) (ed.) *Embodiment and Experience: The Existential Ground of Culture and Self*. Cambridge: Cambridge University Press.

Dale, R. and Pires, E. (1984) 'Linking people and jobs: the indeterminate place of educational credentials', in P. Broadfoot (ed.) *Selection, Certification and Control*. Lewes: Falmer.

Dalton, K. (1979) *Once a Month*. London: Fontana.

Dana, M. (1987) 'Boundaries: One-way mirror to the self', in M. Lawrence (ed.), *Fed Up and Hungry*. London: The Women's Press.

David, M. (1980) *The State, the Family and Education*. London: RKP.

Davies, B. (1989) 'Education for sexism. A theoretical analysis of the sex/gender bias in education', *Educational Philosophy and Theory*, 21: 1–19.

Davies, B. (1990) 'The problem of desire', *Social Problems*, 37(4): 501–16.

Davis, F. (1989) 'Of maids' uniforms and blue jeans: the drama of status ambivalences in clothing and fashion', *Qualitative Sociology*, 12(4): 337–55.

Dawe, A. (1979) 'The two sociologies', *British Journal of Sociology*, 21(2): 207–18.

Dawkins, R. (1976) *The Selfish Gene*. London: Paladin.

De Swaan, A. (1990) *The Management of Normality: Critical Essays in Health and Welfare*. London: Routledge.

Deem, R. (1986) *All Work and No Play? The Sociology of Women and Leisure*. Milton Keynes: Open University Press.

Della Fave, L.R. (1991) 'Ritual and the legitimation of inequality', *Sociological Perspectives*, 34: 21–38.

Delphy, C. (1984) *Close to Home: A Materialist Analysis of Women's Oppression*. London: Hutchinson.

Descartes, R. (1974) *The Philosophical Works of Descartes*. Trans. E. Haldene and G. Ross. Cambridge: Cambridge University Press.

Dews, P. (1987) *Logics of Disintegration: Post-Structuralist Thought and the Claims of Critical Theory*. London: Verso.

Diamond, I. and Quinby, L. (eds) (1988) *Feminism and Foucault: Reflections on Resistance*. Boston, Mass.: Northeastern University Press.

Diamond, N. (1985) 'Thin is the feminist issue', *Feminist Review*, 19: 46–64.

Dore, R. (1976) *The Diploma Disease*. London: Allen and Unwin.

Douglas, A. (1977) *The Feminization of American Culture*. New York: Alfred A. Kopf.

Douglas, M. (1966) *Purity and Danger, An Analysis of the Concepts of Pollution and Taboo*. London: RKP.

Douglas, M. (1970) *Natural Symbols: Explorations in Cosmology*. London: The Cresset Press.

Douglas, M. and Isherwood, B. (1979) *The World of Goods: Towards an Anthropology of Consumption*. London: Allen Lane.

Doyal, L. and Gough, I. (1991) *A Theory of Human Need*. Houndmills: Macmillan.

Dreyfus, H. and Rabinow, P. (1982) *Michel Foucault: Beyond Structuralism and Hermeneutics*. Brighton: Harvester.

Dull, D. and West, C. (1991) 'Accounting for cosmetic surgery: the accomplishment of gender', *Social Problems*, 38(1): 54–70.

Dunning, E., Murphy, P. and Williams, J. (1988) *The Roots of Football Hooliganism*. London: RKP.

Durkheim, E. (1938) *The Rules of the Sociological Method*. New York: Free Press.

Durkheim, E. (1951 [1897]) *Suicide: A Study in Sociology*. Glencoe, IL: Free Press.

Durkheim, E. (1984 [1893]) *The Division of Labour in Society*. London: Macmillan.

Durkheim, (1995 [1912]) *The Elementary Forms of Religious Life*. Trans. Karen E. Fields. New York: Free Press.

Duroche, L. (1990) 'Male perception as a social construct', in J. Hearn and D. Morgan (eds), *Men, Masculinities and Social Theory*, London: Hyman.

Dutton, D. (1986) 'Social class, health and illness', in I. Aitkin and D. Mechanic (eds), *Applications of Social Science to Clinical Medicine and Health Policy*. New Brunswick, NJ: Rutgers University Press.

Dyer, R. (1986) *Heavenly Bodies: Film Stars and Society*. New York: St Martin's Press.

Ehrenreich, B. (1983) *The Hearts of Men: American Dreams and their Flight from Commitment*. London: Pluto.

Ehrenreich, B. and English, D. (1988) *For Her Own Good. 150 Years of the Expert's Advice to Women*. London: Pluto.

Eisenstein, H. (1984) *Contemporary Feminist Thought*. London: Allen and Unwin.

Eisenstein, Z. (1988) *The Female Body and the Law*. Berkeley, CA: University of California Press.

Elias, N. (1978a [1939]) *The Civilizing Process*, vol. 1: *The History of Manners*. Oxford: Basil Blackwell.

Elias, N. (1978b) 'The civilizing process revisited', *Theory and Society*, 5: 243–53.

Elias, N. (1978c) 'On transformations of aggressiveness', *Theory and Society*, 5: 229–42.

Elias, N. (1978d) *What is Sociology?* London: Hutchinson.

Elias, N. (1982 [1939]) *The Civilizing Process*, vol. 2: *State Formation and Civilization*. Oxford: Basil Blackwell.

Elias, N. (1983) *The Court Society*. Oxford: Basil Blackwell.

Elias, N. (1985) *The Loneliness of the Dying*. Oxford: Basil Blackwell.

Elias, N. (1987a) 'On human beings and their emotions: a process sociological essay', *Theory, Culture and Society*, 4: 339–61.

Elias, N. (1987b) 'The changing balance of power between the sexes - a process-sociological study: the example of the Ancient Roman State', *Theory, Culture and Society*, 4: 287–316.

Elias, N. (1988) 'Violence and civilization: the state monopoly of physical violence and its infringement', in J. Keane (ed.), *Civil Society and the State*. London: Verso.

Elias, N. (1991) *The Symbol Theory*. London: Sage.

Elias, N. and Dunning, E. (1986) *Quest for Excitement: Sport and Leisure in the Civilizing Process*. Oxford: Basil Blackwell.

Elias, N. and Scotson, J. (1965) *The Established and the Outsiders*. London: Frank Cass.

Elling, R. (1986) *The Struggle for Workers' Health: A Study of Six Industrialized Countries*. Farmingdale, NY: Baywood.

Engel, G. (1971) 'Sudden and rapid death during psychological stress: folklore of a folk wisdom', *Annals of Internal Medicine*, 74: 771–82.

Epstein, B. (1987) 'Women's anger and compulsive eating', in M. Lawrence (ed.), *Fed Up and Hungry*. London: The Women's Press.

Evans, J. and Hall, S. (1999) *Visual Culture: The Reader*. London: Sage.

Evans, M. and Lee, E. (2002) *Real Bodies*. Houndmills: Palgrave.

Fairhurst, E. (1998) '"Growing old gracefully" as opposed to "mutton dressed as lamb"', in S. Nettleton and J. Watson (eds), *The Body in Everyday Life*. London: Routledge.

Falk, P. (1985) 'Corporeality and its fates in history', *Acta Sociologica*, 28: 115–36.

Falk, P. (1991) 'Le Livre de la chair', in C. Garnier (ed.), *Le corps rassemble*. Montreal/Quebec, Université du Quebec á Montreal, Editions D'Arc.

Fanon, F. (1970) *A Dying Colonialism*. New York: Grove Press.

Fanon, F. (1984 [1952]) *Black Skin, White Masks*. London: Pluto Press.

Featherstone, M. (1982) 'The body in consumer culture', *Theory, Culture and Society*, 1: 18–33.

Featherstone, M. (1987) 'Leisure, symbolic power and the life course', in J. Horne, D. Jary and A. Tomlinson (eds), *Sport, Leisure and Social Relations*. London: RKP.

Featherstone, M. (1990) 'Perspectives on consumer culture', *Sociology*, 24(1): 5–22.

Featherstone, M. (1991) *Consumer Culture and Postmodernism*. London: Sage.

Featherstone, M. (1995) 'Post-bodies, ageing and virtual reality', in M. Featherstone and A. Wernick (eds), *Images of Ageing*. London: Routledge.

Featherstone, M. and Burrows, R. (1995) 'Cultures of technological embodiment: an introduction', *Body and Society*, 1(3–4): 1–20.

Featherstone, M. and Hepworth, M. (1983) 'The midlifestyle of "George and Lyn": notes on a popular strip', *Theory, Culture and Society*, 1: 85–92.

Featherstone, M. and Hepworth, M. (1988) 'Ageing and old age: reflections on the postmodern life-course', in B. Blytheway, T. Keit, P. Allatt and A. Byrman (eds), *Becoming and Being Old*. London: Sage.

Featherstone, M. and Hepworth, M. (1991) 'The mask of ageing and the postmodern life course', in M. Featherstone, M. Hepwroth and B.S. Turner (eds), *The Body: Social Process and Cultural Theory*. London: Sage.

Featherstone, M., Hepworth, M. and Turner, B. (eds) (1991) *The Body: Social Process and Cultural Theory*. London: Sage.

Fedigan, L. (1992) 'The changing role of women in models of human evolution', in G. Kirkup and L. Smith Keller (eds), *Inventing Women: Science, Technology and Gender*. Cambridge: Polity Press.

Feher, M., Naddaff, R. and Tazi, N. (1989a) *Fragments for a History of the Human Body*, Part I. New York: Zone.

Feher, M., Naddaff, R. and Tazi, N. (1989b) *Fragments for a History of the Human Body*, Part II. New York: Zone.

Feher, M., Naddaff, R. and Tazi, N. (1989c) *Fragments for a History of the Human Body*, Part III. New York: Zone.

Ferrer, G. (1992) 'A double-breasted boost', *The Guardian*, 22 January.

Finch, J. (1983a) 'Dividing the rough and respectable: working class women and pre-school playgroups', in E. Garmarnikow, D. Morgan, J. Purvis and D. Taylorson (eds), *The Public and the Private*. London: Heinemann Educational Books.

Finch, J. (1983b) *Married to the Job*. London: Allen and Unwin.

Finch, J. (1984) *Education as Social Policy*. London: Longman.

Finkler, K. (1989) 'The universality of nerves', in D. Davis and S. Low (eds), *Gender, Health and Illness: The Case of Nerves*. New York: Hemisphere Publishing Corporation.

Firestone, S. (1971) *The Dialectic of Sex*. London: Jonathan Cape.

Fletcher, S. (1984) *Women First: The Female Tradition in English Physical Education 1880–1980*. London: The Athlone Press.

Foucault, M. (1973) *The Birth of the Clinic*. London: Tavistock.

Foucault, M. (1974) *The Archaeology of Knowledge*. London: Tavistock.

Foucault, M. (1977) *Language, Counter-Memory, Practice: Selected Essays and Interviews*. Oxford: Blackwell.

Foucault, M. (1979a) *Discipline and Punish: The Birth of the Prison*. Harmondsworth: Penguin.

Foucault, M. (1979b) 'Governmentality', *Ideology and Consciousness*, 6: 5–22.

Foucault, M. (1980) 'Body/Power', in C. Gordon (ed.), *Michel Foucault: Power/Knowledge*. Brighton: Harvester.

Foucault, M. (1981) *The History of Sexuality*, vol. 1: *An Introduction*. Harmondsworth: Penguin.

Foucault, M. (1982) 'The subject and power', in H. Dreyfuss and P. Rabinow (eds), *Michel Foucault: Beyond Structuralism and Hermeneutics*. Brighton: Harvester.

Frank, A. (1990) 'Bringing bodies back in: a decade review', *Theory, Culture and Society*, 7: 131–62.

Frank, A. (1991) 'For a sociology of the body: an analytical review', in M. Featherstone, M. Hepworth and B. Turner (eds), *The Body: Social Process and Cultural Theory*. London: Sage.

Frank, A. (1995) *The Wounded Storyteller: Body, Illness and Ethics*. Chicago: The University of Chicago Press.

Frankenberg, R. (1990) 'Review article: Disease, literature and the body in the era of AIDS - a preliminary exploration', *Sociology of Health and Illness*, 12(3): 351–60.

Frankenberg, R. 'Risk: anthropological and epidemiological narratives of prevention', in S. Lindenbaum and M. Lock (eds), *Knowleldge, Power and Practice in Medicine and Everyday Life*. Berkeley CA: California University Press.

Frankenhauser, M. and Gardell, B. (1976) 'Underload and overload in working life: outline of a multidisciplinary approach', *Journal of Human Stress*. 2: 35–46.

Freund, P. (1982) *The Civilized Body: Social Domination, Control and Health*. Philadelphia, PA: Temple University Press.

Freund, P. (1988) 'Understanding socialized human nature', *Theory and Society*, 17: 839–64.

Freund, P. (1990) 'The expressive body: a common ground for the sociology of emotions and health and illness', *Sociology of Health and Illness*, 12(4): 454–77.

Freund, P. and McGuire, M. (1991) *Health, Illness and the Social Body*. Englewood Cliffs, NJ: Prentice-Hall.

Friday, N. (1991) *Women on Top*. London: Hutchinson.

Friedman, M. and Rosenman, R. (1974) *Type A Behaviour and Your Heart*. New York: Fawcett Crest.

Fuss, D. (1990) *Essentially Speaking: Feminism, Nature and Difference*. London: Routledge.

Fussell, S. (1991) *Muscle: Confessions of an Unlikely Body Builder*. New York: Poseidon Press.

Gallagher, C. and Laqueur, T. (eds) (1987) *The Making of the Modern Body. Sexuality and Society in the Nineteenth Century*. Berkeley, CA: University of California Press.

Gallup, G. (1982) 'Permanent breast enlargement in human females: a sociobiological analysis', *Journal of Human Evolution*, 11: 597–601.

Game, A. (1991) *Undoing the Social: Towards a Deconstructive Sociology*. Milton Keynes: Open University Press.

Garland, D. (1990) *Punishment and Modern Society*. Oxford: Clarendon Press.

Gehlen, A. (1969) *Moral and Hypermoral*. Frankfurt: Athenaeum.

Gerber, R. (1992) 'Manipulated lady', *The Independent on Sunday*, 12 July, 44–6.

Gergen, K. (1991) *The Saturated Self: Dilemmas of Identity in Contemporary Life*. New York: Basic Books.

Giddens, A. (1976) *New Rules of Sociological Method*. London: Hutchinson.

Giddens, A. (1979) *Central Problems in Social Theory*. Houndmills: Macmillan.

Giddens, A. (1981) 'Agency, institution and time-space analysis', in K. Knorr-Cetina and A.V. Cicourel (eds), *Advances in Social Theory and Methodology*. London: RKP.

Giddens, A. (1984) *The Constitution of Society*. Cambridge: Polity Press.

Giddens, A. (1987) 'Structuralism, post-structuralism and the production of culture', in A. Giddens and J. Turner (eds), *Social Theory Today*. Cambridge: Polity Press.

Giddens, A. (1988) 'Goffman as a systematic social theorist', in P. Drew and A. Wootton (eds), *Erving Goffman. Exploring the Interaction Order*. Cambridge: Polity Press.

Giddens, A. (1990) *The Consequences of Modernity*. Cambridge: Polity Press.

Giddens, A. (1991) *Modernity and Self-Identity*. Cambridge: Polity Press.

Gilmore, D. (1990) *Manhood in the Making: Cultural Concepts of Masculinity*. New Haven, Conn.: Yale University Press.

Gilroy, P. (2000) *Between Camps: Nations, Cultures and the Allure of Race*. London: Penguin.

Gilroy, S. (1989) 'The emBody-ment of power: gender and physical activity', *Leisure Studies*, 8: 163–71.

Gimlin, D. (2002) *BodyWork: Beauty and Self-Image in American Culture*. Berkeley: University of California Press.

Goffman, E. (1956) 'Embarrassment and social organisation', *American Journal of Sociology*, LXII(3): 264–71.

Goffman, E. (1963) *Behaviour in Public Places: Notes on the Social Organization of Gatherings*. New York: The Free Press.

Goffman, E. (1968) *Stigma: Notes on the Management of Spoiled Identity*. Harmondsworth: Penguin.

Goffman, E. (1969) *The Presentation of Self in Everyday Life*. Harmondsworth: Penguin.

Goffman, E. (1974) *Frame Analysis: An Essay on the Organization of Experience*. New York: Harper and Row.

Goffman, E. (1977) 'The arrangement between the sexes', *Theory and Society*, 4: 301–31.

Goffman, E. (1979) *Gender Advertisements*. London: Macmillan.

Goffman, E. (1983) 'The interaction order', *American Sociological Review*, 48: 1–17.

Goffman, E. (1987) 'The arrangement between the sexes', in M. Deegan and M. Hill (eds), *Interaction*. Winchester, Mass.: Allen and Unwin.

Goffman, E. (1990 [1963]) *Stigma. Notes on the Management of Spoiled Identity*. London: Penguin.

Goldberg, S. (1973) *The Inevitability of Patriarchy*. New York: William Morrow.

Golden, J. and Hope J. (1991) 'Storm over virgin births', *Daily Mail*, 11 March.

Goldsmith, F. and Kerr, L. (1982) *Occupational Safety and Health*. New York: Human Sciences Press.

Goodger, J. and Goodger, B. (1989) 'Excitement and representation: toward a sociological explanation of the significance of sport in modern society', *Quest*, 41(3): 257–72.

Gordon, C. (1980) *Michel Foucault: Power/Knowledge*. Brighton: Harvester Press.

Gordon, R. (2001) 'Eating disorders East and West: a culture bound system unbound', in M.

Nasser, M. Katzman and R. Gordon (eds), *Eating Disorders and Cultures in Transition*. East Sussex: Brunner-Routledge.

Gordon, S. (1985) 'Micro-sociological theories of emotion', in S. Helle and S. Eisenstadt (eds), *Micro Sociological Perspectives on Sociological Theory*, vol. 2. London: Sage.

Goudsblom, J. (1987) 'The domestication of fire as a civilizing process', *Theory, Culture and Society*, 4: 457–76.

Gould, S.J. (1981) *The Mismeasure of Man*. Harmondsworth: Penguin.

Graham, H. (1984) *Women, Health and the Family*. Brighton: Wheatsheaf.

Grant, L. (1992) 'A distortion of physical reality', *The Independent on Sunday*, 12 January.

Graydon, J. (1983) '"But it's more than a game. It's an institution." Feminist perspectives on sport', *Feminist Review*, 13: 5–16.

Green, E. and Hebron, S. (1988) 'Leisure and male partners', in E. Wimbush and M. Talbot (eds), *Relative Freedoms: Women and Leisure*. Milton Keynes: Open University Press.

Green, H. (1986) *Fit for America: Health, Fitness, Sport and American Society*. New York: Pantheon.

Greer, G. (1971) *The Female Eunuch*. London: Paladin.

Gregory, M. (1978) 'Epilogue', in M. Gregory, A. Silvers and D. Sutch (eds), *Sociobiology and Human Nature*. San Francisco, CA: Jossey Bass.

Griffin, C. (1985) *Typical Girls?* London: RKP.

Griffin, C., Hobson, D., MacIntosh, S. and McCabe, T. (1982) 'Women and leisure', in J. Hargreaves (ed.), *Sport, Culture and Ideology*. London: RKP.

Griffin, S. (1978) *Women and Nature: The Roaring Inside Her*. New York: Harper and Row.

Grogan, S. (1999) *Body Image*. London: Routledge.

Grosz, E. (1990) 'A note on essentialism and difference', in S. Gunew (ed.), *Feminist Knowledge. Critique and Construct*. London: Routledge.

Grosz, E. (1994) *Volatile Bodies: Toward a Corporeal Feminism*. Bloomington, IN: Indiana University Press.

Grosz, E. and Lepervanche, M. (1988) 'Feminism and science', in B. Caine et al. (eds), *Crossing Boundaries: Feminisms and the Critique of Knowledges*. Sydney: Allen and Unwin.

Gruchow, W. (1979) 'Catecholamine activity and infectious disease episodes', *Journal of Human Stress*, 5: 11–17.

Gusterson, H. (1991) 'Nuclear war, the gulf war, and the disappearing body', *Journal of Urban and Cultural Studies*, 2: 45–55.

Haferkamp, H. (1987) 'Reply to Stephen Mennell', *Theory, Culture and Society*, 4: 562.

Hall, C. (1992) 'Girls aged nine "are obsessed by weight"', *The Independent*, 10 April.

Hall, S., Critcher, C., Jefferson, T., Clarke, J. and Roberts, B. (1978) *Policing the Crisis. Mugging, the State and Law and Order*. Houndmills: Macmillan.

Hall, S. and Gieben, B. (eds) (1992) *Formations of Modernity*. Cambridge: Polity Press.

Hall, S. and Jameson, F. (1990) 'Clinging to the wreckage', *Marxism Today*, September, pp. 28–31.

Harburg, E., Blakelock, E. and Roeper, P. (1979) 'Resentful and reflective coping with arbitrary authority and blood pressure', *Psychosomatic Medicine*, 41: 189–202.

Harburg, E., Haunstein, L., Chare, C., Schull, W. and Short, M. (1973) 'Socio-ecological stress, suppressed hostility, skin color and black-white male blood pressure: Detroit', *Psychosomatic Medicine*, 35: 276.

Hargreaves, D. (1969) *Social Relations in a Secondary School*. London: RKP.

Hargreaves, J. (1986) *Sport, Power and Culture*. Cambridge: Polity Press.

Hargreaves, J.A. (1987) 'Victorian familialism and the formative years of female sport', in J.A. Mangan and R.J. Park (eds), *From 'Fair Sex' to Feminism: Sport and the Socialization of Women in the Industrial and Post-Industrial Eras*. London: Frank Cass.

Hargreaves, J.A. (1990) 'Changing images of the sporting female', *Sport and Leisure*, July-August, pp. 14–17.

Harker, R., Mahar, C. and Wilkes, C. (eds) (1990) *An Introduction to the Work of Pierre Bourdieu: The Practice of Theory*. London: Macmillan.

Hartmann, H. (1979) 'The unhappy marriage of marxism and feminism. Towards a more progressive union', *Capital and Class*, 8: 1–33.

Hartwig, A. and Eckland, J. (1990) 'Current implementation and practice of educational policy for HIV-positive children: a national study', *The Urban Review*, 22(3): 221–38.

Harvey, J. and Sparks, R. (1991) 'The politics of the body in the context of modernity', *Quest*, 43(2): 164–89.

Haug, F. (1987) *Female Sexualization*. London: Verso.

Head, H. (1920) *Studies in Neurology*. Oxford: Oxford University Press.

Hearn, J. (1987) *The Gender of Oppression: Men, Masculinity and the Critique of Marxism*. Brighton: Wheatsheaf.

Hearn, J. and Morgan, O. (eds) (1990) *Men, Masculinities and Social Theory*. London: Unwin Hyman.

Heim, M. (1995) 'The design of virtual reality', *Body and Society*, 1(3): 65–77.

Helm, D. (1982) 'Talk's forms: comments on Goffman's *Forms of Talk*', *Human Studies*, 5: 147–57.

Henley, N. (1977) *Body Politics*. Englewood Cliffs, NJ: Prentice-Hall.

Hepworth, M. and Featherstone, M. (1982) *Surviving Middle Age*. Oxford: Basil Blackwell.

Heritier-Auge, F. (1989) 'Older women, stout-hearted women, women of substance', in M. Feher, R. Naddaff and N. Tazi (eds), *Fragments for a History of the Human Body*, Part III. New York: Zone.

Hertz, R. (1960 [1909]) *Death and the Right Hand*. London: Cohen and West.

Hewitt, M. (1983) 'Bio-politics and social policy: Foucault's account of welfare', *Theory, Culture and Society*, 2: 67–84.

Hills, S. (ed.) (1987) *Corporate Violence*. NJ: Rowman and Littlefield.

Hirst, P. and Woolley, P. (1982) *Social Relations and Human Attributes*. London: Tavistock.

Hochschilld, A. (1983) *The Managed Heart: Commercialization of Human Feeling*. Berkeley, CA: University of California Press.

Hochschild, A. (1989) 'Reply to Cas Wouter's review essay on the Managed Heart', *Theory, Culture and Society*, 6(3): 439–45.

Hoff, L.A. (1990) *Battered Women As Survivors*. London: Routledge.

Honneth, A. and Joas, H. (1988 [1980]) *Social Action and Human Nature*. Cambridge: Cambridge University Press.

Huntingdon, R. and Metcalf, P. (1979) *Celebrations of Death*. Cambridge: Cambridge University Press.

Illich, I. (1976) *Limits to Medicine*. London: Marion Boyars.

Jaggar, A. (1984) 'Human biology in feminist theory: sexual equality reconsidered', in C. Gould (ed.), *Beyond Domination*. NJ: Rowman and Allenheld.

James, A. (1990) 'The good, the bad and the delicious: the role of confectionery in British society', *The Sociological Review*, 38(4): 666–88.

Jameson, F. (1984) 'Postmodernism: Or the cultural logic of late capitalism', *New Left Review*, 146: 53–92.

Jameson, F. (1985) 'Postmodernism and the consumer society', in H. Foster (ed.), *Postmodern Culture*. London: Pluto.

Jary, D. (1987) 'Sport and leisure in the "civilizing process"', *Theory, Culture and Society*, 4: 563–70.

Jeffords, S. (1989) *The Remasculinization of America: Gender and the Vietnam War*. Bloomington, Ind.: Indiana University Press.

Joas, H. (1983) 'The intersubjective constitution of the body-image', *Human Studies*, 6: 197–204.

Joas, H. (1996) *The Creativity of Action*. Cambridge: Polity.

Joas, H. (1997) *G.H. Mead: A Contemporary Re-examination of his Thought*. Cambridge, MA: The MIT Press.

Johnson, D. (1983) *Body*. Boston: Beacon Press.

Johnson, J. and Sarason, I. (1978) 'Life stress, depression and anxiety: internal-external control of a moderator variable', *Journal of Psychosomatic Research*, 22: 205–8.

Johnson, M. (1987) *The Body in the Mind: The Bodily Basis of Meaning, Imagination and Reason*. Chicago: University of Chicago Press.

Jones, C. (1977) *Immigration and Social Policy in Britain*. London: Tavistock.

Jordan, W. (1982) 'First impressions: initial English confrontations with Africans', in C. Husband (ed.), *'Race' in Britain*. London: Hutchinson.

Jordanova, L. (1989) *Sexual Visions: Images of Gender in Science and Medicine Between the Eighteenth and Twentieth Centuries*. New York: Harvester Wheatsheaf.

Kamerman, J. (1988) *Death in the Midst of Life*. Englewood Cliffs, NJ: Prentice-Hall.

Kanneh, K. (1992) 'Feminism and the Colonial Body', in B. Ashcroft, G. Griffiths and H. Tiffin (eds), *The Post-Colonial Studies Reader*. London: Routledge.

Kant, I. (1985 [1797]) *Foundations of the Physics of Morals*. London: Macmillan.

Kaplan, G. and Adams, C. (1989) 'Early women supporters of National Socialism: the reaction to feminism and to male-defined sexuality', in J. Milfull (ed.), *The Attractions of Fascism*. New York: Berg.

Kaplan, G. and Rogers, L. (1990) 'The definition of male and female. Biological reductionism and the sanctions of normality', in S. Gunew (ed.), *Feminist Knowledge, Critique and Construct*. London: Routledge.

Keddie, N. (1971) 'Classroom knowledge', in M. Young (ed.), *Knowledge and Control*. London: Collier-Macmillan.

Keith, V. and Herring, C. (1991) 'Skin tone and stratification in the black community', *American Journal of Sociology*, 97: 760–78.

Kelleman, S. (1985) *Emotional Anatomy: The Structure of Experience*. Berkeley, CA: Center Press.

Kelly, D. (1980) *Anxiety and Emotions*. Springfield, Ill.: Charles C. Thomas.

Kelly, K. (1994) *Out of Control: The New Biology of Machines*. London: Fourth Estate.

Kierkegaard, S. (1941) *Concluding Unscientific Postscript*. Princeton, NJ: Princeton University Press.

Kierkegaard, S. (1944) *The Concept of Dread*. London: Macmillan.

Kimbrell, K. (1993) *The Human Boy Shop*. London: Harper Collins.

Kimmel, M. (ed.) (1987) *Changing Men. New Directions in Research on Men and Masculinity*. Newbury Park, CA: Sage.

King, D. (1987) 'Social constructionism and medical knowledge: the case of transsexualism', *Sociology of Health and Illness*, 9: 351–77.

Kirkup, G. and Keller, L.S. (1992) *Inventing Women: Science, Technology and Gender*. Cambridge: Polity Press.

Kissling, E. (1991) 'One size does not fit all, or how I learned to stop dieting and love the body', *Quest*, 43: 135–47.

Klein, A. (1991) *Sugarball: The American Game, the Dominican Dream*. New Haven, Conn.: Yale University Press.

Kroker, A. and Kroker, M. (1988) *Body Invaders: Sexuality and the Postmodern Condition*. Houndmills: Macmillan.

Kushner, H. (1989) *Self Destruction in the Promised Land: A Psychocultural Biology of American Suicide*. New Brunswick, NJ: Rutgers University Press.

Kuzmics, H. (1987) 'Civilization, state and bourgeois society: the theoretical contribution of Norbert Elias', *Theory, Culture and Society*, 4: 515–37.

Kuzmics, H. (1988) 'The civilizing process', in J. Keane (ed.), *Civil Society and the State*. New York: Verso.

Kuzmics, H. (1991) 'Embarrassment and civilization: on some similarities and differences in the work of Goffman and Elias', *Theory, Culture and Society*, 8: 1–30.

Lacey, C. (1970) *Hightown Grammar*. Manchester: Manchester University Press.

Lakoff, G. (1987) *Women, Fire and Dangerous Things*. Chicago: University of Chicago Press.

Lakoff, G. (1991) 'Metaphor and war: the metaphor system used to justify war in the gulf', *Journal of Urban and Cultural Studies*, 2(1): 59–72.

Laqueur, T. (1987) 'Orgasm, generation, and the politics of reproductive biology', in C.

Gallagher, and T. Laqueur (eds), *The Making of the Modern Body. Sexuality and Society in the Nineteenth Century*. Berkeley, CA: University of California Press.

Laqueur, T. (1989) '"Amor veneris, vel dulcedo appeletur"', in M. Feher, R. Naddaff and N. Tazi (eds), *Fragments for a History of the Human Body*, Part III. New York: Zone.

Laqueur, T. (1990) *Making Sex: Body and Gender from the Greeks to Freud*. Cambridge. Mass.: Harvard University Press.

Lasch, C. (1991) *The culture of Narcissism*. New York: Norton.

Lash, S. (1984) 'Genealogy and the body: Foucault/Deluze/Nietzsche', *Theory, Culture and Society*, 2: 1–18.

Lash, S. (1990) *Sociology of Postmodernism*. London: Routledge.

Lauer, R. (1973) 'The social readjustment scale and anxiety: a cross-cultural study', *Journal of Psychosomatic Research*, 17: 171–4.

Lawrence, M. (ed.) (1987) *Fed Up and Hungry. Women, Oppression and Food*. London: The Women's Press.

Laws, S. (1990) *Issues of Blood: The Politics of Menstruation*. Houndmills: Macmillan.

Leder, D. (1990) *The Absent Body*. Chicago: University of Chicago Press.

Leedham, R. (1991) 'Is this the short cut to perfection?' *The Guardian*, 6 September.

Lees, S. (1984) *Losing Out. Sexuality and Adolescent Girls*. London: Hutchinson.

Lennerlof, L. (1988) 'Learned helplessness at work', *International Journal of Health Studies*, 18: 207–22.

Lenskyj, H. (1986) *Out of Bounds: Women, Sport and Sexuality*. Toronto: The Women's Press.

Lessor, R. (1984) 'Consciousness of time and time for the development of consciousness: health awareness among women flight attendants', *Sociology of Health and Illness*, 6: 191–213.

Levine, D. (1995) *Visions of the Sociological Tradition*. Chicago: University of Chicago Press.

Lewontin, R. et al. (1984) *Not In Our Genes*. New York: Pantheon Books.

Livesay, J. (1989) 'Structuration theory and the unacknowledged conditions of action', *Theory, Culture and Society*, 6: 263–92.

Lock, M. (eds), *Knowledge, Power and Practice in Medicine and Everyday Life*. Berkeley, CA: California University press.

Locke, S. et al. (eds) (1985) *Foundations of Psychoneuroimmunology*. New York: Aldine.

Lowe, M. (1983) 'The dialectic of biology and culture', in M. Lowe and R. Hubbard (eds), *Women's Nature*. New York: Pergamon Press.

Luckmann, T. (1967) *The Invisible Religion*. New York: Macmillan.

Lukes, S. (1973) *Emile Durkheim: His Life and Work*. London: Allen Lane.

Lyman, S. (1990) 'Race, sex, and servitude: images of blacks in American cinema', *International Journal of Politics, Culture and Society*, 4(1): 49–77.

Lynch, J. (1979) *The Broken Heart*. New York: Basic Books.

Lynch, J. (1985) *The Language of the Heart*. New York: Basic Books.

Lyotard, J-.F. (1988) Le Postmoderne expliqué aux enfants: Correspondance, 1982–1985. Paris: Galilée.

MacDougall, J., Dembroski, T., Dimsdale, J. and Hackett, T. (1985) 'Components of type A, hostility, and anger-in: Further relationships to angiographic findings', *Health Psychology*, 4: 137–52.

Mackenzie, J. (1987) 'The imperial pioneer and hunter and the British masculine stereotype in late Victorian and Edwardian times', in J. Mangan and J. Walvin (eds), *Manliness and Morality: Middle-Class Masculinity in Britain and America, 1800–1940*. Manchester: Manchester University Press.

Mangan, J. (1987) 'Social Darwinism and upper-class education in late Victorian and Edwardian England', in J. Mangan and J. Walvin (eds), *Manliness and Morality: Middle-Class Masculinity in Britain and America, 1800–1940*. Manchester: Manchester University Press.

Mangan, J. and Park, R. (eds) (1987) *From 'Fair Sex' to Feminism: Sport and the Socialization of Women in the Industrial and Post-Industrial Eras*. London: Cass.

Mangan, J. and Walvin, J. (1987) *Manliness and Morality: Middle-Class Masculinity in Britain and America, 1800–1940*. Manchester: Manchester University Press.

Mannheim, K. (1991) *Ideology and Utopia*. London: Routledge.

Marable, M. (1983) *How Capitalism Underdeveloped Black America*. London: Pluto.

Marsh, P., Rosser, E. and Harre, R. (1978) *The Rules of Disorder*. London: RKP.

Martin, E. (1989 [1987]) *The Woman in the Body*. Milton Keynes: Open University Press.

Marx, K. (1954 [1887]) *Capital*, vol. 1. London: Lawrence and Wishart.

Marx, K. and Engels, F. (1970 [1846]) *The German Ideology*. London: Lawrence and Wishart.

Mauss, M. (1973 [1934]) 'Techniques of the body', *Economy and Society*, 2: 70–88.

Maynard, M. (1990) 'The re-shaping of sociology? Trends in the study of gender', *Sociology*, 24(2): 269–90.

McCarty, R., Horwatt, K. and Konarska, M. (1988) 'Chronic stress and sympatheticadrenal medullary responsiveness', *Social Science and Medicine*, 26: 333–41.

McCrone, K. (1988) *Sport and the Physical Emancipation of English Women 1870–1914*. London: Routledge.

McDonough, R. and Harrison, R. (1978) 'Patriarchy and the relations of production', in A. Kuhn and A.M. Wolpe (eds), *Feminism and Materialism*. London: RKP.

McIntosh, P. (1952) *Physical Education in England Since 1800*. London: G. Bell and Sons.

McIntosh, P. (1981) 'Landmarks in the history of PE since World War Two', in P. McIntosh et al. (eds), *Landmarks in the History of Physical Education*. London: RKP.

McLaren, P. (1988) 'Schooling the postmodern body: Critical pedagogy and the politics of enfleshment', *Journal of Education*, 170(3): 53–99.

McRobbie, A. (1978) 'Working class girls and the culture of femininity', in CCCS Women's Study Group (eds), *Women Take Issue*. London: Hutchinson.

McRobbie, A. (ed.) (1989) *Zoot Suits and Second Hand Dresses*. London: Macmillan.

Mead, G.H. (1907) 'Concerning animal perception', *Psychological Review*, 14: 383–90.

Mead, G.H. (1932) *The Philosophy of the Present*, ed. A.E. Murphy. Chicago, IL: La Salle.

Mead, G.H. (1934) *Mind, Self and Society*. Chicago: University of Chicago Press.

Mead, G.H. (1938) *The Philosophy of the Act*. Chicago: University of Chicago Press.

Mead, M. (1963 [1935]) *Sex and Temperament in Three Primitive Societies*. New York: Morrow.

Mellor, P. (1990) 'Self and suffering: deconstruction and reflexive definition in Buddhism and Christianity', *Religious Studies*, 27: 49–63.

Mellor, P. (1993) 'Death in high modernity: the contemporary presence and absence of death', in D. Clark (ed.), *The Sociology of Death*. Oxford: Blackwell.

Mellor, P. and Shilling, C. (1993) 'Modernity, self-identity and the sequestration of death', *Sociology*, 27(3).

Mellor, P.A. and Shilling, C. (1997) *Re-forming the Body: Religion, Community and Modernity*. London: Sage.

Mennell, S. (1985) *All Manners of Food. Eating and Taste in England and France from the Middle-Ages to the Present*. Oxford: Basil Blackwell.

Mennell, S. (1987) 'On the civilizing of appetite', *Theory, Culture and Society*, 4: 373–403.

Mennell, S. (1989) *Norbert Elias: Civilization and the Human Self-Image*. Oxford: Basil Blackwell.

Mennell, S. (1990) 'Decivilising processes: theoretical significance and some lines of research', *International Sociology*, 5(2): 205–23.

Mercer, K. and Race, I. (1988) 'Sexual politics and black masculinity: A dossier', in R. Chapman and J. Rutherford (eds), *Male Order, Unwrapping Masculinity*. London: Lawrence and Wishart.

Merleau-Ponty, M. (1962) *The Phenomenology of Perception*. London: Routledge.

Messner, M. (1987) 'The life of a man's seasons. Male identity in the life course of the jock', in M. Kimmel (ed.), *Changing Men. New Directions in Research on Men and Masculilnity*. Newbury Park, CA: Sage.

Metcalf, P. and Huntingdon, R. (1991) *Celebrations of Death: The Anthropology of Mortuary Ritual*, 2nd edn. Cambridge: Cambridge University Press.

Midgely, M. (1979) *Beast and Man: The Roots of Human Nature*. London: Methuen.

Miles, A. (1987) *The Mentally Ill in Contemporary Soceity*. Oxford: Basil Blackwell.

Miles, A. (1988) *Women and Mental Illness: The Social Context of Female Neurosis*. Brighton: Wheatsheaf.

Miles, A. (1991) *Women, Health and Medicine*. Milton Keynes: Open University Press.

Miles, M. (1992) *Carnal Knowledge*. Tunbridge Wells: Burns and Oakes.

Miller, N. (1979) 'Psychosomatic effects of learning', in E. Meyer and J. Brady (eds), *Research in the Psychobiology of Human Behaviour*. Baltimore, MD: Johns Hopkins University Press.

Mitchell, J. (1987) '"Going for the burn" and "pumping iron": What's healthy about the current fitness boom?', in M. Lawrence (ed.), *Fed Up and Hungry. Women, Oppression and Food*. London: The Women's Press.

Monks, J. and Frankenberg, R. (1994) '"Being ill and being me": self, body, and time in MS narratives', in B. Ingsted and S. White (eds), *The Anthropology of Disability*. CA: California University Press.

Moore, R. (1989) 'Education, employment and recruitment', in B. Cosin, M. Flude and M. Hales (eds), *School, Work and Equality*. London: Hodder and Stoughton.

Morris, D. (1969) *The Naked Ape*. St Albans: Panther.

Morris, M. and Patton, P. (eds) (1979) *The Pirate's Fiancée: Michel Foucault: Power, Truth and Strategy*. Sydney: Feral.

Moss, G. (1973) *Illness, Immunity and Social Interaction*. New York: John Wiley.

Munrow, A. (1981) 'Physical education in the USA', in P. McIntosh et al. (eds), *Landmarks in the History of Physical Education*. London: RKP.

Murcott, A. (1983) '"It's a pleasure to cook for him": Food, mealtimes and gender in some South Wales households', in E. Gamarnikow et al. (eds), *The Public and the Private*. London: Heinemann.

Nead, L. (1992) 'Framing and freeing: Utopias of the female body', *Radical Philosophy*, 60 (Spring): 12–15.

Nettleton, S. (1991) 'Wisdom, diligence and teeth: discursive practices and the creation of mothers', *Sociology of Health and Illness*, 13(1): 98–111.

Nettleton, S. (1992) *Power, Pain and Dentistry*. Milton Keynes: Open University Press.

Nettleton, S. and Watson, J. (1998) (eds) *The Body in Everyday Life*. London: Routledge.

Newby, H. (1991) 'One world, two cultures: sociology and the enivronment', *Network*, 50 (February).

Nicholson, M. and McLaughlin, C. (1987) 'Social constructionism and medical sociology: a reply to M.R. Bury', *Sociology of Health and Illness*, 9: 107–26.

O'Brien, M. (1979) 'Reproducing Marxist man', in L. Clark and L. Lange (eds), *The Sexism of Social and Political Thought*. Toronto: University of Toronto Press.

O'Brien, M. (1981) *The Politics of Reproduction*. London: RKP.

O'Brien, M. (1989) *Reproducing the World*. Boulder, CO: Westview Press.

O'Neill, J. (1985) *Five Bodies. The Human Shape of Modern Society*. Ithaca, NY: Cornell University Press.

O'Neill, J. (1989) *The Communicative Body*. Evanston: Northwestern University Press.

Oakes, G. (1991) *The Soul of the Salesman*. Atlanta Highlands, NJ: Humanities Press.

Oakley, A. (1972) *Sex, Gender and Society*. London: Temple Smith.

Oakley, A. (1974) *The Sociology of Housework*. London: Martin Robertson.

Oakley, A. (1984) *The Captured Womb: A History of the Medical Care of Pregnant Women*. Oxford: Basil Blackwell.

Orbach, S. (1988 [1978]) *Fat is a Feminist Issue*. London: Arrow Books.

Ostrander, G. (1988) 'Foucault's disappearing body', in A. Kroker and M. Kroker (eds), *Body Invaders. Sexuality and the Postmodern Condition*. London: Macmillan.

Ots, T. (1990) 'The silent Körper – the loud Leib'. Draft paper for AES Spring Meeting, Atlanta, Georgia, cited in R. Frankenberg, 'Review article: Disease, literature and the body in the era of AIDS – a preliminary exploraion', *Sociology of Health and Illness*, 12: 351–60.

Park, R. (1985) 'Sport, gender and society in a transatlantic Victorian perspective', *British Journal of Sports History*, 2: 5–28.

Parsons, T. (1968 [1937]) *The Structure of Social Action*. New York: Free Press.

Parsons, T. (1969) *Politics and Social Structure*. New York: Free Press.

Parsons, T. (1978) *Action Theory and the Human Condition*. New York: Free Press.

Parsons, T. (1991 [1951]) *The Social System*. London: Routledge.

Pennington, S. (1991) 'Chewing out the fat', *The Guardian*, 23 May.

Pettingale, K. (1985) 'Towards a psychosocial model of cancer: biological considerations', *Social Science and Medicine*, 20: 779–87.

Pfohl, S. (1993) 'Venus in microsoft: male mas(s)ochism and cybernetics', in A. Kroker and M. Kroker (eds), The *Last Sex: Feminism and Outlaw Bodies*. Basingstoke: Macmillan.

Phizacklea, A. (1990) *Unpacking the Fashion Industry*. London: Routledge.

Pleck, E. and Pleck, J. (eds) (1980) *The American Man*. Englewood Cliffs, NJ: Prentice-Hall.

Pleck, J. and Sawyer, J. (eds) (1974) *Men and Masculinity*. Englewood Cliffs, NJ: Prentice-Hall.

Poster, M. (1984) *Foucault, Marxism and History: Mode of Production versus Mode of Information*. Cambridge: Polity Press.

Prendergast, S. (2000) '"To become dizzy in our turning": girls, body-maps and gender as childhood ends', in A. Prout (ed.), *The Body, Childhood and Society*. Houndmills: Macmillan.

Pringle, R. (1989a) *Secretaries Talk: Sexuality, Power and Work*. London: Verso.

Pringle, R. (1989b) 'Bureaucracy, rationality and sexuality: the case of secretaries', in J. Hearn, D. Shepard, P. Tancred-Sheriff and G. Burrell (eds), *The Sexuality of Organization*. London: Sage.

Prior, L. (1989) *The Social Organization of Death*. London: Macmillan.

Puner, M. (1978) *To the Good Long Life*. London: Macmillan.

Rheingold, H. (1991) *Virtual Reality*. London: Secker and Warburg.

Rheingold, H. (1994) *The Virtual Community*. London: Secker and Warburg.

Rich, A. (1976) *Of Woman Born*. New York: Norton.

Rich, A. (1980) 'Compulsory heterosexuality and lesbian experience', *Signs*, 5: 631–60.

Richardson, J. (1991) 'The menstrual cycle and student learning', *Journal of Higher Education*, 62(3): 317–40.

Robins, K. (1995) 'Cyberspace and the world we live in', *Body and Society*, 1(3–4): 135–55.

Robertson, R. (1990) 'Mapping the global condition: globalization as the central concept', *Theory, Culture and Society*, 7(3–2): 15–30.

Rogers, L. (1988) 'Biology, the popular weapon: sex differences in cognitive function', in B. Caine et al. (eds), *Crossing Boundaries: Feminisms and the Critique of Knowledges*. Sydney: Allen and Unwin.

Rogers, W. (1991) *Explaining Health and Illness*. New York: Harvester Wheatsheaf.

Rose, N. (1989) *Governing the Soul: The Shaping of the Private Self*. London: Routledge.

Rose, S. (1976) 'Scientific racism and ideology: the IQ racket from Galton to Jensen', in H. Rose and S. Rose (eds), *The Political Economy of Science*. London: Macmillan.

Rose, S. (1984) 'Biological reductionism: its roots and social functions', in L. Birke and J. Silvertown (eds), *More than the Parts*. London: Pluto.

Rosen, B. (1989) *Women, Work and Achievement*. London: Macmillan.

Rosen, T. (1983) *Strong and Sexy: The New Body Beautiful*. London: Columbus Books.

Rosenzweig, M. and Schultz, T. (1991) 'Who receives medical care? Income, implicit prices, and the distribution of medical services among pregnant women in the United States', *Journal of Human Resources*. 26(3).

Rothfield, P. (1990) 'Feminism, subjectivity and sexual experience', in S. Gunew (ed.), *Feminist Knowledge, Critique and Construct*. London: Routledge.

Rouselle, A. (1989) 'Personal status and sexual practice in the Roman Empire', in M. Feher, R. Naddaff and N. Tazi (eds), *Fragments for a History of the Human Body*, Part III. New York: Zone.

Rucker, R., Sirius, R. and Queen, M. (eds) (1993) *Mondo 2000: A User's Guide to the New Edge*. London: Thames and Hudson.

Rudofsky, B. (1986 [1971]) *The Unfashionable Human Body*. New York: Prentice-Hall.

Rutherford, J. (1988) 'Who's that man', in R. Chapman and J. Rutherford (eds), *Male Order, Unwrapping Masculinity*. London: Lawrence and Wishart.

Salter, B. and Tapper, T. (1981) *Education, Politics and the State*. London: Grant Mclntyre.

Sawicki, J. (1991) *Disciplining Foucault: Feminism, Power and the Body*. New York: Routledge.

Scarry, E. (1985) *The Body in Pain*. Oxford: Oxford University Press.

Schiebinger, L. (1987) 'Skeletons in the closet: the first illustrations of the female skeleton in eighteenth-century 'anatomy', in C. Gallagher and T. Laqueur (eds), *The Making of the Modern Body: Sexuality and Society in the Nineteenth Century*. Barkeley, CA: University of California Press.

Schilder, P. (1978 [1935]) *The Image and Appearance of the Human Body: Studies in the Constructive Energies of the Psyche*. New York: International Universities Press.

Schudson, M. (1984) 'Embarrassment and Erving Goffamn's idea of human nature', *Theory and Society*, 13: 633–48.

Schutz, A. (1970) *On Phenomenology and Social Relations*. Chicago: Chicago University Press.

Schwartz, H. (1986) *Never Satisfied: A Cultural History of Diets*, Fantasies and Fats. New York: Free Press.

Searle, G. (1971) *The Quest for National Efficiency*. Oxford: Basil Blackwell.

Segal, L. (1990) *Slow Motion: Changing Masculinities*, Changing Men. London: Virago.

Seligman, M. (1975) *Helplessness: On Depression*, Development and Death. San Francisco: W.H. Freeman.

Sennett, R. (1974) *The Fall of Public Man*. Cambridge: Cambridge University Press.

Sennett, R. (1992 [1974]) *The Fall of Public Man*. New York: W.W. Norton and Co.

Sennett, R. (1994) *Flesh and Stone: The Body and the City in Western Civilization*. London: Faber and Faber.

Sharp, K. (1992) 'Biology and social science: a reply to Ted Benton', *Sociology*, 26: 219–24.

Shilling, C. (1991) 'Educating the body: physical capital and the production of social inequalities', *Sociology*, 25: 653–72.

Shilling, C. (1992) 'Schooling and the production of physical capital', *Discourse*, 13(1): 1–19.

Shilling, C. (1999) 'Towards an embodied understanding of the structure/agency relationship', *British Journal of Sociology*, 50(4): 543–62.

Shilling, C. (2001) 'Embodiment, experience and theory: in defence of the sociological tradition', *The Sociological Review*, 49(3): 327–44.

Shilling, C. (2002a) 'Culture, the "sick role" and the consumption of health', *British Journal of Sociology*, 53(4): 621–38.

Shilling, C. (2002b) 'The two traditions in the sociology of emotions', in J. Barbalet (ed.), *The Sociology of Emotions*. Sociological Review Monograph Series. Oxford: Blackwell.

Shilling, C. (2003) 'Embodiment, emotions and the foundations of social order: Durkheim's enduring contribution', in J. Alexander and P. Smith (eds), *The Cambridge Companion to Emile Durkheim*. Cambridge: Cambridge University Press.

Shilling, C. (2004) *The Body in Culture, Technology and Society*. London: Sage.

Shilling, C. and Mellor, P.A. (1996) 'Embodiment, structuration theory and modernity: mind/body dualism and the repression of sensuality', *Body and Society*, 2(4): 1–15.

Shilling, C. and Mellor, P.A. (2001) *The Sociological Ambition: Elementary Forms of Social and Moral Life*. London: Sage.

Shils, E. (1981) *Tradition*. London: Faber and Faber.

Shuttleworth, S. (1990) 'Female circulation: medical discourse and popular advertising in the mid-Victorian era', in M. Jacobus, E. Keller and S. Shuttleworth (eds), *Body/Politics: Women and the Discourses of Science*. London: Routledge.

Sica, A. (1984) 'Sociogenesis versus psychogenesis: the unique sociology of Norbert Elias', *Mid American Review of Sociology*, 9: 49–78.

Simmel, G. (1950) *The Sociology of Georg Simmel*. Glencoe, IL: Free Press.

Simmel, G. (1971 [1918]) 'The conflict in modern culture', in D. Levine (ed.), *Georg Simmel On Individuality and Social Forms*. Chicago: University of Chicago Press.

Simmel, G. (1990 [1907]) *The Philosophy of Money*. London: Routledge.

Simon, B. and Bradley, I. (eds) (1975) *The Victorian Public School*. Dublin: Gill and Macmillan.

Singer, L. (1989) 'Bodies, pleasures, powers', *Differences*, 1: 45–65.

Sinha, M. (1987) 'Gender and imperialism: colonial policy and the ideology of moral imperialism in late nineteenth century Bengal' in M. Kimmel (ed.), *Changing Men. New Directions in Research on Men and Masculinity*. Newbury Park, CA: Sage.

Smith, T.S. (1992) *Strong Interaction*. Chicago: University of Chicago Press.

Snyder, M. (1987) *Public Appearances, Private Realities: The Psychology of Self-Monitoring*. New York: W.H. Freeman.

Solomon, G. (1985) 'The emerging field of psychoneuroimmunology', *Advances: Journal of the Institute for the Advancement of Health*, 2: 6–19.

Sontag, S. (1979) *Illness as Metaphor*. New York: Vintage.

Soper, K. (1995) *What is Nature?* Oxford: Blackwell.

Springer, C. (1991) 'The pleasure of the interface', *Screen*, 32(3): 303–23.

Stacey, M. (1988) *The Sociology of Health and Healing*. London: Unwin Hyman.

Stanley. L. (1984) 'Should "sex" really be "gender" – or "gender" really be "sex"?', in R. Anderson and W. Shurrock (eds), *Applied Sociological Perspectives*. London: Allen and Unwin.

Staples, R. (1982) *Black Masculinity: The Black Male's Role in American Society*. San Francisco: Black Scholar Press.

Stoller, P. (1997) *Sensuous Scholarship*. Philadelphia, PA: University of Pennsylvania Press.

Suter, S. (1986) *Health Psychophysiology: Mind-Body Interaction in Wellness and Illness*. Hillsdale, NJ: Lawrence.

Tancred-Sheriff, P. (1989) 'Gender, sexuality and the labour process', in J. Hearn, D. Shappard, P. Tancred-Sheriff and G. Burrell (eds), *The Sexuality of Organization*. London: Sage.

Therberge, N. (1991) 'Reflections on the body in the sociology of sport', *Quest*, 43: 123–34.

Theweleit, K. (1987 [1977]) *Male Fantasies vol. I: Women, Floods, Bodies, History*. Minneapolis, MN: University of Minnesota Press.

Theweleit, K. (1989 [1978]) *Male Fantasies vol. 2: Male Bodies: Psychoanalysing the White Terror*. Minneapolis, MN: University of Minneapolis Press.

Tiefer, L. (1987) 'In pursuit of the perfect penis: the medicalization of male sexuality', in M. Kimmel (ed.), *Changing Men. New Directions in Research on Men and Masculinity*. Newbury Park, CA: Sage.

Tiger, L. and Fox, R. (1978) 'The human biogram', in A. Caplan (ed.), *The Sociobiology Debate*. New York: Harper and Row.

Tolson, A. (1977) *The Limits of Masculinity: Male Identity and Women's Liberation*. New York: Harper and Row.

Tomas, D. (1991) 'Old rituals for new space', in M. Benedikt (ed.), *Cyberspace: First Steps*. London: MIT Press.

Toulmin, S. (1990) *Cosmopolis: The Hidden Agenda of Modernity*. Chicago: University of Chicago Press.

Townsend, P., Davidson, N. and Whitehead, M. (1988) *Inequalities in Health: 'The Black Report and The Health Divide'*. Harmondsworth: Pelican.

Trivers, R (1978) 'The evolution of reciprocal altruism', in A. Caplan (ed.), *The Sociobiology Debate*. New York: Harper and Row.

Tseelon, E. (1992) 'Is the presented self sincere? Goffman, impression management and the postmodern self', *Theory, Culture and Society*, 9: 115–28.

Tseelon, E. (1995) *The Masque of Femininity*. London: Sage.

Turner, B.S. (1982) 'The discourse of diet', *Theory, Culture and Society*, 1: 23–32.

Turner, B.S. (1983) *Religion and Social Theory*. London: Heinemann Educational Books.

Turner, B.S. (1984) *The Body and Society*. Oxford: Basil Blackwell.

Turner, B.S. (1987) *Medical Power and Social Knowledge*. London: Sage.

Turner, B.S. (1991a) 'Recent developments in the theory of the body', in M. Featherstone, M.

Hepworth and B. Turner (eds), *The Body: Social Process and Cultural Theory*. London: Sage.

Turner, B.S. (1991b) Paper presented to the British Sociological Association's conference on *Health and Society*, April.

Turner, B.S. (1992a) *Regulating Bodies: Essays in Medical Sociology*. London: Routledge.

Turner, B.S. (1992b) *Max Weber: From History to Modernity*. London: Routledge.

Turner, B.S. (1996) 'Introduction to the second edition', in *The Body and Society*, 2nd edn. London: Sage.

Turner, B.S. (1999) 'An outline of a general sociology of the body', in B.S. Turner (ed.), *The Blackwell Companion to Social Theory*, 2nd edn. Oxford: Blackwell.

Turner, T. (1986) 'Review of the body and society – Explorations in social theory', *American Journal of Sociology*, 92: 211–13.

Urry, J. (1990) 'The "consumption" of tourism', *Sociology*, 24: 23–35.

Van der Vliet, R. (1991) 'Love without ties: A new phase in the sexual life course', *The Netherlands Journal of Social Sciences*, 27(2): 67–79.

Van Stolk, B. and Wouters, C. (1987) 'Power changes and self-respect: a comparsion of two cases of established-outsider relations', *Theory, Culture and Society*, 4: 477–88.

Vance, C. (1984) *Pleasure and Danger: Exploring Female Sexuality*. London: Pandora.

Vance, C. (1989) 'Social construction theory: problems in the history of sexuality', in A. van Kooten Nierker and T. van der Meer (eds), *Homosexuality, which Homosexuality?* London: GMP Publishers.

Vigarello, G. (1989) 'The upward training of the body from the age of chivalry to courtly civility', in M. Feher, R. Naddaff and N. Tazi (eds), *Fragments for a History of the Human Body*, Part II. New York: Zone.

Virey, J. (1823) *De la Femme, Sous Ses Rapports Physiologique, Moral et Litteraire*, Paris, cited in F. Heritier-Auge, (1989) 'Older women, stout-hearted women, women of substance', in M. Feher, R. Naddaff and N. Tazi (eds), *Fragments for a History of the Human Body*, Part III. New York: Zone.

Walby, S. (1989) 'Theorizing patriarchy', *Sociology*, 23: 213–34.

Walter, T. (1991) 'Modern death: taboo or not taboo?', *Sociology*, 25: 293–310.

Walvin, J. (1982) 'Black caricature: the roots of racialism', in C. Husband (ed.), *'Race' In Britain*. London: Hutchinson.

Walvin, J. (1987) 'Symbols of moral superiority: slavery, sport and the changing world order, 1800–1950', in J. Mangan and J. Walvin (eds), *Manliness and Morality: Middle-Class Masculinity in Britain and America, 1800–1940*. Manchester: Manchester University Press.

Warr, P. (1987) Work, Unemployment and Mental Health. Oxford: Clarendon Press.

Washburn, S. (1978) 'Animal behaviour and social anthropology', in M. Gregory, A. Silvers and D. Sutch (eds), *Sociobiology and Human Nature*. San Francisco, Jossey Bass.

Watney, S. (1988) 'Visual AIDS – advertising ignorance', in P. Aggleton and H. Homans (eds), *Social Aspects of AIDS*. London: Falmer.

Watt, I. (1957) *The Rise of the Novel*. London: Chatto and Windus.

Wearne, P. and Jones, J. (1992) 'Use it or loss it', *The Guardian*, 27–28 June, pp. 12–13.

Weber, M. (1948 [1919]) 'Science as a vocation', in H. Gerth and C.W. Mills (eds), *From Max Weber*. London: Routledge.

Weber, M. (1985 [1904–5]) *The Protestant Ethic and the Spirit of Capitalism*. London: Counterpoint.

Weeks, J. (1977) *Coming Out: Homosexual Politics in Britain from the Nineteenth Century to the Present*. London: Quartet.

Weeks, J. (1992) 'The body and sexuality', in R. Bocock and K. Thompson (eds), *Social and Cultural Forms of Modernity*. Cambridge: Polity Press.

Wegner, G. (1991) 'Schooling for a new mythos: race, anti-semitism and the curriculum materials of a Nazi race educator', *International Journal of the History of Education*, 27: 189–213.

Weinstein, H. (1985) 'The health threat in the fields', *Nation*, 240: 558–60.

Whitbeck, C. (1984) 'A different reality: feminist ontology', in C. Gould (ed.), *Beyond Domination: New Perspectives on Women and Philosophy*. NJ: Rowman and Allanheld.

White, A. (1989) *Poles Apart? The Experience of Gender*. London: J.M. Dent and Sons.

Wilkes, C. (1990) 'Bourdieu's class', in J. Harker, C. Mahar and C. Wilkes (eds), *An Introduction to the work of Pierre Bourdieu*, Houndmills: Macmillan.

William, S. and Bandelow, G. (1998) *The Lived Body*. London: Routledge.

Willis, P. (1974) 'Performance and meaning – a sociocultural view of women in sport', in I. Glaister (ed.), *Physical Education – An Integrating Force*. London: ATCDE.

Willis, P. (1977) *Learning to Labour*. Farnborough: Saxon House.

Willis, P. (1985) 'Women in sport in ideology', in J. Hargreaves (ed.), *Sport, Culture and Society*. London: RKP.

Wilson, E. (1975) *Sociobiology: The New Synthesis*. Cambridge, Mass.: Harvard University Press.

Wilson, E. (1978a) *On Human Nature*. London: Tavistock.

Wilson, E. (1978b) 'Introduction: What is sociobiology?', in M. Gregory, A. Silvers and D. Sutch (eds), *Sociobiology and Human Nature*. San Francisco, Jossey Bass.

Wittig, M. (1982) 'The category of sex', *Feminist Issues*, Fall, pp. 63–8.

Wolf, N. (1991) *The Beauty Myth*. London: Vintage.

Woods, P. (1980a) *Teacher Strategies*. Beckenham: Croom Helm.

Woods, P. (1980b) *Pupil Strategies*. Beckenham: Croom Helm.

Wouters, C. (1986) 'Formalization and informalization: changing tension balances in civilizing processes', *Theory, Culture and Society*, 3(2): 1–18.

Wouters, C. (1987) 'Developments in the behavioural codes between the sexes: the formalization of informalization in the Netherlands 1930–85', *Theory, Culture and Society*, 4: 405–27.

Wouters, C. (1989a) 'The sociology of emotions and flight attendants: Hochschild's managed heart', *Theory, Culture and Society*, 6(1): 95–123.

Wouters, C. (1989b) 'Response to Hochschild's reply', *Theory, Culture and Society*, 6(3): 447–50.

Wouters, C. (1990) 'Social stratification and informalization in global perspective', *Theory, Culture and Society*, 7: 69–90.

Wright, E. (1989) 'Rethinking, once again, the concept of class structure', in E. Wright et al. (eds), *The Debate on Classes*. London: Verso.

Wright, G.H. Von (1980) *Culture and Value*. Oxford: Blackwell.

Young, I.M. (1990) *Throwing Like a Girl*. Bloomington, IN: Indiana University Press.

Index

Abercrombie, N. 153, 156
absent-presence of body 70–1,
    87, 172, 179–82; see also
    sociology
abstract systems 158, 171
action, and meaning 152–4
'action problem' 15
actual social identity 75–6
Adams, C. 54
Adams, P. 70
Africans and naturalistic body
    49–52
ageing 14, 20, 28, 31, 35
    and death 162, 168–70
    mask of 76, 195–6
    physical capital 121–3
agency, embodied see action
agoraphobia 80
AIDS and HIV 30, 52, 159,
    165, 169, 170
Alcorn, K. 52
Alexander, R. 45
Allan, G. 120
Althusser, L. 26
animals 89
anorexia nervosa 58, 81,
    101
anxiety and fear 32
    about ageing 122, 168–70
    and civilized body 132
    and death 162, 168–70
    of men about women
        58–9
    and skin colour see racism
    of urban areas 80
    of women about body shape
        see eating disorers
        under food; see also
        image, body
appearance see image, body
Archer, M. viii, 207
Ardill, S. 55
Ardrey, R. 45
Ariès, P. 163, 192
Armstrong, D. 66, 69
artificial insemination 3, 33
asceticism 79, 83–5, 134,
    155–6
Australia, discrimination in 43

Bakhtin, M. 192
Ball, S. 68
Banner, L. 5
Barrett, M. 13, 55
Barrows, S. 41
Bartky, S. 74, 193
Bartrop, R. 102
Baudrillard, J. 190
Bauman, Z. 24, 32
    on death 7, 150, 155, 162,
        166–7, 170
beauty see image
Beck, U. 5, 64–5, 176
Beckford, J. 153, 156
behaviour 135–41
Bell, D. 4
Bendann, E. 162
Bendelow, G. 8
Benedikt, M. 189
Bengal 51
Bentham, J. 67
Benton, T. 46, 91, 92, 149
Berger, J. 99–100
Berger, P. 16, 17, 21, 152–6,
    161
Bernstein, B. 119
Berridge, V. 98
biology
    controlled see civilized body
    sociolobiology and genetics
        43–8
    see also death; health and
        illness; naturalistic
        body; social
        inequalities
bipedalism 92
Birke, L. 47, 60, 96
birth 83, 176
    and naturalistic body 39,
        53–5
    see also children
Bleier, R. 45
Bloch, M. 164
'bodily order' 15, 63, 78–83,
    202–3
body
    -building see sport
    definitions 35
    as latent 183–7

as mask 193–8
as option 189–91
projects see project, body as
regimes 157–60, 187,
    191–3; see also image;
    sport
work 103–4
see also non-verbal
    communication;
    sociology of body
Bogner, A. 15, 133
Booth, C. 32
Bordo, S. 185, 193
Bourdieu, P. 178
    on social reproduction 9,
        176, 186, 205
    cultural capital and
        schooling 19, 130
    death 153, 161–3
    individualization of body 1
    male body images 31
    symbolic value and physical
        capital 13, 65, 109–12,
        126
        changing bodies 116–18
        conversion of physical
            capital 118–20
        legitimate body 126
        social class and
            inequalities 114–16,
            120, 123–6, 150–1
        social field 128
        social formation 121–2
        sport 112–14, 117–20,
            123
        structuration theory
            205
        transmission and control
            of physical capital
            124–6
Bovey, S. 58–9
Bradley, I. 59, 96
Bray, A. 30
breakdown of civilized body
    146–8
Broca, P. 50
Brohm, J.-M. 34
Brown, B. 70
Brown, P. 49

Brubaker, R. 9, 113, 127–8
Bryant, C. 174
Bryson, L. 59
Buffery, A. 45
bureaucracy 22, 34
bureaucratization of spirit 74
Burkitt, I. 160, 175, 207, 210
Burns, T. 73, 75, 76
Burrows, R. 190
Bury, M. 64
Butler, J. 181, 182, 203
Buytendijk, F. 101
Bynum, C.. 83, 134, 191

Calnan, M. 115
Campling, J. 20
Camporesi, P. 191
Cannon, W.B. 93
capital, body as see physical capital
capitalism 9–10, 24, 25
    and civilized body 171–2
    and naturalistic body 47–9
    Protestant ethic 27–8, 90
    and socially constructed body 78, 91, 92
Caplan, A. 45
Carby, H. 51
Carrington, B. 119
categorization 99
changing body and physical capital 116–18
changing value of physical capital 121–4
Charles, N. 39, 58
Chernin, K. 56–60, 81
children 68
    bodily and psychological distance from adults 140, 143–4
    and dieting 7
    language learning 92–5
    new-born, sex of 47–8
    see also birth; socialization
Christianity
    and control 49
    and death 155–6, 163–6
    and sexuality 67–8
    see also Protestants
civil inattention 74
civilized body 131–51
Clark, J. 174
Clarke, J. 119
class see social class
classical sociology 7–10, 21–6
Collins, R. 77, 103 121
Collinson, D. 103, 106
colonialism 50–2

commodification of body 81, 161
    of black people 50–2
    of women 29
    see also consumer culture; image; physical capital; social inequalities
communicating body and action 84–6
competition, status 137–9
compulsive eating see eating disorders under food
Comte, A. 180
Connell, R. 8, 30, 44, 46–8, 60, 94–100
conscience of body and work 110
consciousness see mind
constraints on body 20, 176
    see also ageing, bodily order death; disability
constructionism see socially constructed body
consumer culture 14, 28, 32
control 24, 25
    as action problem 83–5
    and death 158–60
    and meaning 3, 4, 28
    self-imposed see civilized body; self-denial
    see also bodily order; discipline; image, body; medicine; power; state
conversion of physical capital 111, 112, 118–20
Corbin, A. 20
Cornwell, J. 115
court society 131, 134–40
Craib, I. 174
craniometry 41, 50
Crawford, R. 5, 115, 158
crime, criminalization and racism 52–3
crisis of knowledge about body 14, 28, 32–5, 159
Crossley, N. 204, 207
culture, cultural capital 19, 111–30

daily life see everyday life
Dale, R. 120
Dalton, K. 43
Dana, M. 60
dangerous 'others' see 'others'
Darwin, C. and Darwinism 41, 43–4
    Social Darwinism 50–1
David, M. 29
Davies, B. 66
Davis, F. 118
Dawkins, R. 45

Dawe, A. 205
death penalty 61
death and self-identity 152–71
Deem, R. 114
Della Fave, L.R. 103
Delphy, C. 70
Descartes, R. 179
demography see population
desire
    as action problem 84–5
    restraint of 78–80
deviation, sexual 68
    see also homosexuality
Dews, P. 71
Diamond, I. 70
Diamond, N. 59
diet see food; slimming
differences in gendered body exaggerated 95–6
Diprose, R. 4, 186
disability 23, 76 see also stigma
discipline
    disciplined body and action 84–5
    Foucault on 14, 66–71
disease see health and illness
disembodied approach see classical sociology
distinction search for 128, 137–41
distorted body 56–60
    see also eating disorders under food
dominant classes
    court society in middle ages 131–9
    and physical capital 114–16
    changing value of 121–4
    conversion 118–20
    transmission and control 124–6
    see also middle classes
domination
    dominating body and action 84–6
    and emotion work 100–3
    see also control; dominant classes; gendered body; men; patriarchy; power
Dore, R. 121
Douglas, A. 164
Douglas, M. 64, 120
Dowsett, G. 8, 68
Doyal, L. 20
dread 160
    see also anxiety and fear
Dreyfuss, H. 66
drives, internalised 134–41

Dunning, E. 142, 144, 147
Durkheim, E. 9, 22–5, 180, 208
Duroche, L. 10, 38, 39, 65, 145
Dutton, D. 108
Dyer, R. 51
dying see death

eating see food
economic capital 111, 118–20, 124–6
education 18, 19
  and control 69
  and gender 41
  physical 19, 59
  and physical capital 120–4
Ehreneich, B. 31, 98
Eisenstein, H. 53
elderly see ageing
Elias, N. 178, 191, 208
  on civilized body 131–3, 142–8
    historical development and historical body 20, 134–6, 148–51
    search for distinction 137–41
    social interdependence 141–3
  on death 149, 153, 161–5
  on emotion 108
  on individualization and development of body 10, 92–3
  on language and consciousness 8
élite see dominant classes
Elling, R. 108
emancipation from nature 158
  symbol 133–4, 140
embarrassment and shame 75–6, 145–6
emotion and civilized body 131–5, 146–7
  commercialized see Hochschild
  emotional body and social inequalities 103–8
employment see work
encounters see social interaction
Engel, G. 102
Engels, F. 190
English, D. 98
Epstein, B. 60
essentialism 178
  discursive 70–1
established-outsider boundaries 146–7

everyday life 20
  challenged by death 154–6
  rituals 108, 157, 164
  socially constructed body in 66, 72–3
  violence in 134–5
evolution 50, 152
  and civilized body 131–3, 146–9
  and social inequalities 91–5
  and sociobiology 43–6
  see also history
exceptionalism, human 149
expert systems 171
externalization see action

face 93
  work see non verbal communication
Falk, P. 103, 144
false consciousness, emotional 110
Fanon, F. 50, 186, 192, 193, 194
Fascism 54
fashion 7, 57
fasting 83–5
fatness see slimming
fear see anxiety and fear
Featherstone, M. 20, 26, 76
  on ageing 122–5, 195, 196
  on death 161, 168
  on image and self-identity 31, 32, 66, 182, 190
Fedigan, L. 49
feeling see emotion
Feher, M. 26, 179
feminism 176
  and naturalistic body 37–8
    distorted body 56–60
  second wave 14, 28–31
    see also under women
  suffrage 41
  see also gendered body; women
Finch, J. 114, 128
Finkler, K. 108
Firestone, S. 28, 53
food 32–3, 68, 79
  eating disorders 56–60
  fasting 83–5
  taboos 111
  see also slimming
force as ideal type of body usage 84–7
  see also violence
Foucault, M. 67–72, 203
foundationalist and anti-foundationalist approaches 10, 89–91

Fox, R. 45
Frank, A. 26, 35, 204
  on death 159
  on human action and body 63, 81–6
  on nature/culture bifurcation 11
Frankenberg, R. 35, 52
Frankenhauser, M. 108
Freund, P. 26, 35, 94, 100, 101, 105, 108, 110, 179
Friedman, M. 102
Fuss, D. 70, 71
Fussell, S. 6
future
  lost see death
  planning for 139

Gallagher, C. 40
Gallup, G. 46
Gardell, B. 108
Gehlen, A. 154
gendered body 12
  and civilized body 140–3, 147
  constructing 94–5
  negating 95–7
  and physical capital 114–21
  reproduction of 98–100
  and social inequalities 97–100
  socialized see under socialization
  see also men; naturalistic body; social inequalites; women
generations, conflict between 122, 123
  see also ageing; children
Gerber, R. 7
Gergen, K. 197
Giddens, A. 12, 66, 85, 153, 157–61, 169, 171, 174, 178, 185, 188, 192
Gieben, B. 2
Gilroy, P. 196
Gilroy, S. 59
Gimlin, D. 199, 204
globalisation 18, 125
Goffman, E. 5, 32, 66, 72–8, 150, 158, 184, 185, 186, 197
Goldberg, S. 46
Golden, J. 4
Goldsmith, F. 108
good and evil, dichotomy between 49–50
Goodger, B. 144
Goodger, J. 144
Gordon, C. 69
Gordon, R. 7

Goudsblom, J. 139
Gough, I. 20
Gould, S.J. 41, 51, 53
Graham, H. 115
Grant, L. 6
Gray, J. 45
Graydon, J. 59
Green, E. 114
Green, H. 27
Greer, G. 29
Gregory, M. 49
Griffin, C. 58, 59
Grogan, S. 7, 195
Grosz, E. 43, 48, 49, 200,
    205–6
Gusterson, H. 110

habitus 111, 124, 127, 128,
    130, 151–62
    defined 113
Haferkamp, H. 151
Hall, C. 7
Hall, S. 2, 53, 125
hand 90
Harburg, E. 108
Hargreaves, D. 124
Hargreaves, J.A. 98
Harrison, R. 29
Hartmann, H. 29
Haug, F. 11
health and illness 4–6, 18, 21,
    30–3, 158–9, 176
    and civilized body 150
    improvements see sport
        (and keep-fit and body-
        building)
    and naturalistic body 41–5,
        52
    panics 32–4
    and physical capital
        114–16
    and social inequalities
        100–6, 107–9
    and socially constructed
        body 68, 79–81
    stress 34, 80–1, 101–2
    and war 1
    see also medicine and
        medical discourse/
        model
Heim, M. 192
Hearn, J. 30, 55, 56
Hebron, S. 114
Henley, N. 74
Hepworth, M. 76, 168, 195,
    196
Heritier-Auge, F. 29, 42
Herring, C. 129
Hertz, R. 90
Hewitt, M. 66
Hills, S. 108

Hirst, P. 92, 93, 179
History 163–4
    of civilized body 134–6
    of naturalistic body 38–40,
        49–53
    of sexuality 66–8
    of socially constructed body
        64–8
    see also evolution
Hobbes, T. 40, 78, 89, 92
Hochschild, A. 15, 34, 94,
    102–8
hollow bodies 181–2
homosexuality 30, 51–2,
    127
Honneth, A. 68, 149, 151,
    154
Hope, J. 4
hormones 44–7
    see also menopause;
        menstruation;
        pregnancy
horror films 34, 35
housework 29
Howson, A. 181
hysteria 48, 68, 80

identification, mutual
    138–40
identity, see self-identity;
    social identity
ideology, asceticism 79, 83–5,
    134, 155–6
    see also religion
idiom, body 77
    see also non-verbal
        communication
Illich, I. 165
illness see health and illness
image, body (self-
    presentation) 1, 4–7, 72
    and civilized body 135
    and consumer culture
        31–2
    and management of stigma
        75–6
    and naturalistic body
        59–60
    and physical capital 112,
        116–17, 124–6
    and social inequalities 96–8,
        105
    and socially constructed
        body 65, 72–7
    see also fashion; under men;
        plastic surgery;
        slimming; sport
imagination 99
immortality 166–7
implants see transplants and
    implants

in vitro fertilization 3, 33
individualization/
    individuation of body 1,
        69, 111, 131–2, 145, 151,
        162–5
    see also civilized body;
        'others'
inequalities see gendered body;
    social inequalities
Inglis, D. 181
institutionalized state 130
institutions 66–9
    see also education; religion;
        state
instrumental relation to body
    see physical capital under
        working classes
intentions/intended outcome
    67, 151
interaction 9
    social 72–81
interdependencies, web of
    163
interest, sociology of see
    physical capital
internalization 134–41, 151,
    154
interviews 120
irreducibility of body 72
Isherwood, B. 120

Jaggar, A. 54
James, A. 57
Jameson, F. 125
Jary, D. 174
Jaspers, K. 155
Jewish people 52
Joas, H. viii, x, 149, 151,
    154
Johnson, D. 179
Johnson, M. 99–100
Jones, C. 52, 53
Jones, J. 97
Jordan, W. 49–50
Jordanova, L. 38, 40

Kamerman, J. 162
Kanneh, K. 194
Kant, I. 179
Kaplan, G. 41, 47, 54
Keddie, N. 119
keep-fit see sport
Keith, V. 129
Kelleman, S. 100
Keller, L.S. 28
Kelly, D. 102
Kennedy, B. 4
Kerr, L. 158
Kerr, M. 29, 58
Kierkegaard, S. 160
Kimmel, M. 30

King, D. 64
Kippax, S. 30
Kirkup, G. 28
Klein, A. 18
knife 136
knowledge and body 70–1
    and reason 171
    and sociology 22, 24–6,
        56
Kroker, A. 35
Kroker, M. 35
Kuzmics, H. 75, 132, 143,
    147

labelling 77, 126–7
    see also stigma
Lacey, C. 124
Lakoff, G. 99
language 133
    learning 93–5
    and sociology 8, 17, 19, 21,
        26–7
    and symbolic interactionism
        62
Laqueur, T. 38–40
Lasch, C. 167, 168
Lash, S. 15, 111, 121
Latent body 183–7
Lauer, R. 102
Lawrence, M. 81, 101
Laws, S. 34
Le Bon, G. 41
learning, capacity for 148–9
Leder, D. 183–7, 204
Lees, S. 29
leisure 97, 103, 114–15, 117,
    144
    see also sport
Lennerlof, L. 102
Lepervanche, M. 43, 48, 49
Lessor, R. 105
Levine, D. xiii
Lewontin, R. 53
'lived body' 13
Locke, J. 40
loneliness of dying 165,
    170
love, and death 169–70; see
    also sexuality
Luckmann, T. 21
Luke, S. 22
Lyman, S. 51
Lynch, J. 102

McCarty, R. 102
McDonough, R. 29
MacDougall, J. 102
McGuire, M. 108
machine
    body as 32–3
    body subordinated to 21

McIntosh, P. 27
McLaughlin, C. 64
McRobbie, A. 119, 125
manageable body 76–8
managed heart see Hochschild
Manga, J. 42
manners 134–40
Mannheim, K. 21
Maplethorpe, R. 51
Marable, M. 51
'marginal situations' 155–6
    see also death
marriage and family
    delayed 78–9
    as goal for women 57, 80
    legitimate 127
    and naturalistic body
        53–8
    and physical capital 120,
        121, 127–8
    and sport 119–20, 128
    see also children
Marsh, P. 118
Martin, E. 7, 29, 34, 40, 41,
    43, 173
Marx, K. 8, 190
Maynard, M. 30
Mauss, M. 20
Mead, G.H. 200–1
Mead, M. 48
meaning
    body as receptor of social see
        socially constructed
        body
    and control 3–4, 28
    and death 153–7, 161–2
    privatization of 2
media 1
    and body image 5–6
    and death 165
    and racism 51
    teledildonics 34
    and uncertainty 34–5
    see also consumer culture
medicine and medical
    discourse/model 4, 33
    and ageing 31
    and civilized body 137
    control 2, 11
    and death 164–6
    and naturalistic body 42–4,
        48, 55, 58
    racism 50–3
    and social inequalities 98
    and socially constructed
        body 69
    see also health and illness;
        plastic surgery;
        transplants
Mellor, P.A. 23, 152, 156,
    171, 180, 187, 192

men
    and body image 6, 30
        see also strength below
    men's studies 30
    naturalistic body as norm
        and superior to female
        38, 40–3, 48–9
        see also naturalistic body
    and physical capital 114–23
    sociologists as 23–4
    strength of bodies 30,
        98–100, 114–16
    see also gendered body;
        patriarchy
Mennell, S.
    on civilized body 142, 148,
        150
    on physical capital 113
menopause 34, 46
menstruation 34, 38, 40–1, 44
Mercer, K. 49, 51, 52
Merleau-Ponty, M. 183, 204
Metcalf, P. 189
Middle Ages, court society
    131–8
    see also asceticism
middle classes 1, 42, 80, 98
    and ageing 122–3
    and civilized body 139
    and physical capital 115–18,
        122
    see also dominant classes
Midgley, M. 92
Miles, A. 29, 48, 115, 150
Miller, N. 102
mind (consciousness)
    and body dichotomy 8, 12,
        49, 157
        see also classical sociology
    and social inequalities
        99–102
    and socially constructed
        body 67, 71, 78
    and sociology 8, 12, 17,
        19–27
mirroring body 84–5, 167–9
    'savages' as mirrors 49
Mitchell, J. 60
mobility see social mobility
monopoly of violence 134,
    141–2, 146
Moore, R. 120
Morgan, O. 33
Morris, D. 45
Morris, M. 70
Moss, G. 102
mother–daughter relationship
    57–8
Murcott, A. 29, 58
Murphy, P. 147
mutual identification 139–40

Nadaff, R. 26
narcissistic body 85
    and death 167–9
naturalistic body 37–61
nature
    and culture dichotomy
        11–12, 22, 39–40,
        175
    emancipation from 158
    see also control
negating body 95–7
Nettleton, S. 66, 204
Newby, H. 22
Nicholson, M. 64
non-verbal communication
    72–8

Oakley, A. 29
O'Brien, M. 37, 54, 55
occupation see work
old people see ageing
O'Neill, J. viii, 33, 35,
    179
ontological security 160–1
oppression see subordination
Orbach, S. 7, 56–60
order see 'bodily order'; social
    order
organic nature of body see
    biology
organizing pricniples, dynamic
    (social field) 121–4
O'Sullivan, S. 55
'others'
    dangerous 49–53
    established-outsider
        boundaries 146–7
    other-relatedness as action
        problem 84–5
    see also individualization;
        racism
Ots, T. 35
overburdened body 29,
    60–1
ownership of body see
    possession

panics, health 33
panopticism 67–70
paradoxes of body and death
    154–7
Parsons, T. 10, 180, 185
Passeron, J-C. 119, 130
passive container, body as
    23
pathology of women's bodies
    40–4
    see also health and illness
patriarchy 28–9
    feminism as threat to
        58–9

and naturalistic body 37, 44,
    46, 53–4
    distorted body 56–60
patriarchal household
    78–80
    see also men
Patton, P. 70
Pennington, S. 105
Pettingale, K. 102
Phizaclea, A. 18
physical capital 111–30
physical education see sport
Pires, E. 120
planning ahead see future
plastic surgery 1, 5–6, 33,
    58
Plato 60
pleasure in violence
    134–6
population
    changes see ageing
    regulation 68–9, 78, 80
reproduction see
    reproduction
possession of body 4, 72
    by spirits 34–5
post-structuralism 62
    see also Foucault
power and socially
    constructed body 66–9
    see also control; discipline
predestination 25
pregnancy 34, 38–9
    see also birth
Prendergast, S. 185
Pringle, R. 106
Prior, L. 137, 164
prisons 67–80, 97
privatization
    and death 163–71
    of meaning 2
privileged body 53–6
project, body as 4–7, 154–5,
    158, 173–4, 187–201
prostitution 29
Protestants 49, 67, 164–5
    ethic 24–5, 79
psychology 21–2
Puner, M. 196
punishment 67–8, 141
    of self see self-denial

Quinby, L. 70

Rabonow, P. 66
Race, I. 49, 51, 52
racism 18, 27–8
    and naturalistic body
        49–53, 61
    and physical capital 118–19,
        128–9

rape 56, 150
    fear of 128
    and racism 51–2
rational choice theory viii, x
rationalization of body 132–51
    and death 162, 167
    see also civilized body;
        control
receptor of social meaning,
    body as 64–6
    see also socially constructed
        body
recognition as ideal type of
    body usage 83–4
reductionism 60–1
    see also naturalistic body;
        socially constructed
        body
reflexivity 3–5
    and civilized body 133,
        145–6
    and death 157–60
Reformation see Protestants
regimentation as ideal type of
    body usage 83–4
relationships see marriage;
    social interaction; social
    relationships
religion
    and death 154–70
    decline 2
    see also Protestants
Renaissance 39, 134
representation of body in
    social space 78–81
    see also image, body
reproduction of gendered body
    98–100
'residual categories' 10
restructuring body 88–94 see
    also project
Rheingold, H. 34, 189
Rich, A. 29
Richardson, J. 41
'risk societies' 64
rituals of everyday life 108,
    157, 164–5
Robins, K. 190
Rogers, L. 43–5
Rogers, W. 33, 115
Rose, S. 50, 53, 60
Rosen, B. 29
Rosen, T. 6
Rosenman, R. 102
Rudofsky, B. 4, 174
Rutherford, J. 49

Salter, B. 120
Sawicki, J. 70
Scarry, E. 184
schema, body 200–1

Schiebinger, L. 40
schizophrenic body in structuration theory 174–6
schooling see education
Schwartz, H. 27
Scotson, J. 140
Searle, G. 27, 49
Segal, L. 50, 53
self see individualization
self-classification 75–7
self control and self scrutiny 49
see also civilized body
self-denial and self-punishment 58–9, 84–5
see also asceticism
self-identity 1, 4–7, 174, 182–202
and civilized body 136, 147
men 30–1
and sexuality 68
and social inequalities 90, 102–3
see also death and self-identity
self-presentation see image, body
self-relatedness as action problem 83–5
self-sacrifice see self-denial
Seligman, M. 102
Sennett, R. 32, 85, 190, 197, 198
separateness see individualization; privatization
service work for women 106–8
sexual division of labour 53–4, 78
sexuality
and Christianity 67–8
and civilized body 135, 139–40
criminal see rape
and death 169–70
deviation 68
homosexuality 30, 51–2, 127
history of 66–8, 70
legitimate see marriage
masturbation 68, 69
of men 30
and naturalistic body 45–6, 49–51, 53–5
problems and social inequalities 105–7
and racism 49–52
and socially constructed body 66–8, 70, 79

teledildonics 34
of women restricted by men 29
see also reproduction
shame, see embarrassment and shame
shared meaning systems 154–7
Sharp, K. 92
Shilling, C. 5, 9, 19, 23, 25, 128, 152, 171, 180, 187, 192, 202
Shuttleworth, S. 40, 42, 43
similarities in gendered body suppressed 95–6
Simmel, G. 9, 25, 200
Simon, B. 59
Singer, L. 29
Sinha, M. 51, 52
slavery 49–51
slimming and body weight 1, 3, 5–6, 81
and naturalistic body 57–9
social capital 112, 117, 119, 120, 123
social class 1, 18–19, 60
and civilized body 131, 134–42
and physical capital 112–16, 127–8
changing body 116–18
changing value of 121–4
transmission and control 118–20
and social inequalities 96–7
status masks 79–80, 102
see also dominant classes; middle classes; working classes
social control see control; state
Social Darwinism 50–1
social differences see social class
social division of labour 141–2
social field 121–5
social figuration 132
social formation of body and physical capital 112–14
social identity
and socially constructed body 74–7
see also self-identity
social inequalities 7, 12–13, 15, 18, 88–110, 173, 176
emotion work 103–7
emotional body 94, 100–3
gendered body
constructing 94–5
reproduction of 98–100
negating body 95–6
restructuring body 88–94

transforming body 96–8
see also physical capital under social class
social institutions see institutions
social interaction 72–8
social interdependence of civilized body 141–2
social location see social class
social meaning see meaning
social mobility 18–19
social order and socially constructed body 78–82
social relationships 37–8
see also marriage; sexuality
social reproduction see physical capital; social class
social sexes 38–40, 47–9
social space, representation of body in 78–81
see also image, body
social stasis 127
socialization 11
and civilized body 131–3, 136, 139–43, 145, 150, 151
class 112–13
and death 162
gender 29, 58–9
and social roles 74
socially constructed body 62–87, 203–4
society, body in see culture; naturalistic body; social inequalities; socially constructed body
sociobiology 43–7
sociology and body 1, 7–13, 17–36, 180–1, 205–10
solitude see loneliness
'somatic society' 1
Sontag, S. 43
sport (and keep-fit and body-building) 3, 6, 30–1, 33–4, 158, 166, 176, 189
and body trading 18
and civilized body 144
and naturalistic body 58–9
and physical capital 114–16, 130
changing value 121–3
physical education in schools 19, 58–9
and social inequalities 96–100
spectating 144
Springer, C. 34
Stacey, M. 103
Stanley, L. 47, 48
Staples, R. 51

state and government control
1, 2, 26–7
and cultural capital 130
monopoly of violence
133–4, 141–2
and socially constructed
body 67–9
status
competition 138–9
masks/shields 79–80, 102–3
see also social class
stigma, management of 66,
72–3, 75–7
structuralism 20–1
structuration theory 66,
174–6
schizophrenic body in
205–6
subordination of women
28–9
and emotion work 100–3
see also control; domination;
gendered body; men;
patriarchy
surrogate motherhood 29
surveillance see panopticism

taboos and civilized body
135–6, 141, 146–7
see also privatization
Tancred-Sheriff, P. 106
Tapper, T. 120
tastes 113, 118, 124, 128
Tazi, N. 26
teledildonics 34
Therberge, N. 81
Theweleit, K. 88, 147
Tiger, L. 45
time-bound body 155
see also death
Tomas, D. 189
tools, use of 90, 92–3, 95
Toulmin, S. 179
Townsend, P. 113
transcendence see transforming
body
transforming body 95–110
transmission of physical capital
124–30

transplants and implants 4, 97
Tseelon, E. 194, 195, 197
Turner, B.S. 1, 10, 26, 32, 35,
69, 97, 170, 185
on ageing 31
on Berger 154–5
on bodily order 63–5,
78–82, 88–91, 179,
203–4
on classical sociology 21–6
Turner, T. 82

uncertain body 3–4
see also crisis of knowledge
unemployment and stress 109
upper classes see dominant
classes
urbanization 80
Urry, J. 115

Vance, C. 62
vanishing body 69–72
violence
and established-outsider
relations 147
in everyday life 134–5
genocide 150
and sport 145
state monopoly of 134, 141,
146–7
towards women see rape
see also force
Virey, J. 42

Walby, S. 29, 127, 128
Walter, T. 164–5, 171
Walvin, J. 49–50
Warr, P. 108
Washburn, S. 46
waste, bodily 23
Watney, S. 52
Watson, J. 204
Watt, I. 190
Wearne, P. 111
Weber, M. 9–10, 25, 188
Weeks, J. 30, 70
Weinstein, H. 108
Wilkes, C. 114–15
Williams, J. 147

Williams, S. 8
Willis, P. 59, 118–19
Wilson, E. 44, 45
Wittig, M. 70
Wolf, N. 81
women
and body image 5–7
see also slimming
and civilized body 140, 142,
150
classical sociologists not 24
and naturalistic body (seen
as inferior) 37–43
distorted body 56–60
see also eating disorders
under food
overburdened body 60–1
privileged body 53–6
and sociobiology 43–8
and physical capital
114–17, 128, 129
and social class see
physical capital
above
and social inequalities
97–110
and socially constructed
body 67, 80–1
violence to see rape
see also feminism; gendered
body; self-denial
Woolley, P. 92–3
work
investment 94–110
working classes 42
control of 21–2, 25
and physical capital
114–15
changing body 116–20
changing value of 121–3
conversion 118–20
Wouters, C. 108, 144, 147
Wright, E. 129
Wright, G.H. von 145

youth
appearance of see image
see also children
Young, I.M. 103, 186, 204